'"I am everywhere," answered the Voice, "but to the eyes of common mortals I am invisible. I will now seat myself upon my throne, that you may converse with me." Indeed, the Voice seemed just then to come straight from the throne itself; so they walked towards it and stood in a row while Dorothy said:

"We have come to claim our promise, O Oz."

"What Promise?" asked Oz.'

L. Frank Baum, *The Wizard of Oz*, 1900

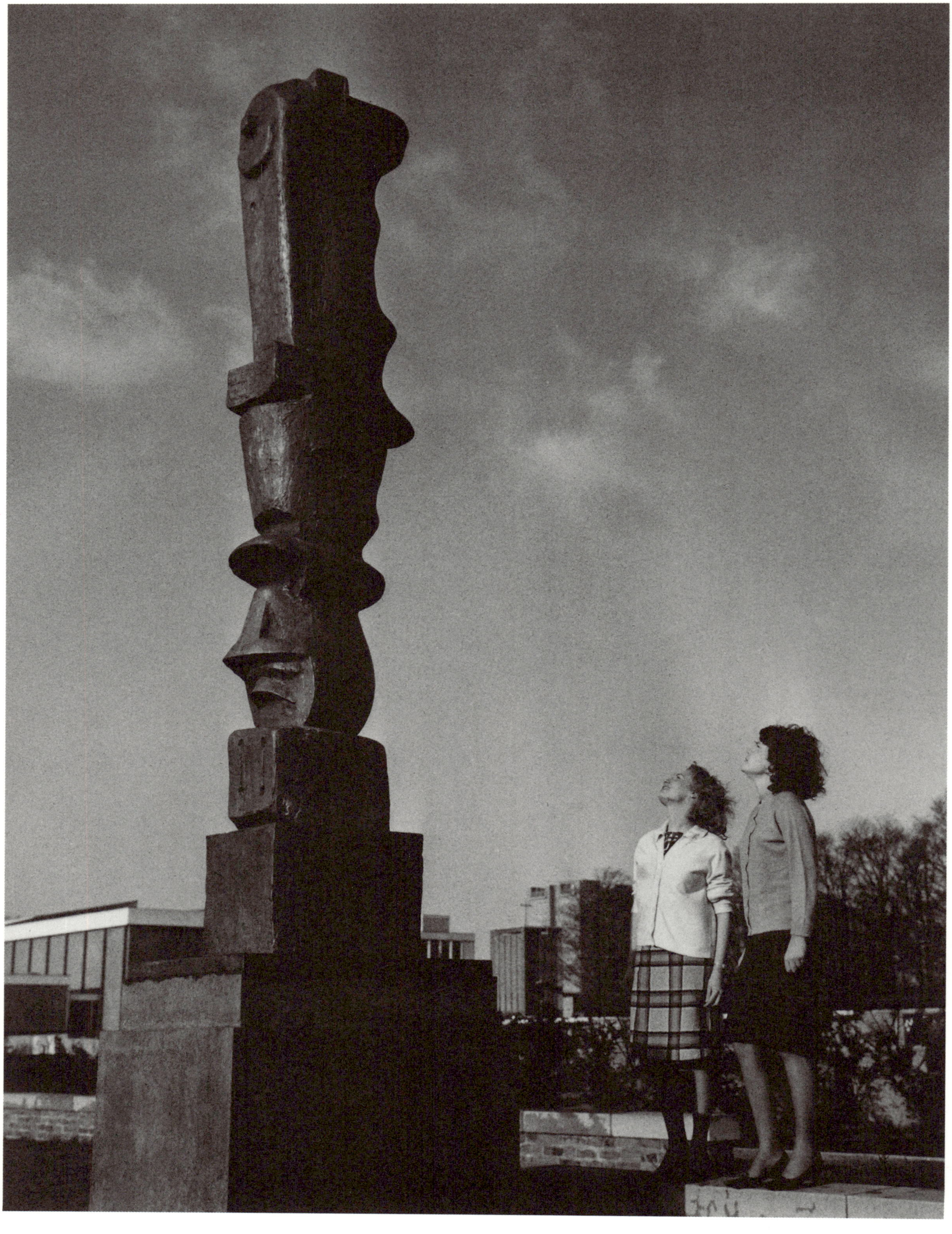

Totem Motif 1964, Photographic print on paper, 30.4 × 42.7 cm, 2014

4
Power, Corruption and Public Sculpture:
Ideologies of Public Art in Britain, 1910 to 2016

8
Competitive Designs for
the Great Tower for London

Part One: This England

13
Study of Blackpool Tower

19
A Balloon for Britain

31
A Better Britain

44
Interview: Robert Hewison

48
I Dream of Dalstonia

Part Two: The Internationale

84
Interview: Lynda Morris

88
Anish and Antony Take Afghanistan

107
The European Monument of Unity

119
The Ekranoplanter

129
Infinite Monument

136
New York Rural

161
Postcards from The Sculpture Park

166
New Values: An International
Public Art for the Future

Power, Corruption and Public Sculpture: Ideologies of Public Art in Britain, 1910 to 2016

by Owen Hatherley

Every era gets the public art it deserves. That is, the works left over after a political moment that has changed have a tendency to speak exceptionally vividly of their time, of the things that a given era held dear and considered to represent itself. Due to the way that its state and private funding is hugely direct and intensive, sculpture and artworks in public places tend to be as deeply connected to 'the powers that build' as its more utilitarian sibling, architecture, and because of that they can tell you a great deal about what power is at any given historical moment. What does it believe, who does it represent, what does it intend to communicate? A quick thought experiment will illustrate this point – what would be the most typical, most predictable and normal piece of public art in a public space in a typical British city in a series of years picked at random – say, in 1910, 1950, 1965, 1982, 2000 and 2015? In each case, it will become clear that any attempt to talk about the 'autonomy of art' in such a context is faintly absurd; though that doesn't mean that the work in question is necessarily more kitsch or of a lower quality than any other. Rather, it simply makes clearer than any other form of fine art the processes of commissioning and patronage that would otherwise remain more opaque.

Public art on a large scale, like most things in British public life, dates from the nineteenth century, and begins, unsurprisingly, with monuments to authority figures – generals, kings, and suchlike, usually in bronze, on plinths. The earlier, classical versions of this are remarkably simple – Grey's Monument in Newcastle or Nelson's Column, where a statue of the figure in question is placed at the top of an enlarged classical column, something for which there's little 'actual' classical precedent. Much in the same way that the architecture of art galleries and art museums pass from austere Greek and Roman temples to more elaborate baroque and Ruskinian Gothic confections, usually with an attendant purpose to edify and improve the tastes of the industrious classes, by the end of the century, though, this had developed into larger, freer compositions, recounting narratives, with experiments in drapery and 'national costume', and that particularly nineteenth century approach to the body, alternately lurid and guilty. The ultimate example of this is of course the Albert Memorial in South Kensington, with its almost pornographic display of imperial power and opulent material (marble, gold). These are mostly passed over unthinkingly, except when they're threatened, when suddenly they are noticed, and the unsavoury things, which they provide a 'narrative' of, are brought to unwelcome attention.

The most famous piece of public art in Fulchester is a 1910 sculptural group that sits in the central square, opposite the Rates Hall, adjacent to the Technical and Trades School. Sculpted by Sir Joshua Rhodes-Boyson RA, consisting of bronze figures on three symmetrical granite plinths it was originally called *Triumph over the Kaffirs*, but has for some time been known by the less inflammatory title *Botswana Campaign 1903*. A moustachioed figure in a tin hat, wielding a bayonet in one hand and a maxim gun in the other places a heavy boot on an African figure; a long-haired, aquiline-nosed woman

grabs his other leg in gratitude, her gauzy drapery falling to reveal a full Edwardian breast. On two lower plinths are personifications of 'grace' and 'military valour', two more women, one of them in a shift, with eyes looking skyward, and the other holding a spear and a shield. The monument has not always been popular – for a time in the 1980s the 'loony left' borough council in Fulchester voted to dismantle what they called a 'racist monument to genocide and imperialism', but a fierce campaign led by SAVE Britain's Heritage and *Private Eye*'s Piloti saw it spot listed by English Heritage, along with all other Edwardian monuments in the centre of the city, a move hailed by Sir John Betjeman as 'a victory for common sense'.

The most important monument to have been built circa 1950 can be found quite far outside of the city centre, in the overspill settlement of New Fulchester. It sits in the main precinct of the development, in the middle of a green square flanked on one side by a row of shops, partly disused, with a bookmaker, a branch of Londis and the Titanic Fish Bar, and on the other by a pitched-roofed block of flats sitting on mosaic-covered pillars, and with windows that were recently refurbished with uPVC. The monument used to be easily accessed from the shops around but large fences were erected around it as part of the New Deal for Communities programme in 2002, and CCTV cameras were placed nearby, something that happened around the time the work of the sculptor, Gareth Hinterland, was being re-evaluated. This example is called *Worker and Land Girl* and consists of two semi-abstract figures, with blank faces and hefty bodies lifting their tools aloft. Initially popular, the monument was heavily attacked as a 'Stalinist' symbol of 'Old Labour', coming in for particularly harsh criticism in Beatrix Campbell's essay 'Fulchester – What Went Wrong?', published in *New Society* in 1984, where she called it a symbol of the 'patriarchal values of old-school socialists still attached to the obsolete idea of full employment'. The veteran local MP Dennis Hardman still speaks well of it, however – 'when I got home tired from pit, looking at that sculpture gave me the strength to follow my dream of becoming Britain's longest serving member of parliament'.

The gradual creation of a public social security system in the first decades of the twentieth century sees the gradual use of the public itself as the subject matter, something that accelerates after the landslide victory of the Labour Party in the 1945 general election. Oddly, given the scale of the programme of social reform that was rolled out over the next three decades, art galleries were not built in any great number, bar a handful of particularly central spaces, such as the various phases of the South Bank complex in London. In some cases, what happened was quite close to the nineteenth century notion of the 'improving' public sculpture, such as the placing of family groups or reclining nudes by Henry Moore, and the like. What was possibly different on this occasion was that the artworks created by the post-war consensus were not themselves consensual, but often jarring, hard to understand, compared with the lurid or sentimental narratives of historic public sculpture. And what happened in some cases – the Water Gardens of Harlow New Town, the South-West area of Peterlee, planned partly by Victor Pasmore, the concrete relief landscape of Hockley Circus in Birmingham, by the prolific William Mitchell, or innumerable less famous murals, mosaics, reliefs and murals on housing estates and schools – was more radical in its attempt to eliminate the divide between 'art' and 'life' than anything else in the British mainstream.

No such controversy was attendant on 1965's most important sculpture in the area, however. The University of Fulchester was opened that year, in the form of several concrete ziggurats, using the CLAMP prefabrication system, with pre-cast, fair-faced beton brut panels, on a meadow compulsorily purchased from a local pit-owner, who later bought the *Daily Sketch* with the compensation proceeds. The buildings were controversial, for a time – the mixed dormitories were soon the subject of a crabs outbreak, leading to prurient local press outrage that only increased when a group of university students threatened to shoot themselves with airguns in solidarity with the victims of Kent State, unless the Vice-Chancellor publicly wiped his backside with a photograph of Spiro Agnew. When the Vice-Chancellor – the biographer of John Ruskin, R.P. Williamson – complied with alacrity, he was fired, after being subject to what he called in his book *Fulchester University – Capitalist Bastards* (Pluto Press, 1975) a 'trial by media'. In all of this, everyone seemed to miss the sculpture that occupied the lowest point of the green hill in between the six ziggurat dormitories – Christopher Nathanson's *Fulcrum*. Made of six sheet-metal tubes welded into a series of interconnected X-shapes, Nathanson made the sculpture out of discarded parts he had obtained from the Fulchester Bic Vero engineering works. Although tall and impressive, the sculpture went unnoticed in the controversy, gradually rusting until it was rediscovered on the release of Jane and Louise Wilson's film exploring Nathanson's 'total environments', *Totalisator* (1998). Nathanson, otherwise best known for his 1989 stained glass panel *Endless Love*, depicting the marriage of Prince Charles and Diana Spencer, refuses to comment on his 1960s sculptures, only adding to his current cachet and mystique.

Art, unlike architecture, did not receive much of the blame for the collapse of the post-war compromise. Architects – and the local authorities that commissioned them – underwent a traumatic process of public humiliation followed by samokritika, after which neither managed to regain any of their former prominence in public life. The particular forms that the majority of post-war public art took – usually, those abstract patterns or Moore-esque and Hepworth-esque sculptures left in picturesque corners in council estates – meant that however vandalised they may have been, they did not suffer from the same level of opprobrium, with exceptions such as Pasmore's *Apollo Pavilion* in Peterlee, which was half-way to being architecture in any case. Another reason for this relative obscurity is the fact that it was always more acceptable to be dismissive of modern architecture in British public life than it was of public art. The 1960s generation that began the dismantlement, destruction and demonisation of public modernism would talk quite freely about 'concrete monstrosities', 'eyesores' and later 'carbuncles', but would usually baulk at 'my five year old could have done that', or indeed 'it's all just a load of noise'. Accordingly modern art in public places never suffered the same massive rejection as modern architecture. However, the ordinary public art that got commissioned after the early 1970s did go through a similar change towards local representation, local stories, figuration, and the increasingly popular notion of 'heritage'.

No such drama has ever accompanied the 1982 relief sculpture *Trades of Old Fulchester*, unveiled by Michael Heseltine that year in celebration of the 200th anniversary of the opening of Fulchester's first worsted mill, notably described by Friedrich Engels in *The Condition of the Working Class in England* as 'quite the worst of the mills in Fulchester, emitting a stench of fear, piss and rotting flesh – workers here dub it 'the mangler', due to the sheer quantity of factory hands who have been maimed or dismembered during the performance of their labours'. The relief sculpture, by Dame Elizabeth Freud, was unveiled by the entrance of the mill after it was reopened as the Fulchester Industrial Heritage Museum. It consists of four panels, in a realistic style, in terracotta to harmonise with the sand-blasted red bricks of the renovated factory buildings. The first panel shows the men and women of the town working cheerfully in the mill, the second depicts them supporting the 'People's Charter', the third depicts them working making munitions (substantially the same as panel one, only with somewhat different clothing and a large Union Jack in relief in the background) and the fourth depicts the same figures working in the gift shop. After a year in which the newly post-industrial town was convulsed by rioting, the sculptures, and the new museum, were greeted as the start of the road to recovery.

Unfortunately, economic recovery had not wholly taken root by 2000, when the fifth and by far the largest of the town's public sculptures was opened to the public. Entitled *Phoenix from the Ruins*, it consists of an enormous, winged Cor-Ten steel figure, designed by Jez Wakefield OBE, one of the most popular sculptors of that decade, described by then-Culture Secretary Andy Burnham as 'the best bloody sculptor in the whole bloody world'. It forms the centrepiece of Quayside Village, a regeneration scheme around the disused Fulchester Harbour, consisting of a mixed development of three towers with sloping roofs, clad in an attractive mixture of red brick, aluminium balconies and purple Trespa panels, which won the phone-in poll for 'best regeneration scheme of the year' on the Channel 4 programme *Brilliant! – The Story of Regeneration*. The flats are mostly empty at the time of writing, but developer Jack Shand, a local to the town, and head of the council Cliff Accrington both moved in early on. Regardless, the housing has always been overshadowed by *Phoenix from the Ruins*, which is now regarded as 'the Icon of Fulchester', appearing on

promotional brochures and the council's official logo. The 450 million pound project was funded by the European Union's Objective 1 Programme, Arts Council England, the Mining Areas Development Agency, and Yes Fulchester.

The return of nineteenth century values in public sculpture of the 1980s – even when, as in Cardiff and Huddersfield, it entails portraying social democratic heroes like Aneurin Bevan and Harold Wilson – does still continue. Particularly in the most important spaces of power and government, notable in the procession of odd Edwardian-Vegas sculptures in Westminster – Lloyd George, Animals at War, Bomber Command, Women of World War II, a motley list – but the main ideology of public art was *a kind of* modernism. It comes out of the improvement-via-abstraction of 1945, out of Cedric Price's mooted *Fun Palace*, out of relational aesthetics and from a particularly strange, almost theological conception of art's ability to raise the spirits, or more often the property values, of a given area. Like the art of the late nineteenth century it accompanied a massive expansion of art galleries and museums, often lottery funded. Some, such as the New Art Gallery in Walsall, made use of existing collections and were designed in such a way as to feel a part of the town or city they were placed in, but more common was something like the Middlesbrough Institute of Modern Art (mima, lower case please), dropped as if from nowhere, a squiggly box with a blank backside you weren't meant to look at, with a giant message-in-a-bottle sculpture (by Claes Oldenburg, not just any hack) outside in 'reference' to near-local Captain Cook.

The public art of the New Labour era resulted in dozens of optimistic, large-scale sculptures speaking of the 'regeneration' of various post-industrial areas of the United Kingdom. In this, as in so much else, Birmingham was the pioneer. In the mid-1990s, even before the election of Tony Blair, the city council sponsored the quintessential regeneration scheme – Brindleyplace, a canal-side, post-industrial scheme that entailed modernist blocks on a traditional, ordered street plan, sparsely designed public spaces and opaque public-private ownership, and the quintessential regeneration sculpture, Antony Gormley's *Iron Man*, an iron figure leaning imposingly over Birmingham's nineteenth century civic heart. It was figurative and yet, in its faceless, abstracted figure, enigmatically modernist; it was 'good taste' art that nonetheless lent itself to a simple interpretation, a 'reference' both to the city's industrial heritage of metal trades, and to its pioneering role in the development of Heavy Metal, something made possible by sheet-metal worker Tony Iommi losing a finger in an industrial accident. It was also, or would soon become, 'iconic', because it was instantly identifiable as 'a Gormley', cast from the dimensions of the man's body. After that, the deluge, with 'Gormleys' appearing in North Greenwich, Gateshead, Crosby and elsewhere, and 'mock-Gormley' appearing as a genre in the Woolwich Arsenal development, south-east London. Usefully, unlike Gareth Hinterland's *Worker and Land Girl*, it has no obvious political content; it is open to many interpretations, all equally banal.

It is curious how sculpture became the main means for conveying 'regeneration'. My first memory of 'regeneration' was an artwork called *Bevis and Ascupart*, opened in the late 1990s in Bevois Valley, an inner-city district of my home town, Southampton. It consists of a billboard on a hill, looking out over a bypass and a skyline of light industry, landfill, wharves and stunted Victorian housing. Two young figures – one black, one white – lurk like giants over the area, their names, 'Bevis' and 'Ascupart' referring to medieval knights who allegedly founded and named the district. This is sort of halfway there, in that it 'refers' to the local area, is optimistic and 'inclusive', but the use of a billboard is unforgivably ephemeral, something that became obvious when the photo-printed image gradually wore down. Another 'almost' would be the giant steel balls which occupy regenerated public spaces in post-industrial cities. One huge example appears in front of the At-Bristol Science Centre in the West Country port, and there are several littered around the 'golden route', a processional series of repaved and expanded public spaces across the centre of Sheffield. None of these have the winning combination of enigma, optimism and popularity of Jez Wakefield's *Phoenix from the Ruins* or Gormley's *Iron Man*.

Not everyone can just imitate Gormley, of course, so other approaches had to be developed, which were more abstract – you can have only so many symbolic figures suggesting that a formerly great and then unfortunately benighted area was going up in the world again. One great example in this respect was provided by non-functional 'engineer' and artist Thomas Heatherwick, with his sculpture *The B of the Bang*, erected on a main road into Manchester for the Commonwealth Games. This series of metal shards, caught seemingly mid-way through an explosion, was titled in reference to a phrase of Linford Christie's, that a sprinter needs to start running as soon as the 'b of the bang' of the starting whistle. So we're a long way from Nathanson's *Fulcrum* and its ilk. Abstraction, for sure, but a new, univocal form of abstraction, which very obviously says something – it speaks, and it speaks optimistically and dramatically of success, or to use the Blair-era buzzword, 'aspiration'. Accordingly, one of the mid-period examples of this trend actually used that very expression as a title. *Aspire* is a sculpture at the heart of the Jubilee Campus of the University of Nottingham, designed in 2007 by the architect Ken Shuttleworth and his firm MAKE; Shuttleworth had made his name as a partner with Norman Foster, where he claimed a major role in that major Blair-era icon, the Swiss, Re 'Gherkin', a hugely successful domestication of the skyscraper.

The Jubilee Campus takes up most of the former Raleigh Bicycle Works, a couple of miles from the centre of Nottingham, a factory well known for its starring role in Alan Sillitoe's *Saturday Night and Sunday Morning*. This is presumably why the sculpture, a net of pink steel members, appears to be 'in reference' to the spokes of a bicycle wheel. The difference is that rather than being circular, it is extruded upwards. Amusingly, a website produced by the architects claimed it to be one of the tallest sculptures in Europe. Its height and its name are designed to work as a 'beacon'. Yes, industry has gone and the jobs that came with it – but aspire enough, and you might get to study here and work in one of the Jubilee Campus' 'business incubators', or if not that, then at least as a cleaner or a barista here. The blurring of the boundaries between architecture and sculpture would become increasingly important. The architecture of a firm like MAKE, or more famous international masters such as Santiago Calatrava, Daniel Libeskind or Frank Gehry, is to do all the things a regeneration sculpture has to do anyway – declare newness, legibility, drama and optimism. An unheralded prophet in this respect is the Portsmouth Spinnaker Tower, a universally ridiculed viewing tower-cum-sculpture that towers over much of Southampton's neighbouring and rival port, resembling part of the Burj-al-Arab hotel in Dubai removed and then dropped near Portsmouth Harbour.

If the Spinnaker Tower is honest kitsch, the same is unlikely to be said about the public art of Anish Kapoor. Beginning with the *The Tees Valley Giants* dropped like alien objects on a dockside site in the especially depressed North East industrial town of Middlesbrough, Kapoor began an unexpected career as court sculptor to late Blairism and its successor. If the 'Teesside Giants' were directly publicly funded as a spur to attract people to the new (and barely finished) architect-designed housing nearby, the successor, *ArcelorMittal Orbit*, was notoriously the result of a meeting in the toilets of Davos, between two members of the global elite, the Mayor of London Boris Johnson and the steel magnate Lakshmi Mittal, who stumped up the cash in return for a towering, free advert. The whimsy of the commissioning process and the ludicrousness of the eventual design by Kapoor and Cecil Balmond, a hot pink entrail curved around a partly-hidden support structure holding up a viewing platform, implies that this work is becoming a lot less high-minded. It is of a piece with other, similar structures in London such as the 'dangleway' cable car or the mooted Garden Bridge cooked up between Johnson, Joanna Lumley and Thomas Heatherwick. These projects, closely associated with the Mayor of London, have a quite novel combination of utter pointlessness and vacuity combined with 'real' engineering, a real 'experience'.

That's one possible future. Another is in a similar vein to Friendly Design's *Quayside Burger Den*. Here, the key examples would be Bold Tendencies' exhibitions of large-scale sculpture in a Peckham car park, or Assemble's 'follies' and 'pop-ups' such as *Folly for a Flyover* in Bow. These blur even further the divide between sculpture and architecture, but conversely, are the product of straitened circumstances and the attempt to recreate some version of a 'public sphere'. In their *Granby Four Streets* project in Liverpool, it connects directly with local activism, over the disastrous Blair-era Pathfinder scheme that condemned dozens of sound streets to dereliction and destruction awaiting a never-begun 'regeneration'. Optimistically, this could mean works that force themselves out of the logic of power and finance altogether, instead rethought as a service, something 'useful'. Looked at critically, this can, like most 'pop-ups' sponsored to cover up the wastelands opened up by creative destruction, appear as a form of trust-funded artistic sticking-plaster, temporarily healing wounds that were opened up brutally and needlessly, and possible only through the work of those not dependent on some form of (even 'creative') wage labour. The future of public art, though, is likely much more to resemble Gormley's transformation into a hotel designer. At the end of the stripped classical facade of the Beaumont Hotel in Mayfair, an inter-war building originally designed as a garage, sits a cubic, humanoid figure, occupying most of one wing of the structure. There's been some attempt to integrate it with the stone facade, but the gap is still obvious. The figure appears to be squatting, folding its arms and staring, blank faced, like a muted, reduced version of an ancient Assyrian sculpture, hieratic, pompous and faintly silly. You can stay, for the expected exorbitant fee, inside the sculpture on the Beaumont Hotel; the bedroom is in the head.

At the time of writing, proposals are being made for a temporary artwork to occupy the currently derelict part of the dockland site just beyond Quayside Village, which was bought by developers Urban Splash in 2007 but which has so far not been built on, after a deal with the Homes and Communities Agency to obtain public funding for a 1,000 unit development of self-designed condominiums unexpectedly fell through due to lack of demand. *Quayside Burger Den* was designed and built by architects Friendly Design in collaboration with volunteer cooks from the Fulchester Craft Burgers Facebook group, and consists of a series of interlocking balsa-wood fair-trade burger bars, is being constructed by local labour, courtesy of a job creation scheme, a partnership between Reed Employment Agency and Fulchester Jobcentre Plus, in order, said the lead partner, Bartlett-educated Tim Chipping, 'to help these poor people re-learn the sort of trades Fulchester was once famous for all over the world'. After the bars have been used in the popular, month-long Fulchester Pop-Up Real Ale Festival, they will be re-used to become self-build housing for the city's homeless. The scheme benefits from the participation of the local office of *The Big Issue*, who are sponsoring the scheme, which is otherwise funded by the parents of one of Friendly Design's partners.

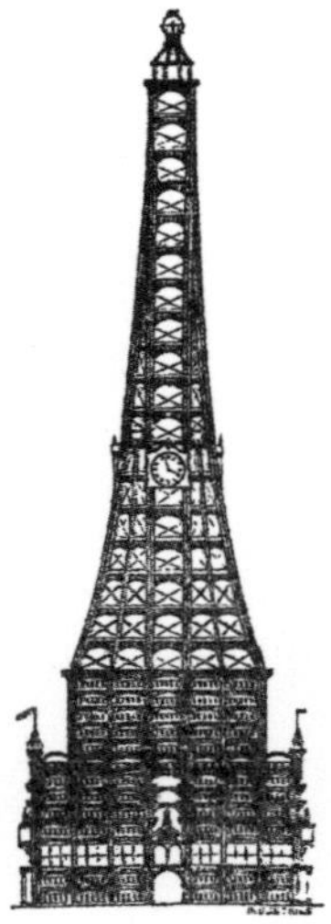
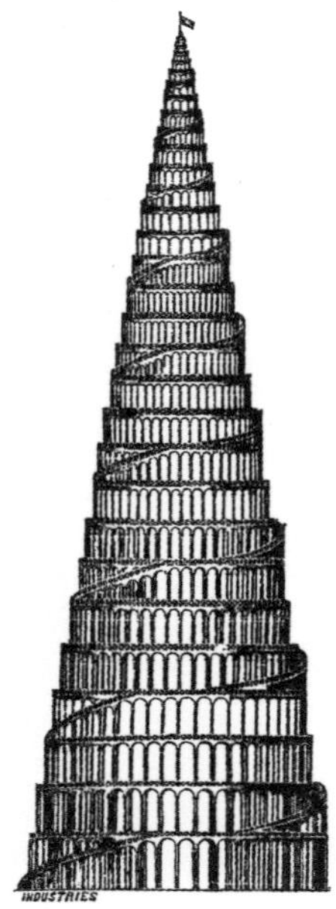
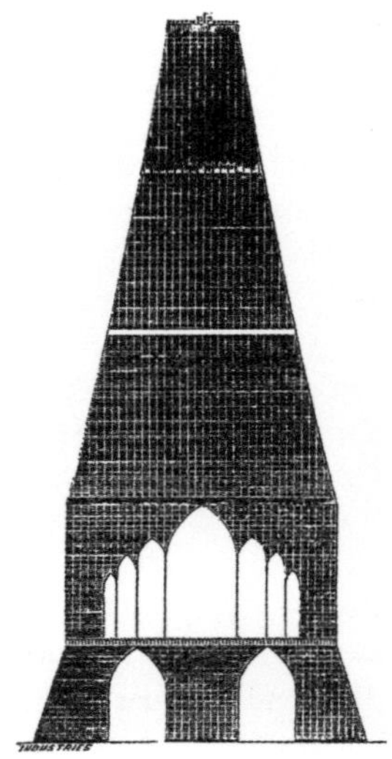
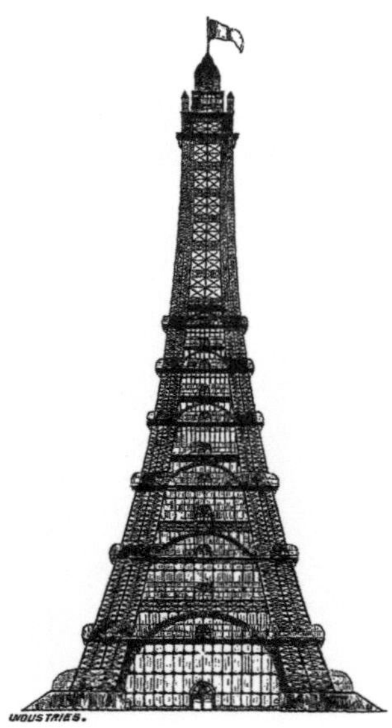
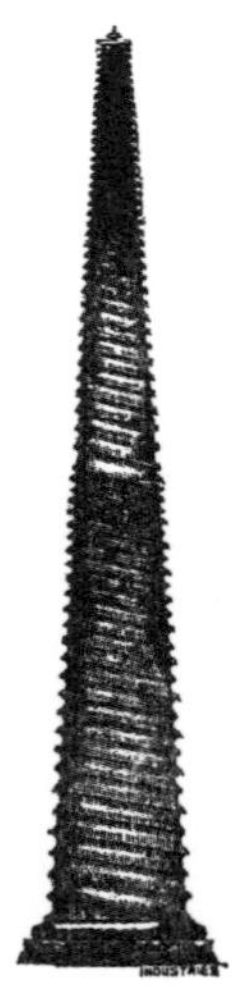
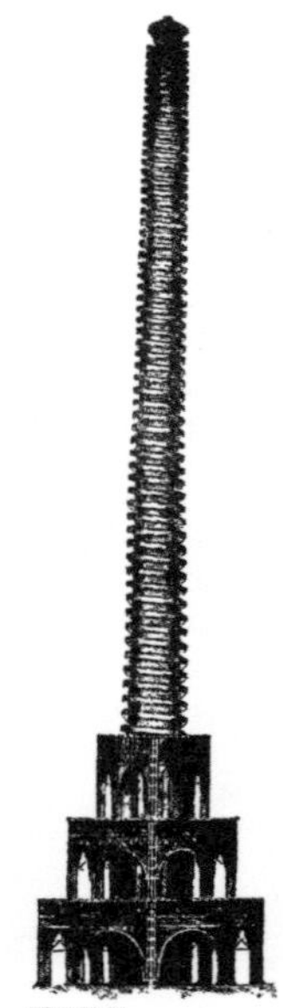

Twelve of the sixty-eight entries from the *Descriptive Illustrated Catalogue of the Sixty-Eight Competitive Designs for the Great Tower for London*, held by Edward Watkin in 1896. Watkin intended to build a monument to rival Paris' Eiffel Tower and invited designs from a wide range of architects from all over the world. Proposals included those that imagined a vegetable garden and a full size steam powered railway. The project was abandoned in 1901 and demolished in 1906.

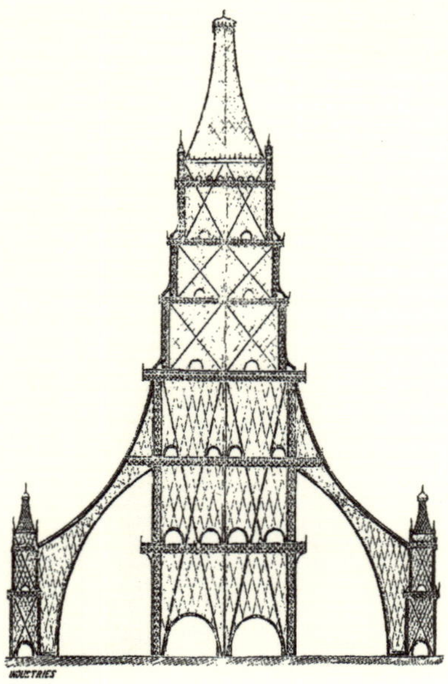

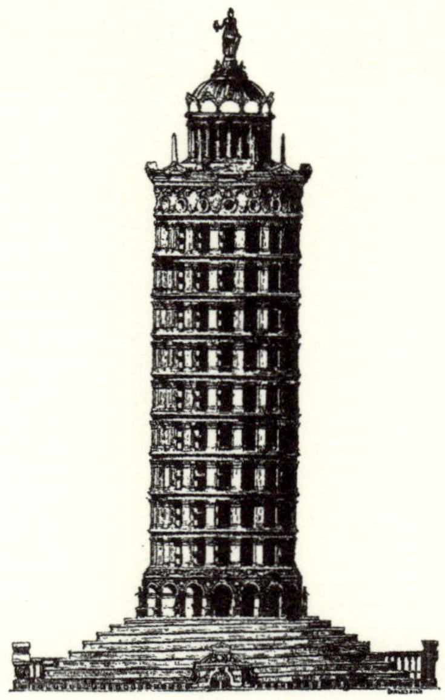

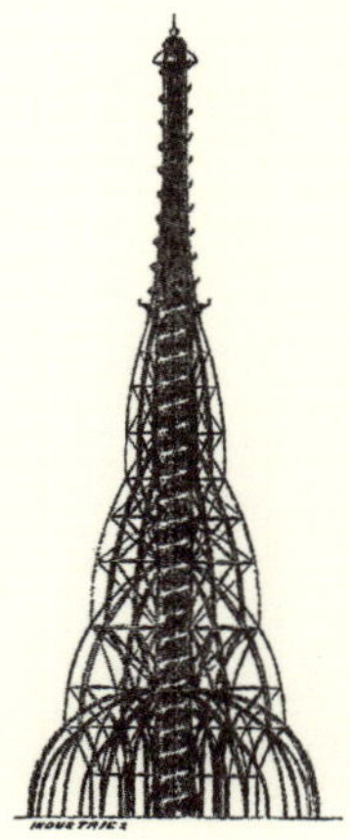

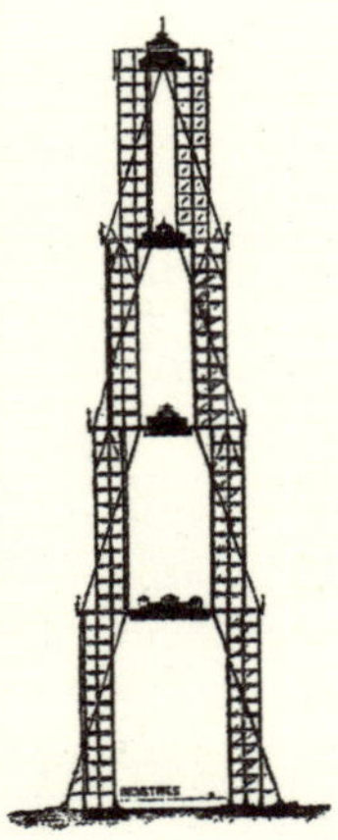

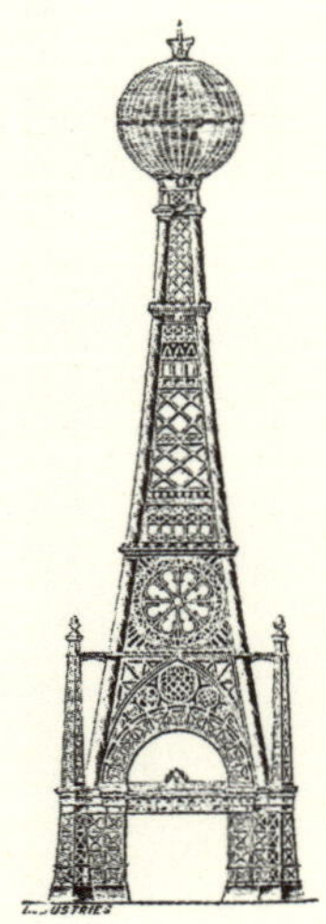

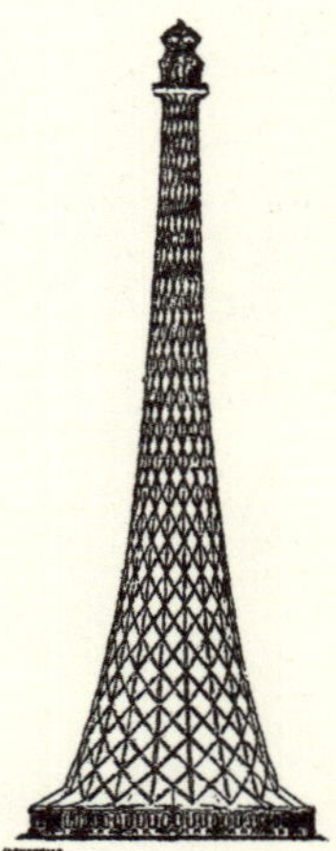

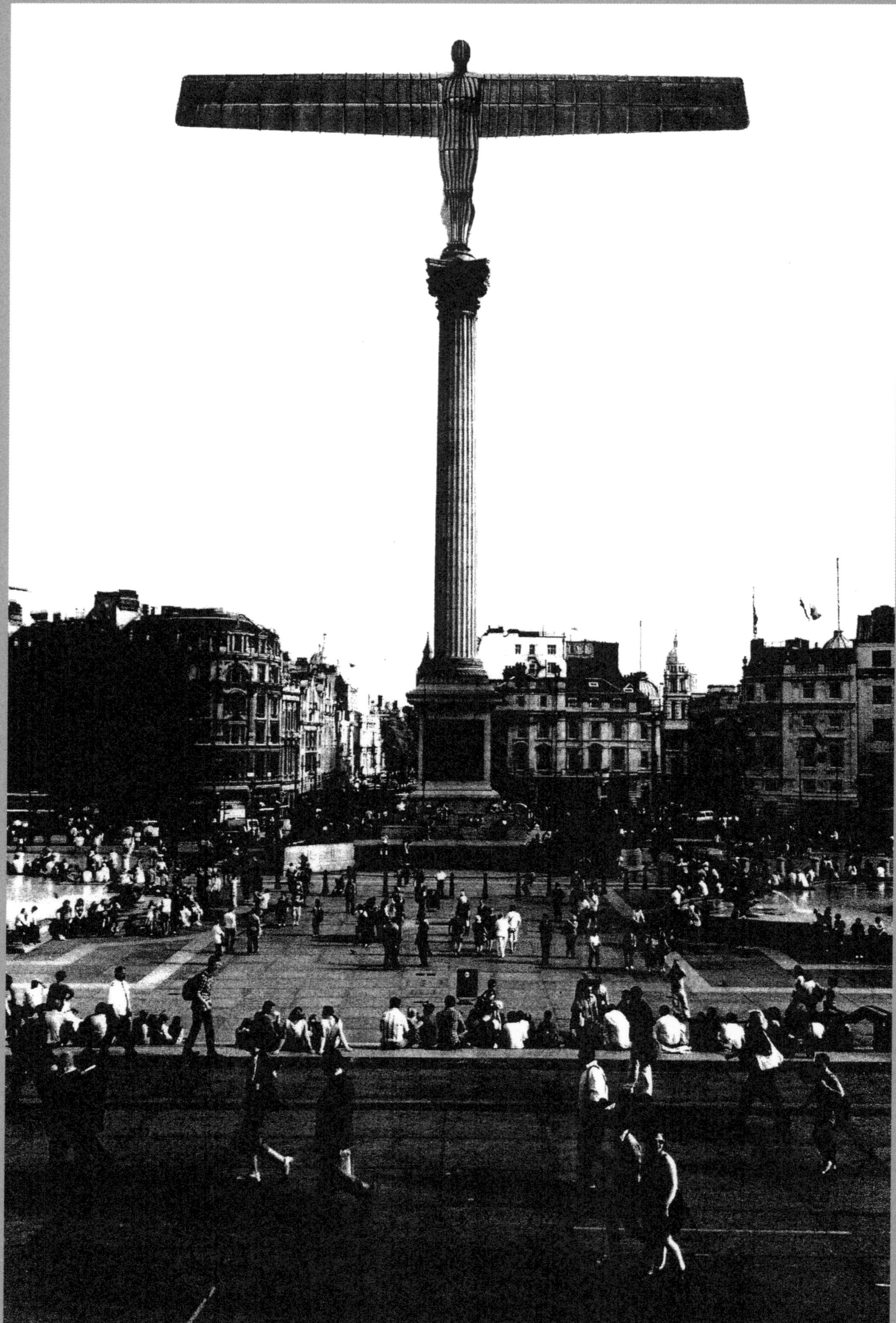

Long Live Death, Inkjet print on paper, 219 × 150 cm, 2012

PART ONE
THIS ENGLAND

STUDY OF BLACKPOOL TOWER

'I had planned to get up early, but not *this* early. I've been pacing my room, smoking, since 4am – all the best hotels here advertise "smoking rooms" – some even boast "smoking throughout". By the time I go down for breakfast four hours later, I feel like I've been out all night; but it's a beautiful winter's morning. As I sit amongst my fellow diners, I couldn't be happier. I fiddle with my camera and make a list of today's goals: photograph B&Bs, backstreet misery, Blackpool Tower, Winter Gardens, dog shit, etc.

So, with this as my agenda, I set out. First, a two-mile hike down the sea-front, just for pleasure. It's fantastic – the gale force fresh air sweeping over the Irish Sea and straight down my throat – a stark contrast to this morning's chain-smoking in my overheated room. I love the British seaside, all of it, at anytime of year. It's the sense of communal nostalgia perhaps, shared memories in towns that never really change – or maybe its the teenage scooter rallies – slow adventures to Yarmouth, Morecambe or Skegness and that very first sense of freedom. Whatever it is, I'm never happier than when in a seaside town and I just walk and walk, immediately forgetting about my misery-agenda. As I walk, I also remember how much I enjoy being alone in strange places – how much it's part of the job of being an artist. If you're lucky enough to have a show in New York, Zurich or Berlin it's almost impossible not to meet someone that you know, not to arrange a drink in a bar – but should you find yourself exhibiting in Breda, Fribourg, Dunkirk or Dundee, the opposite applies: there's no chance at all of bumping into someone you know and anyone you do meet, you'll most likely never see again. I'm excited to be all alone. It's alone in these strange towns, sat in a bar over a notebook with hours if not days to kill, that I find myself to be at my most creative. Separated from real life, and with no one to talk to, I become an endless font of ideas, and I love it.

After two hours I am absolutely bored shitless. It's only just gone ten o'clock and the band don't get here till four. I've already been to the tower and the Winter Gardens (both closed). I've wandered up and down the back-streets photographing the lunatic B&Bs; I've photographed the dog shit, the spew and the semi-defunct rock shops. Now what do I do? Time has almost stood still and every ten minutes seems to take an hour. I've even contemplated all-day drinking, but was put off by a non-legged man parked outside Wetherspoons. I sit on a bench high up in the town and flick back through my photographs – they're all terrible – predictable clichés of northern misery – they look like Morrissey's holiday snaps. I seriously consider giving up and just going back to bed. But then – then – I notice that at least half of my pictures have Blackpool Tower in the background – and this gives me an idea.

For the next three hours, I am the happiest man in Lancashire. I've decided to photograph Blackpool Tower from every point that it becomes visible in a half-mile, half-radius as I walk up through the town: the tower always the same size and in the same place in every shot. I know exactly what I'm doing. My idea is a composite of many influences (John Baldessari, Guy Debord and Victor Burgin to name three), but ultimately, *absolutely*, it is mine: I am making original ART. Not only that, I've found an objective way to document the daylight misery of Blackpool without having to seek it out: the red brick chip shop terraces are all essential but ultimately incidental. I've applied the essence of Conceptual Art's objectivity to a grotty Social Realism, and I'm very pleased with myself. I even have a brilliant idea for a title "Majestic Karaoke Nihilism".'

Extract from 'December 14 & 15 2013: Alone in Blackpool, Waiting for Sleaford Mods' by Scott King for *Arena Homme +*, 2014.

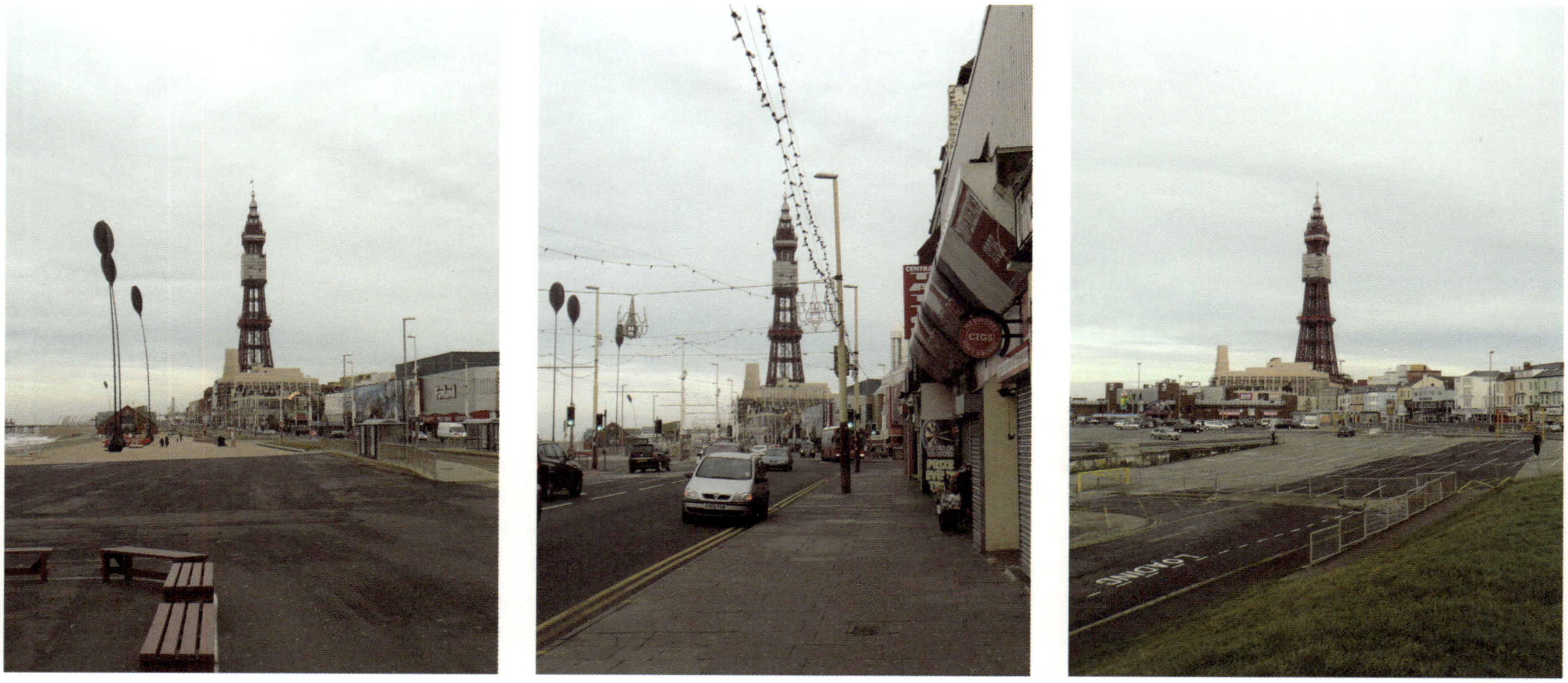

Study of Blackpool Tower, Inkjet prints on paper, Twelve of fourteen parts, Each: 40 × 30 cm, 2014

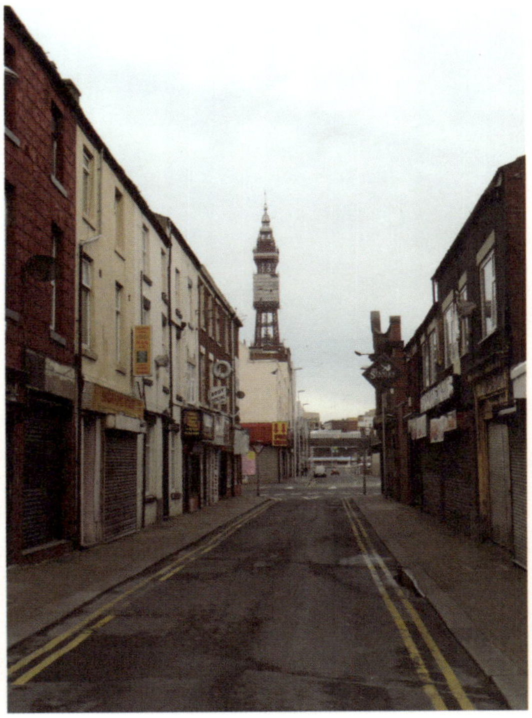

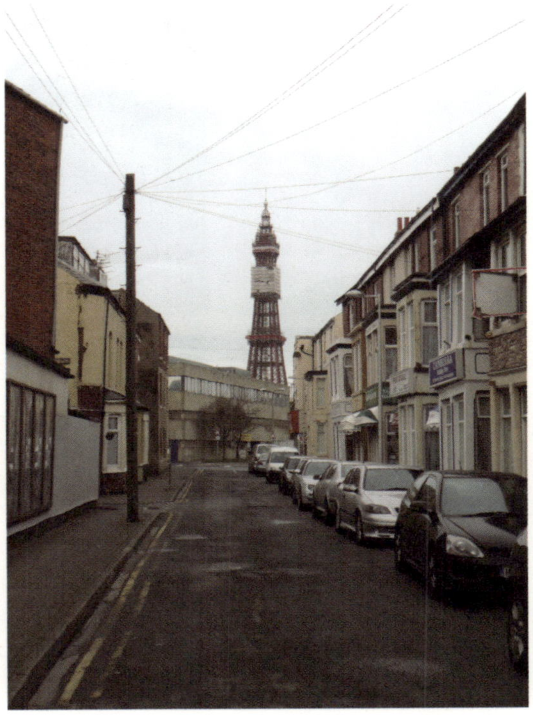

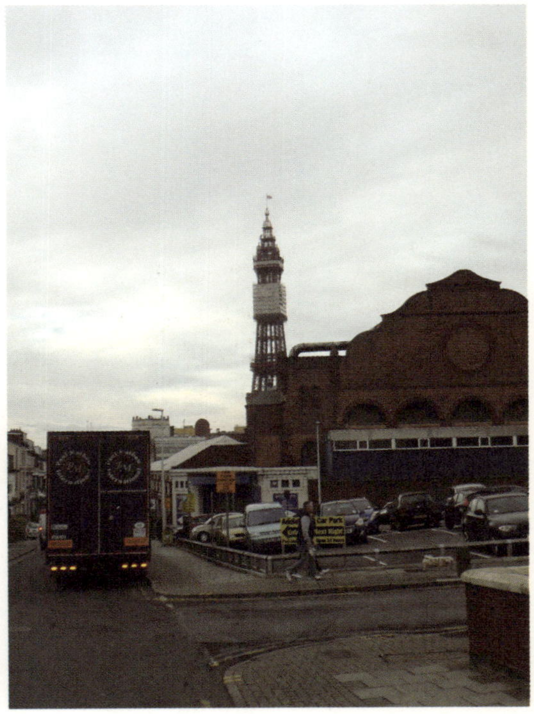

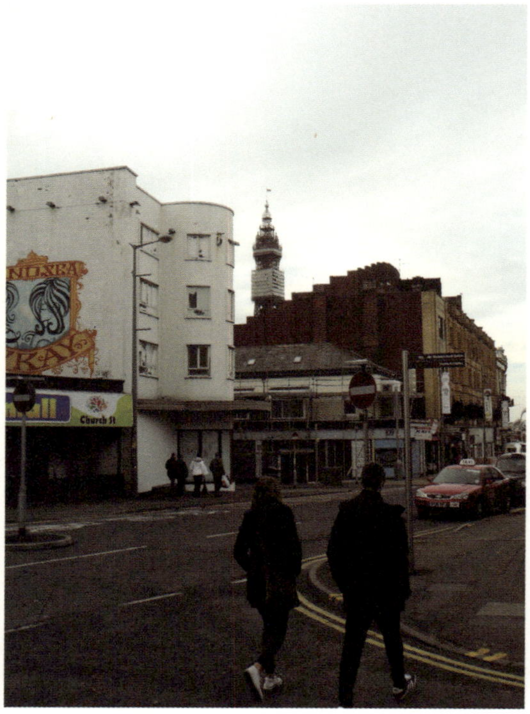

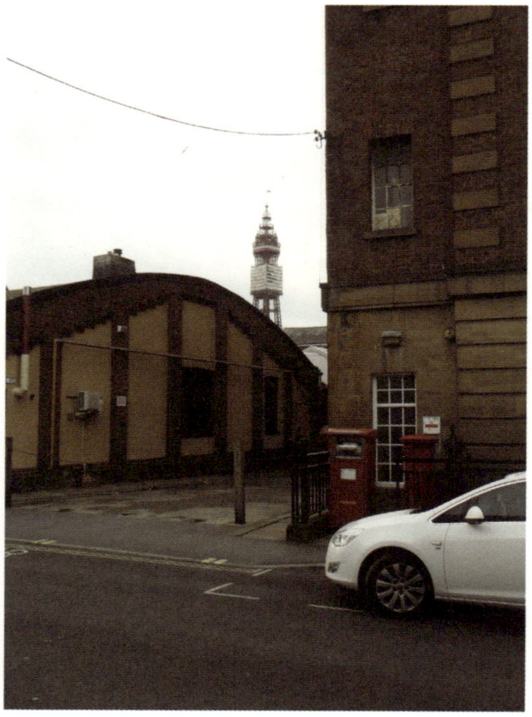

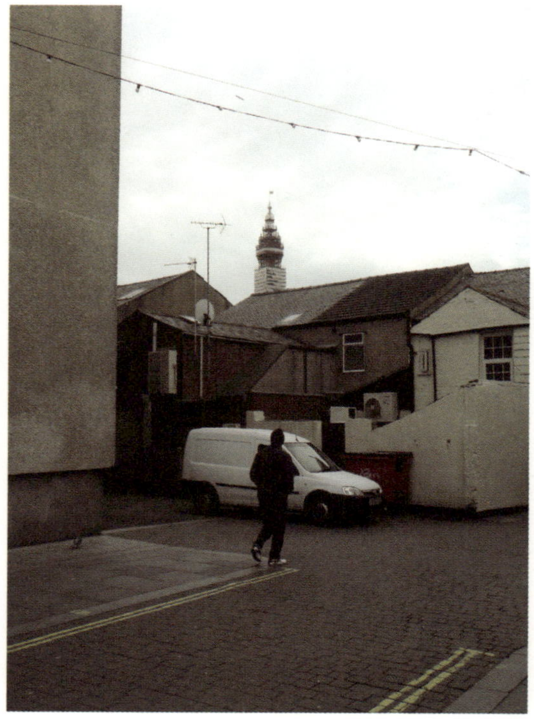

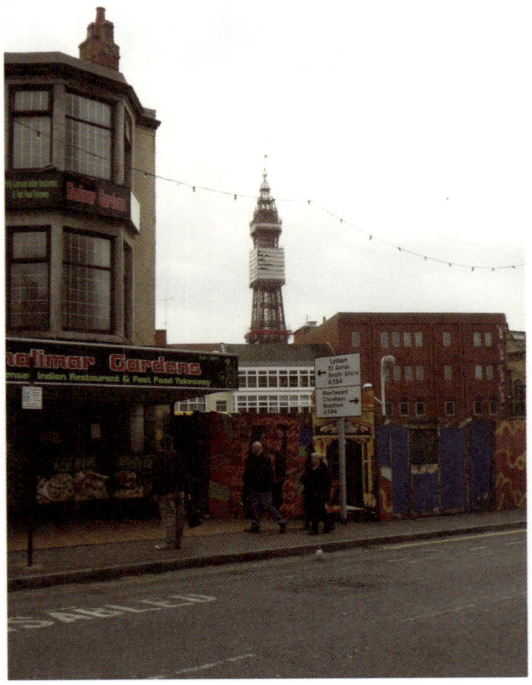
Indian Restaurant & Fast Food Takeaway

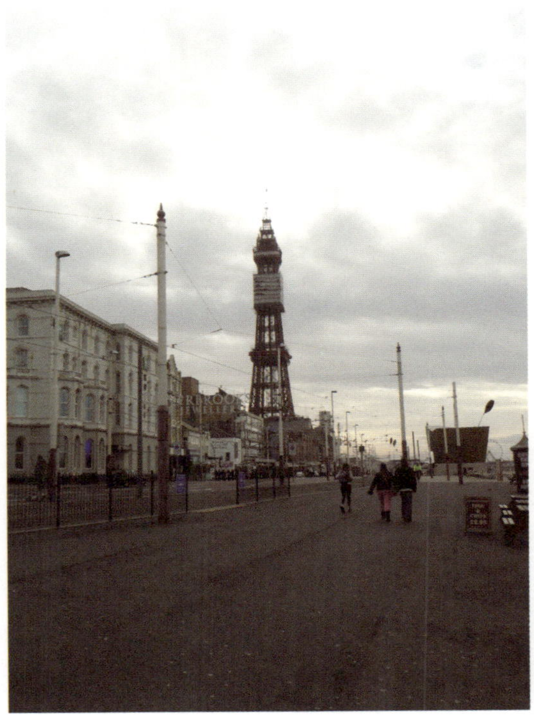

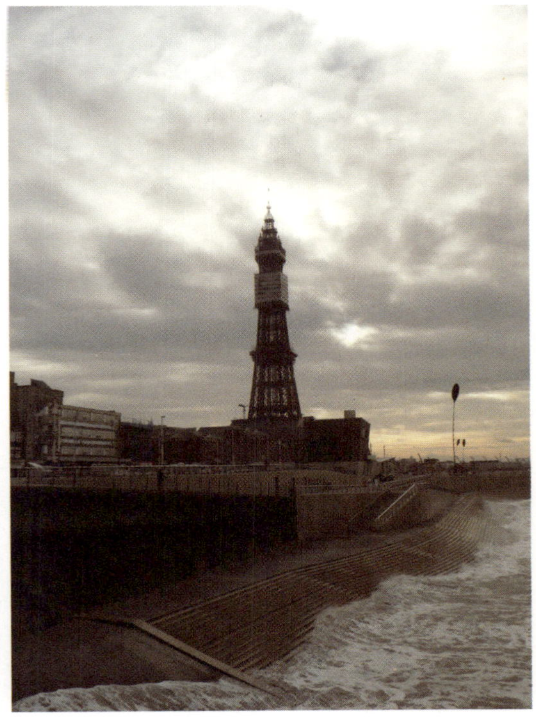

A BALLOON FOR BRITAIN

'Making sure that everyone has access to great art is the Arts Council's ambition, and it's one that we can only realise in partnership with Local Government. An inspiring cultural life is vital to the success of every local community, and increasingly councils are also investing in culture because they realise that it brings a real economic return. Our world class cultural sector is at the heart of growth in tourism and the creative industries – it is the hallmark of successful regeneration from Liverpool to St Ives, Margate to Gateshead. This publication [*Driving growth through local government investment in the arts*, Local Government Association, 2013] demonstrates local government's track record and ongoing commitment in putting arts at the heart of economic growth. I look forward to working with councils to achieve this.'

Sir Peter Bazalgette
Chair, Arts Council England
January 2013 to January 2017

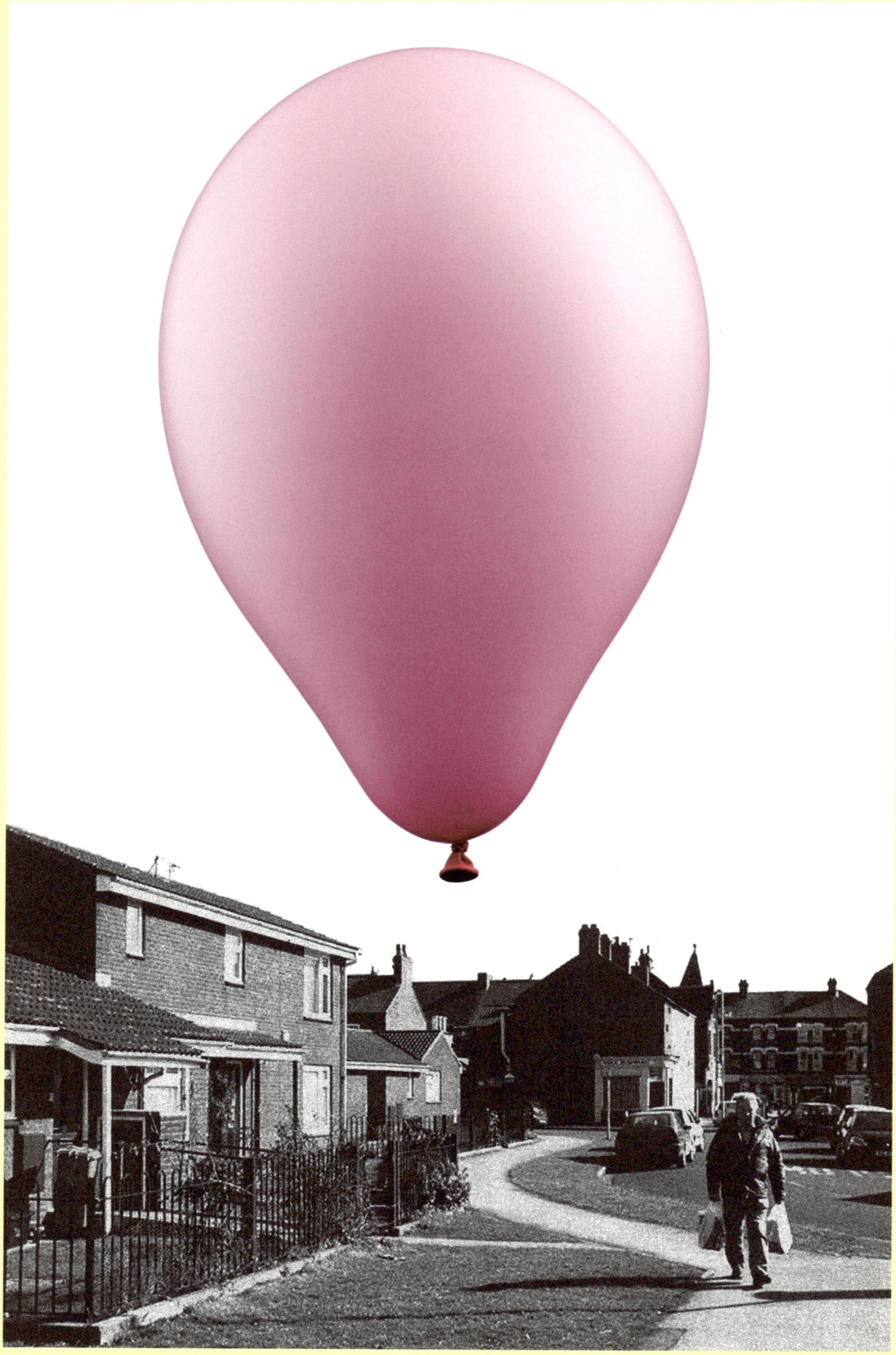

Kingston upon Hull

A Balloon for Britain, Photographic prints on paper, Ten parts, Each: 45 × 30 cm, 2012

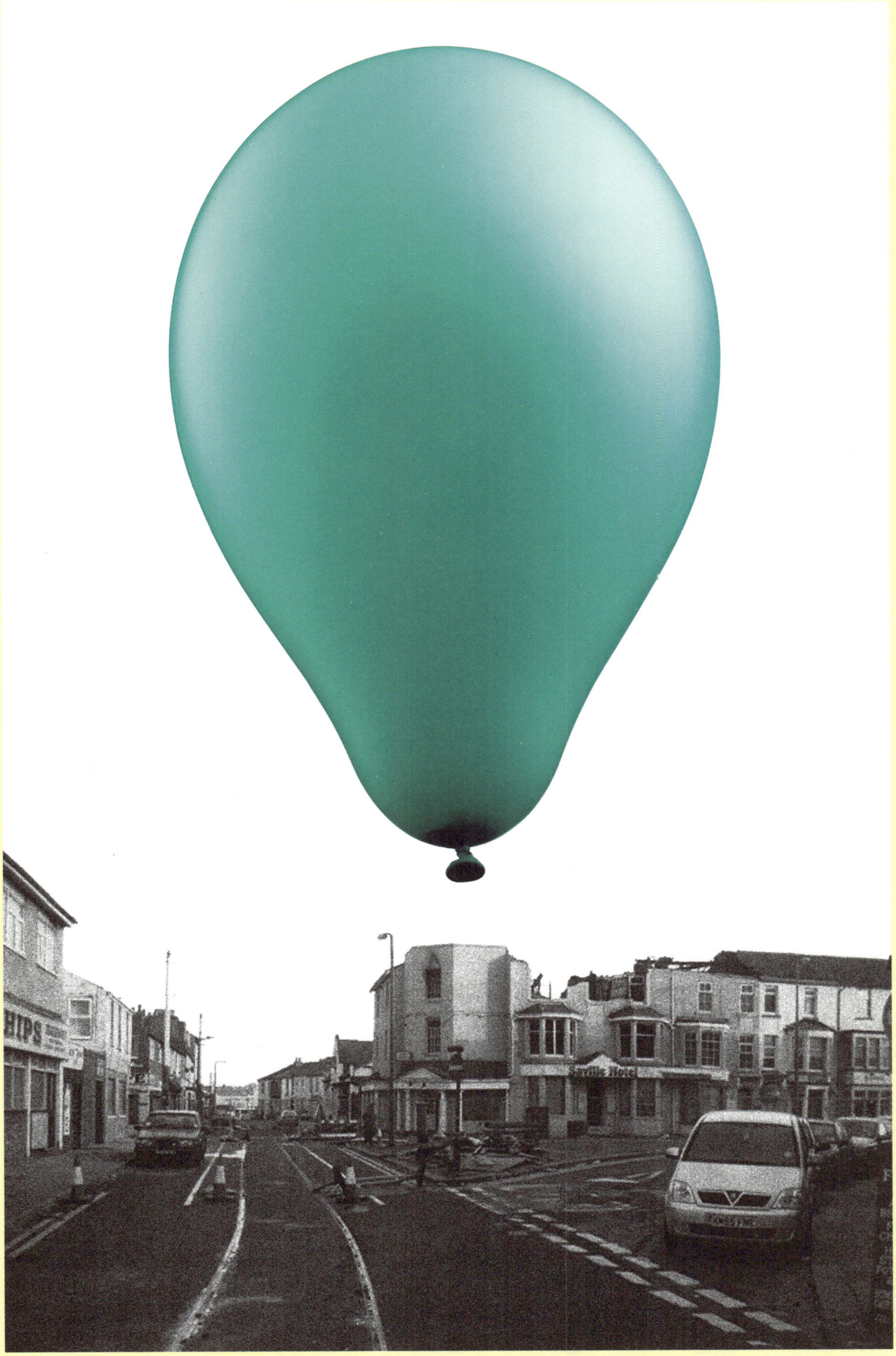

Blackpool

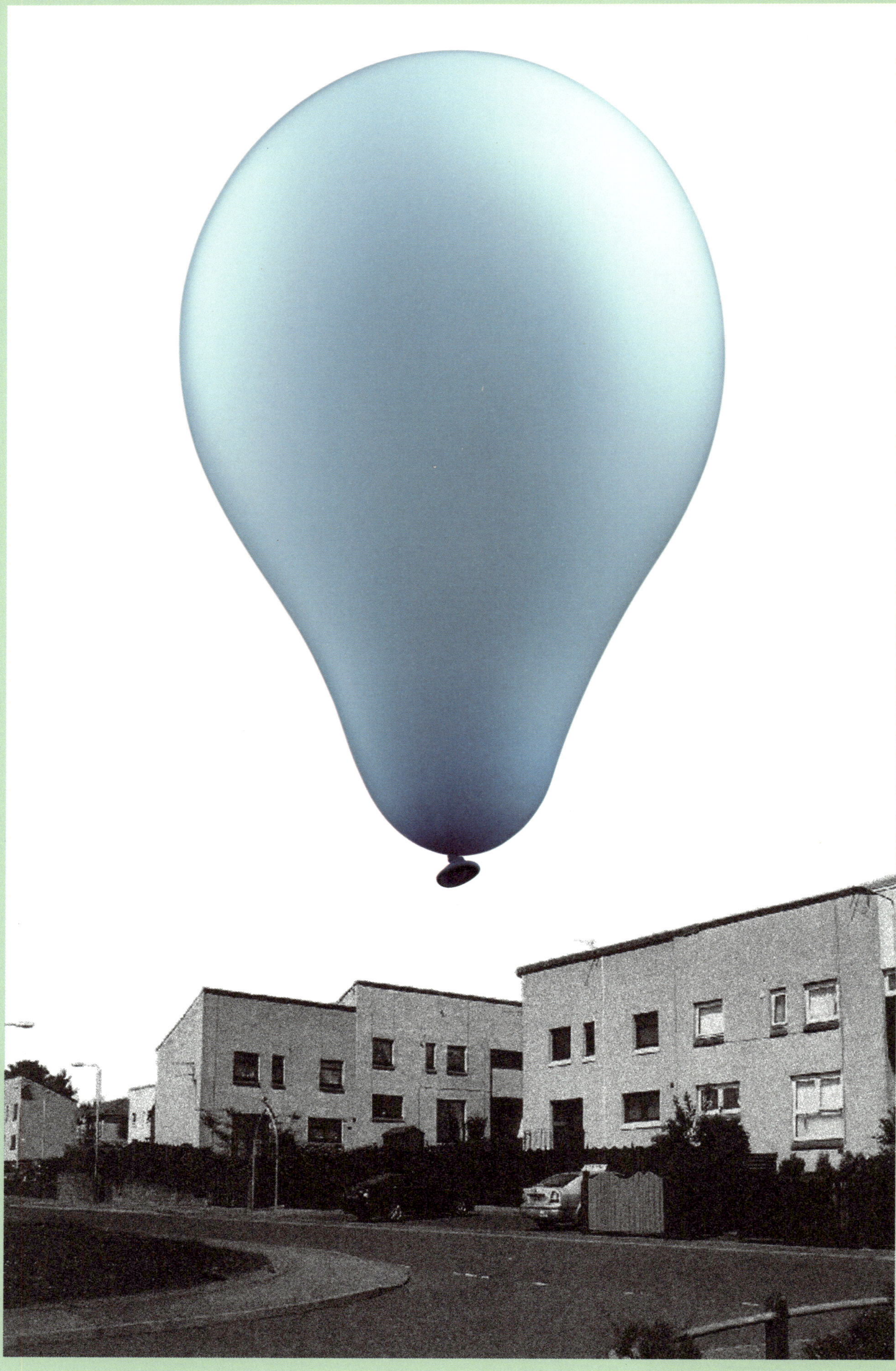

Dundee

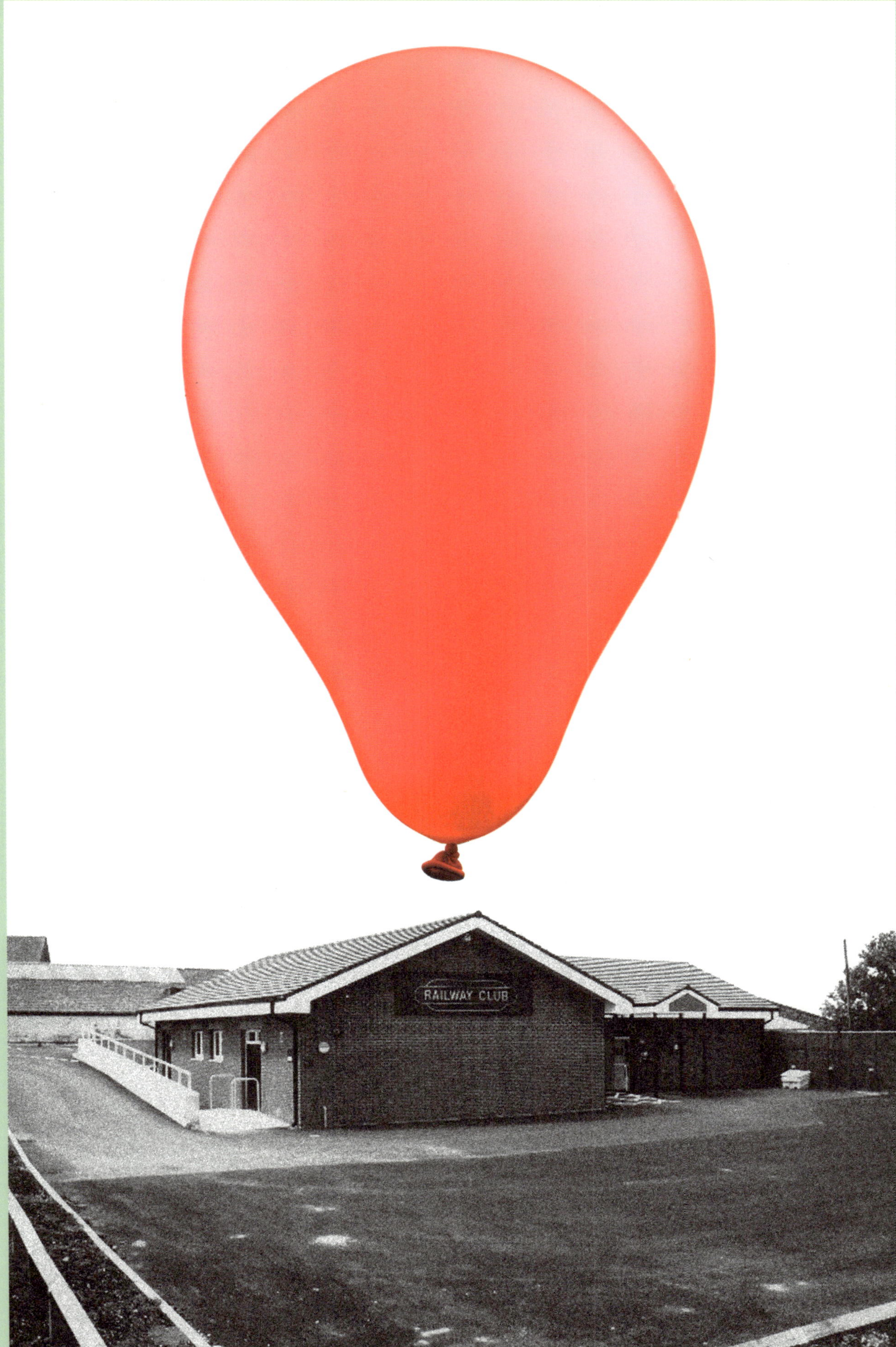

Blackburn

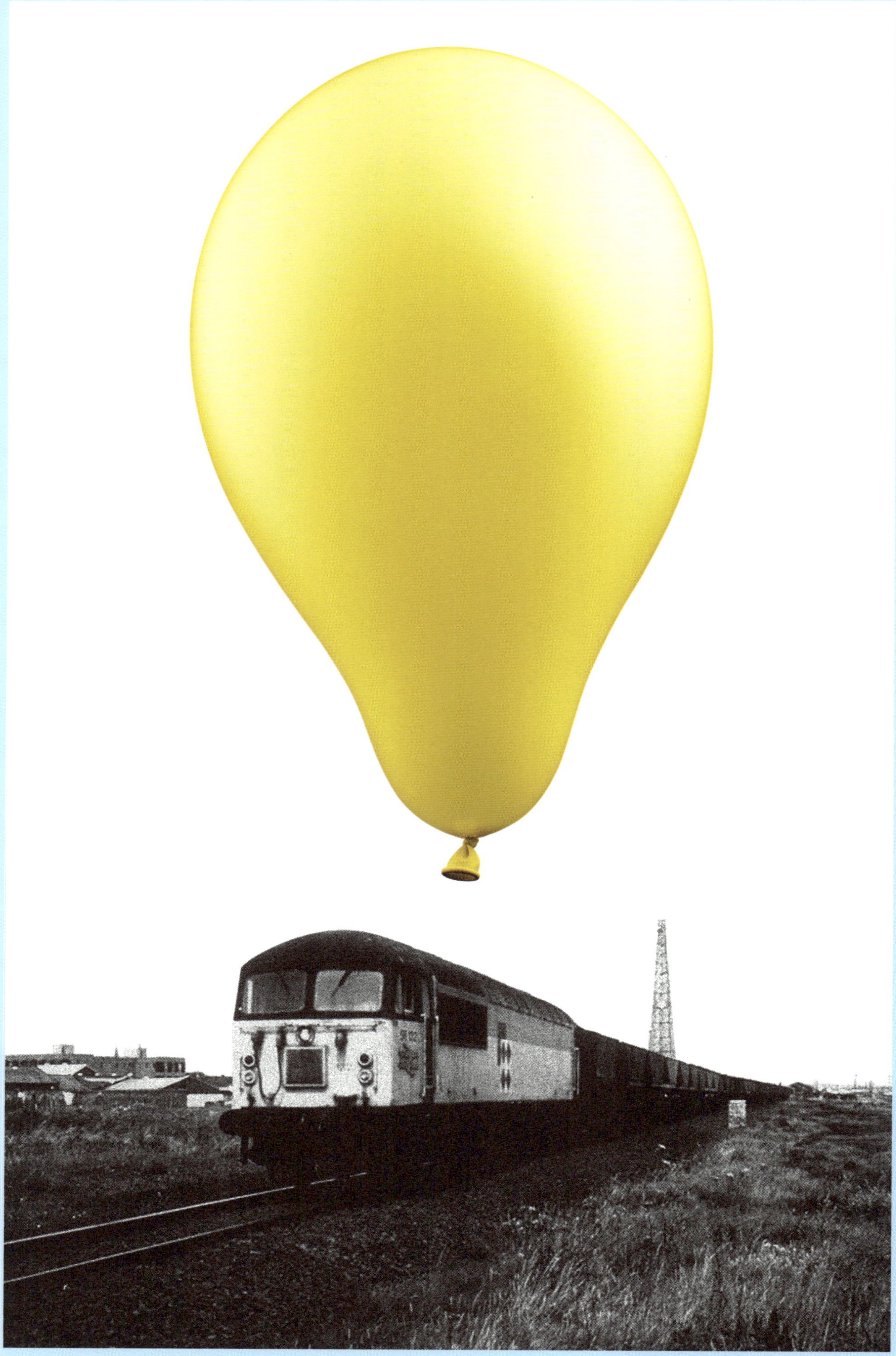

Sunderland

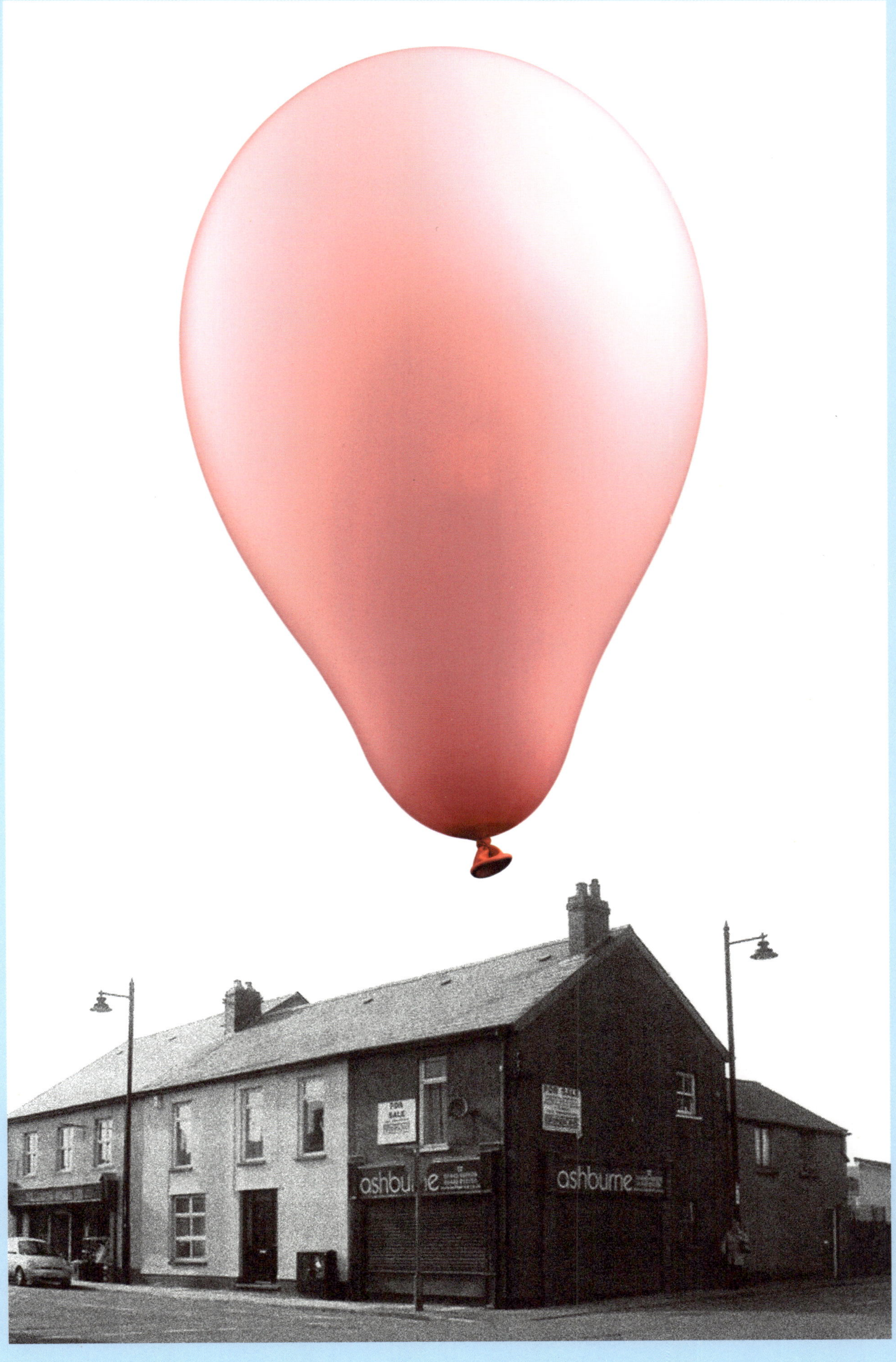

Caerphilly

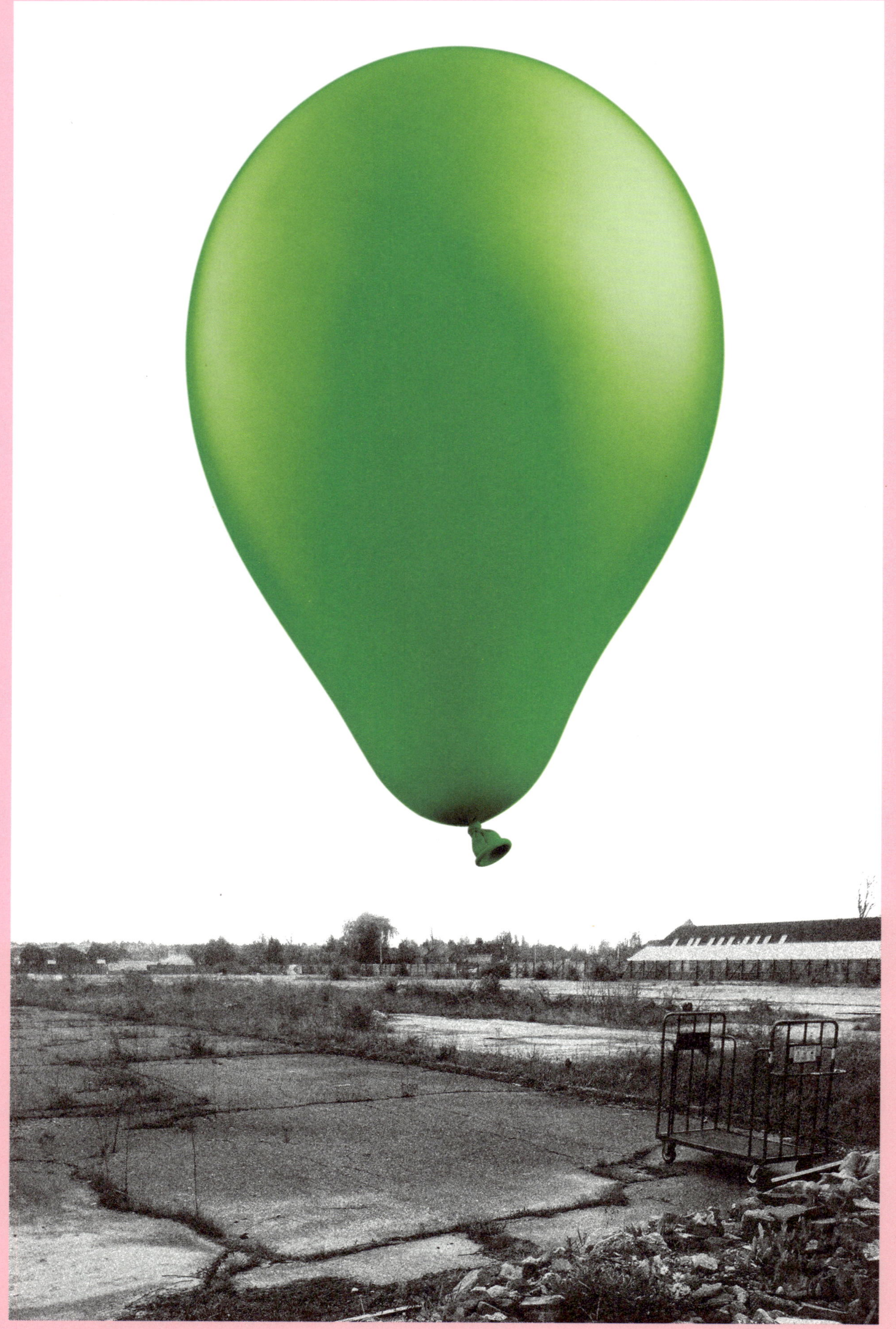

Knowsley

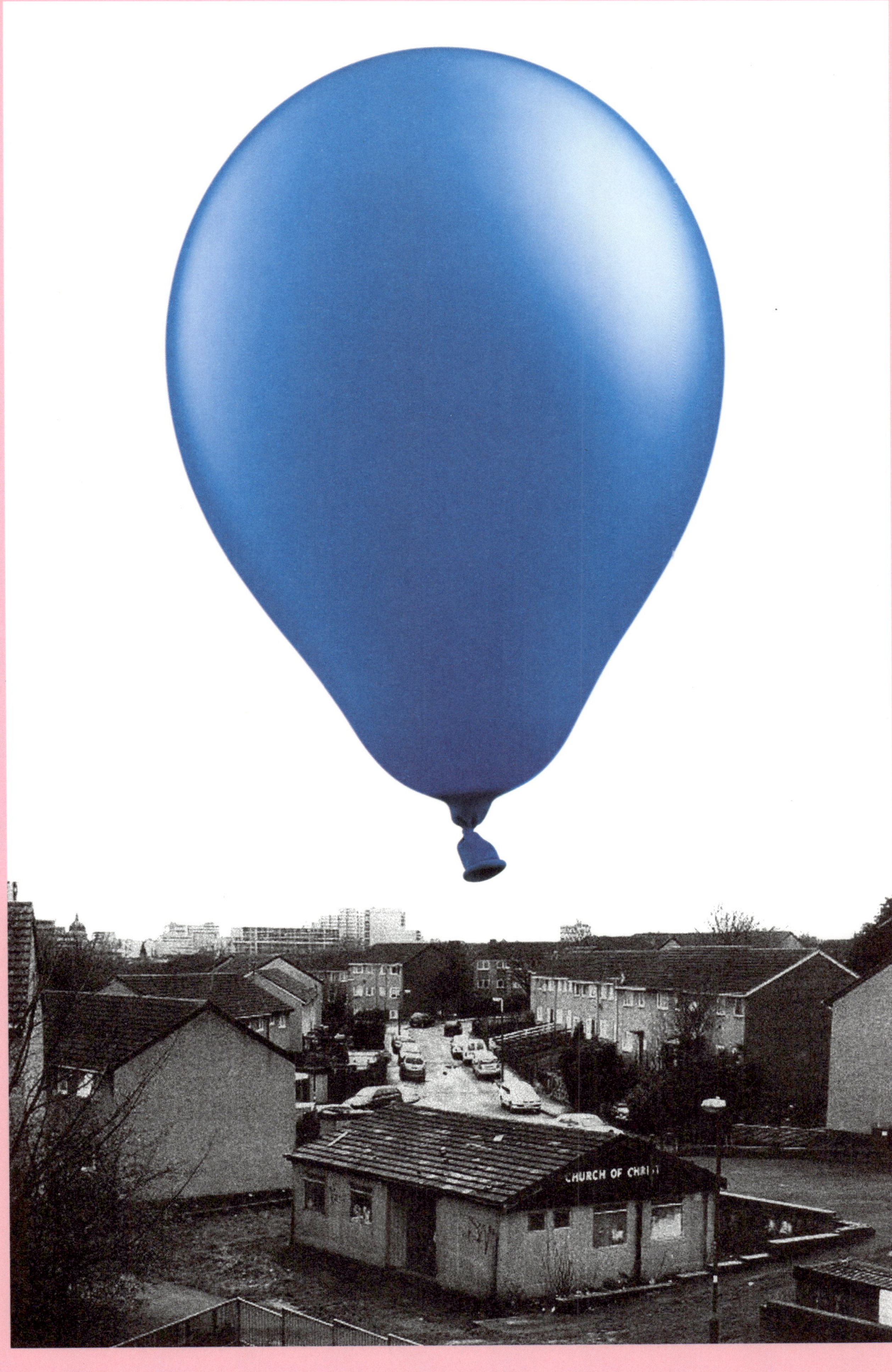

Nottingham

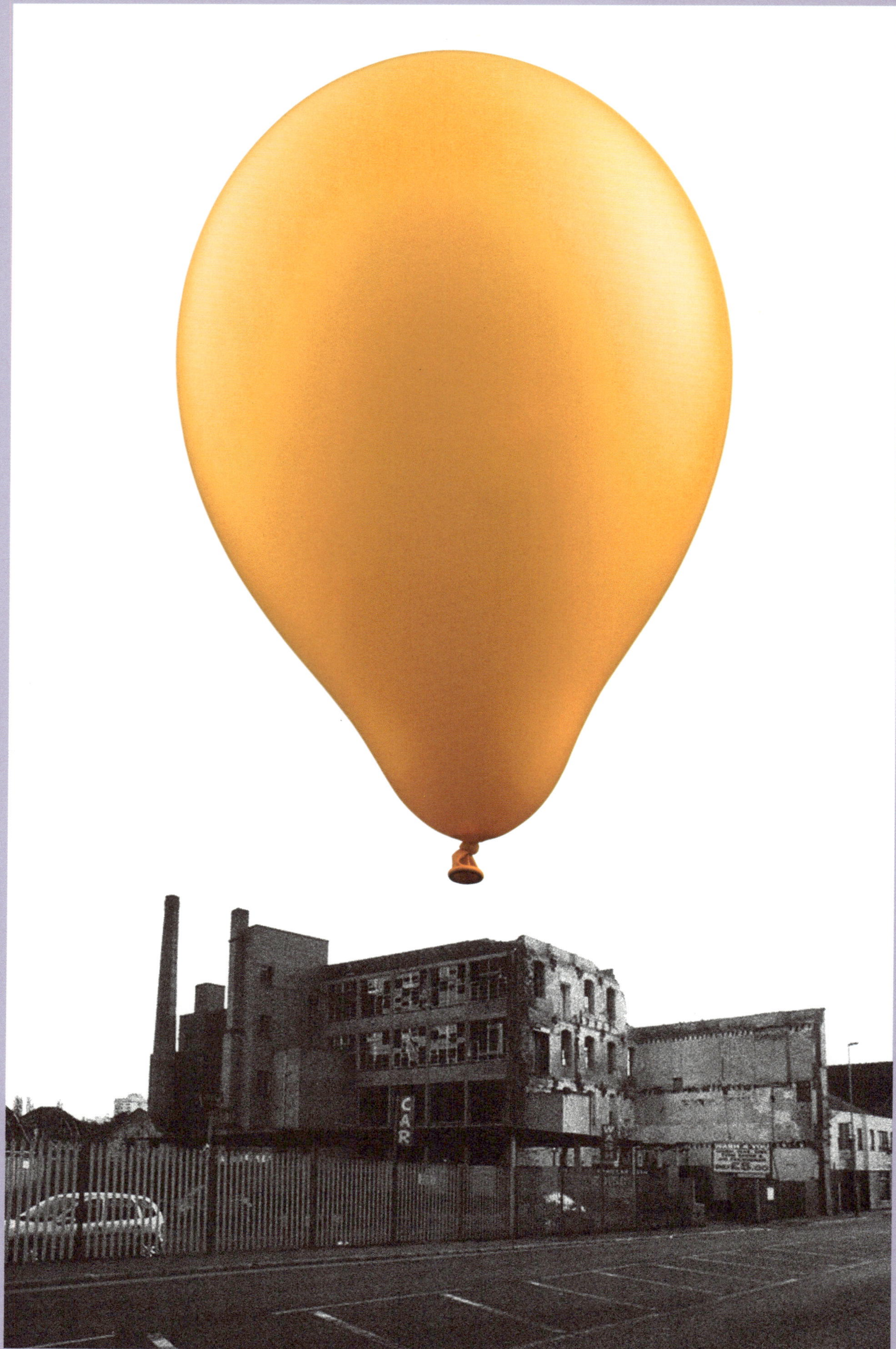

Leicester

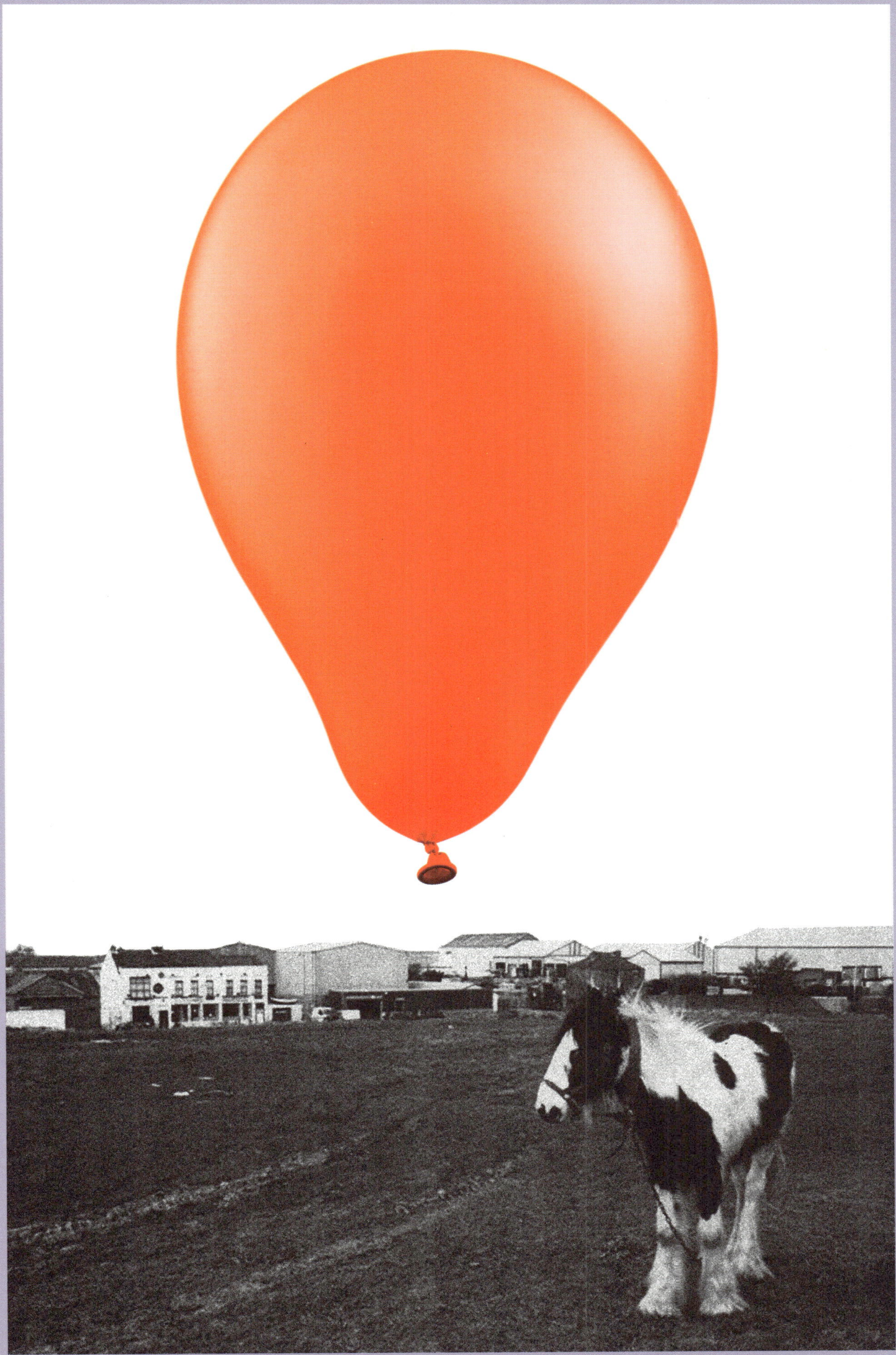

Middlesbrough

A Better Britain
One people, one country, one vision

A map of the world that does not include Utopia is not worth even glancing at - William Hague, Foreign Secretary of Great Britain

These are exacting times. The economic crisis is cutting deep and outlets for cultural innovation are feeling the brunt of the government spending cuts. Educational establishments, public funding bodies and state-supported exhibition spaces will all need to economise, streamline and re-evaluate their remits over the next few years. Art production, its cultural point-and-purpose, will no doubt come under greater scrutiny as budgets tighten and political attention is turned to regenerating – rather than celebrating – Britain's battered polity.

Artists can, of course, respond to this in a variety of ways. They may choose to keep their heads down and simply plough on as best they can; they could get politicised and campaign against the Con-Lib agenda; some will opt to engage with the market solutions and conceptual precepts of the modern Tory party – the Big Society, the mending of Broken Britain, the pre-eminence of the private sector in forging innovation and generating wealth. Whatever, an artist's cultural capital must now be seen less as representative of his or her 'power' and more as a measure of their investment potential and market worth. Like it or not, each and every response to the shifting ideological climate will inform Britain's political and cultural future. Here, then, are twelve projects designed to seek a way out of what many foresee to be dark days ahead; twelve ways to turn the imagination into a source of renovation; twelve ways to re-imagine Britain's cultural mission; twelve ways to build a Better Britain. **Scott King and Matthew Worley**

Scott King and Matthew Worley, *A Better Britain*, Xerox prints, Thirteen of twenty-five parts, Each 29.7 × 21 cm, 2010

No Glass Ceiling

Urban regeneration will alleviate poverty

Art and pop music have already made a significant contribution to the regeneration of Britain's most depressed areas. Both have offered working people a creative escape route from their seemingly predetermined lives; both have allowed cities – such as Liverpool – to benefit from their cultural heritage. More recently, the creation of large sculptures in the north of England have served to raise the quality of life for people living in some of Britain's most deprived areas. According to one recent independent survey, large public sculptures are directly attributable to drops in the crime rate, to better health among the unemployed community, and to improvements in the education of school children between 7 and 11 years of age.

We propose, then, to combine the cultural and regenerative potential of pop and art by building ten large sculptures based on the cover of Mike Oldfield's seminal *Tubular Bells* lp (1973). The lp's status as a cultural treasure has already been verified by its inclusion in a collection of stamps depicting classic British albums. Thus, by floating a large but twisted tubular bell over the town centres of those places recently listed to be among Britain's poorest (Hull, Leicester, Sunderland, Middlesbrough and Knowsley), so we believe potential investors and retailers will be drawn to the aforementioned towns as musical connoisseurs were to the original lp. As importantly, the construction of the sculptures will offer employment and succor to the local community, building a work ethic and a sense of *joie de vivre* that simply throwing money at public services will fail to achieve. If the immediate cost of the project seems excessive, then the long-term impact of the finished work will stand as a testament to the entrepreneurial spirit of the British culture industry.

Tubular Bell for Hull
One of 10 Tubular Bell sculptures set to dominate wasteland in Britain's 10 poorest towns and cities

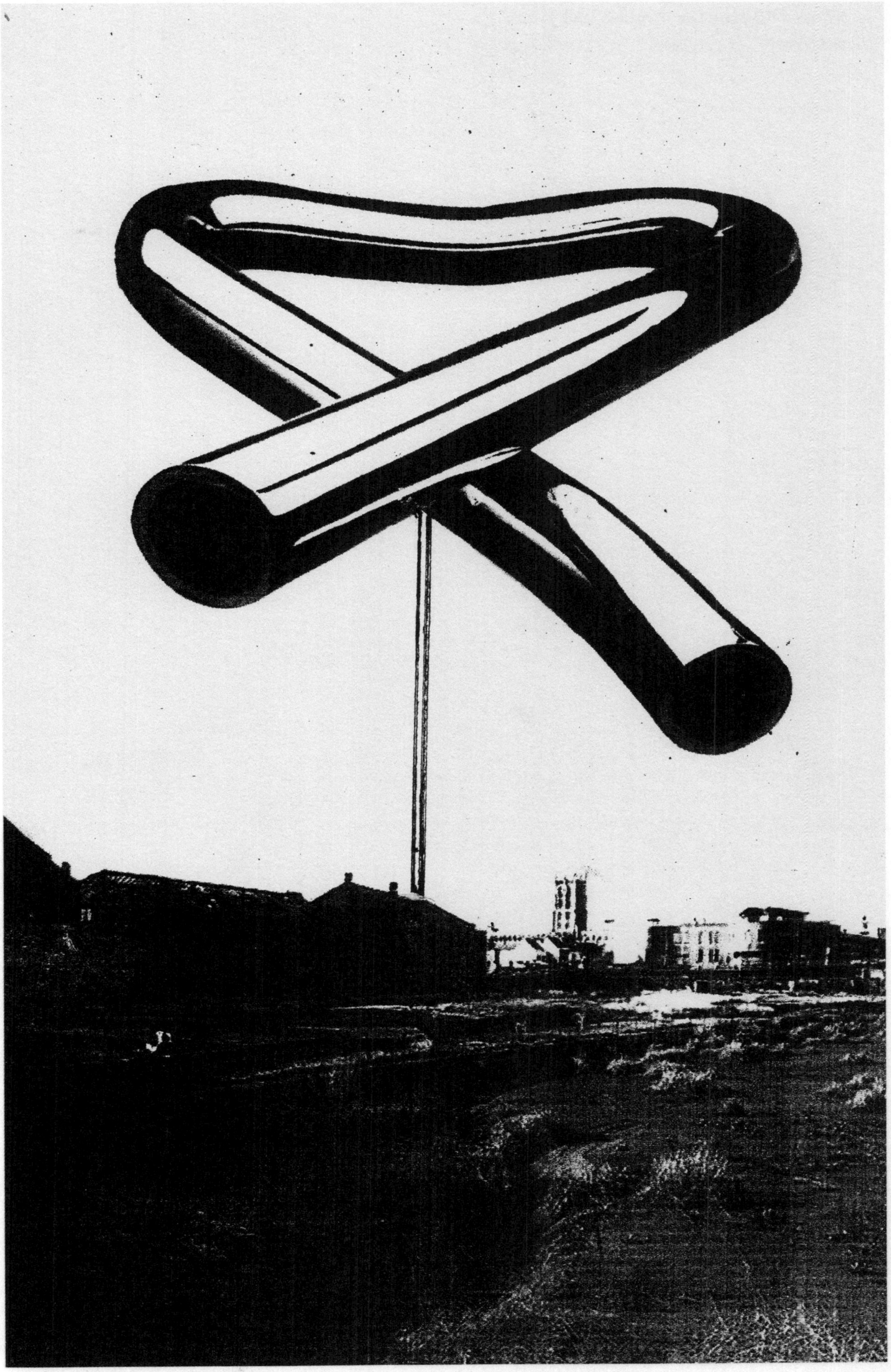

When The Rubber Meets The Road

Motorhead 76: A celebration of the wheel

A necessary consequence of the economy measures introduced to solve the financial crisis is unemployment. But unemployment can also create opportunity. For business there is a ready pool of people desperate for work whatever the wage rate; for the unemployed there is the chance to experience flexible working patterns or to reinvent their lifestyle choice; and for the government there is an opportunity to undertake various low-cost projects necessary to patch up Britain's ageing infrastructure. Prisoners, obviously, can be made to work for their keep. But low-wage labour may also allow for modest work schemes designed to renovate public buildings or improve Britain's transport network.

Transport is important: commerce needs to move. And now that the war against the motorist has been defeated by those standing beneath the standard of Jeremy Clarkson, so the government would be wise to repay its foot soldiers by designing a new motorway network to better connect Britain. After some analysis, this would appear to work best by following the tour undertaken by Motorhead in 1976. The motorway should be built in the spirit of the band: no corners, accepting no obstacle to its route, and attuned to speed. No doubt Lemmy will appreciate the echoes of the autobahn, but for the British motorist it will rekindle the freedom of the road that seemed perilously close to being snuffed out.

Built For Speed
Image illustrates exciting new motorway that will connect Dudley to Bolton

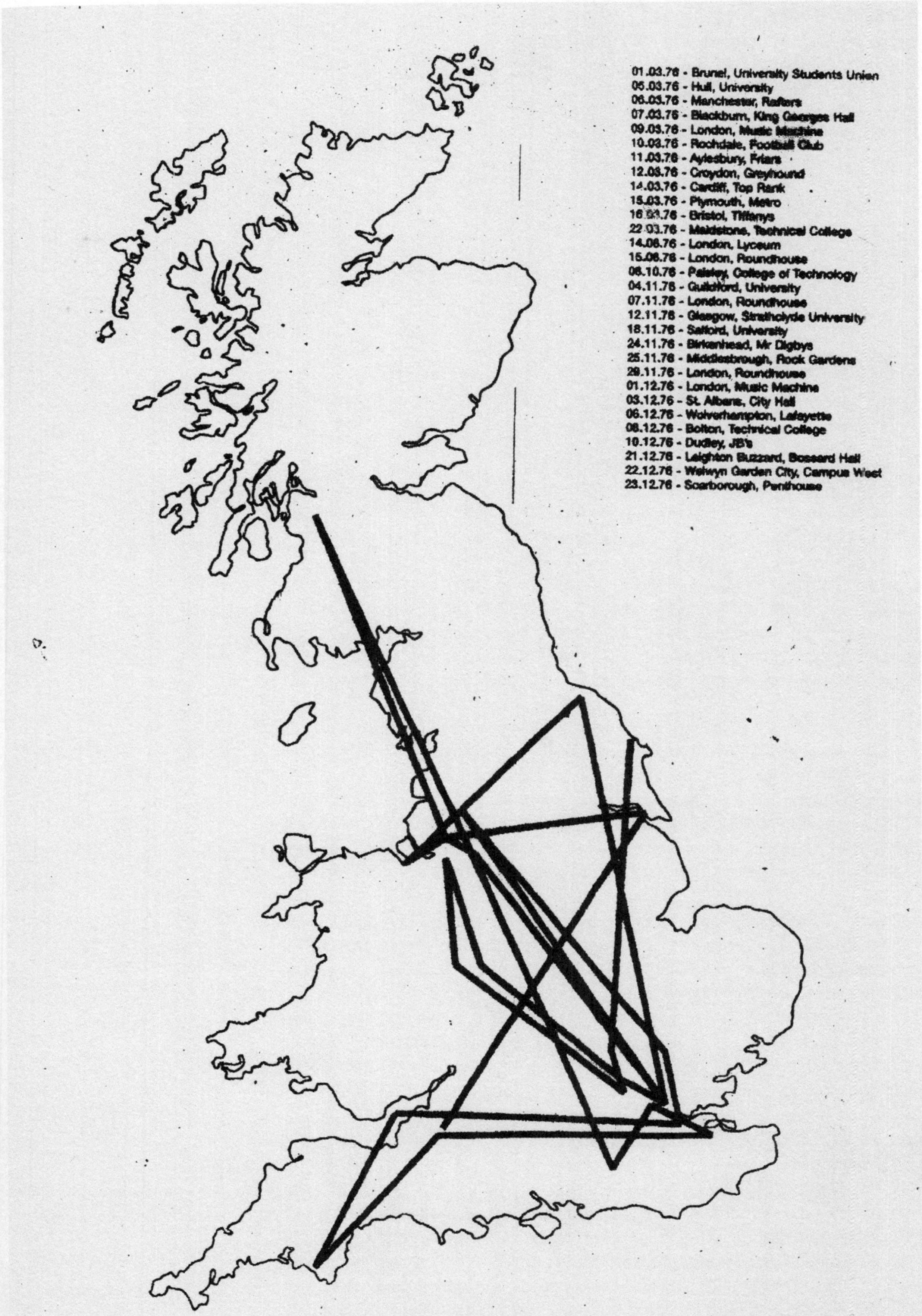
01.03.76 - Brunel, University Students Union
05.03.76 - Hull, University
06.03.76 - Manchester, Rafters
07.03.76 - Blackburn, King Georges Hall
09.03.76 - London, Music Machine
10.03.76 - Rochdale, Football Club
11.03.76 - Aylesbury, Friars
12.03.76 - Croydon, Greyhound
14.03.76 - Cardiff, Top Rank
15.03.76 - Plymouth, Metro
16.03.76 - Bristol, Tiffanys
22.03.76 - Maidstone, Technical College
14.06.76 - London, Lyceum
15.06.76 - London, Roundhouse
08.10.76 - Paisley, College of Technology
04.11.76 - Guildford, University
07.11.76 - London, Roundhouse
12.11.76 - Glasgow, Strathclyde University
18.11.76 - Salford, University
24.11.76 - Birkenhead, Mr Digbys
25.11.76 - Middlesbrough, Rock Gardens
29.11.76 - London, Roundhouse
01.12.76 - London, Music Machine
03.12.76 - St. Albans, City Hall
06.12.76 - Wolverhampton, Lafayette
08.12.76 - Bolton, Technical College
10.12.76 - Dudley, JB's
21.12.76 - Leighton Buzzard, Bossard Hall
22.12.76 - Welwyn Garden City, Campus West
23.12.76 - Scarborough, Penthouse

Thought Leader

Man or myth?: A celebration of individuality

The importance of communal memory, and the oral passing of information from generation to generation, has long been of interest to historians of folk memory and tradition. This project therefore seeks to explore and capitalise on a crucial example of this: namely, to celebrate the maverick figures of provincial Britain whose (real or imagined) life stories have become weaved into the fabric of the community to which they were at once a part of and detached from.

The logistics of the project would require only modest investment. Up to 25 localities would be targeted across the UK. A 'Great British Eccentric' would then be identified and information gathered as to their name, background and the myths that had grown around them. A 50 x life-size statue would then be erected to dominate the area of their most regular sightings. Two examples may include:

Cue Gary (Goole) – Cue Gary's name stems from the fact that he has carried a snooker cue around with him everyday for the past 25 years, though no-one has ever seen him play snooker. He is also known to ride a bicycle with no chain.

Marigold (Norwich) – a black man in yellow washing-up gloves who walked around the ring road directing the traffic; sometimes carrying a broom. Rumour had it that his hands were rotting away beneath the gloves and that his 'condition' was caused by a blow to the head by a helicopter.

Such a project would obviously be designed to celebrate diversity within communities and applaud individuality. It would cultivate understanding within local communities, bringing awareness of social exclusion to the fore and thereby serving to provide policy solutions that help the socially disadvantaged. It would also help ensure that the chosen maverick at last 'gave back' something to the community that sustained him or her throughout their eccentric and ultimately unproductive lives.

Cue Gary (Goole Leisure Centre)
An artist's impression of one of 25 proposed monuments that will celebrate local mavericks

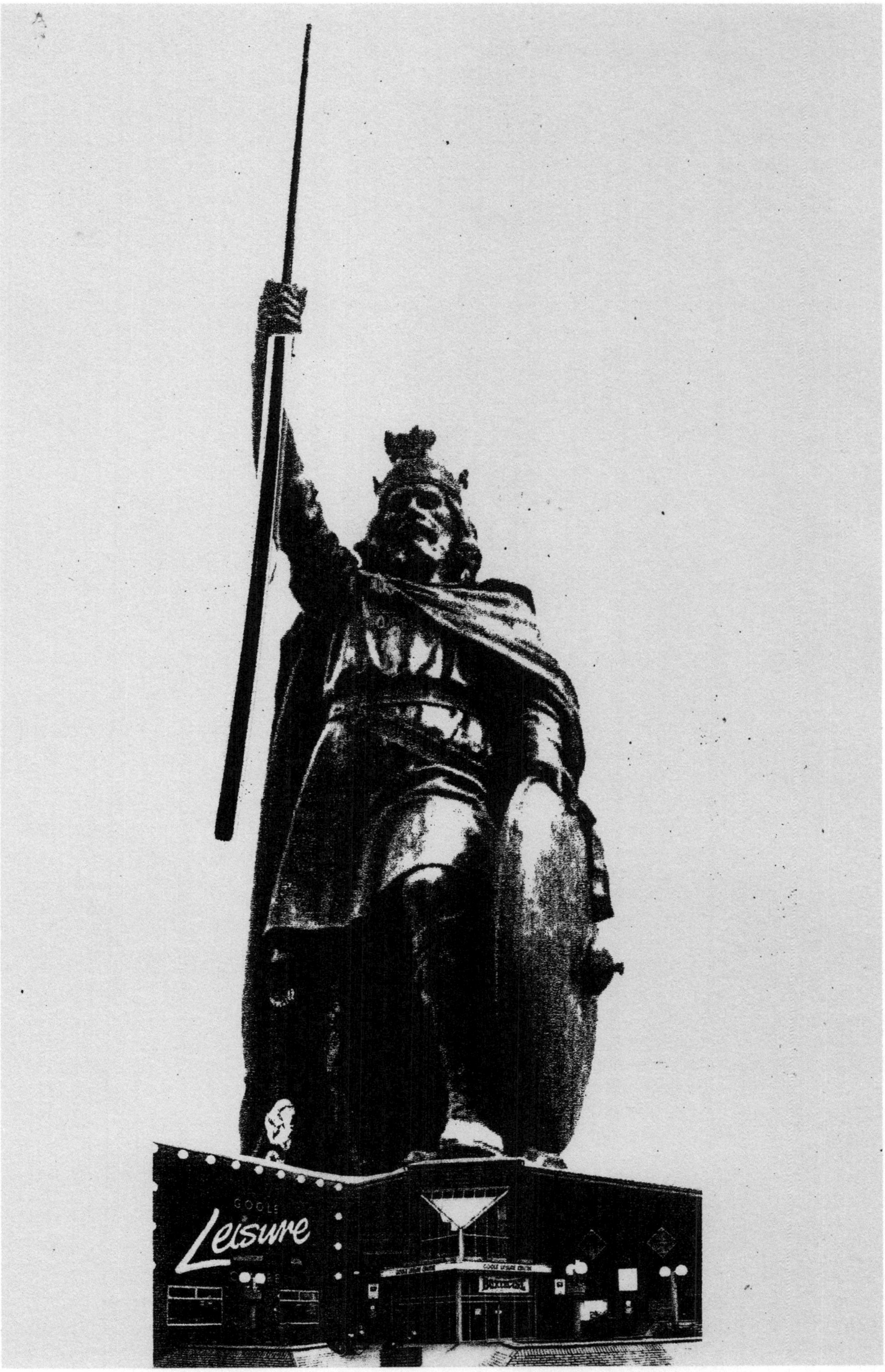
GOOLE
Leisure

Blue Sky Thinking

Ailing icons given new lease of life

Britain is a small country, and in an age of high-speed travel and technological innovation it is easy to see why tourists are beginning to look elsewhere for their summer thrills. One whistle-stop week is all that is needed to tick Britain's key tourist attractions off any 'must-see' list. Quite clearly, the time has come for reinvigoration. Bath's baths have changed little for hundreds of years, and a new range of postcards will not fool the modern-day tourist. Not dissimilarly, one Tudor-themed street is much like another; why go to York and Norwich when doing just one will serve you fine. In our fast-moving world, how many cathedrals can the average tourist stomach; and who exactly are the old soldiers on horses in Whitehall? One solution would be to initiate temporary attractions or introduce elements of 'surprise'. Placing sculptural figures on rooftops has proven itself both press worthy and popular. Thus, perhaps, figures of contemporary significance could be used to revitalise ailing tourist sites. Statues of Saddam could be brought back from Iraq to add visual spice to Edinburgh Castle; a life-size figure of Robbie Williams could stand atop Tower Bridge; the cast of Dr Who could be dressed in tunics to brighten up Colchester's historic streets. If Britain wants to better itself, it must become a centre of innovation – it must entice tourists by relating its historic traditions to the needs and desires of the modern age.

A New Horizon
Recycled and populist statues will rejuvenate Edinburgh Castle and other forgotten landmarks

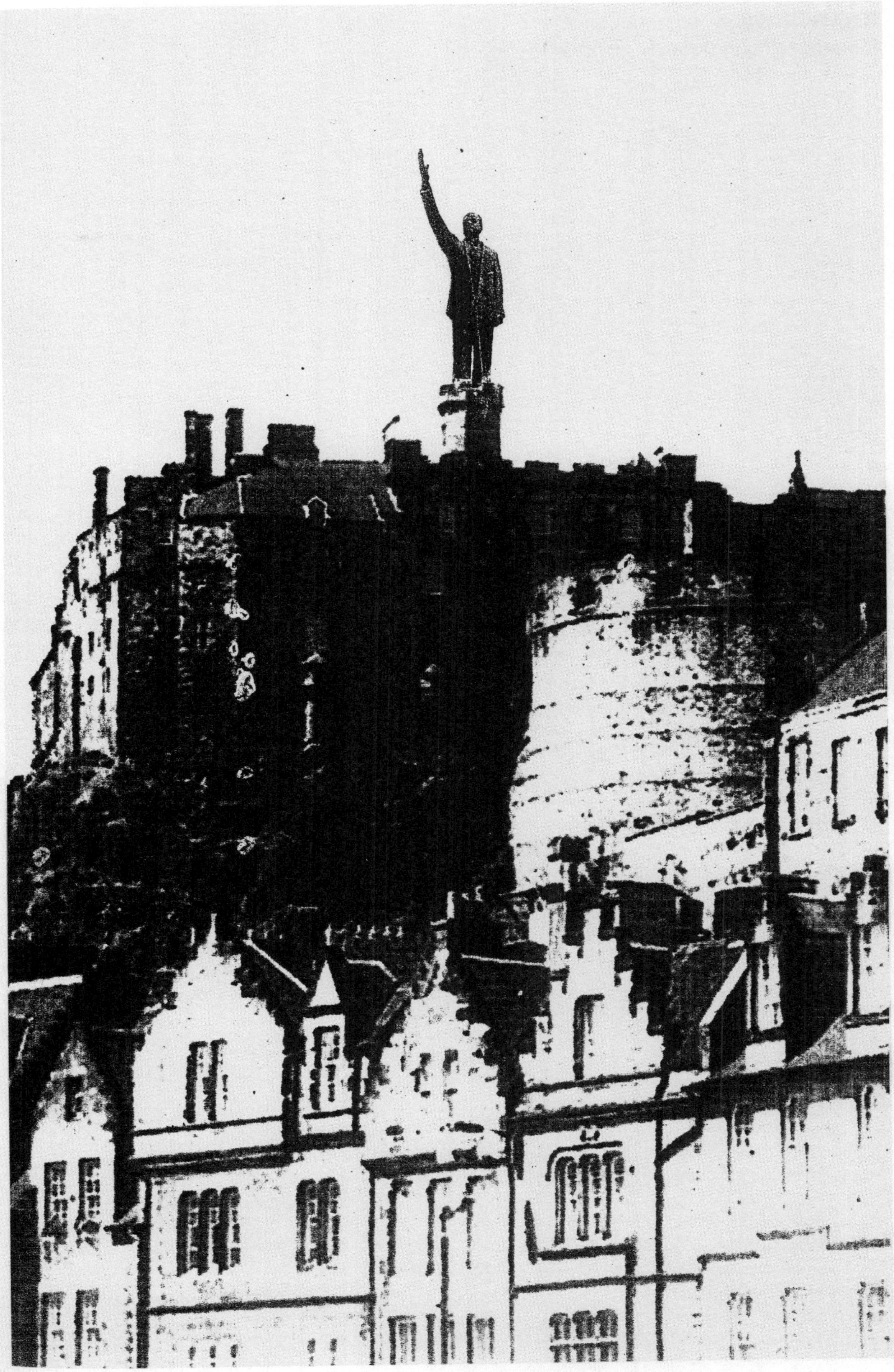

Market Driven

Strength through diversity: Driving for freedom

Over the past fifty years, Britain has learned to celebrate its diversity. No longer is disability, ethnicity, gender or sexuality judged by any divergence from an imagined, or Whitehall prescribed, norm. Instead, differences in sexual preference, skin colour, religion and physicality are embraced. They are, within a society defined by consumption, a potential font of cultural capital to be exploited; or a recognized lifestyle to be catered for by the ever-flexible parameters of the free market. Britain, in the twenty-first century, is a testament to the 60s slogan of the personal being political – we are all different but all accepted; we are all individuals now.

This project seeks to celebrate the complexities of such diversity within a society proud of its inclusivity by proposing that the M1 is demarcated along lines of personal identity. Thus, motorists will be expected to drive in lanes designated as 'Gay', 'Black', 'White', 'Christian' and so on. An element of 'choice' will of course be allowed: a gay Chinese man with a disability will be able to choose which lane he drives down. But the project serves primarily to instigate a sense of individuality without any accompanying sense of isolation.

In terms of finance, money will be needed to widen the M1 to accommodate the diverse range of identities that inform the UK. We estimate that this will amount to some £2 billion. However, the cost of the project will be offset by its impact on the cultural well-being of the nation, on its ability to connect communities, and its contribution to keeping unemployment to a respectable level.

The M1x12
Major artery widening will become a monument to modernity

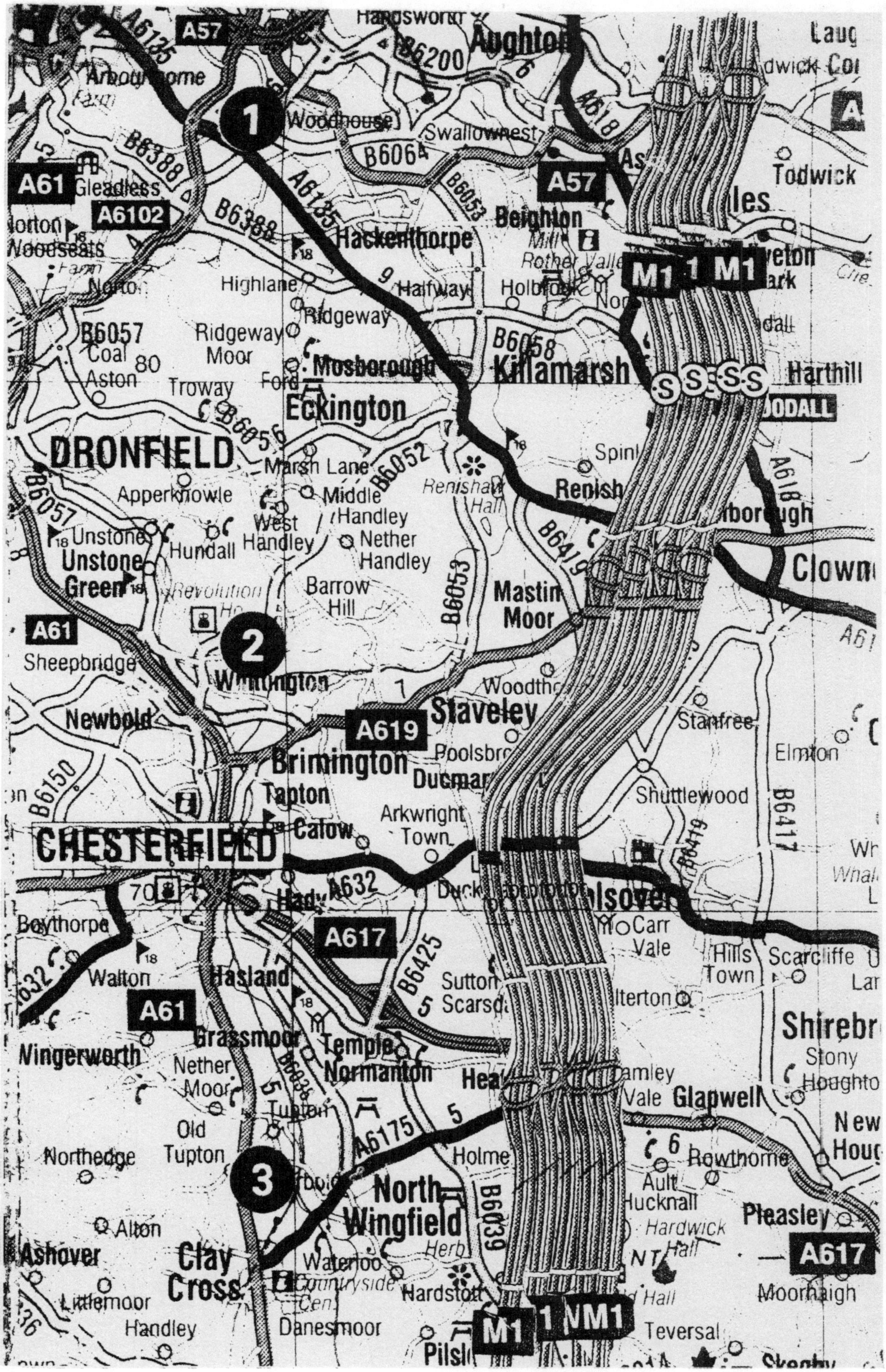
A57
Aughton
B6200
1
Woodhouse
Swallownest
B6064
A61
Gleadless
A6102
B6388
A6135
Hackenthorpe
Beighton
Todwick
A57
M1
1
M1
Highlane
Halfway
Holbrook
Ridgeway
Ridgeway Moor
B6057
Coal Aston
Troway
Mosborough
Killamarsh
B6058
Harthill
Eckington
DRONFIELD
Marsh Lane
B6052
Apperknowle
Middle Handley
Renishaw Hall
Unstone
Hundall
West Handley
Nether Handley
Unstone Green
Barrow Hill
B6053
Mastin Moor
Clown
A61
2
Sheepbridge
Staveley
Woodthorpe
Newbold
A619
Brimington
Stanfree
Elmton
Tapton
Calow
Arkwright Town
Shuttlewood
B6417
B6419
CHESTERFIELD
A632
Carr Vale
Hasland
A617
B6425
Sutton Scarsdale
Hills Town
Scarcliffe
Walton
A61
Grassmoor
Temple Normanton
Shirebrook
Stony Houghton
Wingerworth
Nether Moor
Glapwell
A6175
Old Tupton
Holme
Rowthorne
Northedge
3
North Wingfield
Ault Hucknall
Hardwick Hall
Pleasley
Alton
B6039
Ashover
Clay Cross
Waterloo
A617
Countryside Cen
Hardstoft
Moorhaigh
Littlemoor
Handley
Danesmoor
M1
1
M1
Teversal

Connected Communities

Ambitious proposal set to unify Essex and Kent

One healthy trend in recent British public sculpture has been its attention to scale. Such a focus has obvious ramifications for the mending of 'Broken Britain', serving to embolden Britain's sense of pride and place in the world. By following the example of Mark Wallinger's proposed 'White Horse', Antony Gormley's 'Angel of the North', and Anish Kapoor's 'ArcelorMittal Orbit' and 'Temenos', Britain can restate its global status as a financial power-house and shed its reputation for being a stagnant state-bureaucracy akin to Hoxha's Albania. Just as the 'Angel of the North' intimidates and impresses those who venture into England's hinterlands, so the French will shrink beneath the shadow of a massive horse. Our idea, then, is to extend this concept and make 'Horse' even more impressive through the addition of Essex's most famous son, The Big Figure. We envisage that, in the future, all ways into Britain, and all major motorway turn-offs, should be signaled by a cultural statement of intent. The message should be: We are British and look what we can do.

Bigger Figures
Dr Feelgood drummer on a large horse will leave a lasting impression on French *Eurostar* passengers traveling through Ebbsfleet

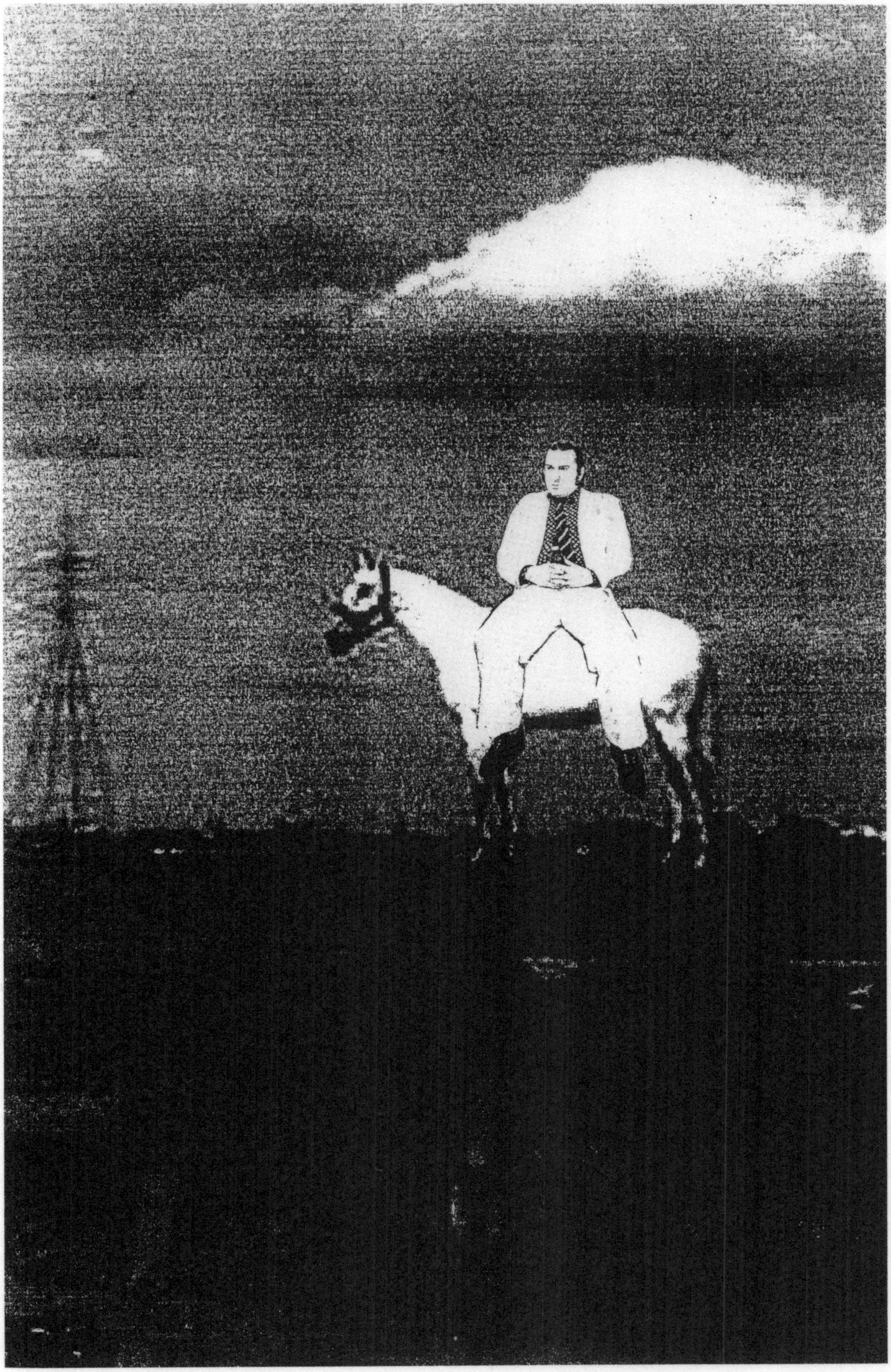

Interview: Robert Hewison

This conversation took place at Robert Hewison's home in Acton, London, on 30 July 2015.

SCOTT KING: To start with Robert, I was wondering if you could explain in simple terms your view of public sculpture and public art under the New Labour government.

ROBERT HEWISON: Well, perhaps the real question is, what is public art? I suggest it's a form of art that engages with the public in a public space. We might ask what that space is, to whom it belongs, and what the conditions are for engagement with it. There have been some great examples where the public – however defined – has been able to engage with a work of art outside a gallery. I think that is what we are talking about, situations where artists position their work outside the walls of a gallery – which, even when museum entrance is free, does not involve the cash nexus in some way. In my book *Cultural Capital* (2014) I ask questions about the nature of that public space, and talk about the mental and physical space of the 'public realm'.

One of the most successful examples of public art in the UK this century has been the fourth plinth series in Trafalgar Square in London. That's a context that we can understand because Trafalgar Square has long been a place of public assembly. What's interesting is that the empty space in the square's northwest corner – which is an eloquently empty site, because the three other corners contain statues of dead white male imperialists – is that the plinth has been offered up as a space of engagement for the public with contemporary sculpture. Many of the commissions have simply been objects that have just stood there – I'm thinking of *Ecce Homo* (1999) the figure of Christ by Mark Wallinger and *Hahn/Cock* (2013) the blue cockerel by Katharina Fritsch, for instance – however, Anthony Gormley's piece *One and Other* was an opportunity for anyone to occupy that space on the plinth for an hour, and do what they liked. What's interesting is that this commission appeared on television and online, so the participation was virtual as well as actual.

I think that Gormley's work represents a very successful use of public art and public space. But that's not really what most public art is. These days it's a form of decoration, which is usually paid for by private interests to secure planning permission for capital projects, so the effect is entirely negative.

SK: I appreciate what you say about Gormley's use of the fourth plinth. Within the period of history we're talking about, Gormley is still the king. However, what *Angel of the North* and other totemic public artworks were trying to achieve was really to create business via collusion between private and government sponsorship in areas decimated by Thatcher's government in the 1980s. The site of Anish Kapoor's *Temenos* in the Middleborough docks is another good example where there was once industry, and now there's none. How much do you think there was a conscious policy by New Labour to use gigantic public sculpture to create business?

RH: Firstly, there's a distinction between public sculpture and public art. After all Jeremy Deller's parade in Manchester was a form of public art, if your definition of public art is something that takes place in a public space, and which isn't filtered by a direct monetary exchange. If we are talking about public sculpture, then this is essentially the cherry on the cake of projects in which 'culture' has been exploited as a form of urban regeneration. Possibly the biggest example of this is not just a single sculpture, but the entire gallery of sculpture that is Tate Modern. This building is emblematic of the transformation that has taken place in London, a situation in which a redundant power station, which nobody had noticed for years – even though it was enormous and situated bang in the centre of the city – was suddenly transformed into a rival cathedral of culture to St. Paul's across the river.

To me, this situation is extremely eloquent, because the Borough of Southwark, in which Tate Modern sits, was one of the poorest places in the UK, yet it is directly opposite one of the richest places in the world, the City of London. The City's fathers were very reluctant about the so-called 'wobbly bridge' being built, with its own public sculpture by Anthony Caro (which is somewhat ignored, neglected and probably not very successful). Their hesitancy was due to the fact that the bridge meant there'd be an easy connection between these two spheres of the north and the south. I used to live in the City of London in the 1970s, and I would walk round Bankside with its total dereliction; now it's just another set of gleaming boxes. What happened was that money poured south, and Southwark has been enormously transformed.

Now, there are three questions we can ask. First of all, was Tate a success in cultural terms? I would argue that it was. Secondly, was the transformation of Southwark a success in economic terms? Well, obviously it was, because the initial refurbishment is gradually drifting south. The third question would be, is the redevelopment and high-end gentrification of Southwark socially beneficial? And to answer this, I think you need to ask further questions about the nature of public space: who is allowed to live in that space and who is making money from it? There's no easy answer.

Tate Modern worked as a way to regenerate an area. However, if you try and do the same thing in West Bromwich by employing Will Alsop, the brilliant visionary architect who also designed Peckham Library, to try and take a very small local community arts organisation that originally functioned out of a double-decker bus – and say 'right, we're going to build a space that will completely transform the area' – it can turn out to be a complete disaster. 'The Public' as it was called, was an example of a public space that, in spite of its original roots in the community, failed to achieve its ambition. It became a vast vanity project driven by the wrong motivations. The Arts Council found itself driving the project, because it felt it had to respond to New Labour policy that believed that art could achieve urban and social regeneration.

SK: A very obvious point is that there's a difference in class and culture between the two locations, as well as scale: in West Bromwich there simply aren't the same level of tourist visitors as at Tate Modern. What was run perfectly successfully from a bus fails when it's translated into a gigantic theme park, because there is only a small percentage of people interested in that kind of culture in the West Bromwich area. Unlike London, there really aren't going to be that many people who are passing West Bromwich that decide to go to The Public.

RH: That's the great irony of the term 'public art' in relation to The Public. It articulates an unsuccessful example of the instrumental use of culture.

SK: In my opinion, the ambition of The Public is a direct reflection of the scale of Tate Modern and relates to the size of Antony Gormley's *Angel of the North*, Anish Kapoor's *ArcelorMittal Orbit* and Mark Wallinger's *White Horse of Ebbsfleet*. What's your view on this type of gigantism?

RH: Well, the spread of gigantism is partially a result of the success of *Angel of the North*. Everybody, including the locals, fought Gormley's monument until it got there and then somehow or other it became adopted, which was a great moment. The fact that *Angel of the North* is built on top of an old coalmine, and is made of steel, is a magical transformation of a lost industrial culture. Having looked at it and seen how it sits in the physical and mental landscape, I think you have to say that it is a success, and part of its success is because it's so big. We have to acknowledge that lottery money was very influential in developing large-scale projects, because it made all of these things possible, including Tate Modern.

In my view, this created the necessary refurbishment of the entire cultural infrastructure of the UK, which was an important and valid thing to have done. Public art is part of that infrastructure; it's a visualisation of the ambition of this refurbishment. But it's not enough to simply refurbish towns and cities, you actually need to have something happening inside them.

ANDREW HUNT: Historically speaking, with property developers and architects occupying positions as chairs and trustees of major arts organisations, such as the National Lottery and Tate, one can see a direct connection between the major gallery capital projects of the 1990s and 2000s, regeneration and the astronomical rise of house prices in the UK. With current cuts to the DCMS and Arts Council, one might ask whether or not these galleries, even the successful ones, have served their purpose and are now unsustainable. Do you think their real aim is to bring art to the people, or are their sometimes predictable programmes simply marketing for urban regeneration?

RH: Well the answer to 'are these buildings and their programmes art or marketing' is that they're both. Let's not be naïve about this. We live in a capitalist society, and there's always been a connection between art, culture, cash and capitalism. When Pope Julius II employed Michelangelo it was marketing: the artist's commissions promoted the papacy and publicised the pope's own reputation and that of his family. It's very difficult to separate out these two things.

What's very interesting is the growth of galleries like The Towner in Eastbourne and Turner Contemporary in Margate. There was a deliberate policy to try and revive seaside towns especially. There is evidence that this has worked in Margate. Clearly due to local politics and funding issues, Firstsite, the new gallery in Colchester, hasn't. We have to accept the fact that culture, or a cultural manifestation such as Turner Contemporary – which is a beautiful building – has certainly done something for Margate. We have to accept that there's a trade-off between the motivations of different people. Surely, if the environment of Margate improves even fractionally as a result of a greater confidence in the town, then I'm not going to say we shouldn't have built the gallery. You have to think of places like Turner Contemporary as a form of public art in its own right, in the sense that they offer something for the public, in a public space, for free.

Now, will it survive? I maintain that there is genuine danger that the flood tide of development and money that has gone into new public art and spaces will become, as it were, stranded by the receding economic tide. As the state withdraws its commitment and responsibilities towards the public realm and public culture and therefore public art – and it looks like we are going to have a very abrasive type of government for some time – I think there is a danger that the economy of public culture will become untenable. I'm very doubtful about to the extent to which other non-government interests might be able to step in.

The danger is not just that the Department for Culture, Media and Sport and Arts Council England are having their funding cut, but that local authorities are being cut too. It's actually the local authorities that keep the whole infrastructure going. As they desperately try to sustain their social responsibilities, their cultural responsibilities will suffer. I know this, because I'm involved in a project here in London, in which Ealing Council is handing over Pitzhanger Manor, a museum and gallery, to a private trust. I joined the trust to learn what it is like under present circumstances to manage a cultural facility – a heritage attraction and a public gallery. We've got to try and keep it going but I'm very sceptical that we can.

SK: I'd like to ask you about the future of public art connected to the new fetish for greenery within cities. For example, Joanna Lumley's idea to build a garden bridge across the Thames, and the High Line, a 1.45 mile-long linear park built in Manhattan on an elevated section of a disused New York Central Railroad spur. There's also the whole hipster culture of the urban-rural with its desire for allotments. Are we looking at the end of cities of the industrial revolution, the great cities of industry?

RH: I don't see how. Regretfully we're going to have to live at ever-greater densities, and therefore we're going to be living more densely in cities. I don't think it's ever going to come to an end. What's very interesting is, even though the technology we have has made it possible for us to work anywhere, we still cluster. The so-called 'creative industries', which is an oxymoron, all gather together. You can see it happening in Shoreditch. People need to come together, and therefore they have to come together within an organised space, which is an architectonic space in the city.

In terms of the new gardens, there's a very interesting difference between the proposed Garden Bridge in London and the High Line in New York. The High Line curiously has 'roots'. It's like Tate Modern, a repurposed piece of architecture. To me, the Garden Bridge is a completely spurious project. The more one learns about it, the more fraudulent it appears. What is being presented as public space may well turn out to be heavily privatised.

SK: I imagine that Joanna Lumley or Thomas Heatherwick wouldn't have even thought of the Garden Bridge without seeing the High Line, it's a terrible simulacra of what they've seen in Manhattan. It's comparable with attempting to translate the success of Tate Modern to West Bromwich. It shows a lack of imagination.

RH: Yes, and of course the Garden Bridge isn't the only proposal. There's another bridge proposed for Vauxhall, which is desperately needed. A vast amount of developments in that area aren't proving economically successful. There's a lot of doubt around the Battersea Power Station renovation. It could be a case of over-extension. Don't forget that Canary Wharf went bust. Olympia and York, the major international property development firm behind it, actually folded, and then later Canary Wharf took off. Eventually, simply because we need the space for housing, it'll be occupied. That great contrarian Simon Jenkins suggests that in twenty years Vauxhall will be a vast teeming slum.

AH: It's interesting that Damien Hirst's new museum designed by Caruso St John has just opened in Lambeth, while Cabinet Gallery, the dealer space, is currently building its new premises there. What do you think the commercial visual arts sector would do for Vauxhall?

RH: Drive up property prices. We're now talking about privately owned art, which is absolutely fascinating to me. It's what I call in my book 'fictitious capital'. Artists like Koons are like large organisations. What we see with the hugely inflated prices for art is simply a form of debt, because capitalism constantly needs to expand. When it creates money, it needs to find somewhere to put it. And parking it in high-priced contemporary art, an extremely fungible, tradable commodity – and it is really only the highest echelons of art and artists that are really making the prices – is a wonderful place to put money which has got nowhere else to go.

Whether collectors actually appreciate or enjoy the art they buy, I really don't know. But when you discover that a lot of art is stored in warehouses and free ports, because that way no one pays any tax on it, you suddenly see that, at the high end, art acts as a fiscal instrument that's open to all forms of illegality, money laundering and tax evasion. Curiously, private art facilitates liberal capitalism. The interesting thing is that even the galleries in Mayfair have been forced out, because of the price of the property.

AH: We have a question about Blackpool Tower because one of the projects in Scott's book is based on the monument and its surrounding area.

SK: Yes, I went to interview a band in Blackpool and I found myself with a lot of spare time, so I started walking around. Of course Blackpool is the second poorest town in Britain, and it got me thinking. The tower was built 1896 and I started to realise that it was possibly a very early example of what *Angel Of The North* was attempting to do. An artist or designer takes somewhere undeveloped – Blackpool at that time was a very small town – and creates a monument that literally becomes the focal point for regeneration. I did this thing called *Study of Blackpool Tower*, in which I walked in a half-mile circle around Blackpool and every time the tower became visible, which is nearly all of the time, I took a photograph with the monument in the centre, like a John Baldessari work.

AH: We thought it was the first symbol of failed regeneration.

SK: I saw parallels between gigantic monuments like *Angel of the North* and Blackpool Tower. Is it my imagination or do you think there's any substance to that?

RH: Well, they both – to use that dreadful term – have 'iconic status'. The term iconic really needs to be explored, because an icon is something you worship. It's possible that there are certain public artworks that are being quietly worshipped by people. But they're only worshipped when they work, when they exercise their magic. I think that the fourth plinth is a good example.

SK: I don't know if it's too early to say, but I think Damien Hirst's sculpture on the quay at Ilfracombe is terrible.

RH: There are some horrible things, like that horse's head at Marble Arch. It makes me feel annoyed every time I pass it. Is that because I'm a snob? Probably.

SK: Well that's the thing with public sculpture; it's often aesthetically very poor. It has to go through so many committees and consultation processes that it often ends up moronic. Two good examples are Mike Wallinger's unrealised *White Horse* and Ryan Gander's public sculpture *Dad's Halo Effect* in Manchester. I think Wallinger and Gander are good artists, but they've been affected by the burden of being asked to make a public sculpture.

RH: And of course, there was Thomas Heatherwick's famous *B of the Bang*. It's a pity that it had to be melted down for scrap, because I thought it was rather a good piece. But unfortunately it was structurally poor and started to fall apart.

What's interesting is the fact that most public sculpture still exists in the form of war memorials, and because of the centenary of the First World War, that purpose is being recalled. Charles Jagger's sculpture in Paddington Station of a soldier reading a letter is a powerful work in its own terms, and it was re-animated by the 14–18 NOW project which invited people to write their versions of what the letter might be saying. Similarly, the poppy sculpture *Wave* by Paul Cummins, was installed in the moat at the Tower of London, and people bought individual poppies to add to it. It became a massive participatory event, which shows that there is an appetite for public art. It seems to me that one of the requisites of public sculpture is that there has to be a genuine connection with people, through place and memory. Through its site and the materials involved, *Angel of the North* activates memory in an interesting manner. If you are going to talk about public art, you have to consider its role, and to succeed it has to be more than developers' decoration.

AH: Another recent development is that large public sculpture is starting to be replaced by regenerative social projects by artist groups such as Assemble. If we're to be generous, this shift represents a radical grass-roots style of community-engaged public art. However, it could also be criticised as a symptom of our increasingly straightened times. If we're to describe previous public art produced under New Labour as a cost-effective way of creating social cohesion whilst covering up the policies that were actually undermining it, could we describe Assemble as anything different under the new Tory administration?

RH: I don't think Assemble's work acts as a sticking plaster. I think they're a manifestation of the idea of co-creation. They're trying to produce collaborative work as a way of bypassing the enormous challenges of producing a vast monument. We can all work collaboratively to allow the public to become part of a work. Again, Gormley's Fourth Plinth commission, *One and Other*, did exactly this.

Community art has always been considered a second-class citizen, simply because its aesthetic purpose is secondary to its social purpose. Art does and should have a social purpose, but at the same time, when you're engaging with these projects, you have to decide whether a work's purpose is essentially social or aesthetic. Arts Council England has always been focused on the aesthetic, while local authorities have always been focused on the social, even when they're at their most negative. You simply have to think clearly about what a work's purpose is, and then ask to what extent it achieves its purpose within a social or aesthetic context.

AH: You suggested in your current book that the current conservative government's policies represent a purer form of neo-liberalism. Can you elaborate on this point?

RH: As I've said, the public realm is a political space, and also a mental space. It's an arena in which people interact socially, creatively and humanely, and an area where people transact independently from the market. My great fear for the future is that the public realm will gradually be eroded as neo-liberal economic interests see a way to make money out of privatising public space. It's an argument that goes back to the enclosure of the commons in the middle ages, where communal space was gradually privatised. Out of this grew an agricultural industry, which was then able to fund the industrial revolution. To my mind, what is astonishing about the financial crisis of 2008 is that, instead of leading to a reform of capitalism, things have become even worse. Essentially, the state is withdrawing from its public responsibility by cutting back on social services. It's also privatising free education, so that students are going to be in debt until they're fifty or sixty years old. It's withdrawing support for those in desperate need of social support: it's basically cutting back on social and educational life. And it is cutting back on our cultural life by withdrawing to the safe citadels of traditional institutions, leaving a periphery of independent organisations to struggle to maintain themselves by engaging with the market.

I'm really concerned about the public realm. Apart from the obvious fact that the rich are getting richer, and the poor are getting much poorer, it seems to me that, under neo-liberalism, truly creative space is gradually shrinking, and it is up to artists to try and push back. I'm not saying that the state should manage the public realm in a Stalinist manner. All I'm saying is that the state has to guarantee free public space, in which a genuine form of public art can continue to flourish.

AH: What would your ideal scenario be to enable culture to flourish?

RH: The real lesson of the New Labour period is that you can't predict creativity. By imposing certain forms of expectation, which are effectively restrictions – in New Labour's terms these expectations were good social outcomes – you actually negate the thing that you were trying to achieve, which is a flourishing contemporary culture. So, I would like to see the state acting as a guarantor of a public culture. And this public culture would consist of a mixed economy. I don't think we are actually going to be able to escape capitalism. But I do think we need a truly mixed economy that acknowledges the state has a role as the guarantor of public space, because, for instance, it's through cultural education that our artists emerge. The 'research and development' argument for funding the arts is absolutely valid. The whole idea that the free market will spontaneously flow into the spaces vacated by public organisations and the culture they support is a complete fantasy.

AH: Finally, what's the most that public art can ever ask for?

RH: That the state is the guarantor, but not the gatekeeper, of public culture.

SK: That's a great answer and a good place to end. Thank you Robert.

I DREAM *of* DALSTONIA

Illustrations by Will Henry

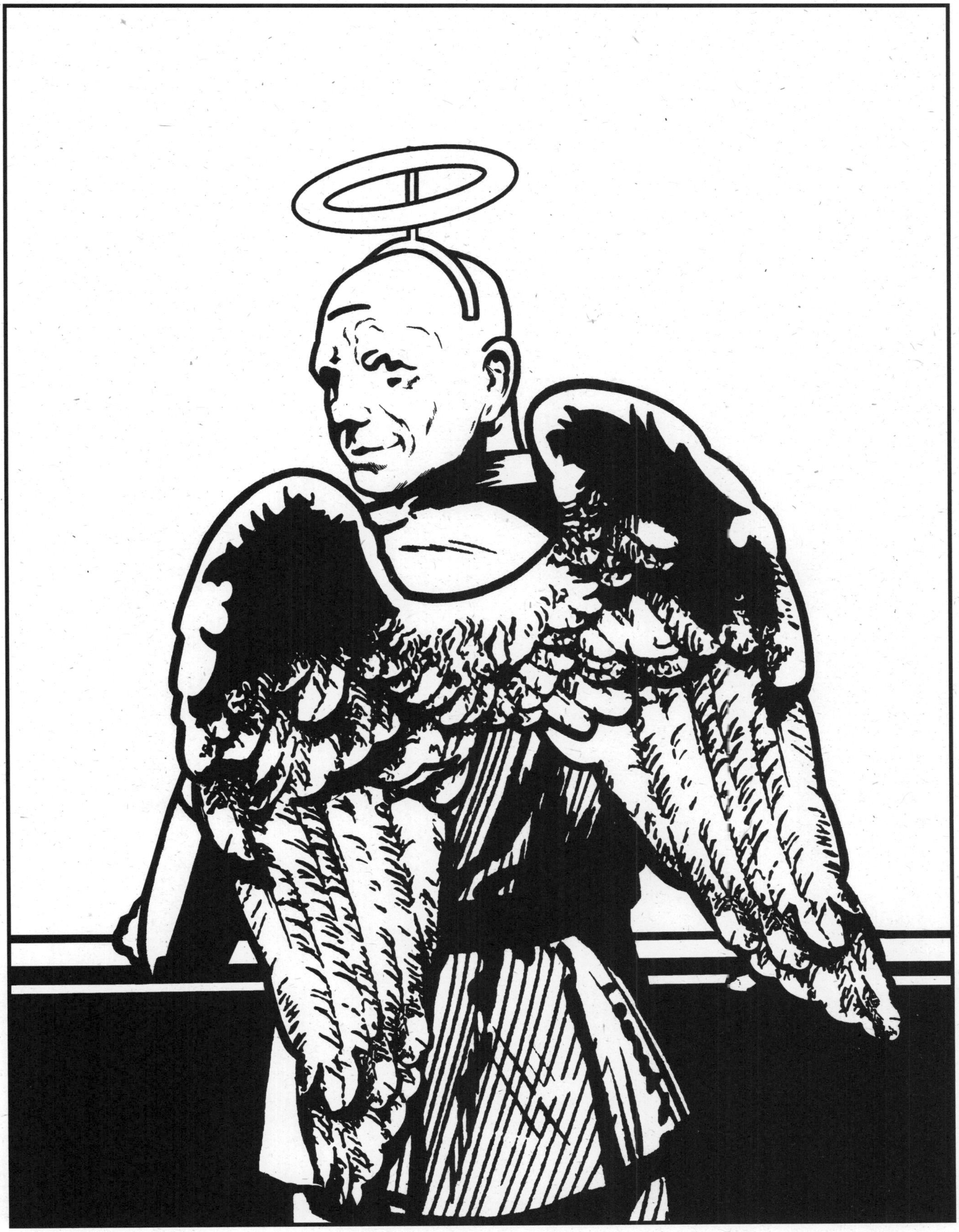

I Dream of Dalstonia, Thirty-one parts, Inkjet prints on paper, 2016

Baron William Hague is at 10 Downing Street, again…

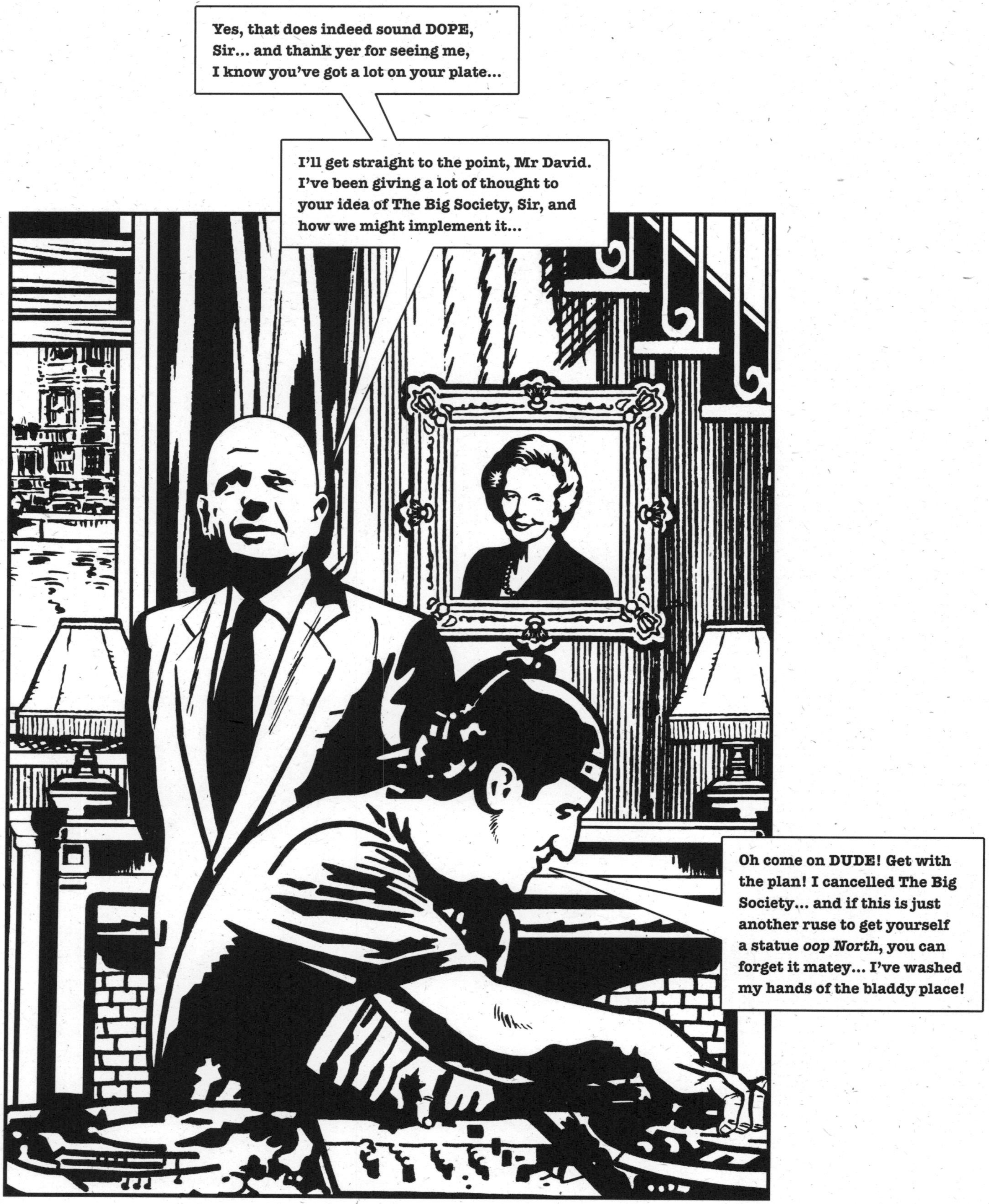

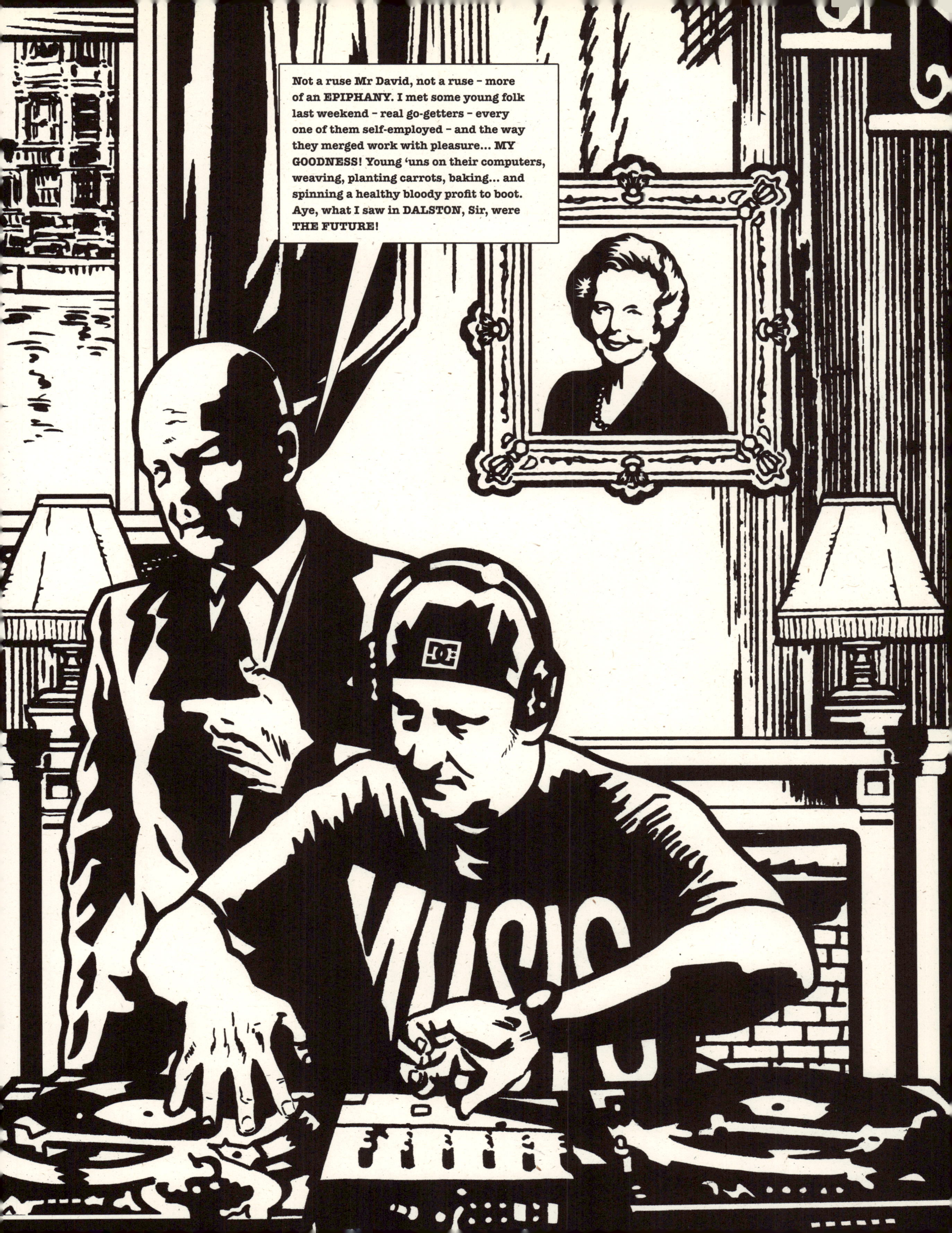
Not a ruse Mr David, not a ruse – more of an EPIPHANY. I met some young folk last weekend – real go-getters – every one of them self-employed – and the way they merged work with pleasure... MY GOODNESS! Young 'uns on their computers, weaving, planting carrots, baking... and spinning a healthy bloody profit to boot. Aye, what I saw in DALSTON, Sir, were THE FUTURE!
MUSIC

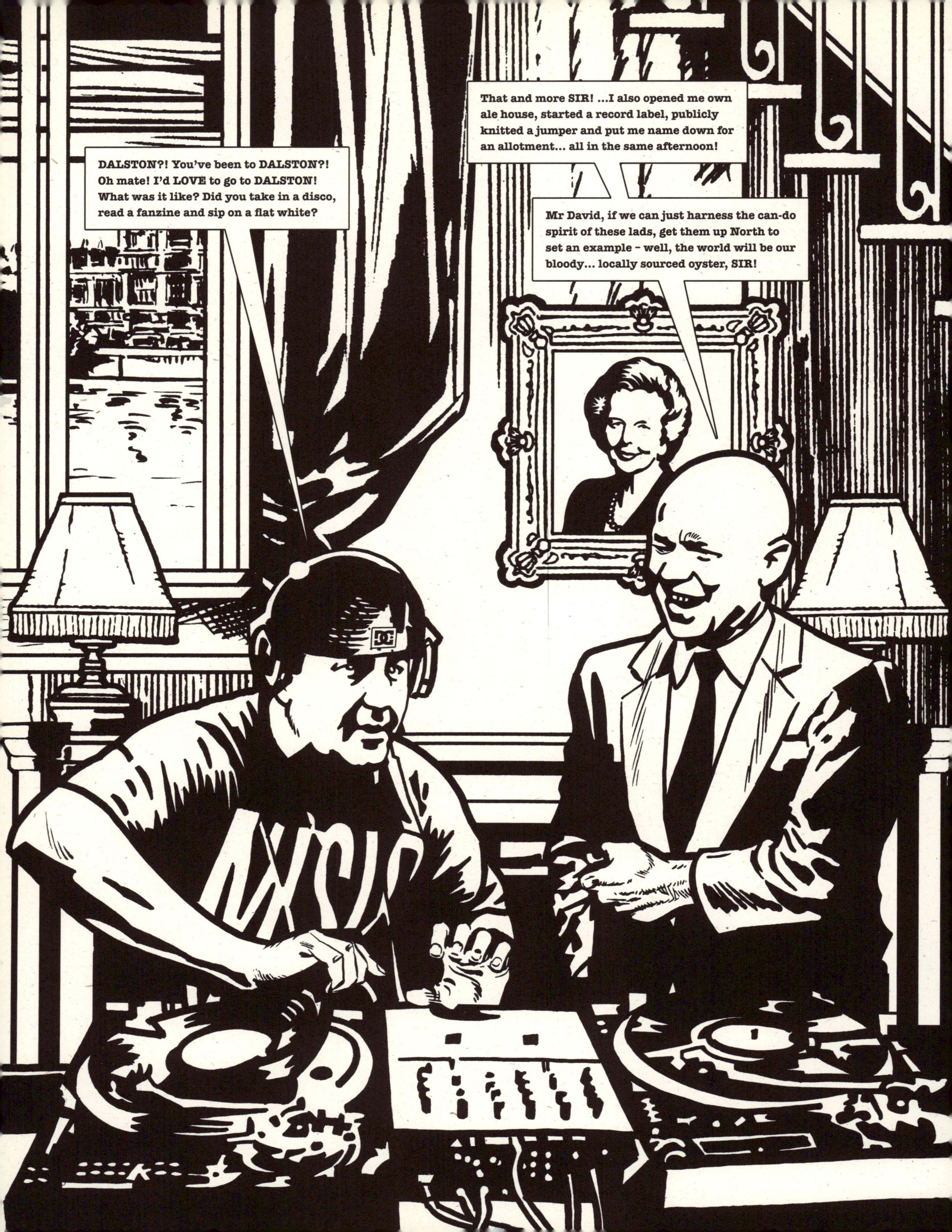
DALSTON?! You've been to DALSTON?! Oh mate! I'd LOVE to go to DALSTON! What was it like? Did you take in a disco, read a fanzine and sip on a flat white?
That and more SIR! ...I also opened me own ale house, started a record label, publicly knitted a jumper and put me name down for an allotment... all in the same afternoon!
Mr David, if we can just harness the can-do spirit of these lads, get them up North to set an example - well, the world will be our bloody... locally sourced oyster, SIR!

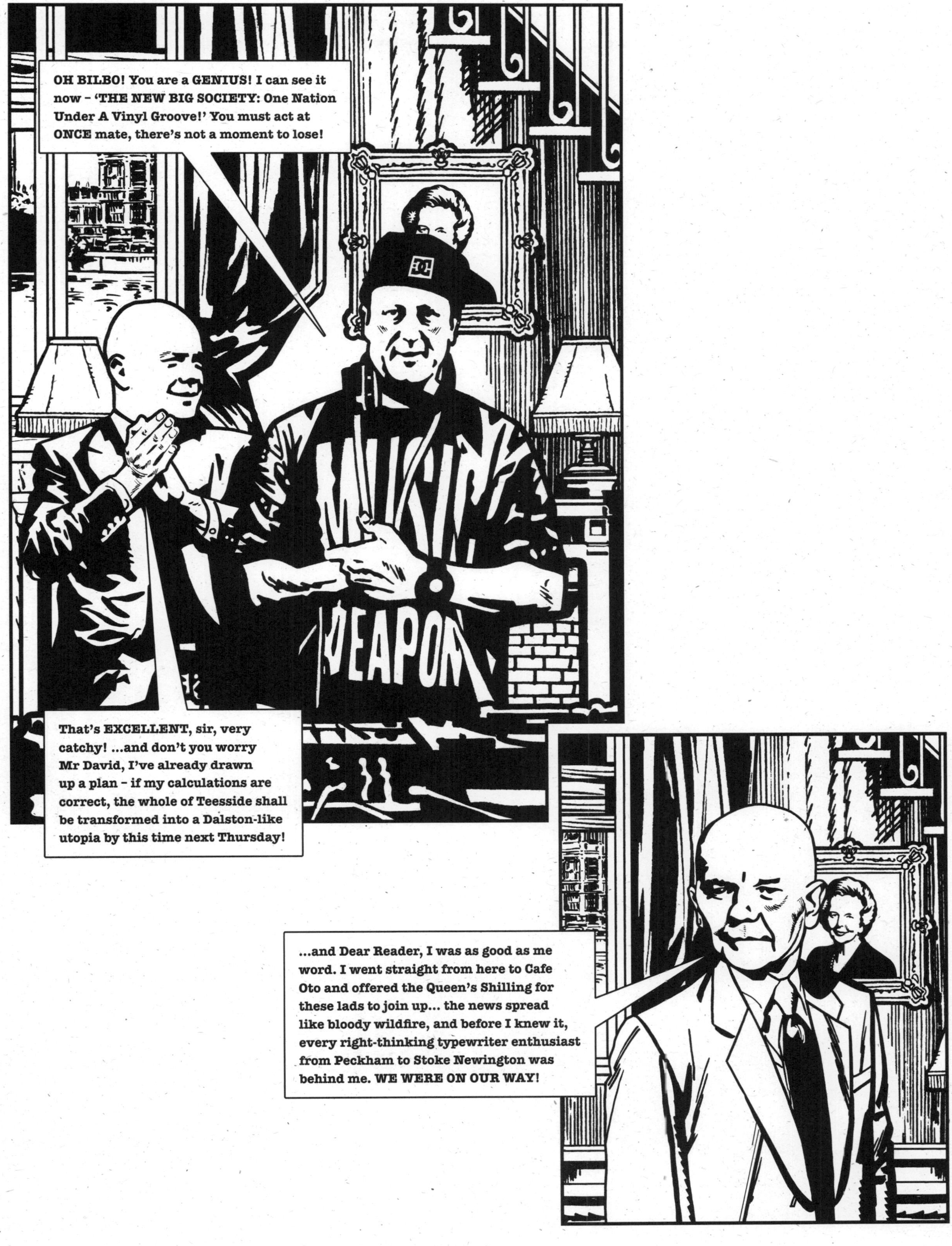
OH BILBO! You are a GENIUS! I can see it now – 'THE NEW BIG SOCIETY: One Nation Under A Vinyl Groove!' You must act at ONCE mate, there's not a moment to lose!
That's EXCELLENT, sir, very catchy! ...and don't you worry Mr David, I've already drawn up a plan – if my calculations are correct, the whole of Teesside shall be transformed into a Dalston-like utopia by this time next Thursday!
...and Dear Reader, I was as good as me word. I went straight from here to Cafe Oto and offered the Queen's Shilling for these lads to join up... the news spread like bloody wildfire, and before I knew it, every right-thinking typewriter enthusiast from Peckham to Stoke Newington was behind me. WE WERE ON OUR WAY!

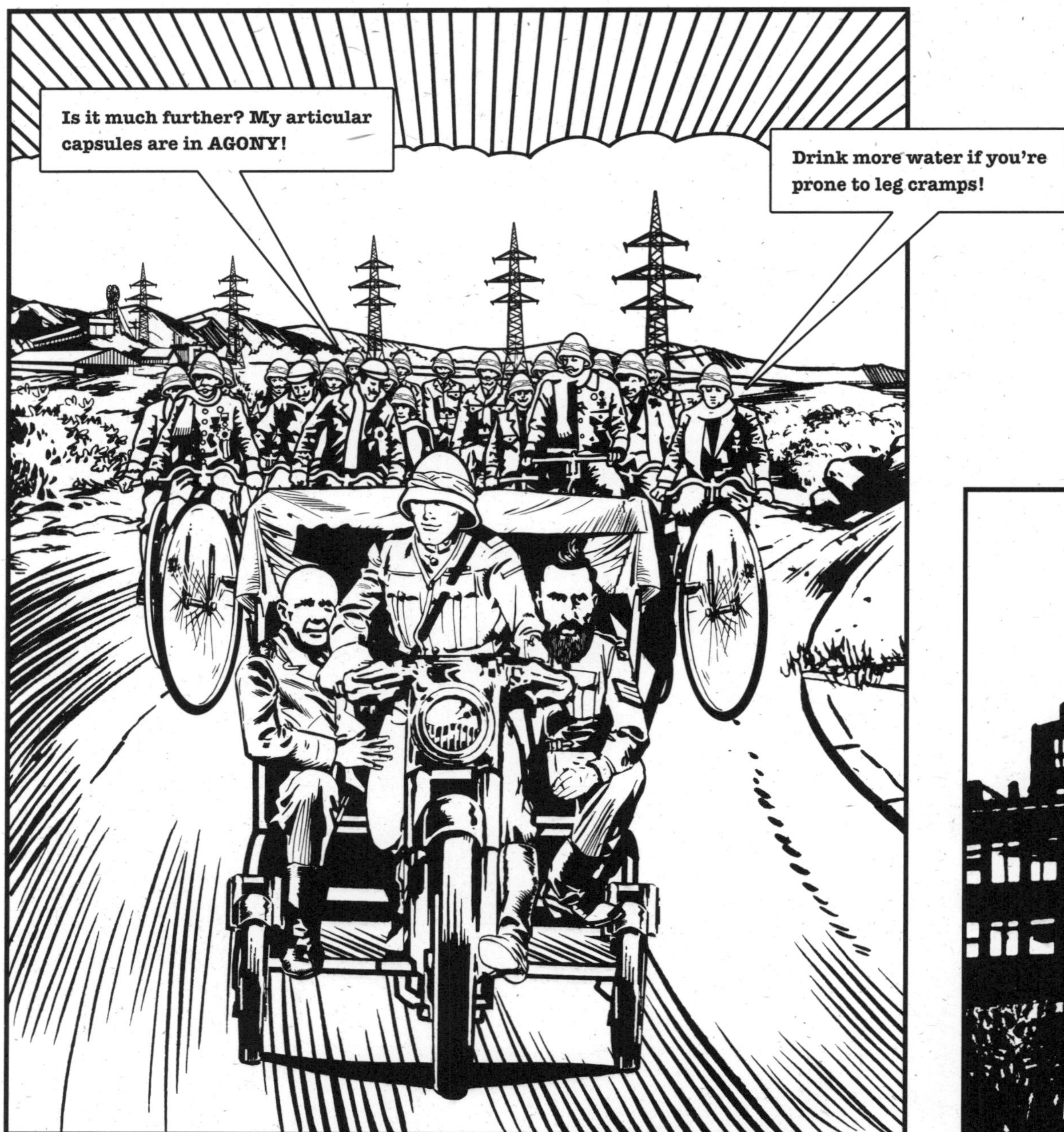

Within two days, the newly formed militia were already eight miles up the A1, heading north, and recruiting stragglers from vintage poster emporiums as they went. But, when Hague's Army finally did reach Teesside, it was not to the heroes' welcome they had expected...

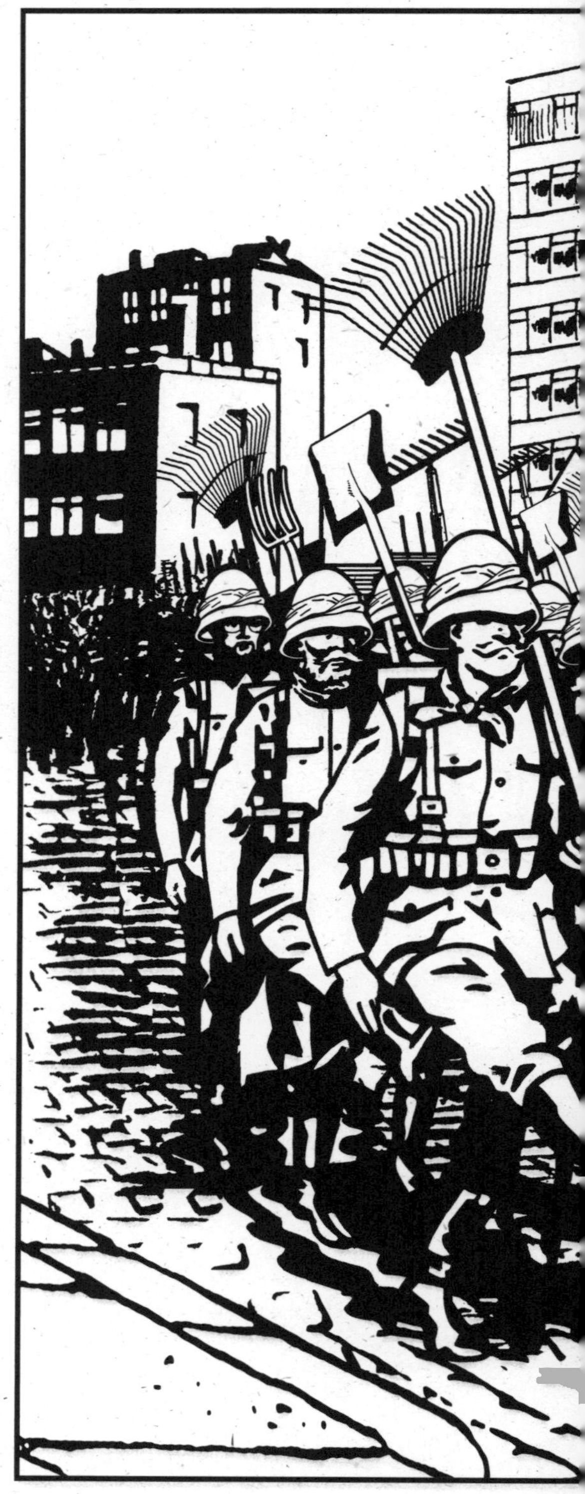

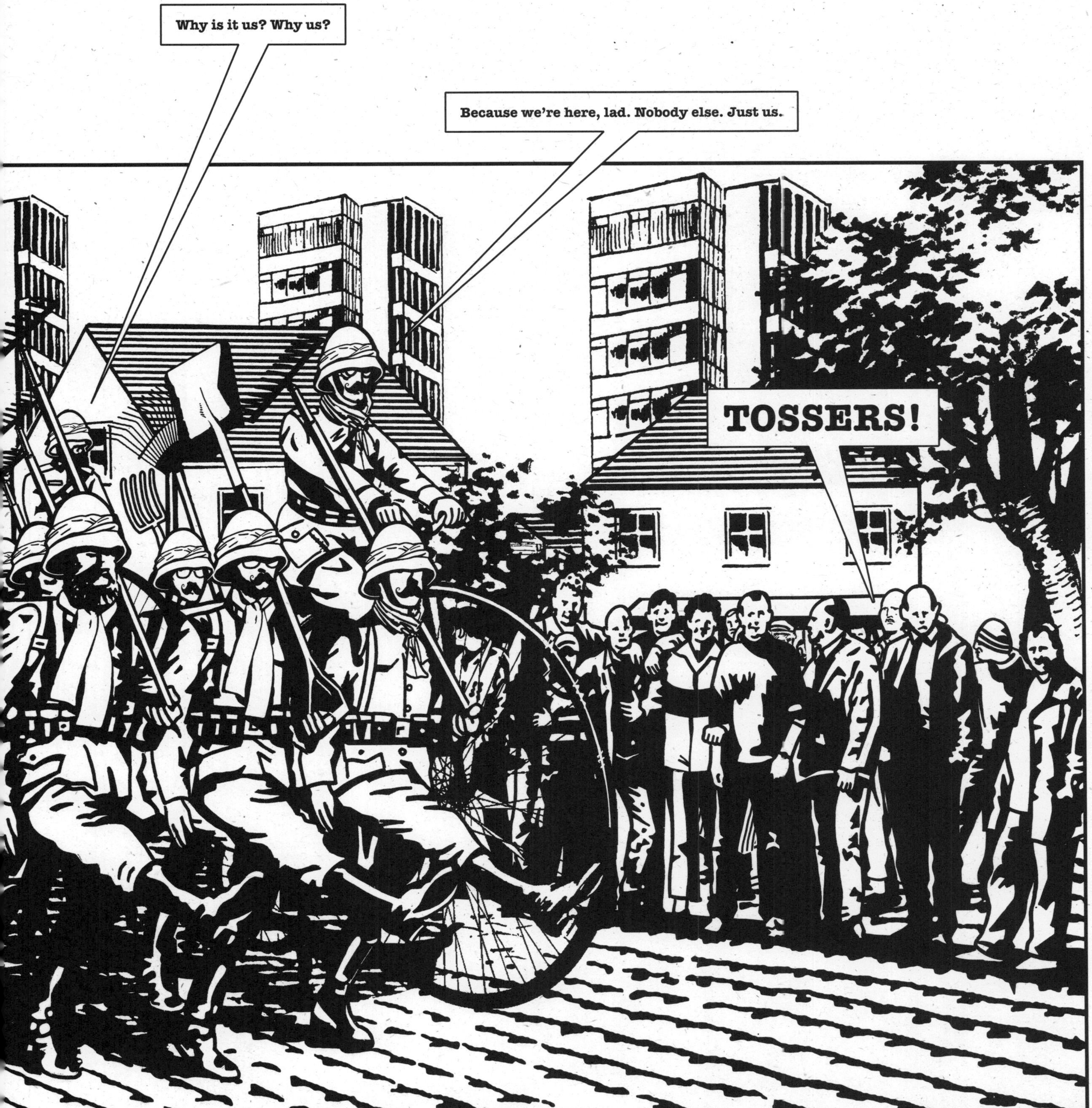
Why is it us? Why us?
Because we're here, lad. Nobody else. Just us.
TOSSERS!

Yet, despite pockets of resistance, a cleverly co-ordinated social media campaign ensured that Hague's first public speech was a triumph.

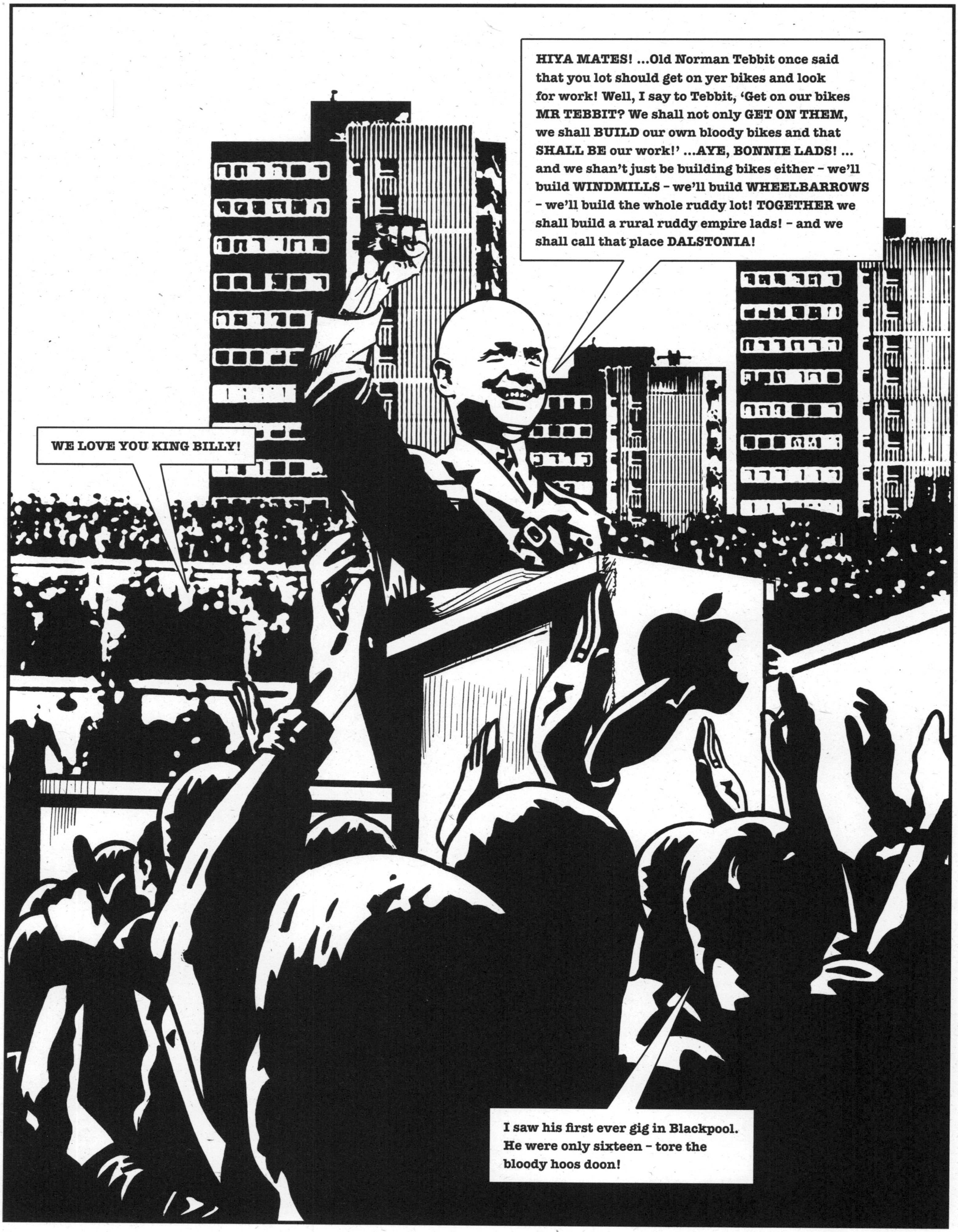

Ten minutes later...

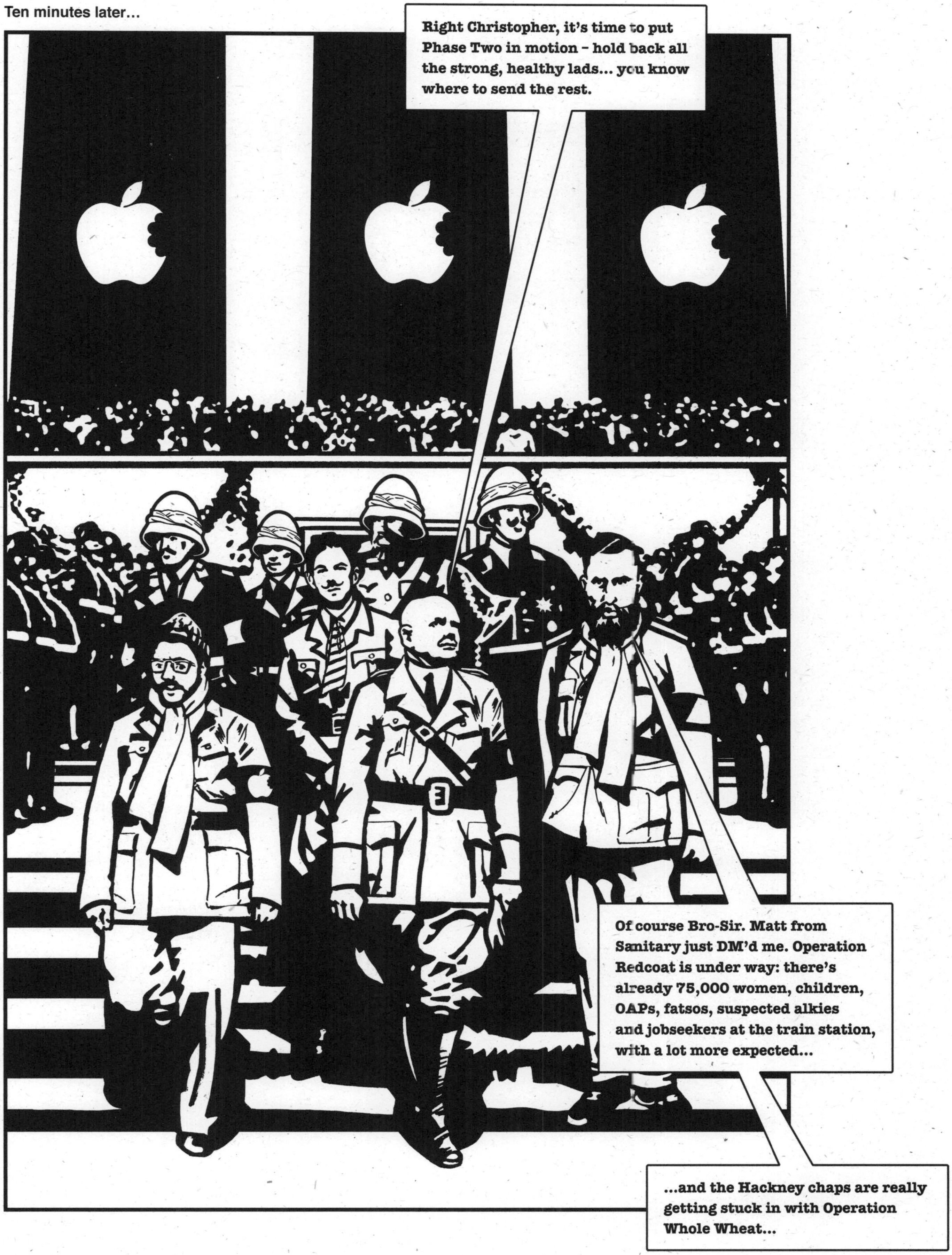

Behind the public facade of inclusivity, Hague began to seek out certain groups for persecution, and it fell to the battle hardened Hackney Bloggers to do this dirty work: a task they undertook with brutal relish.

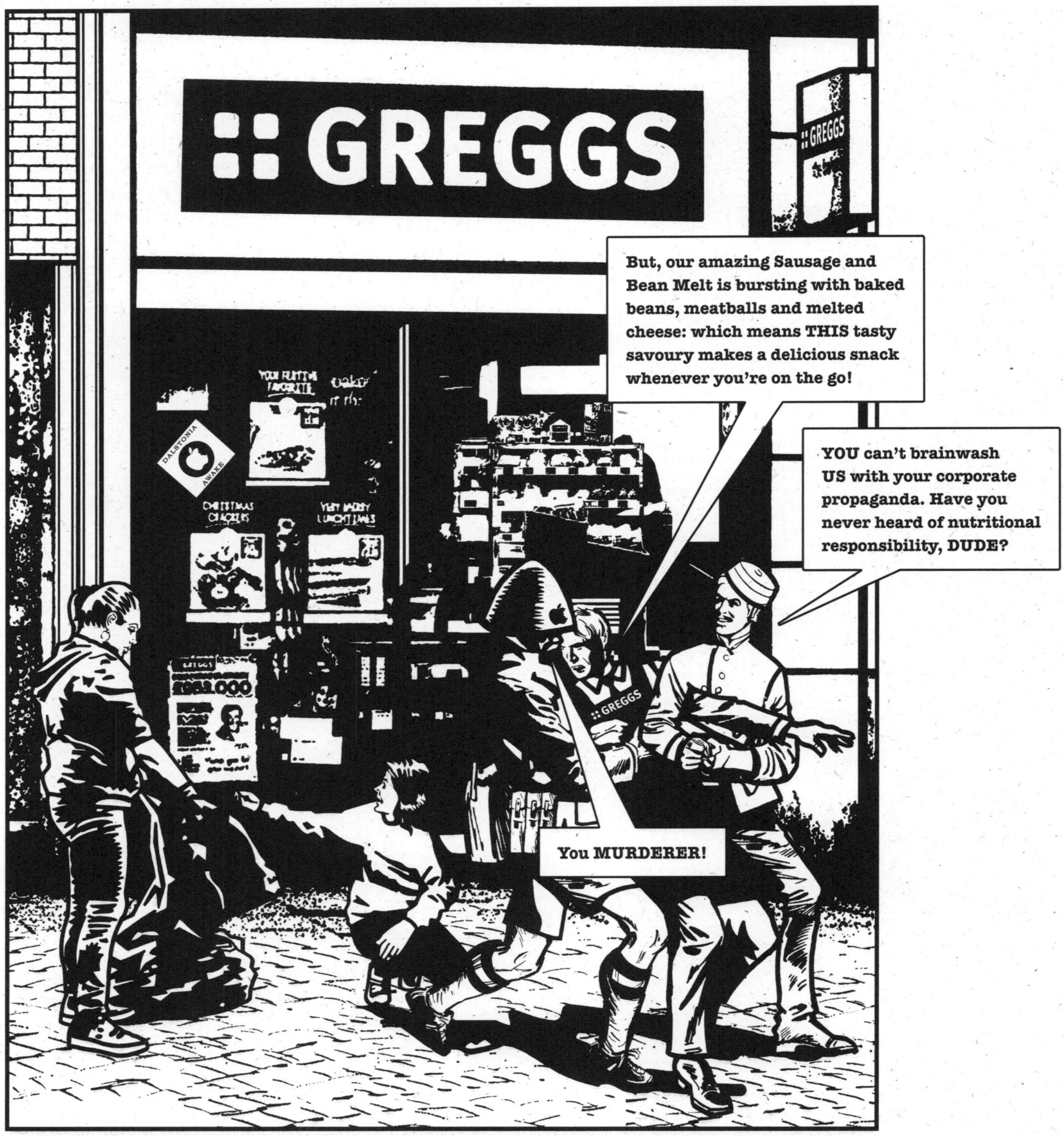

... while sub-contracted property developers were tasked with destroying unsightly housing stock and reclaiming dockside warehouses.

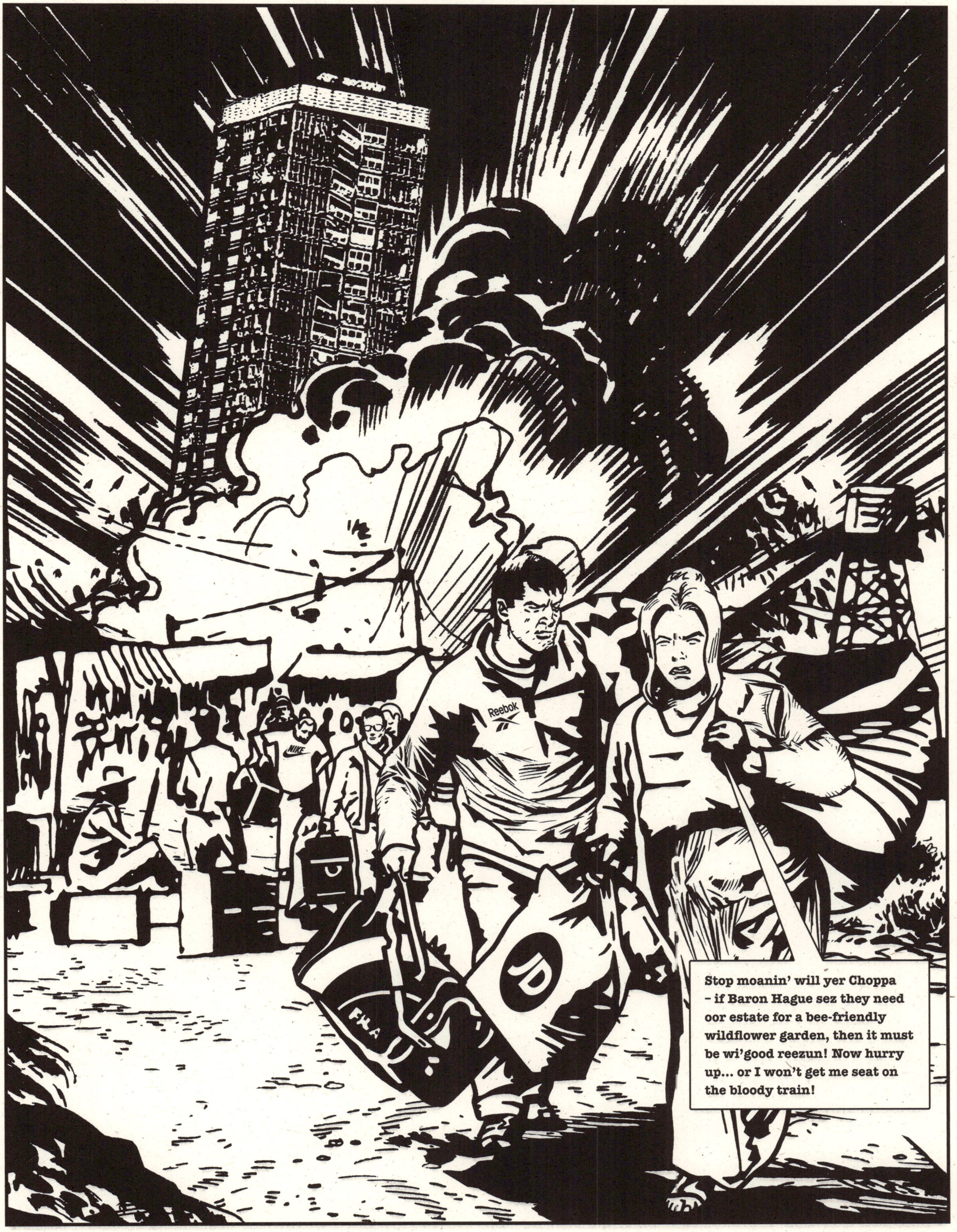

Heavily promoted in discount supermarkets, Hague offered a free SuperBreakDeal to those he considered undesirables. By Deal-Day, every station in the North East was a scene of chaotic excitement as an estimated 250,000 locals boarded trains and headed south.

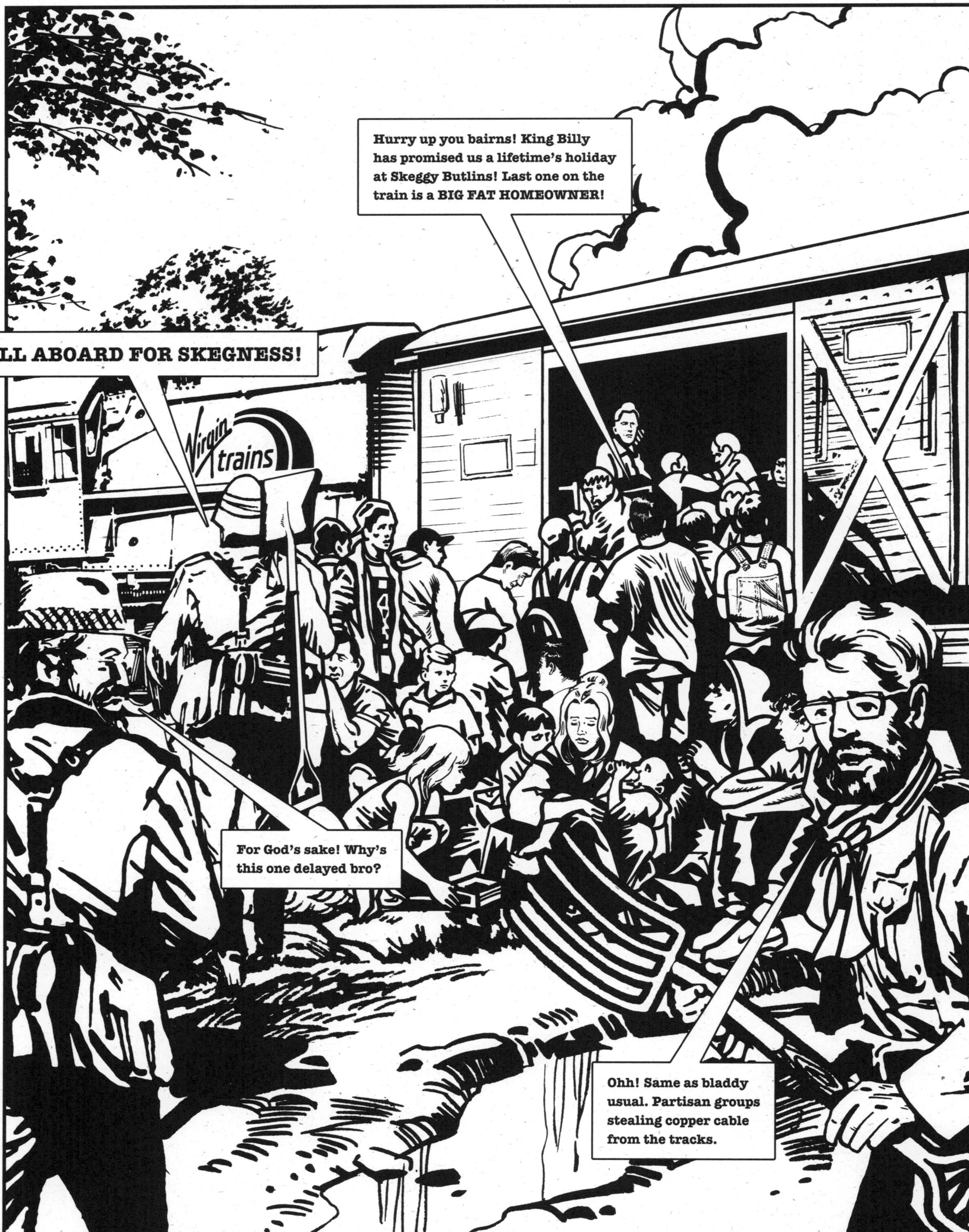

But cracks soon began to appear: Hague's cultural blitzkrieg of the North East, though not initially of great importance to Downing Street, did become a cause for concern when – without permission – his army swept south and invaded the traditionally middle class stronghold of York.

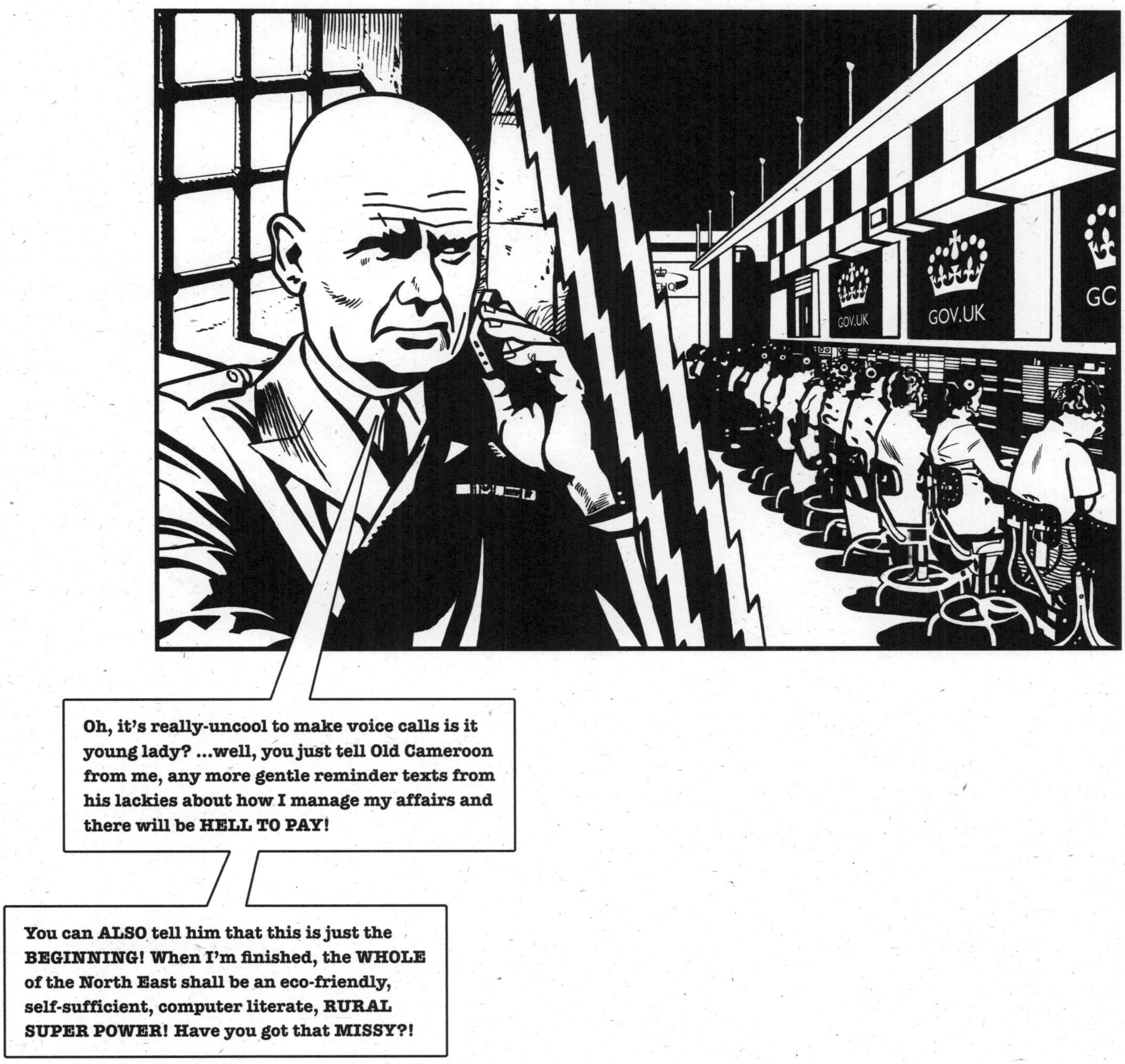

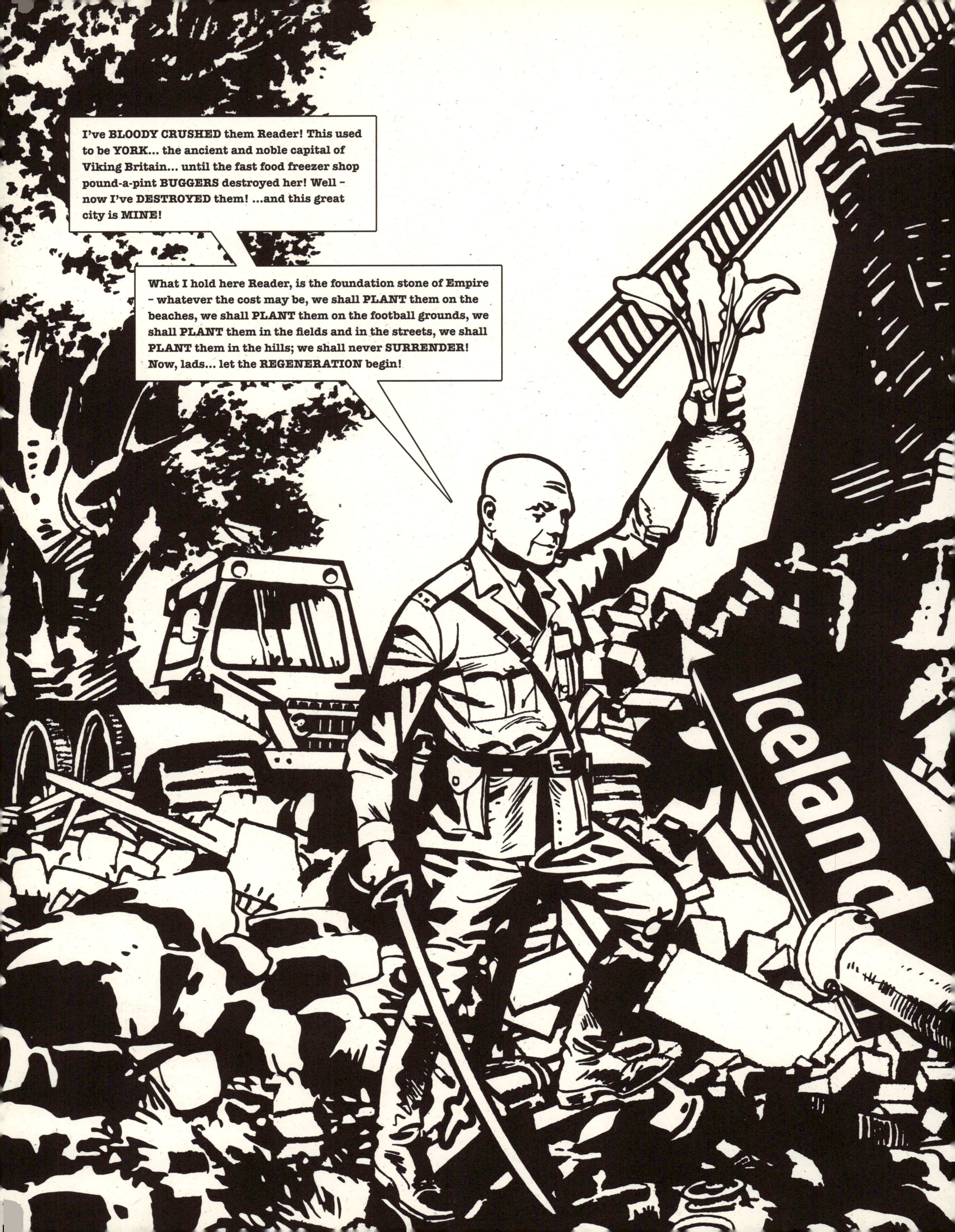
I've BLOODY CRUSHED them Reader! This used to be YORK... the ancient and noble capital of Viking Britain... until the fast food freezer shop pound-a-pint BUGGERS destroyed her! Well – now I've DESTROYED them! ...and this great city is MINE!
What I hold here Reader, is the foundation stone of Empire – whatever the cost may be, we shall PLANT them on the beaches, we shall PLANT them on the football grounds, we shall PLANT them in the fields and in the streets, we shall PLANT them in the hills; we shall never SURRENDER! Now, lads... let the REGENERATION begin!
Iceland

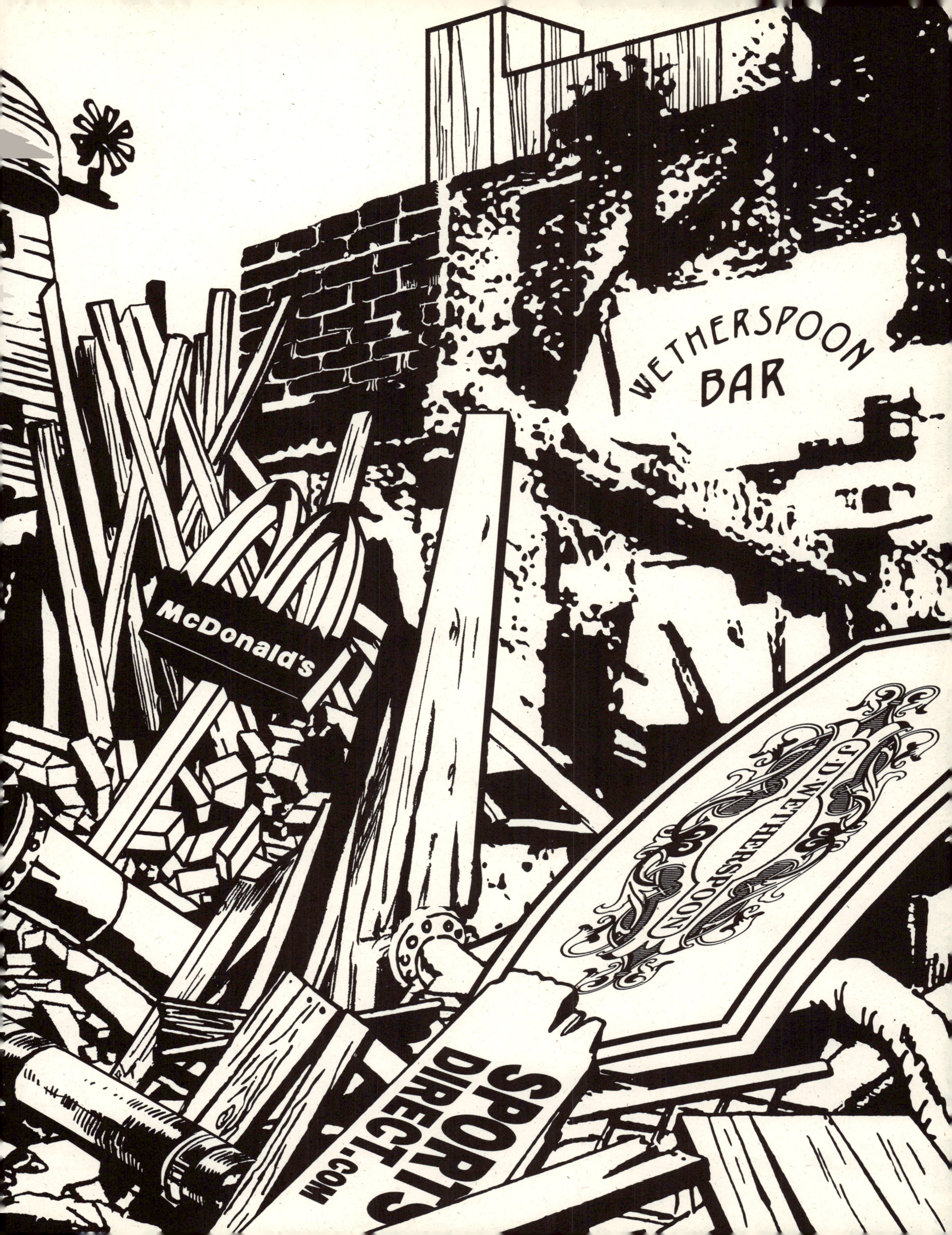
WETHERSPOON
BAR
McDonald's
J.D. WETHERSPOON
SPORTS
DIRECT.COM

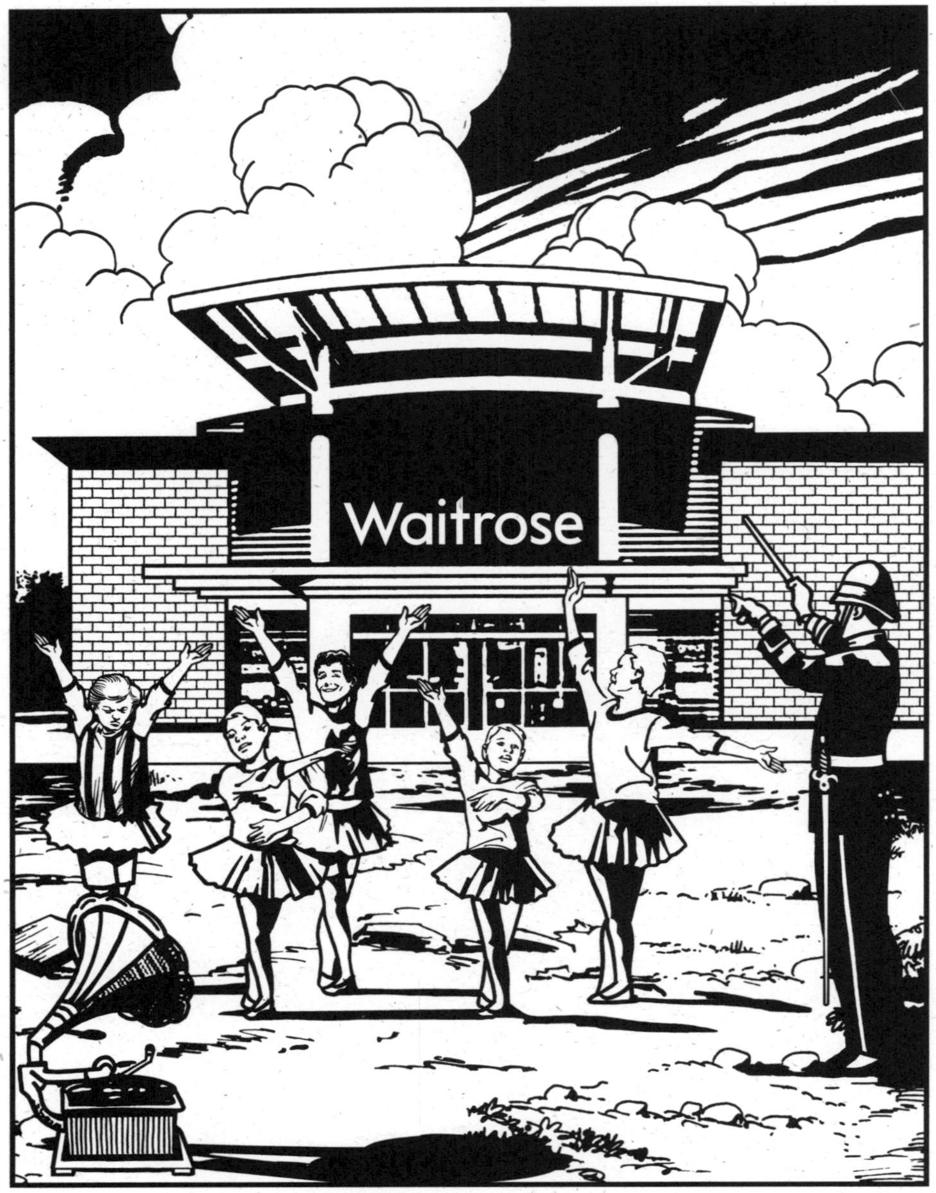

...and regeneration did begin, all across this once impoverished region. Of vital importance in Dalstonia was the immediate assimilation of the few remaining locals. Those too young to be conscripted were heavily schooled in all aspects of culture; daily ballet, street theatre, pottery workshops and barista training were made compulsory for all children under the age of twelve...

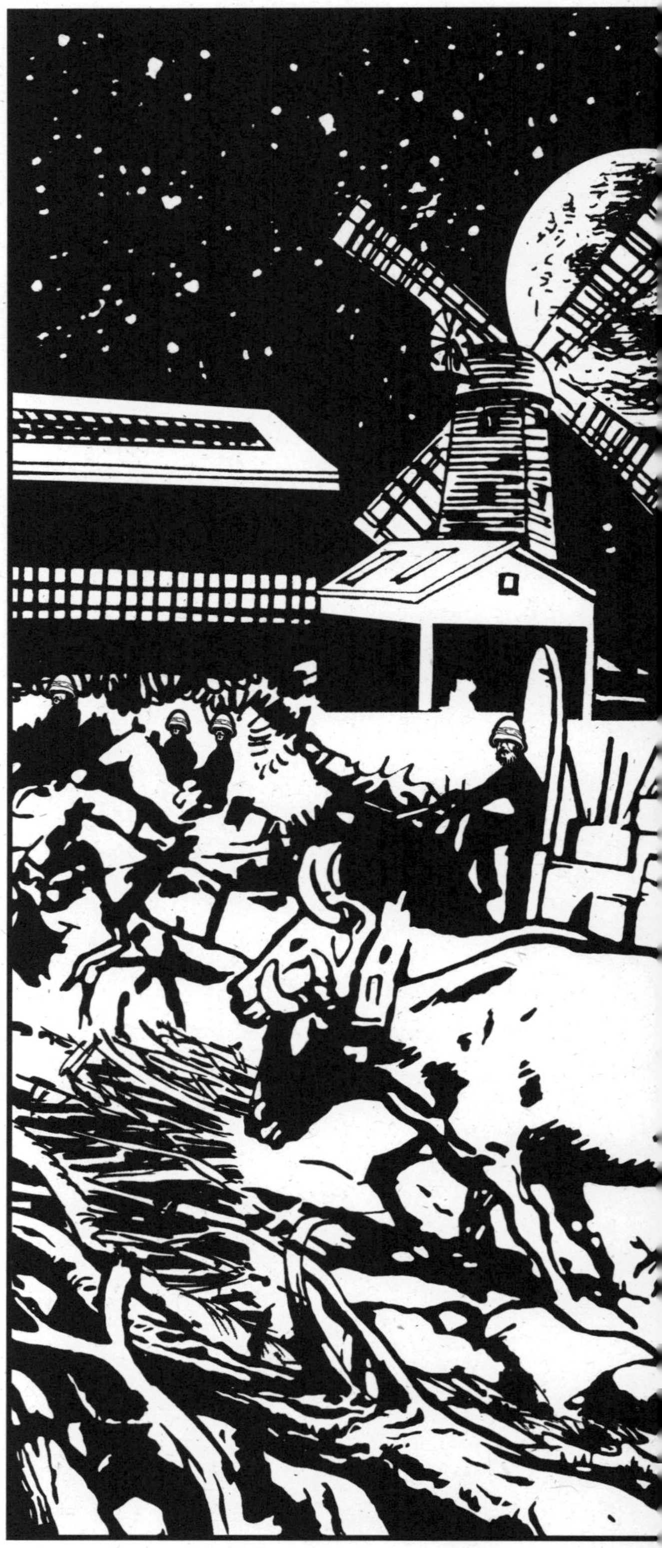

...while the lads worked tirelessly around the clock, determined to create the ambience of an Edwardian hamlet across the entire North East of England.

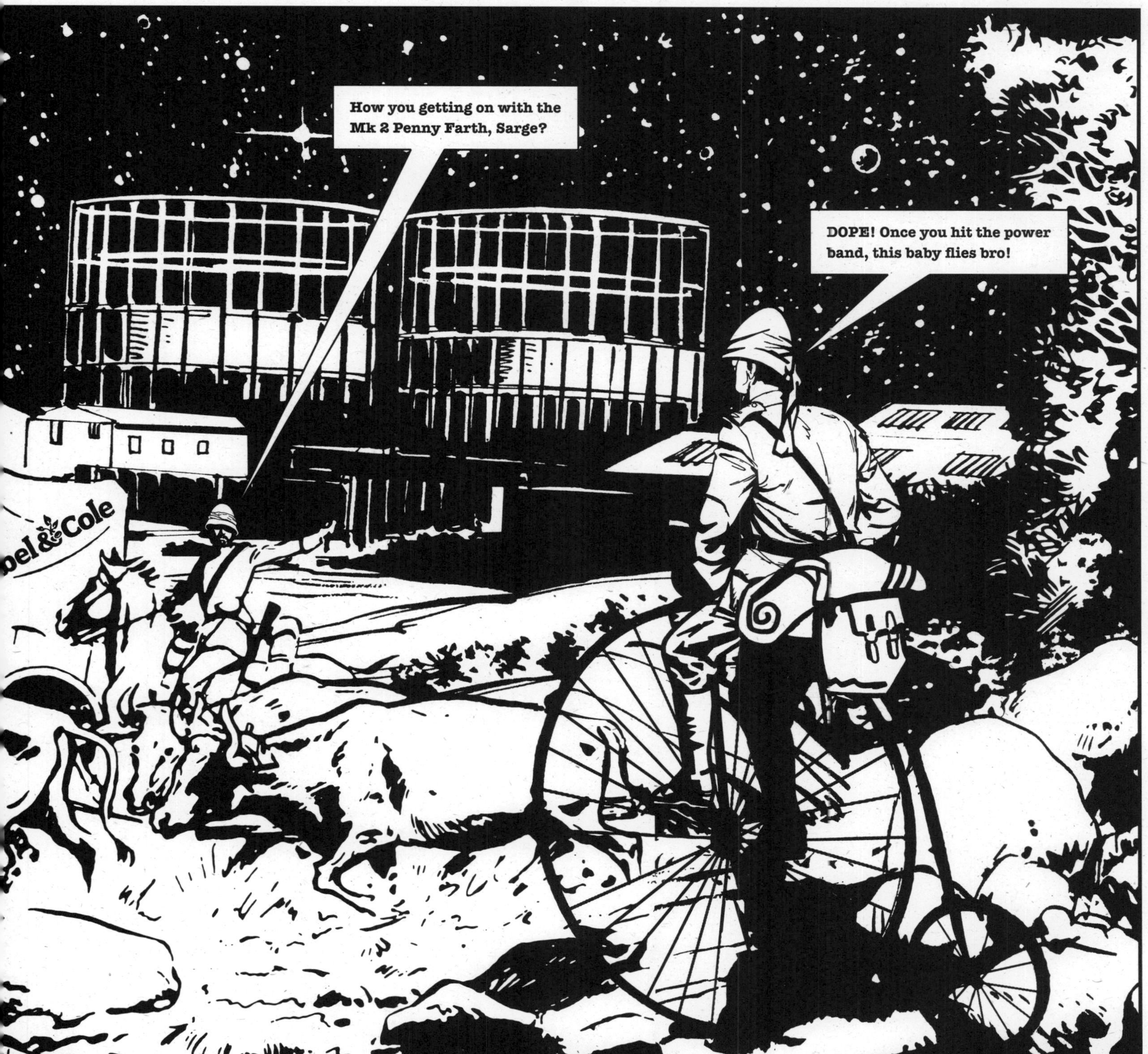

The few chain stores that remained standing were re-opened as independents, ugly shopping precincts were converted into prison farms and the Humber Bridge was divided up into highly desirable suspension allotments.

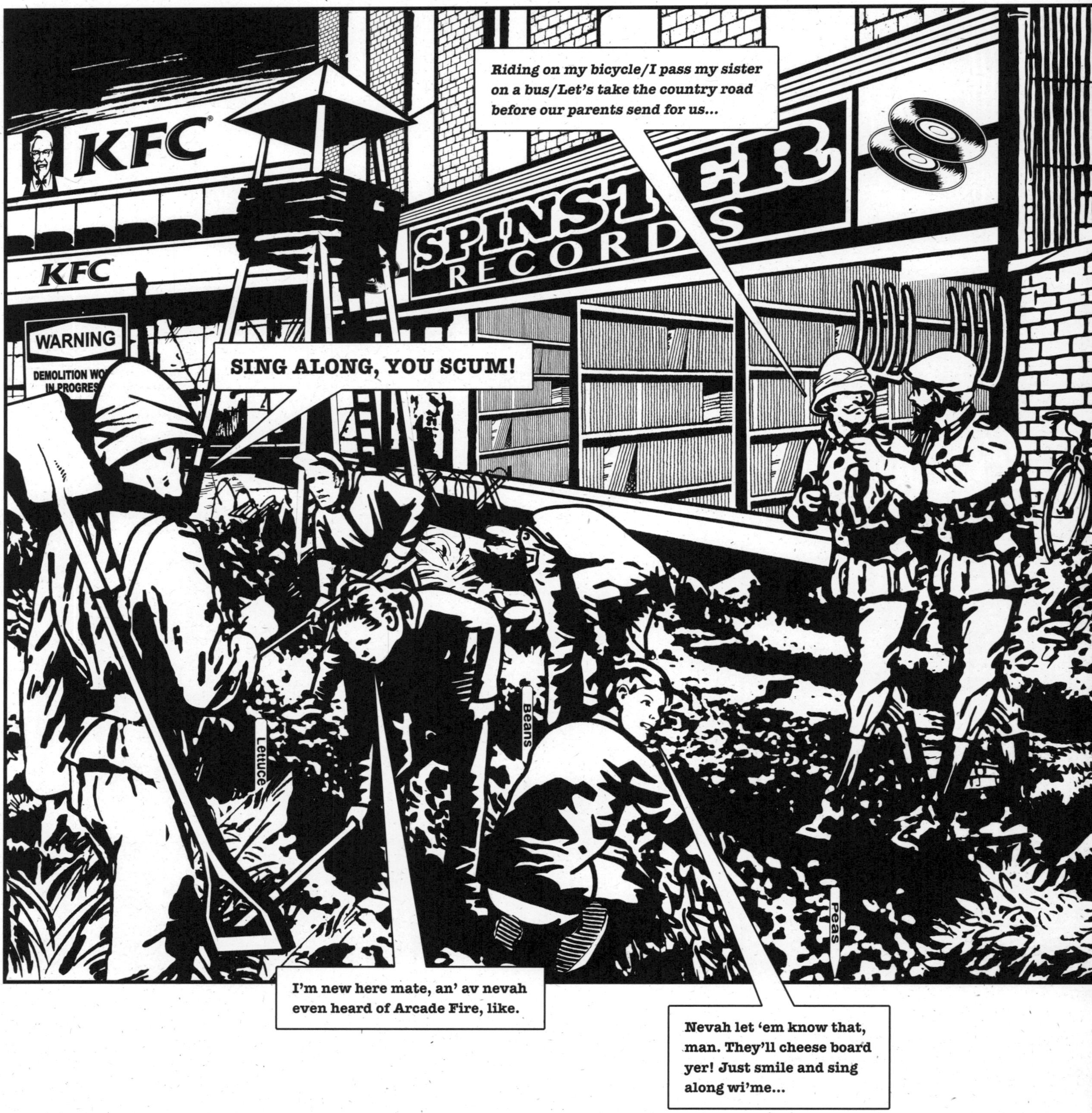

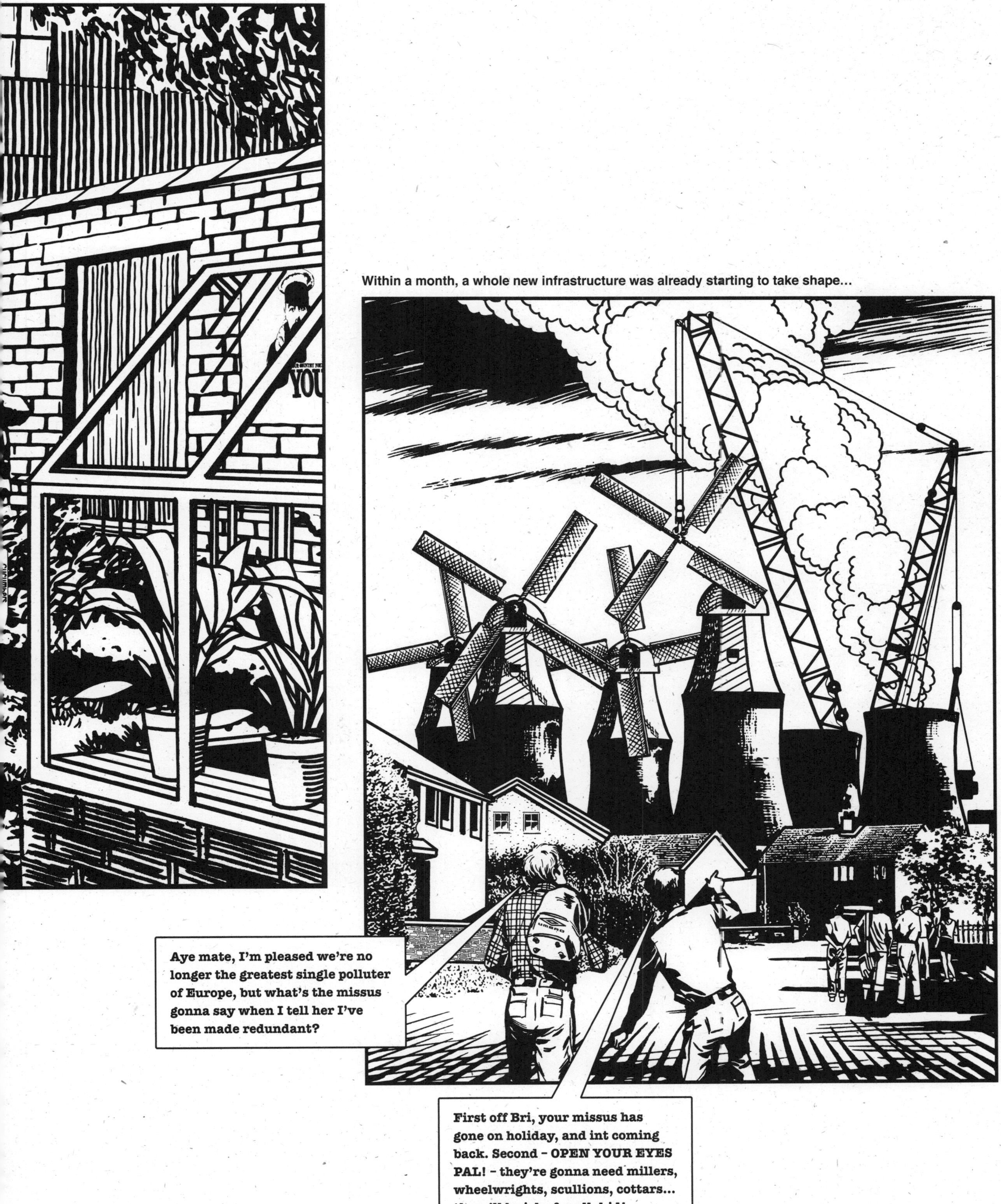

YOU
Within a month, a whole new infrastructure was already starting to take shape...
Aye mate, I'm pleased we're no longer the greatest single polluter of Europe, but what's the missus gonna say when I tell her I've been made redundant?
First off Bri, your missus has gone on holiday, and int coming back. Second – **OPEN YOUR EYES PAL!** – they're gonna need millers, wheelwrights, scullions, cottars... there'll be jobs for all, kid!

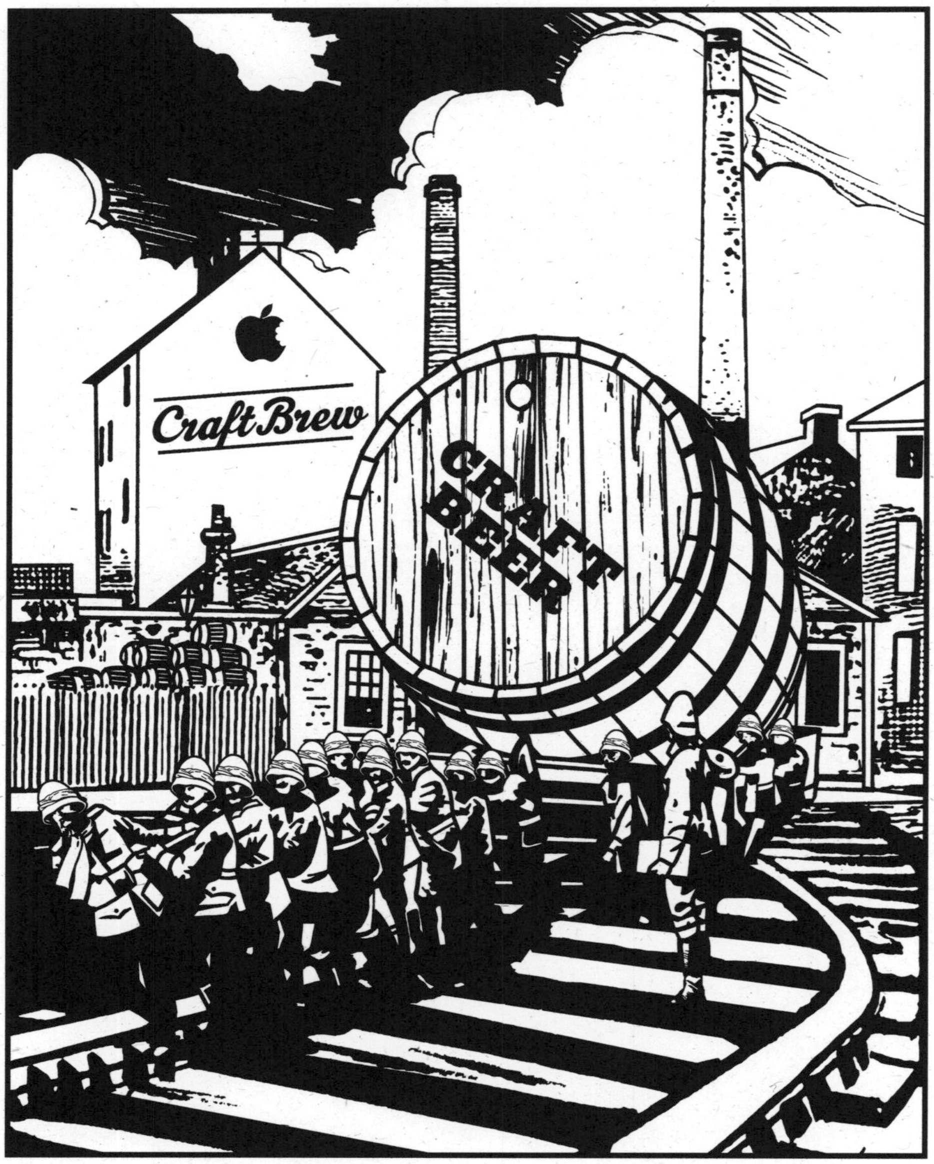

However, amongst the upper echelons of the regime, decadence did not only creep in, it became a daily occurrence: heavy drinking, light drug use and constant 'partying' became the norm…

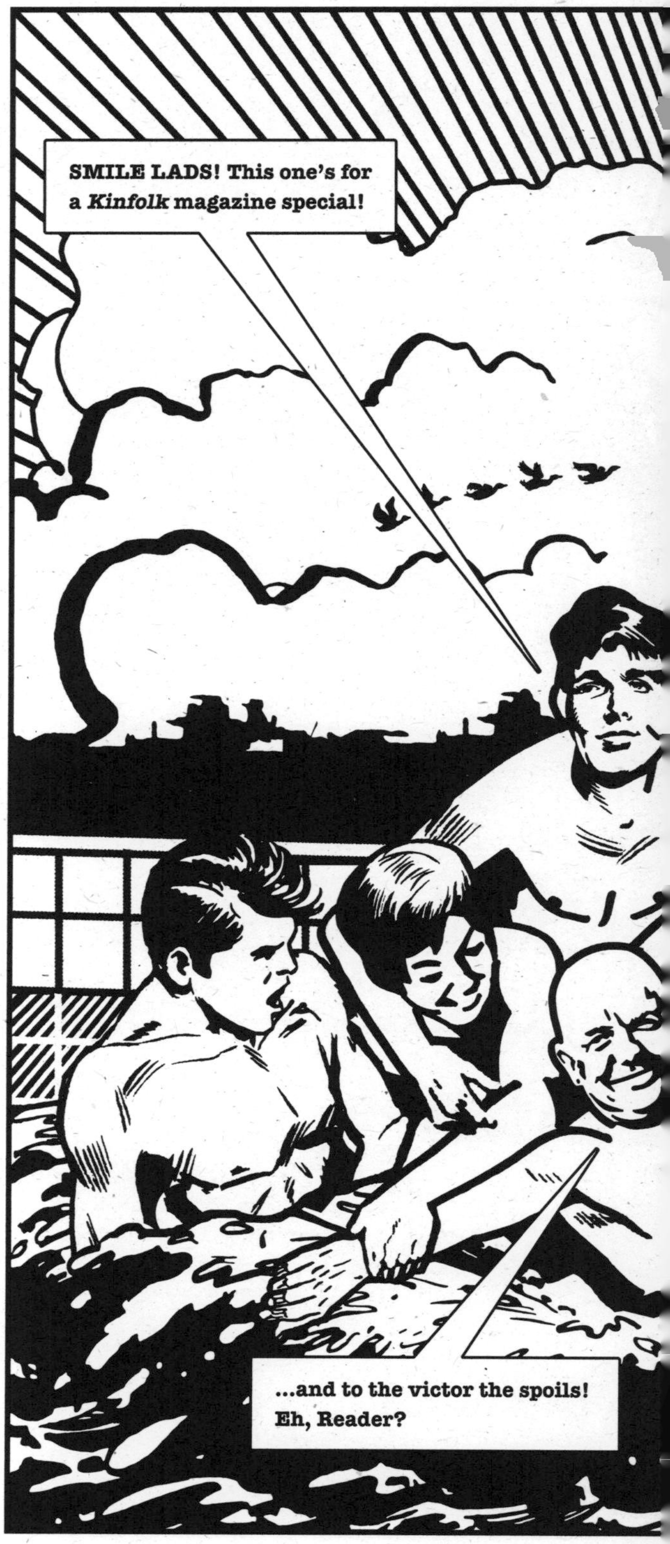

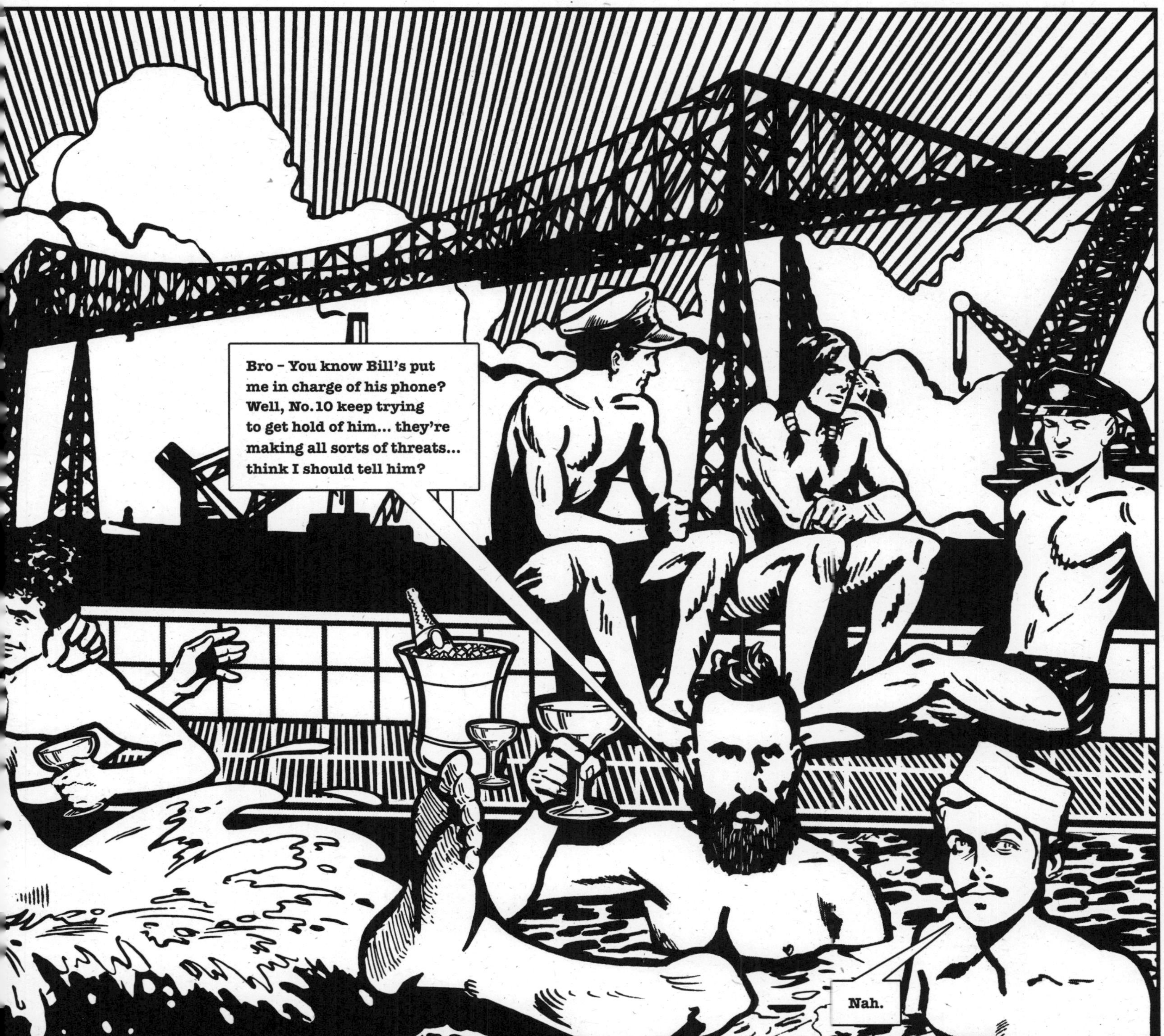
Bro – You know Bill's put me in charge of his phone? Well, No.10 keep trying to get hold of him... they're making all sorts of threats... think I should tell him?
Nah.

Three weeks later...

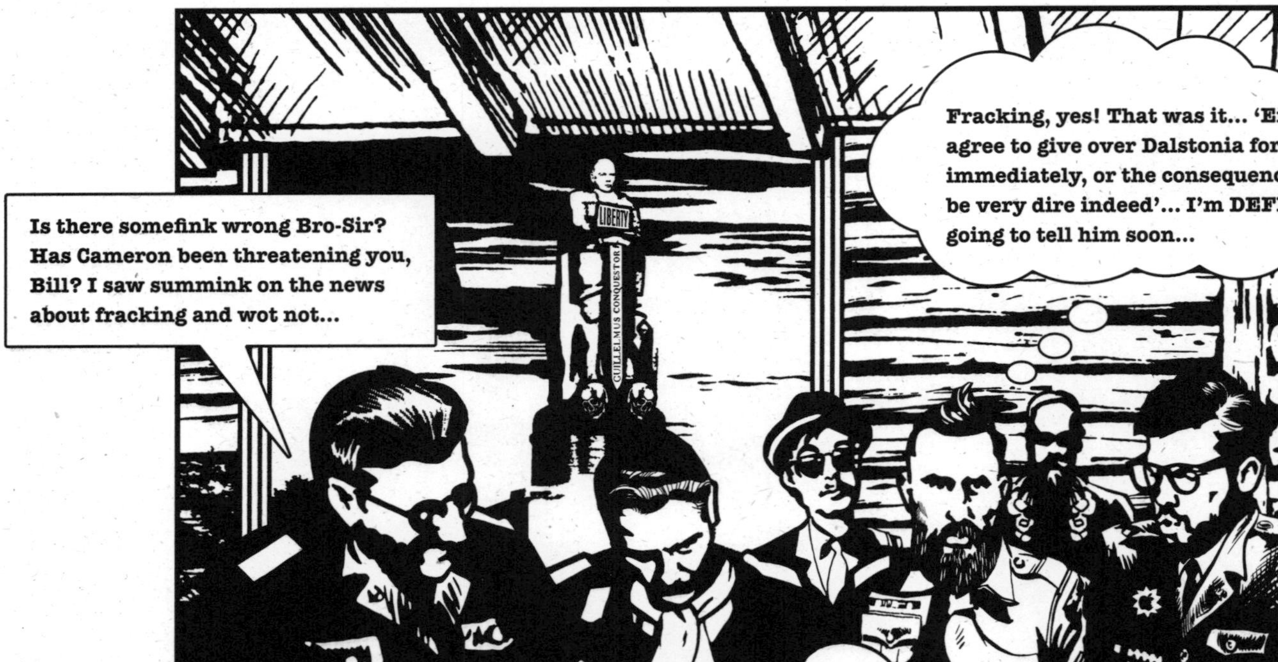

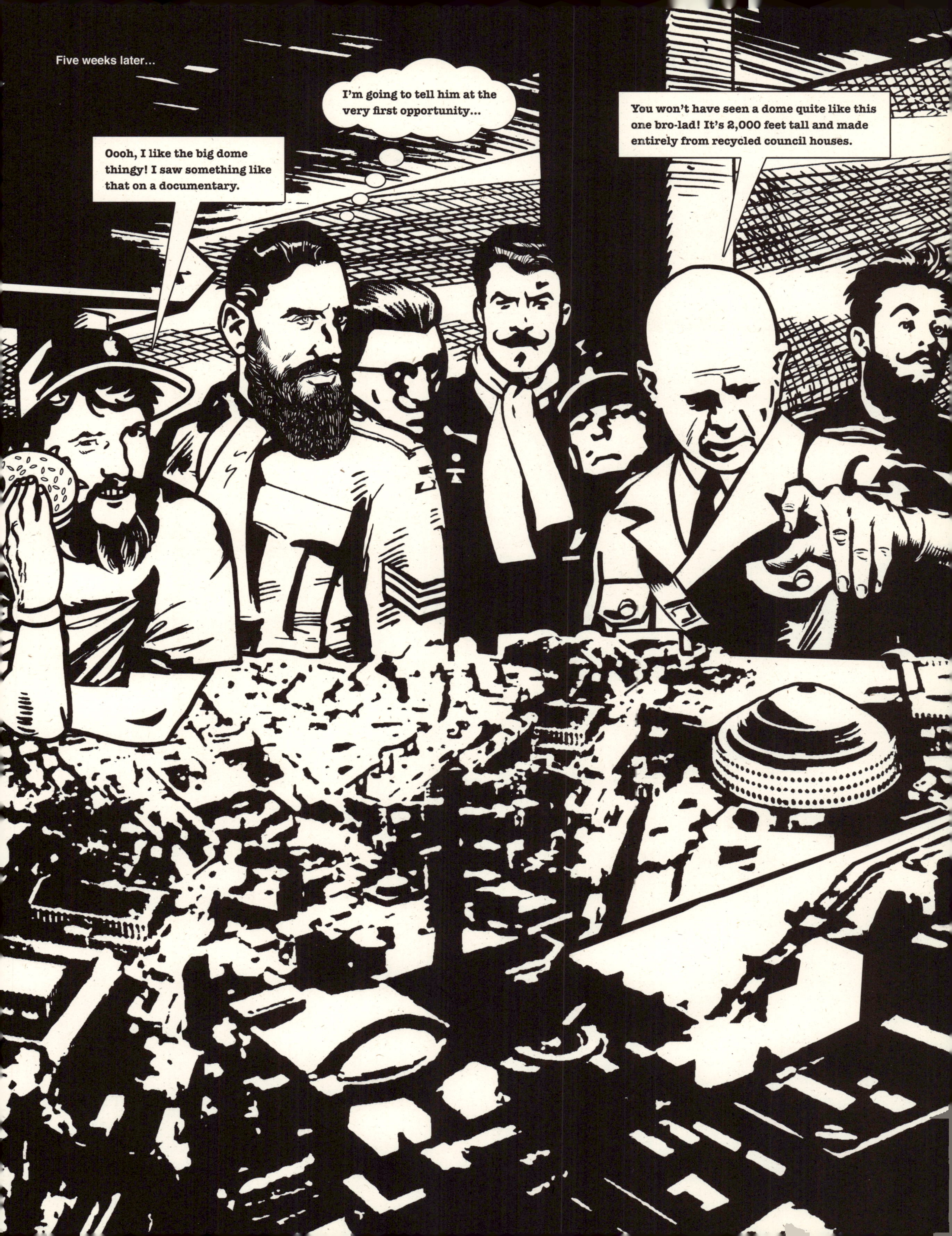
Five weeks later...
Oooh, I like the big dome thingy! I saw something like that on a documentary.
I'm going to tell him at the very first opportunity...
You won't have seen a dome quite like this one bro-lad! It's 2,000 feet tall and made entirely from recycled council houses.

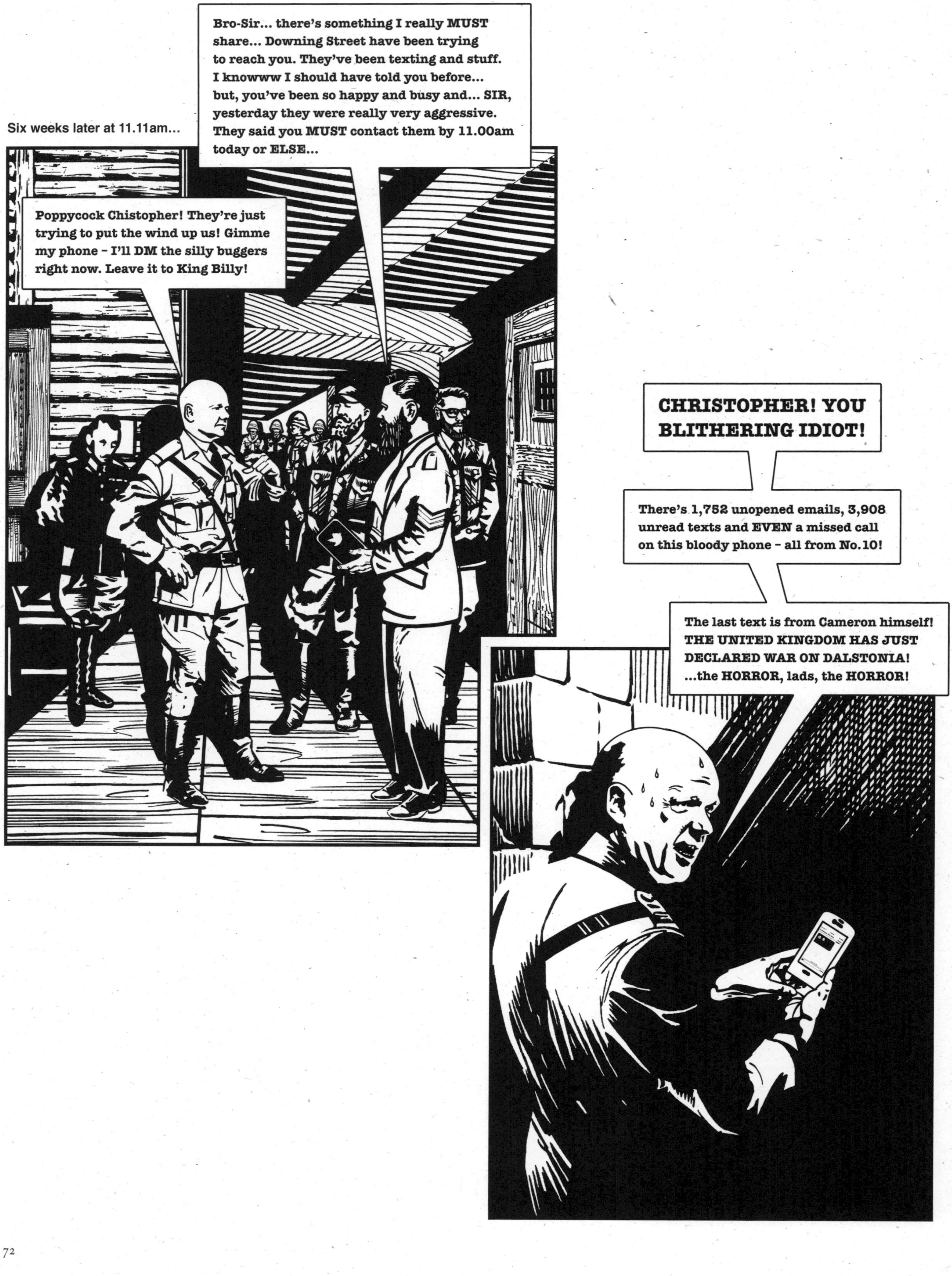
Six weeks later at 11.11am...
Bro-Sir... there's something I really MUST share... Downing Street have been trying to reach you. They've been texting and stuff. I knowwww I should have told you before... but, you've been so happy and busy and... SIR, yesterday they were really very aggressive. They said you MUST contact them by 11.00am today or ELSE...
Poppycock Chistopher! They're just trying to put the wind up us! Gimme my phone – I'll DM the silly buggers right now. Leave it to King Billy!
CHRISTOPHER! YOU BLITHERING IDIOT!
There's 1,752 unopened emails, 3,908 unread texts and EVEN a missed call on this bloody phone – all from No.10!
The last text is from Cameron himself! THE UNITED KINGDOM HAS JUST DECLARED WAR ON DALSTONIA! ...the HORROR, lads, the HORROR!

Knowing that Cameron could attack at once, Hague demanded that his Special Forces prepare for action immediately…

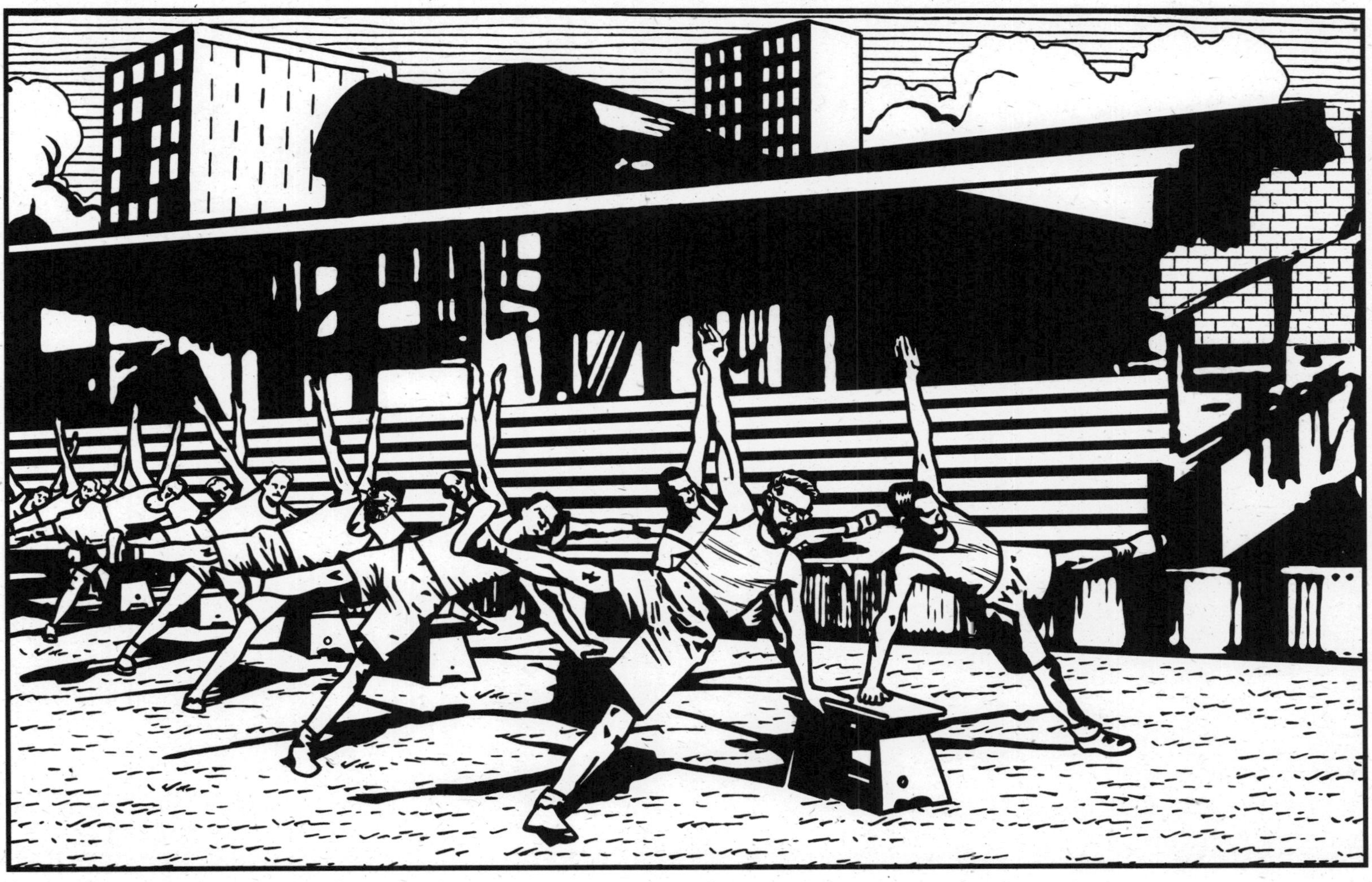

...while he addressed the rank and file in The Village Square...

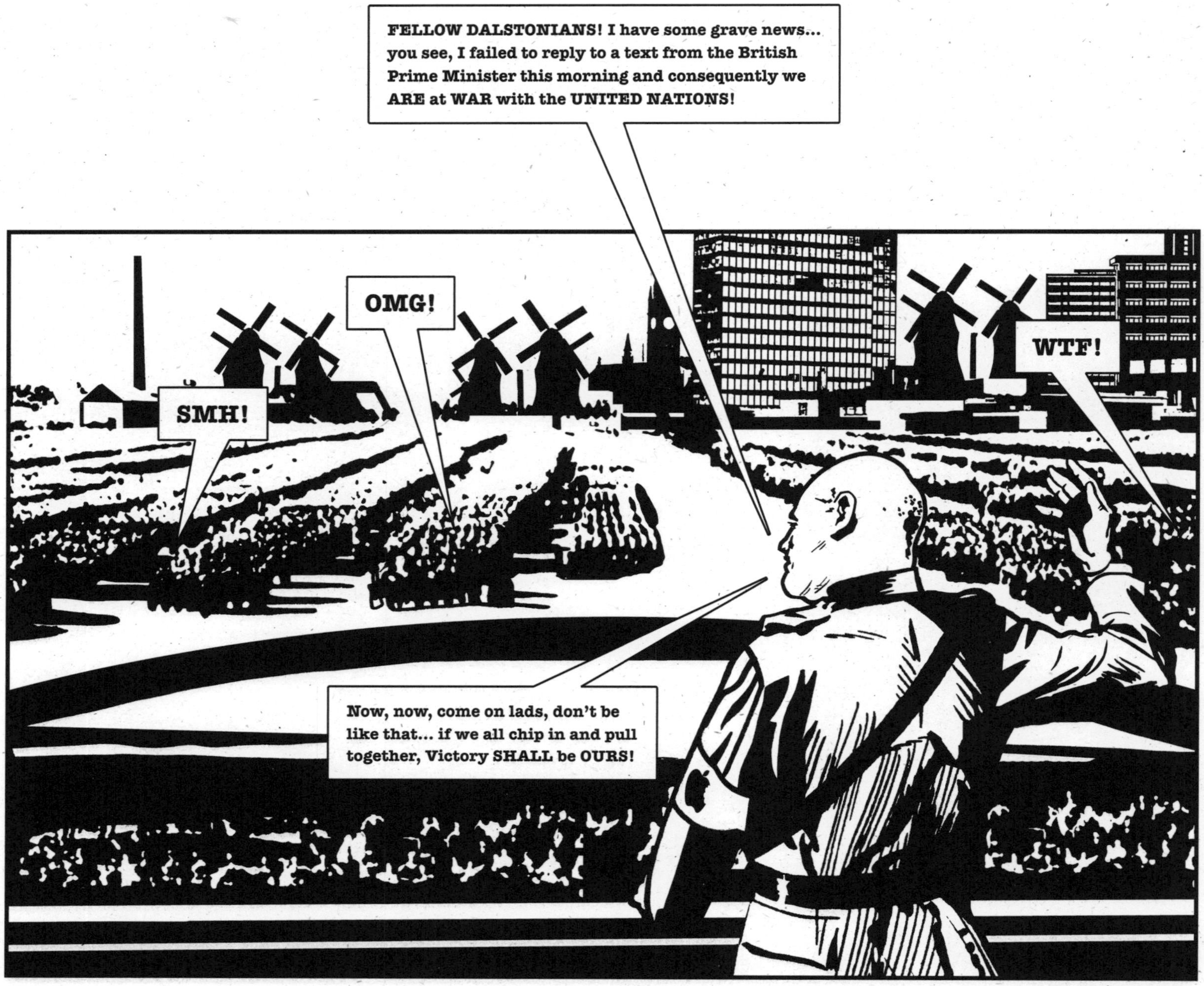

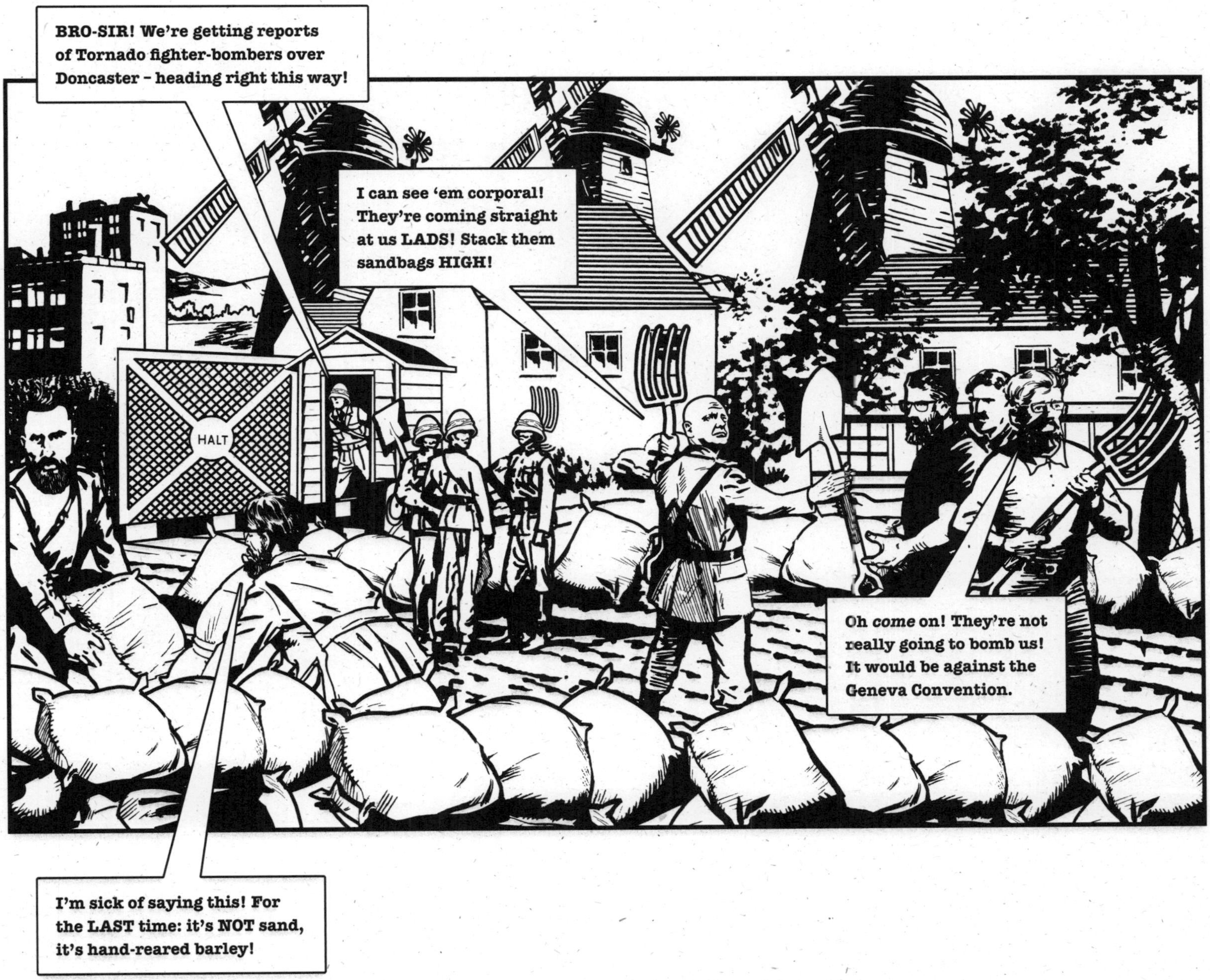
BRO-SIR! We're getting reports of Tornado fighter-bombers over Doncaster – heading right this way!
I can see 'em corporal! They're coming straight at us LADS! Stack them sandbags HIGH!
HALT
Oh *come* on! They're not really going to bomb us! It would be against the Geneva Convention.
I'm sick of saying this! For the LAST time: it's NOT sand, it's hand-reared barley!

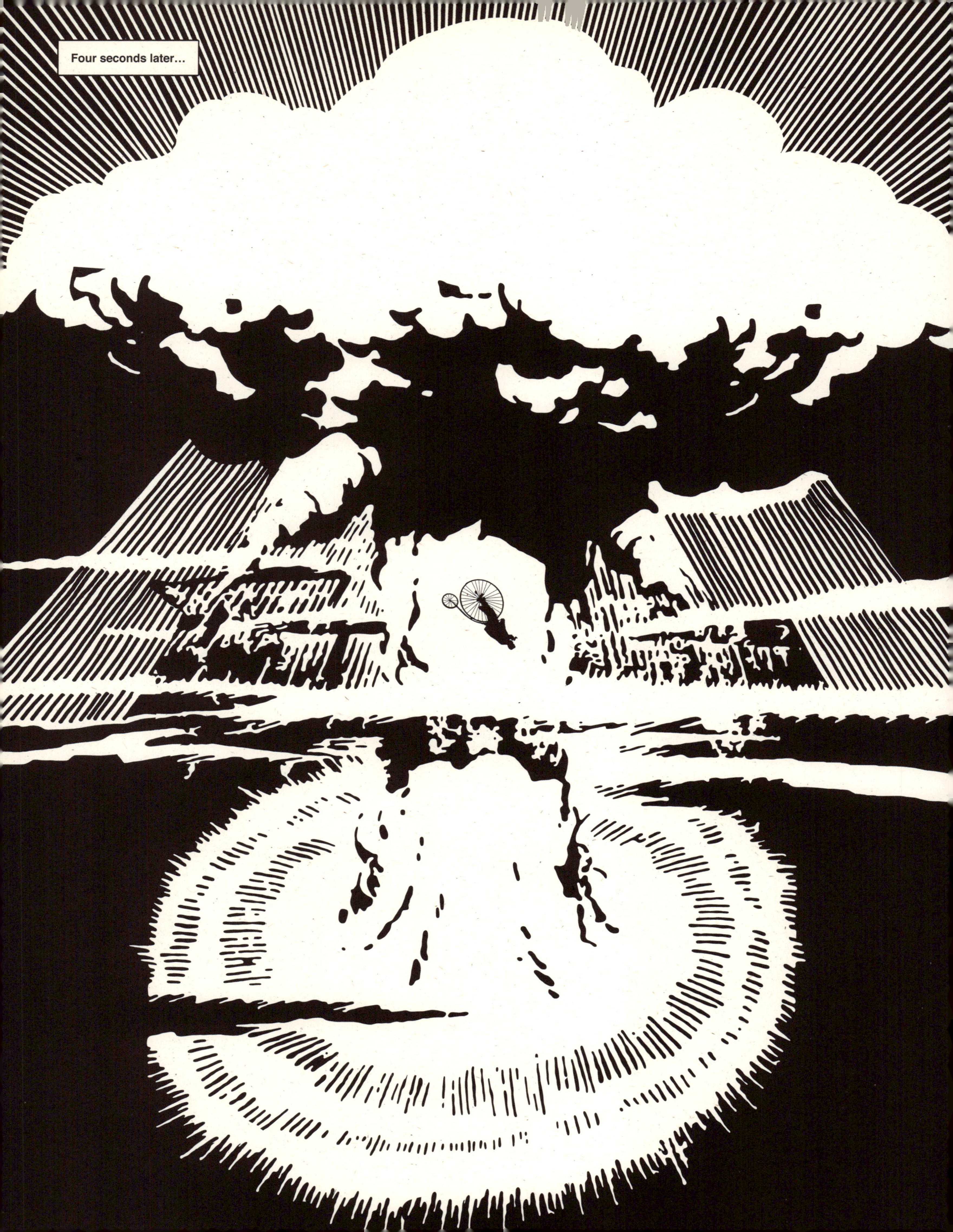
Four seconds later...

The

END

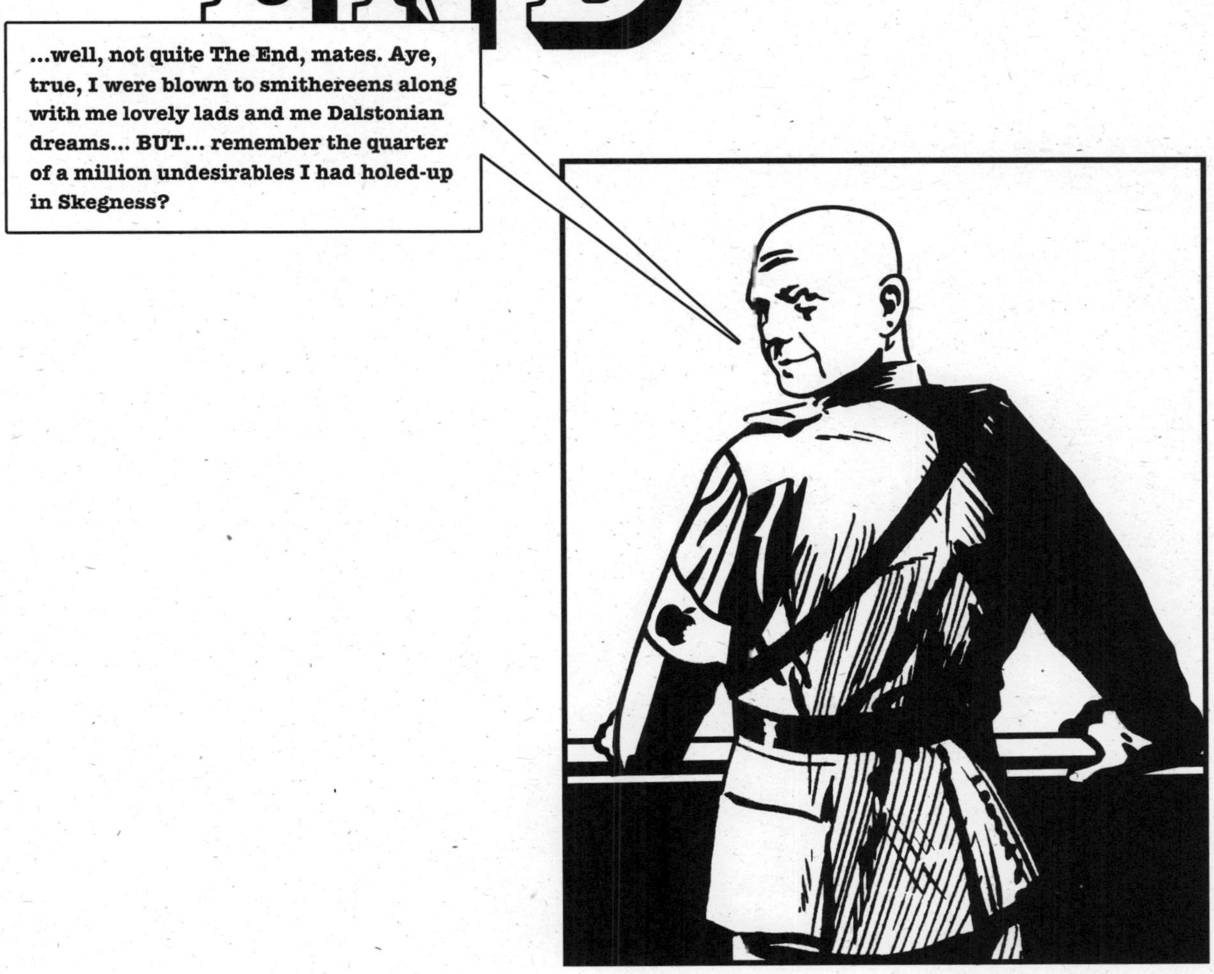
...well, not quite The End, mates. Aye, true, I were blown to smithereens along with me lovely lads and me Dalstonian dreams... BUT... remember the quarter of a million undesirables I had holed-up in Skegness?

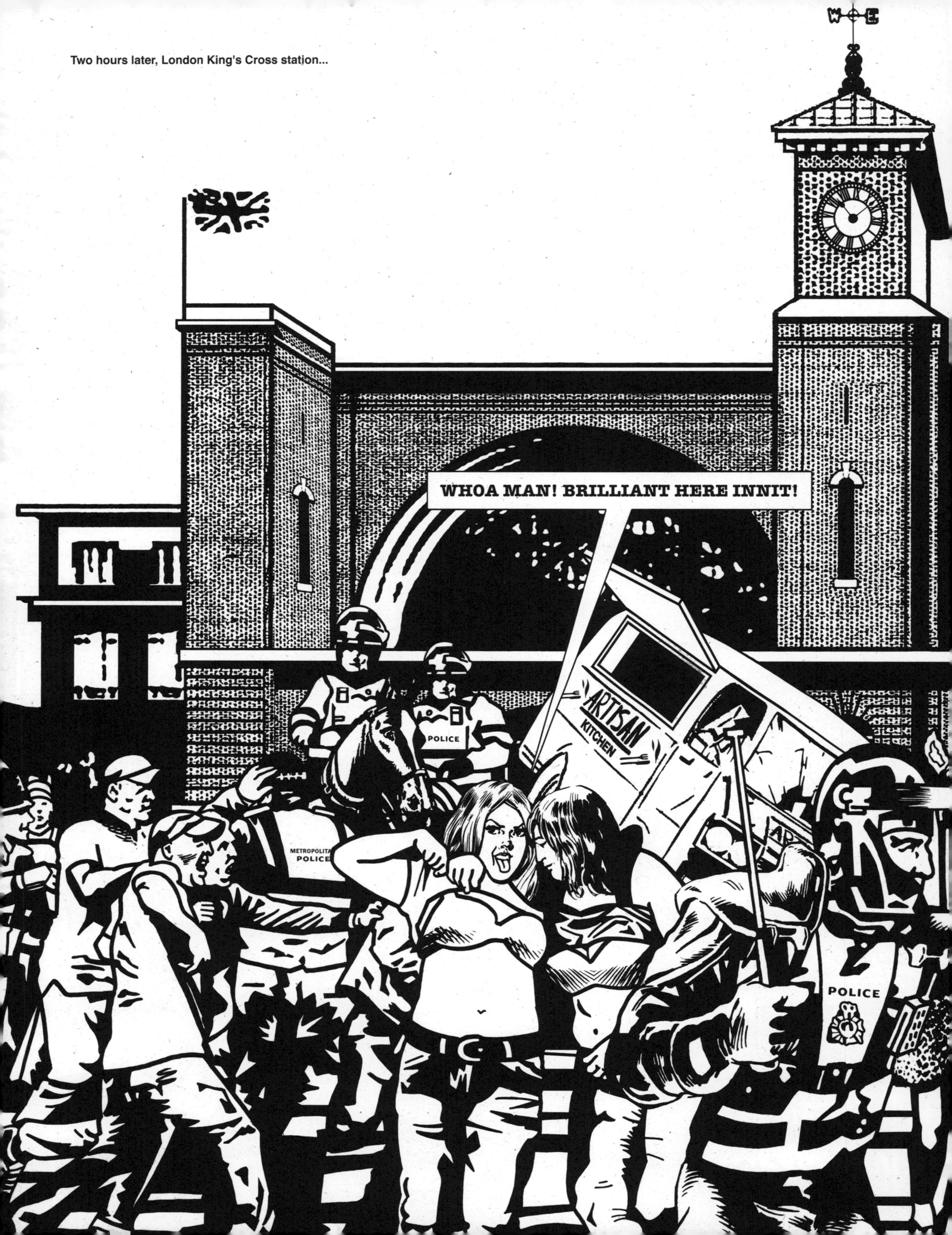
Two hours later, London King's Cross station...
WHOA MAN! BRILLIANT HERE INNIT!
POLICE
ARTISAN
KITCHEN
METROPOLITA
POLICE
POLICE

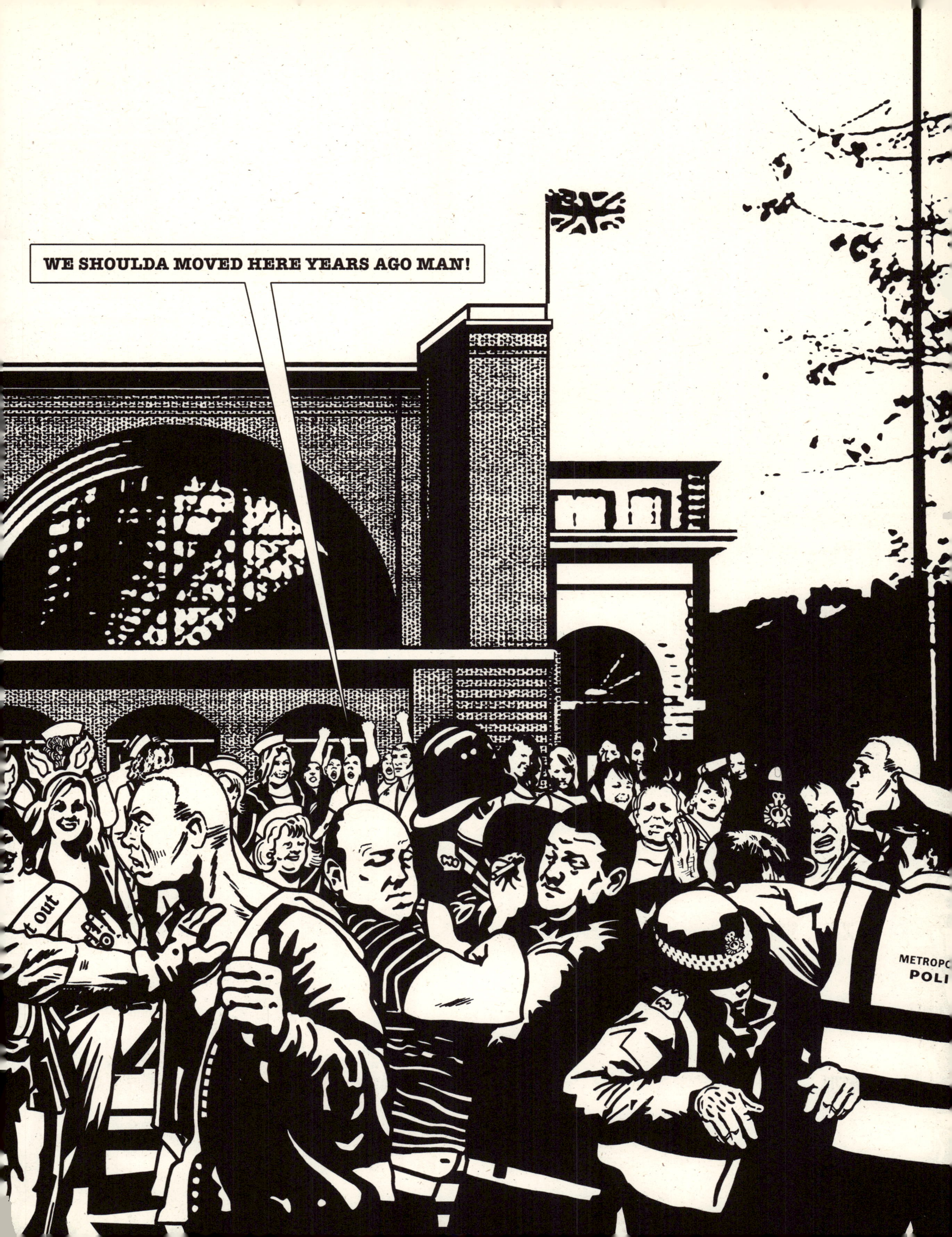
WE SHOULDA MOVED HERE YEARS AGO MAN!

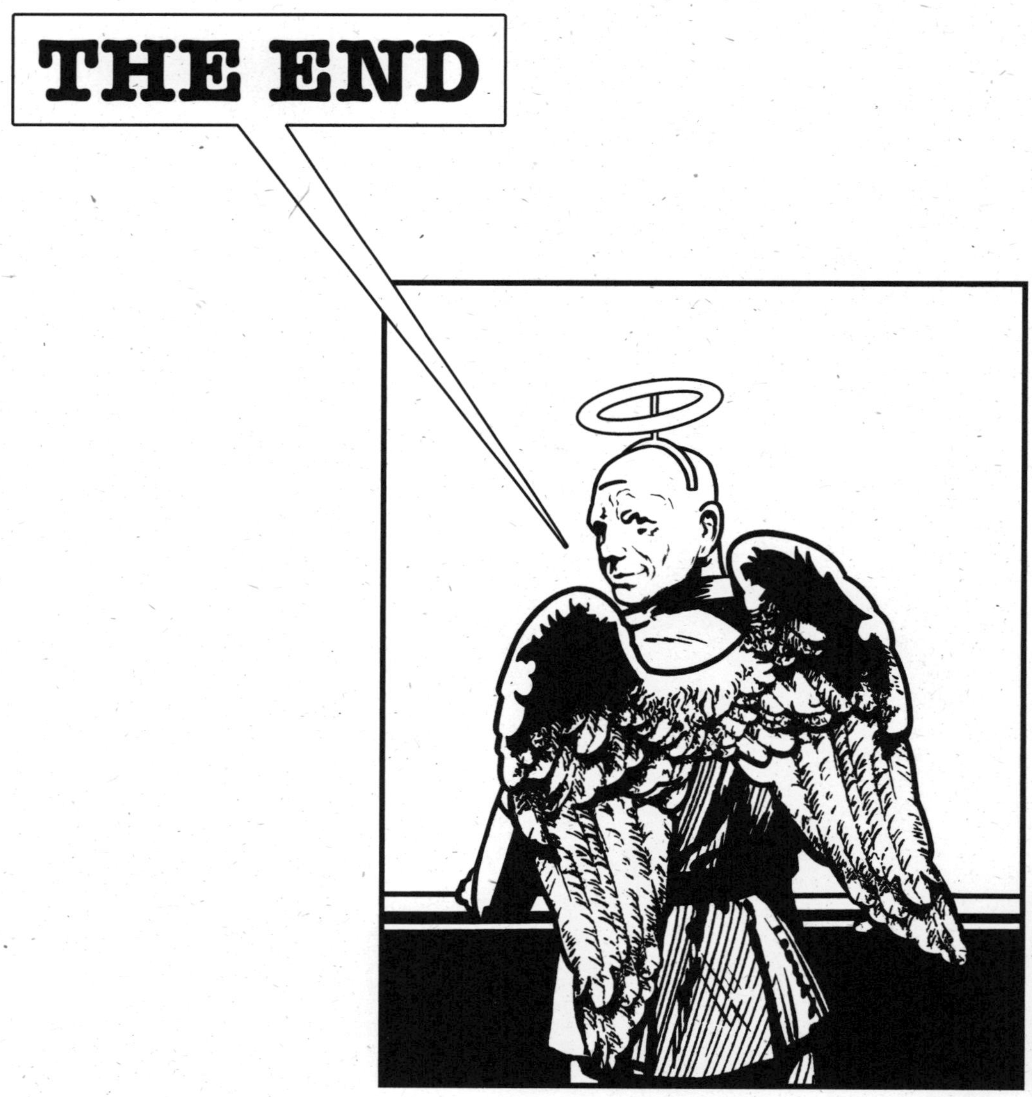
THE END

PART TWO
THE INTERNATIONALE

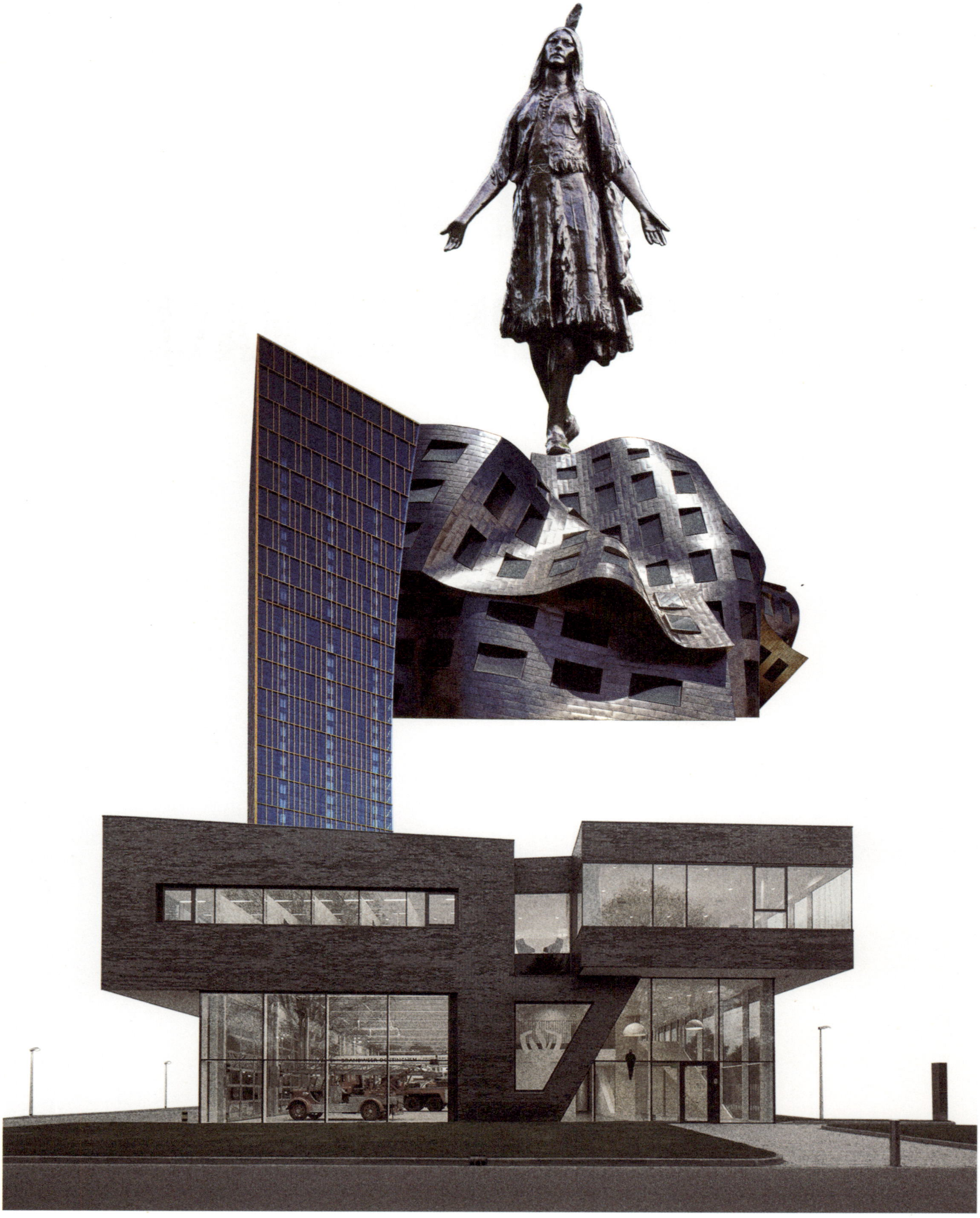

Pocahontas (Fire House Wing, Jamestown, Virginia), Photographic print, 26.5 × 21 cm, 2015
Early prototype of *Hot Wings* project – later discarded, before elements
of this design were incorporatred into *The Ekranoplanter* scheme

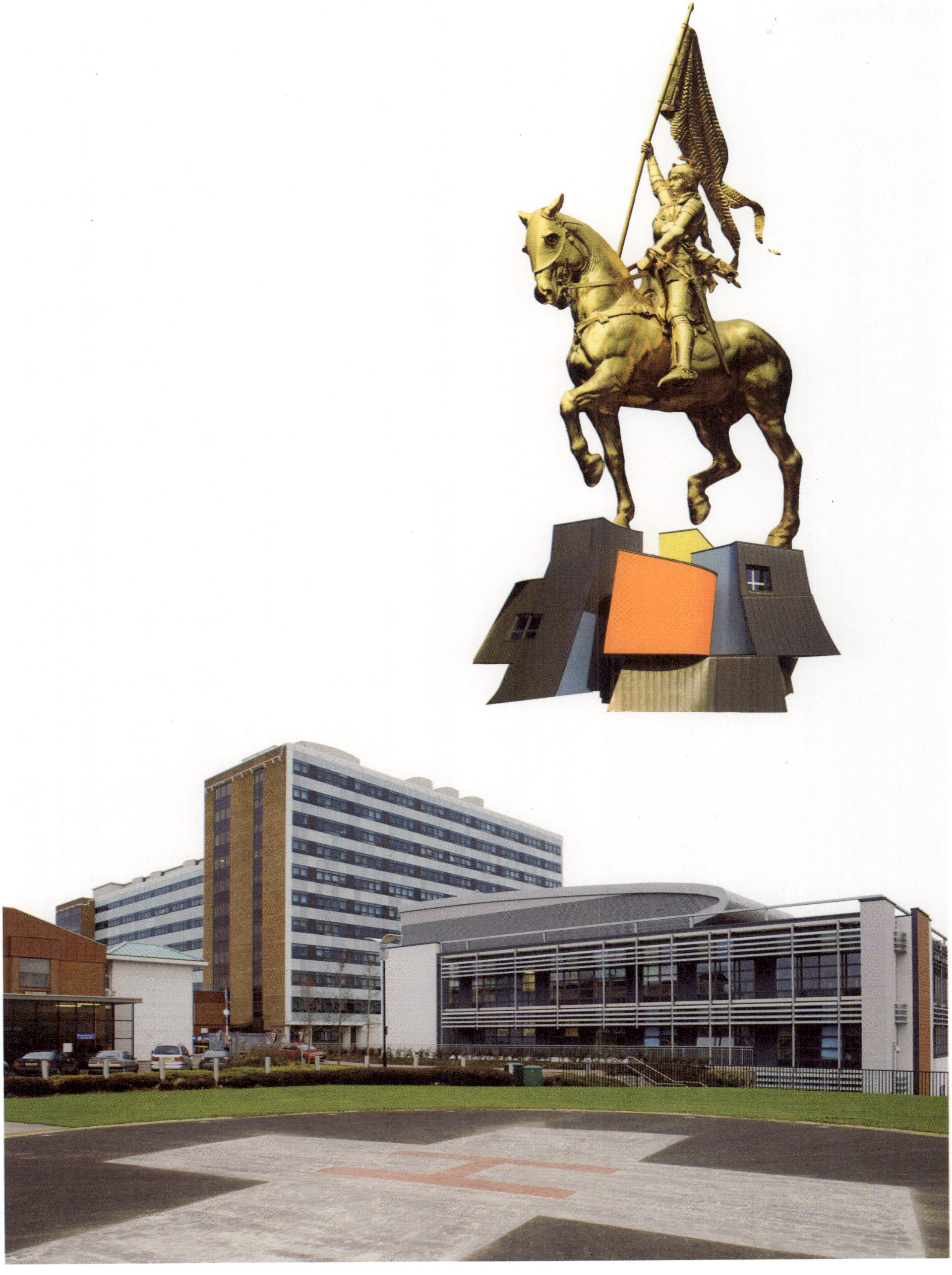

Joan of Arc (Floating Hospital Wing, Rouen, Normandy), Photographic print, 26.5 × 21 cm, 2015
Early prototype of *Hot Wings* project – later discarded, before elements
of this design were incorporatred into *The Ekranoplanter* scheme

Interview: Lynda Morris

This conversation took place at Scott King's home in Highbury, London, on 13 October 2015.

SCOTT KING: Tell us about the late 1960s and if there was a European dream. What fired you and what did you find there?

LYNDA MORRIS: I was born in 1947, so I'm a war baby. I grew up in Dover, which was more or less a bombsite at the time. My dad was very anti-war. He'd been in Germany and Belgium at the end of World War Two, and there was a haunted quality in the stories he told me. I've been thinking about this recently and I have been trying and put it in perspective. The whole of Europe from Greece through to Norway, and from Moscow through to Marseille, was occupied during World War Two, and occupation does strange things to people. It's very difficult. The two countries that were never occupied were Britain and the US, and I don't think it's a coincidence that these were the first two countries into Iraq and Afghanistan in the early 2000s.

Going forward twenty years from World War Two into the 1960s, I found working on 'When Attitudes Become Form' at the ICA very interesting, for the reason it was international, US artists, Germans and Italians, mostly organised by Germans. It was an example of artists and curators attempting to heal post-war wounds. I subsequently went to Documenta V in 1972, then to Cologne for the art fair, and then to Düsseldorf to be a student of Joseph Beuys, but Beuys got kicked out of the Academie, so I came back with loads of newspapers containing all of the photographs and the coverage of that event.

There was a geographical triangle in Northern Europe in the late 1960s between Amsterdam, Ghent and Brussels, and Cologne and Düsseldorf and most of the museums and galleries that supported the new Conceptual Art came from that area. I started to think about my father's experience in that triangle in the 1940s, which saw some of the very worst fighting at the end of World War Two. I have a particular interest in Konrad Fischer, who was the main dealer in Düsseldorf. He pulled the whole thing together with his friend Kasper Koenig, who was living in New York. Fischer did an interview for *Studio International*, saying his ideal way to create a new international art world was to pay for artists to come over from the US and the UK rather than to send crates with their work. Artists could stay in Fischer's flat for three weeks and he would help them make new work – made in Düsseldorf, which was a steel city – and they'd all go to the bar in the evening with his German artist friends, such as Sigmar Polke and Gerhard Richter. When they made trips to New York, they already knew Carl Andre and Sol LeWitt. Fischer said it helped them get over their inferiority complexes. I thought that was a really beautiful statement. We've never understood this idea fully in Britain, that there was this whole ethical position on what Conceptual Art was doing.

SK: Presumably there was a lot of talk about how art might affect society. Was there any sense of this in terms of art being situated outside of the gallery?

LM: That generation, who were about twenty-seven years old at the time, and who had been four or five year old boys at the end of the World War Two, had all been part of Schmeller's Gallery in Düsseldorf. Schmeller showed Fluxus artists, so postal art and the circulation of pieces of paper outside of the gallery was already happening. I think these artists automatically took on board the idea of art moving outside of the gallery. This really came in with the 1972 'Documenta V' and 'Sonsbeek', the big show of public sculpture in The Netherlands in 1971.

SK: I think that it's a very British attitude that Fluxus became recognised in mainstream popular culture through Seditionaries punk t-shirts. Art was very much separate from the people, the public.

LM: But you gradually had art that dealt with everyday life coming in. I remember Konrad telling me a story about the first time he met Richard Long at an exhibition that Paul Maenz – a graphic designer for the advertising agency Young & Rubicam in New York, who later opened a gallery in Cologne – had organised. Konrad said he was introduced to Richard by Jan Dibbets, and said: 'what's your work like?' and Richard replied: 'well, I go for walks.' Konrad said he didn't know where to look, so he looked down. He said Richard had the largest feet he'd ever seen, so he felt there was something genuine there.

ANDREW HUNT: What's interesting is that many British artists had to go to mainland Europe for their first solo exhibitions because there was no support in the UK. I've just seen a piece of digital marketing by Modern Art Oxford showing shots of an exhibition by Richard Long from 1971 or 1972, as if it was a groundbreaking project. But these institutions were simply riding on the coattails of the European dealers.

LM: Oh yes, Richard was showing overseas in 1968 and 1969. Art & Language couldn't get a show in the UK. Their first exhibition at Lisson Gallery was in 1973. Barry Flanagan was showing with Art & Project. Gilbert & George weren't allowed to be in 'When Attitudes Become Form' in 1969, but they simply turned up for the opening at the ICA with gold and silver paint on their hands and faces. I watched from across the foyer as Konrad met them for the first time. He took them to Düsseldorf and the rest, as they say, is history. It was in early 1970 that Nigel Greenwood showed *The Singing Sculpture*, whereas Konrad was in there already.

SK: So there was a seriousness in mainland Europe for Performance Art and Land Art that didn't exist here?

LM: There were a few people like Nigel and the Lisson who started to watch what was going on in Europe, and they realised that it was quite special.

SK: You mentioned art started to happen increasingly outside of the gallery, as well as the idea of the sculpture park, which I have a real problem with. Are you a fan of public sculpture?

LM: Not really, no. With 'When Attitudes Become Form', Charles Harrison made a great thing about Robert Smithson tipping dirt into the countryside. And Gerry Schum made important videos with Land Artists. Mario Merz was making spirals out in the open air. But it's the immateriality of Conceptual Art that really interests me. Things like Stanley Brouwn going for a walk and recording the precise amount of steps taken in various cities.

SK: A lot of the things we address in this book are the precise opposite, the co-option of monumental sculpture, particularly of sculpture by government or business.

LM: Yes, and that's what also really interests me at this moment in time, in terms of how public art has affected private property. If a young couple, like my son and his girlfriend, Fred and Emma, are able to buy an attic in Highgate, they are really lucky. In terms of art, they haven't even got the room to hang small pieces of paper on their wall. Paradoxically, British art since the early 1990s has all been about vast great pieces of work, yet the only people that can buy and hang them are corporations, which have got great big buildings.

SK: Which is very much the New York model.

LM: Yes. Recently, up in Manchester, I became really interested in English science fiction and *New Worlds* magazine, which includes contributions by Richard Hamilton and Eduardo Paolozzi. English science fiction was very different to the US idea of the robot man on Mars. *New Worlds*' idea was that we are already living in the future, it's already here with men on the moon in 1969.

SK: Speculative architecture, such as Archigram, is essentially science fiction as reality. Yet that view of the future came to an end.

LM: Well it's there in 'This Is Tomorrow', the Whitechapel Art Gallery show of 1951. That sense of modernity interests me a lot, together with the fact that we're all having to shrink where we live. None of us have got room for Tate's idea of art. What really interests me about Tate is what they treat as a 'minor' department, which is the material in the archives. These pieces of paper from Fluxus to Conceptualism are absolutely wonderful. I always wonder why this doesn't affect what comes out of the art schools. But it's because students aren't being encouraged to make the kind of art that people who spend their life with kids in two rooms are going to be able to collect.

AH: You've previously talked about the international Conceptual movement being bastardised by Britain. What did you mean by this?

LM: Well for me Conceptual Art took place between 1967 and 1973. It was over by 1973. In 1979 Anthony D'Offay opened his gallery in London and that really was the end of it. Everything then became larger and perfect. One of the beautiful pieces by Richard Long from 1968 was simply a piece of paper torn from a lined school book. You can see the holes where the compass points have pierced, five concentric circles and a little map taken from an atlas at the top. That's all it is. And suddenly D'Offay took over ten years later and Long's work became enormous photographs framed under glass.

SK: So the position became commodified. One of the things I really wanted to ask you about was Victor Pasmore's Apollo Pavilion, a piece of public art that was built in the new town of Peterlee in 1955. What's your position on this?

LM: I've actually done a lot of work on Pasmore, because he was a member of the Coldstream Committee. I am not a fan, I think Stuart Brisley's work at Peterlee in 1976 and1977 covers the problem. I'm very fond of Coldstream and I particularly like his involvement with film. I found this wonderful poem from W.H. Auden to 'William Coldstream Esq' written in 1937, about the idea of the eye of the camera that 'we discussed in Soho Square'. The relationship between Hamilton and Gerhard Richter and painting and photography is similar. I introduced them to each other, to drop a name or two. I was Hamilton's assistant for his Guggenheim show and I remember they talked about Hamilton's Kent State University image, and the shooting of the students. Richard told the story of taking Polaroid photographs from his television set and the new technology that enabled images to be sent over the Atlantic via cable, which he found really exciting. Richter was also really excited about this. And of course eight years later Richter made the Baader-Meinhof paintings from CCTV images. Depicting images from television is of course what Richter's fuzziness is about. We used to talk about 'the snow' and the reception on TV, which is contained in his portraits of the Baker family.

SK: The snow has now completely gone, along with all of the programmes.

LM: The important idea is that a photograph is unstable and a constantly evolving and changing thing. Coldstream's idea of the future of art education was filmmaking alongside painting and drawing from life. However, Pasmore ruled the day, and this is the reason why you have the legacy of architecture and the Bauhaus as a sense of basic design in public art. In opposition to this, the stuff I really like currently comes from graphics rather than fine art. Peter Wollen had this idea of the history of contemporary art as the twin avant-gardes. Abstraction, design and architecture, together with figurative painting, photography and cinema twirling around each other. The whole time, people have taken one side or the other without trying to deal with the fact that they are intertwined.

SK: I've got an assistant who is twenty-two years old, and he has no interest in boundaries. To come back to Pasmore, I wanted to ask you about the fact that it's been endlessly vandalised. What do you think of this?

LM: Well people don't like being told what to do. I did a show with Stuart Brisley after his residency programme in Peterlee when I was in Nottingham.

Pasmore wanted everyone on the estate to paint their doors certain colours according to his artistic programme, and of course, people were furious. They wanted each door their own colour. Have you got a positive thing about Pasmore?

SK: Yes, a story that I read on the internet a few years ago really struck a chord in me. There are some Neolithic ruins in Shetland. Several thousand years after they were erected, a Viking ship docked in rough seas and the invaders scrawled all over them. Victorians unearthed their graffiti. This is really interesting, because you've got three levels of time, ancient history, Viking history and a Victorian account of it. Certainly man has an inability to move on from the idea of vandalising monuments. This struck me as a parallel to the short history of Victor Pasmore's modernist structure. For me, vandalism from 1968 would be just as interesting as the artwork because of the cultural references within the graffiti. Being based in Norwich, what's your experience of the interface between the real public and art?

LM: Well, first of all I think public art works well in Germany, but we have a different relationship to it in this country. I remember taking my kids to Documenta, and they spent the whole time at a swimming pool, but when we went onto the Münster Sculpture Park (Skulptur Projekte Münster) they loved it. The success is contained in the experience of discovering places with a map. Public art can work quite nicely in that way. Part of the approach to new public sculpture in Germany comes from the fact that they had to get rid of their previous statues, because of the war. But in the UK we still have ceremonial sculpture everywhere. In Norwich I was very conscious of the city's Puritan Quaker tradition: Elizabeth Fry for example, who was an English social reformer and a Christian philanthropist. Edith Cavell, the British nurse that helped around 200 allied soldiers escape from German-occupied Belgium during the First World War, is also from Norwich. This is the sort of thing that I like about the place. There aren't many statues, apart from the one built in Victorian times of Sir Thomas Browne in the market square. Browne gave evidence in 1662 against two women charged with witchcraft, so it has connotations. For 'EAST*international*' in 1997, the Japanese artist Tazro Niscino built a domestic living room around the statue. You could go up a staircase and meet Thomas Browne and sit inside. It had 9,000 visitors over the course of the summer.

SK: My long-term collaborator Matt Worley is a professor of modern history at the University of Reading. One of our ideas is that public art should celebrate the local. There is a man, 'Cue Gary', that lives in Goole, my home town. He's called that because he always walks around with a snooker cue in his hand. We think that there should be a statue erected to him. Matt said there should also be a statue erected in Norwich to celebrate 'Marigold', the guy famed for wearing rubber gloves and directing traffic on the city's inner ring road in the early 1990s. He died recently.

LM: Oh yes, I remember him well, he was black, which was rare in Norwich. I've got a press cutting from when he died.

SK: Matt thinks the Marigold statue would be a tribute to a specific character that everybody in the city identifies with, hence it's a genuinely public form of art.

LM: Ruth Ewan came to Norwich and made a nice piece about Kett's Oak, a tree in Hetherset on the outskirts of the city. Robert and William Kett, who the tree is named after, assembled their men for the Peasant's Revolt at the tree in 1549, before marching on Norwich. When I first came to Norwich, there was a chapel in the cathedral that contained a plaque congratulating the city on defeating the Peasant's Revolt, but thankfully it was removed. To celebrate Kett's Oak, Ruth composed a tune for folk groups in the area, and made a film.

SK: The idea that public art can be quite small in scale, be palatable and make a subtle and genuine protest is exciting. The New Labour version of public art – *Angel of the North* and *AccelorMitalOrbit* – is obviously very phallic, and it connects with the artist as architect. That of course wouldn't happen under the Tory government, you're not going to see them commission enormous public sculpture.

LM: I have a nice story that connects with recent developments. I was very lucky to know Marcel Broodthaers when he lived in London in the early 1970s. I did a project with him at the Slade, showing his film *Figures of Wax* (1973), in which he talks to the wax figure of Jeremy Bentham and explores Bentham's revolutionary traditions and the chaos in exchange rates. Broodthaers was very involved with the Tervuren museum, which is the Royal Congo Museum in Brussels. Broodthaers' palm trees were about colonialism. Similarly, his *Museum of Modern Art, Department of Eagles* (1970–71) wasn't about museology, as the American journal *October* and the theorist Benjamin Buchloh would have us believe. The work traces the history of the use of the image of an eagle from Assyria to Egypt, to the Roman Legions the Austro-Hungarian Empire, the Russian Empire, Napoleon and then Hitler. Today it's the USA that still uses the symbol of the Eagle, on top of the US Embassy in Grosvenor Square.

SK: The demonstration against the Vietnam War outside the US Embassy?

LM: Yes, there are plans to move the US embassy, and I wonder what will happen to the concrete eagle? I have been thinking that Vietnam has been taken out of the demonstrations in 1968, it's just become a small local French thing that happened in May of that year. The Rolling Stones were there for that demo in London. Jagger and Richards went home that evening and wrote *Street Fighting Man*, a fact that has now been lost on us.

So, Broodthaers was immensely political. And that set me off to look at colonialism, which I'd never really considered. In Hannah Arendt's *The Origins of Totalitarianism* (1951) there are three volumes on the search for gold. First you've got medieval alchemy, then you've got European colonialism in Africa, India and China, and then you've got the Nazi search for Jewish gold. Just think of the surplus time that we created through slavery. Arendt says that the population of the Congo went from around forty million down to around eight million in a twenty-year period leading up to the First World War. Sir Roger Casement went up the Congo with Joseph Conrad of *Heart of Darkness* (1899) fame and wrote a report about what was happening. He was sent back to Ireland, where he led the Easter Rising in 1916 and was eventually executed. Recently a historian at UCL revealed Cameron's family's connections with slavery. You couldn't make it up.

The main point is how famine was used by the military in empire. Mike Davis, who is at UCLA, wrote a book called, *City of Quartz: Excavating the Future in Los Angeles* (1990) on the way that museums were constructed in Los Angeles to reclaim parts of the city from local Spanish Americans. His study is all about how public art and museums are closely connected to property developers. One could claim that this is exactly what Tate has been doing in London since 1988. Davis also wrote a book called *Late Victorian Holocausts* (2000), where he looks at Britain and the use of hunger to control our colonies. If you compare this to the way in which the British upper classes, 'The Officer Class', are still so in charge of the contemporary art world and the idea of what public sculpture is, then you can start to identify the various forms of duplicity about what large public artworks and galleries do.

AH: Do you think there is a similar management of the working class areas of Britain through public art?

SK: Well, Margate is definitely an example of that. There are now two Margates: there's a bubble of gentrification on the seafront next to Turner Contemporary. On one level you could argue that this is very good for the area, but you could also say that one section has simply been colonised by a new form of bourgeois culture, because the rest of the town is exactly the same as it was.

AH: What do you think the future of public art will be under the Tories?

LM: Well I see public art as part of the welfare state. It's part of the system that was brought in after 1945. In the same way that the health service has started to be privatised, there's a privatisation in the way that all of the committees that fund public art are becoming more closely related to the commercial interests of the main dealer galleries. From my perspective, this is extraordinary. After 1979 – and particularly since Tate Modern opened in 2000 – an enormous gap has opened up between what is considered to be contemporary art in the US and in Europe on one side, and what contemporary art is seen to be in the UK on the other. I mean, I love the fact that Gilbert & George have refused to have anything to do with Tate Britain. They don't see themselves as being British artists.

In terms of recent projects in London, I thought Hans Haacke's fourth plinth commission in Trafalgar

Square might be interesting. But it didn't really work, did it? There was a missed opportunity for a direct political conversation about the city. All you could see was a piece of tape around the ankle of a horse. Not many of the fourth plinth commissions have been political, or have included artists that really matter internationally. I think that the whole problem with public art in this country is held in the fact that the artists and curators that would push everything aren't getting a voice.

SK: Given the context, I actually quite like what Haacke did. Do you think the committee quashed any genuine sentiment?

LM: Yes, maybe they stopped the real story about the work coming out. I mean, Haacke was never really forgiven by the art establishment for the work that contained the portrait of Thatcher, which showed that Saatchi & Saatchi held the account of the South African Nationalist Party at the same time that they held the account of Thatcher and her government during the ban on having anything to do with apartheid. We all stopped buying South African oranges, but Saatchi and Saatchi continued their support, because for them it was normal. Haacke did a similar piece about South Africa and Land Rover at Modern Art Oxford.

I haven't really got a real interest in public art because my idea of what's important today is what young people like Fred and Emma are collecting, which are those small pieces of paper that reflect back to the 1970s, and to Conceptualism.

SK: That's interesting.

LM: It's what young people can connect with. I like the idea of Richard Hamilton making 5,000 copies of an editioned print of Kent State. Instead of asking who would you most like to see producing a single public sculpture, my question would be, who are the five artists in this country that you'd like to make an editioned print? You, Gilbert & George and Jeremy Deller continue this line of thinking.

AH: A new symptom within public art comes in the work of the artists' group Assemble, who are on the shortlist for this year's Turner Prize. They create small, low-level socially-engaged temporary architectural work. What are your thoughts on this type of practice?

LM: Well I see architects as the enemy. All architects. Going back to British science fiction, when I walked from London Bridge to White Cube in Bermonsey last night, it felt like I was walking through a science fiction film. I remember Konrad thumping the table when he selected 'EAST*international*' in 1993. He said art had nothing to do with fashion whatsoever, and I feel the same way about architecture, because architects have tried to turn themselves into artists.

SK: What about seeing this situation in reverse, where the artist becomes a do-gooder or urban planner? There's a sense with Kapoor that the artist has become an architect. And at ground level, artist groups such as Assemble have become local philanthropists. What's your feeling on this type of engagement?

LM: I just see this work as decoration for larger architectural development and planning. People are paying £1,000 a month for somewhere to live. In London, the whole housing market has its roots in the profile of architects. There was a certain point when Peter Palumbo – a major property developer, and one of my bêtes noires – was appointed to Nicholas Serota's committee at the Whitechapel Gallery. After his links with Serota and the Whitechapel, Palumbo was appointed chairman of the Tate Trustees. I knew Palumbo from my days working for Nigel Greenwood. He bought the most expensive works by Jasper Johns and he also bought houses; he had a Frank Lloyd Wright house and Marcel Breuer house in the US, and a Le Corbusier house in France. Palumbo was collecting houses like people collect art objects, and he was a big developer. When he became the chairman of the Tate Trustees he gave an interview to *The Observer* the same weekend, in which he said that the Tate needed a new director, someone young and thrusting like Serota. Alan Bowness was the director at the time and Palumbo had to resign because he couldn't be the chairman of the Tate Trustees and go against the existing Director. However, within two years Thatcher made Palumbo the Chairman of the Visual Arts Panel of the Arts Council of Great Britain, which was to decide the rules for the National Lottery Funding. The Committee under Palumbo determined that lottery funding had to go towards new buildings. The alternative proposal, made by officers at the Arts Council and the artists running Air and Space – who were wonderful back in the 1970s – was slung out. They were interested in creating sustainable post-industrial developments in twenty-five regional cities around Britain, including artist-run gallery spaces, low-cost housing and studios for artists. They're the people who should be up for the Turner Prize. Instead National Lottery money went into architectural developments such as Tate Modern, Baltic, Ikon and gigantic public artworks.

AH: Other galleries on the list include Turner Contemporary in Margate and Firstsite in Colchester – the latter has been in financial difficulties since it opened.

LM: Palumbo eventually became Lord Palumbo. Tate appointed the architect Richard Rogers as the new chair. Then there was the exhibition 'London as it Could Be' at the Royal Academy in 1986, in which Rogers proposed a radical overhaul of the capital.

AH: There's also the book *A New London* by Richard Rogers and the labour MP Mark Fisher from 1990. The plans that appear in the book were realised over the next twenty or so years. It's interesting that the exhibition and the book represent the first time that a garden bridge was mooted for the Thames.

LM: And Tate Modern, the Millenium Dome and the London Olympics all took place, which are a property developer's dream come true. For me, public art is really the glorification of those building projects that are dominated by the architectural establishment.

SK: Yes, one could say that the whole idea of public sculpture is the icing on the cake of a new build, such as Kapoor's work in the piazza of IBM. Public art is often the final corporate twiddling of the dicky bow.

AH: I've got one final question about the future, within the utopian aspect of Conceptualism. What would your ideal scenario be for the future of visual art outside of government and market forms of instrumentalisation?

LM: In reality, the future is all about how we can empower young people to love the art that makes sense to them again. That's really what I care about. I did this in Norwich by helping all of the key people in the city to form a committee to create Outpost Gallery, and there is an article in *Frieze* about the young artists that came through as technicians in the 'EAST*international*' exhibitions. This is the type of thing that young people need, and it's the future of art. For me, the work that's being included in the British Art Shows and shown at Tate – with notable exceptions – comes from the past. I'm interested in the future.

SK: Okay, that's a good place to end, thanks for your time Lynda.

ANISH & ANTONY TAKE AFGHANISTAN

Illustrations by Will Henry

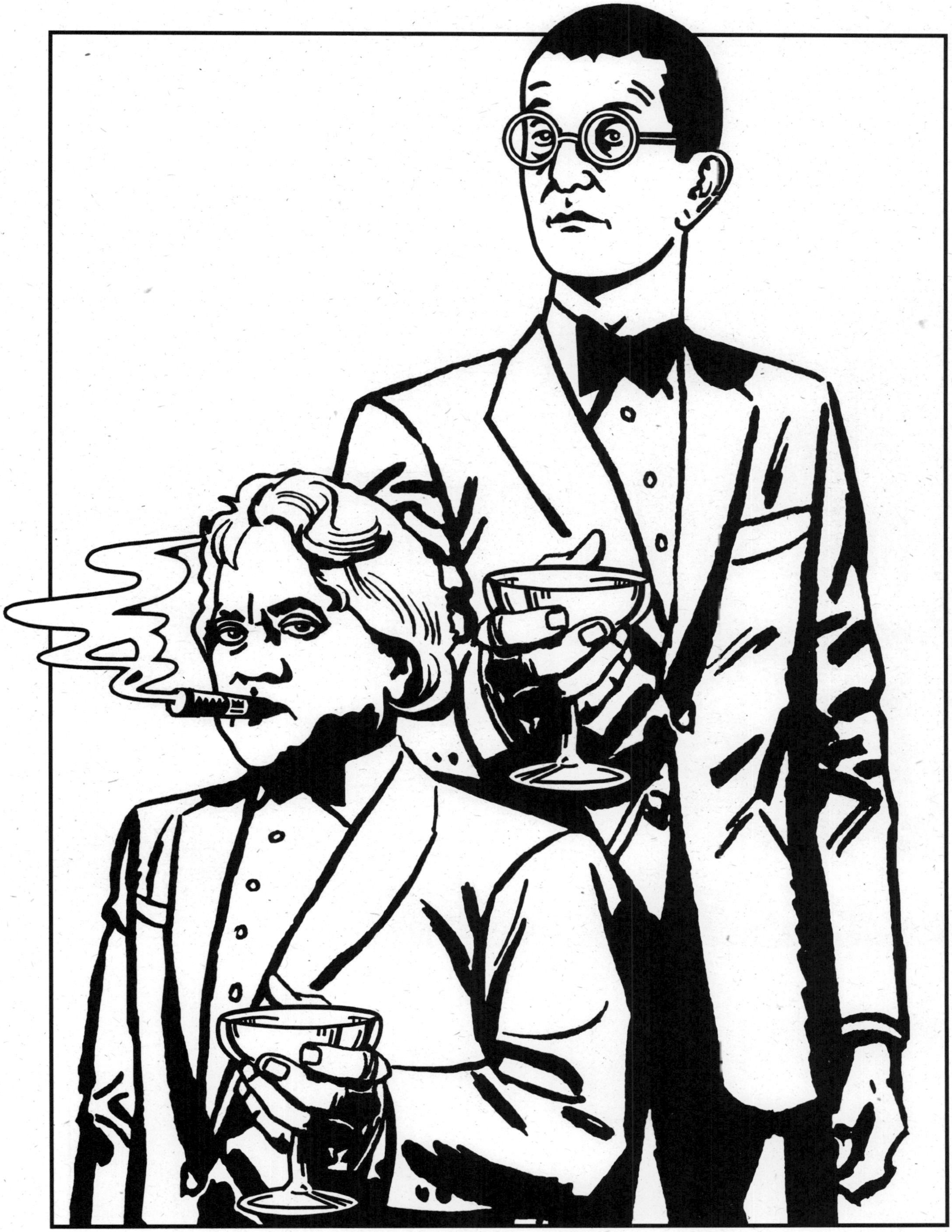

Anish & Antony Take Afghanistan, Inkjet prints on paper, Thirty-two parts. 2014

Afghanistan yesterday…

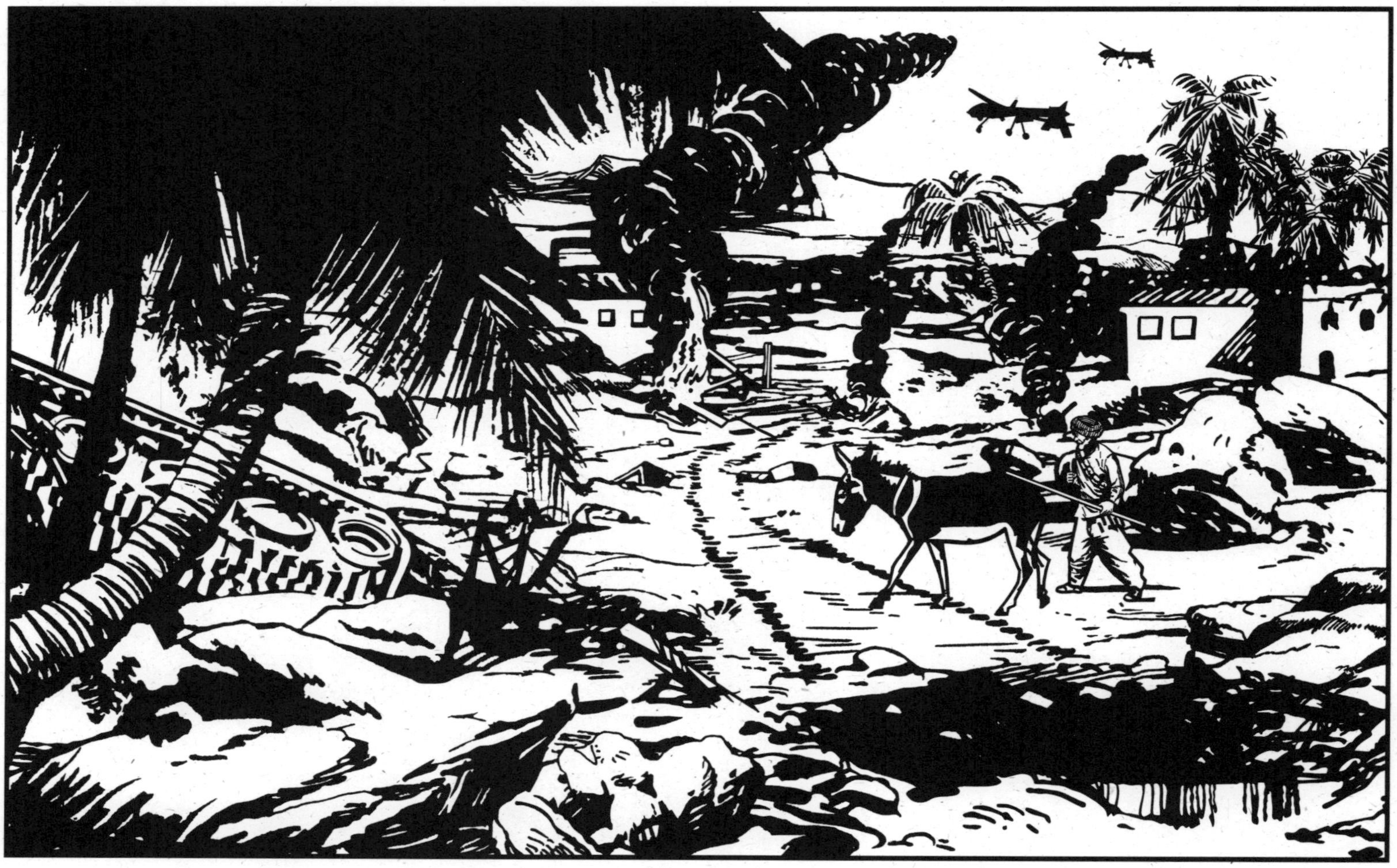

Meanwhile, at the United Nations Headquarters...

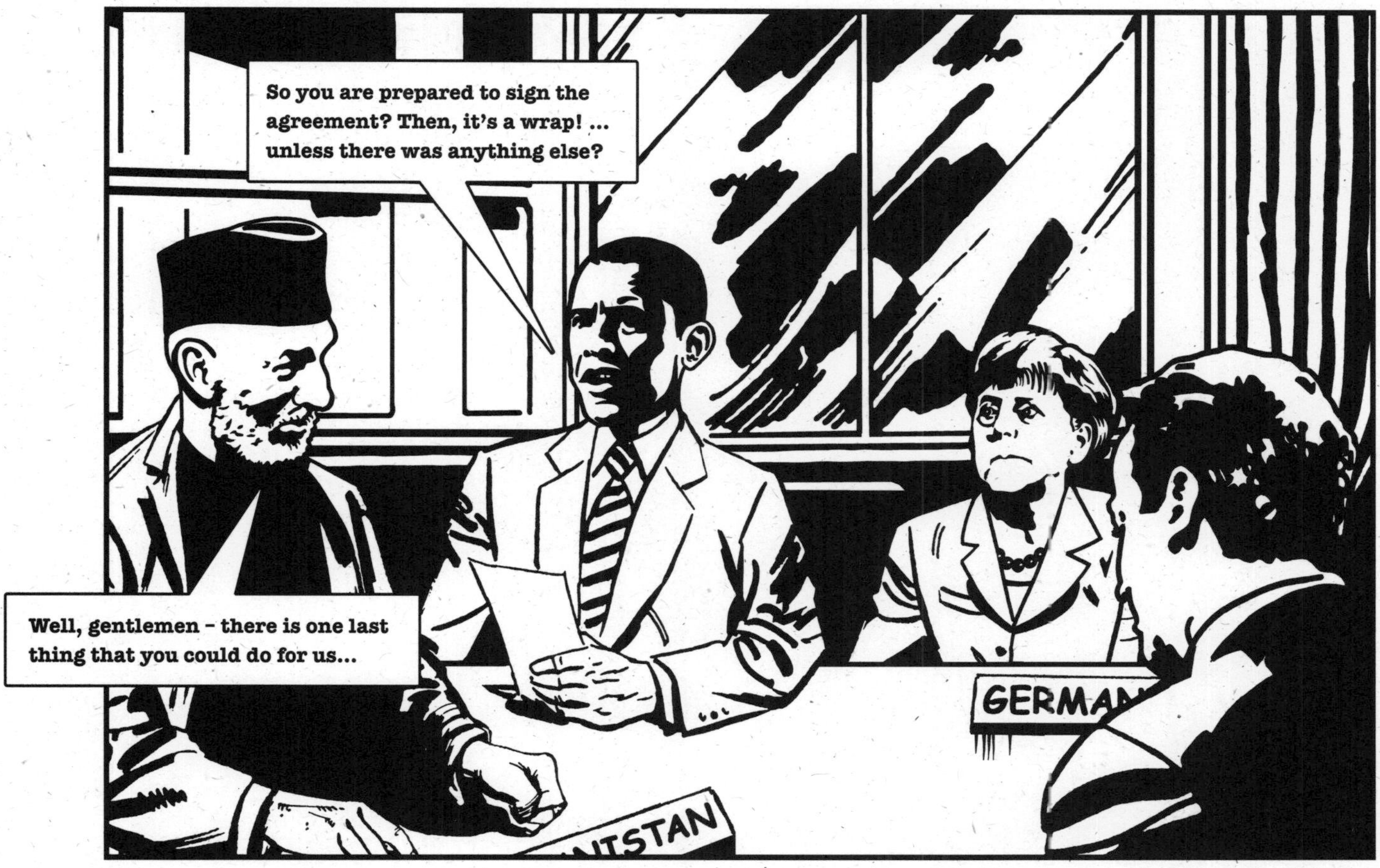

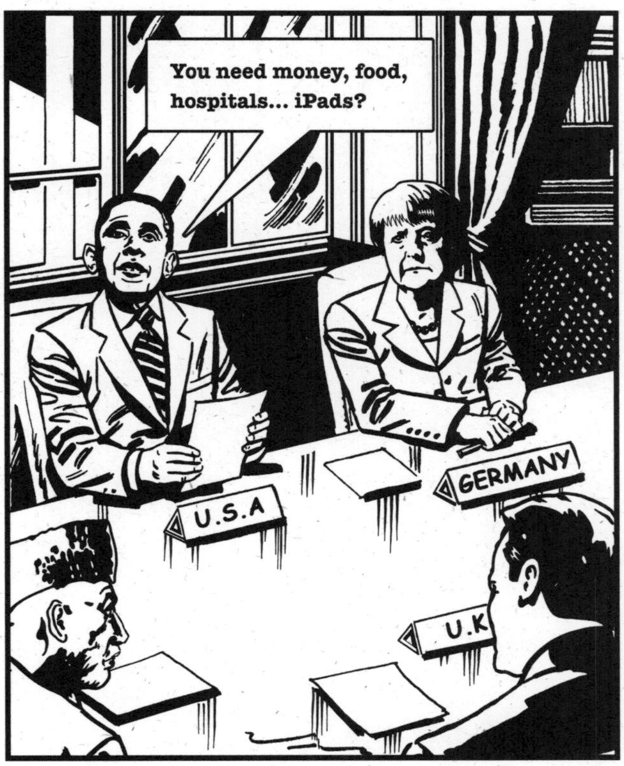

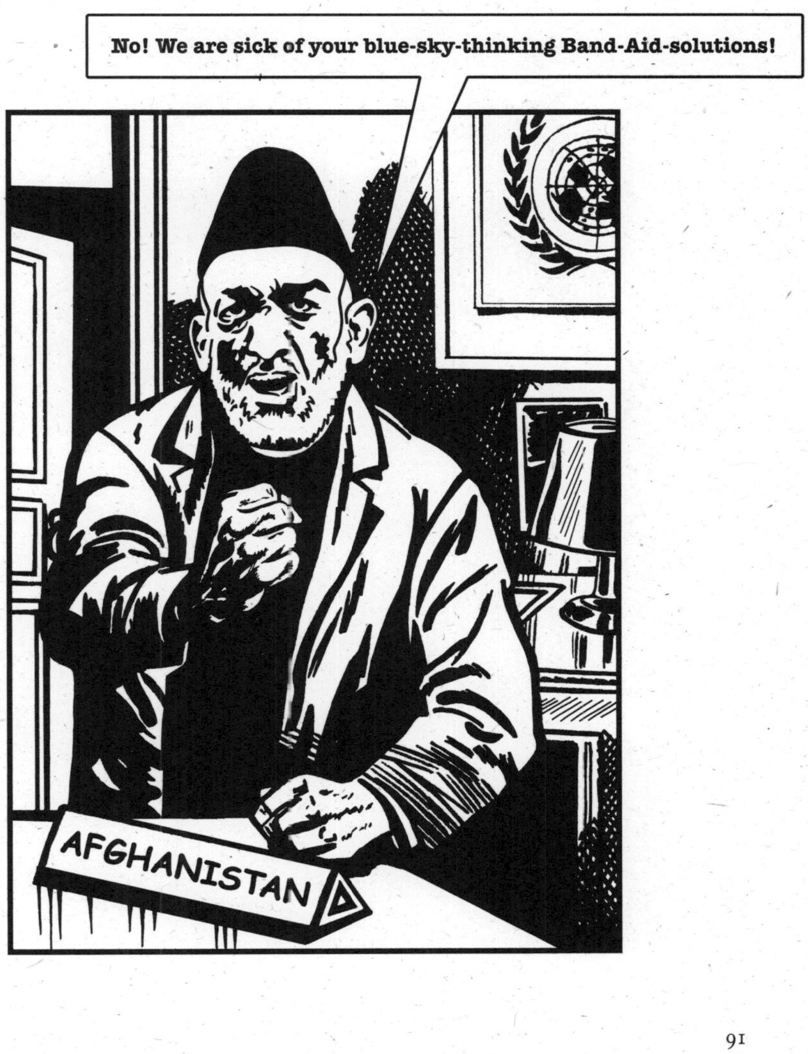

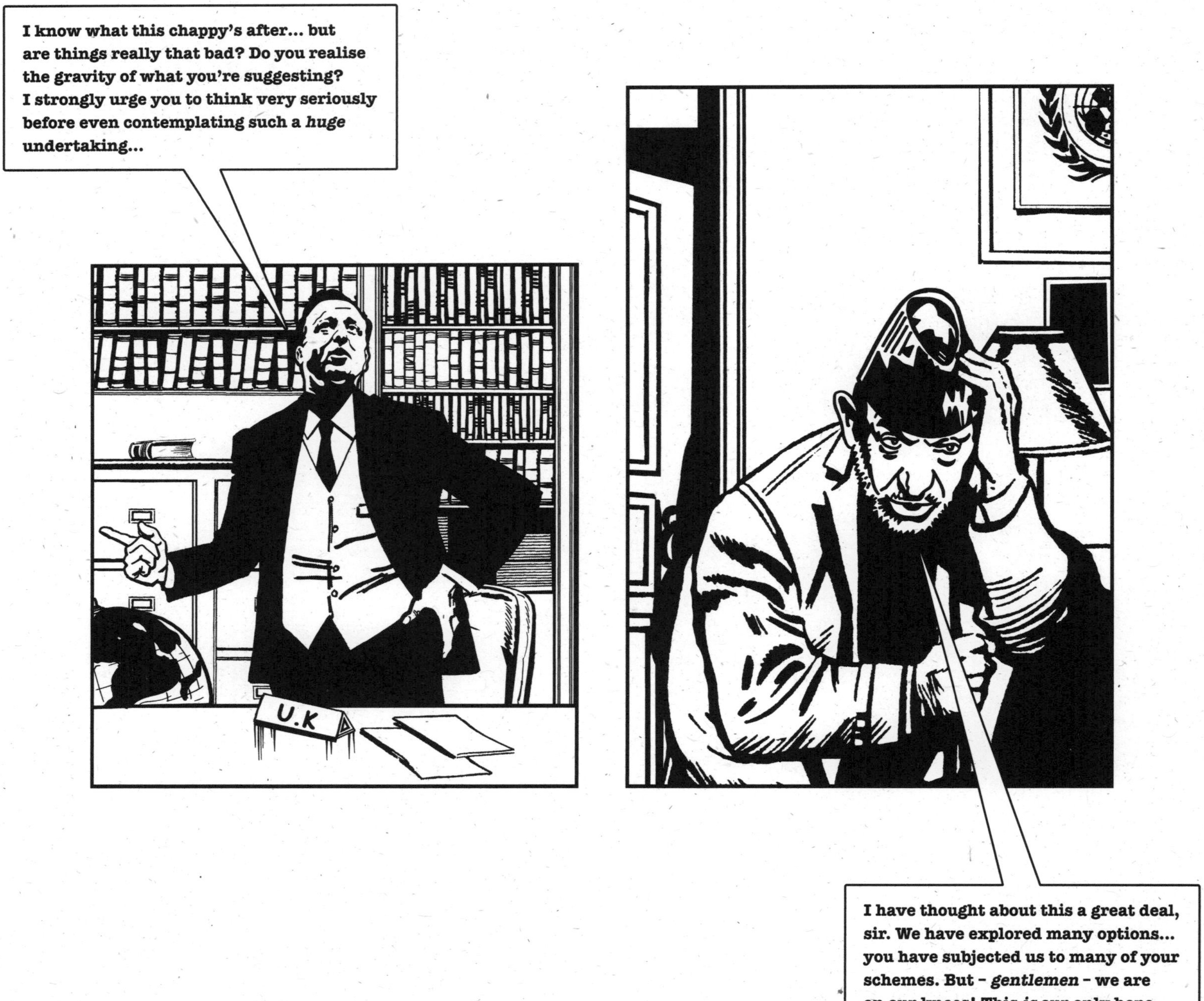
I know what this chappy's after... but are things really that bad? Do you realise the gravity of what you're suggesting? I strongly urge you to think very seriously before even contemplating such a *huge* undertaking...
U.K
I have thought about this a great deal, sir. We have explored many options... you have subjected us to many of your schemes. But – *gentlemen* – we are on our knees! This *is* our only hope.

Soon after, at the Empire Club, Mayfair…

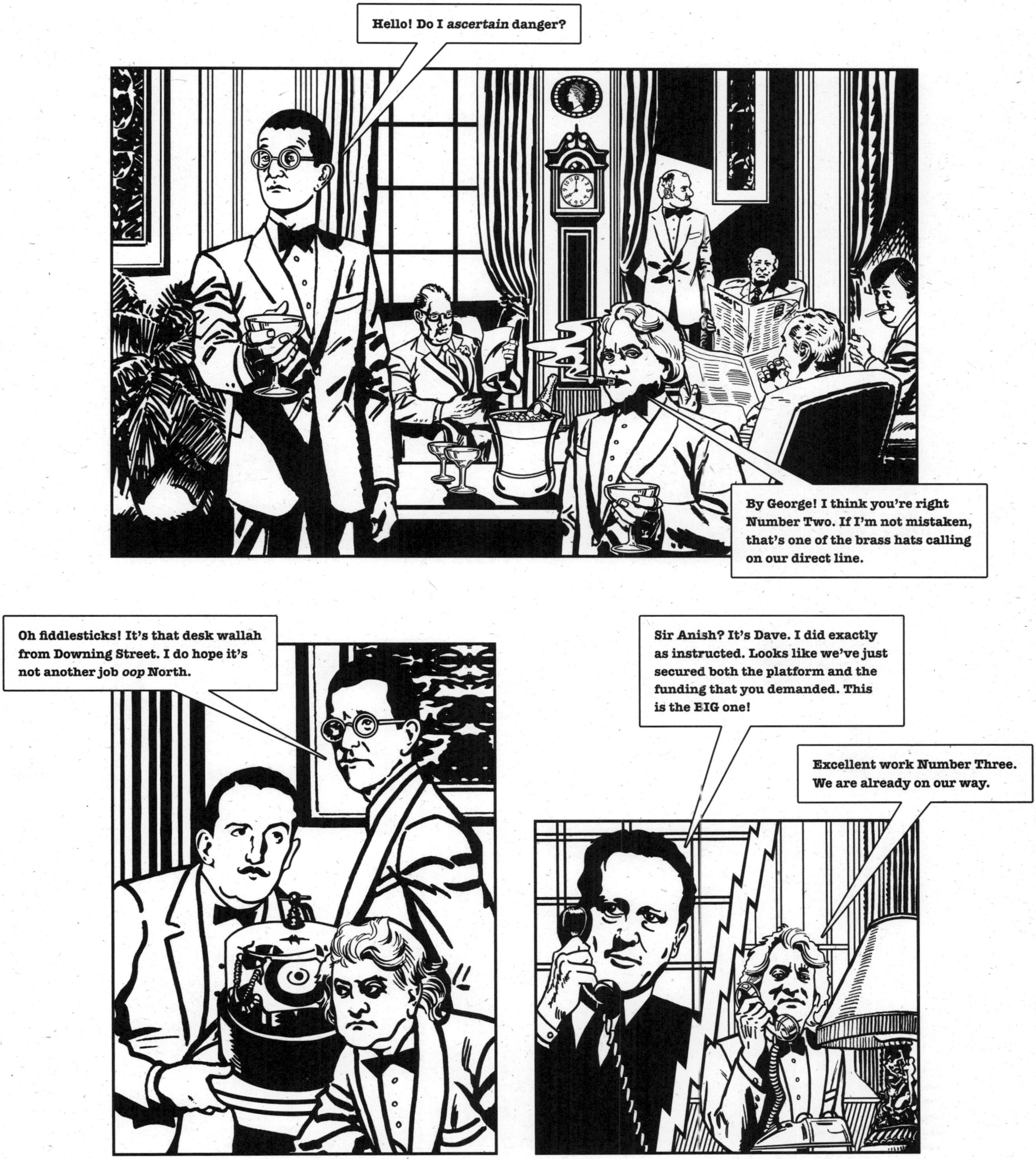

Not since D-Day had such a vast armada set sail from British shores... nor since the Berlin Blockade had so many aircraft flown so many round-the-clock missions.

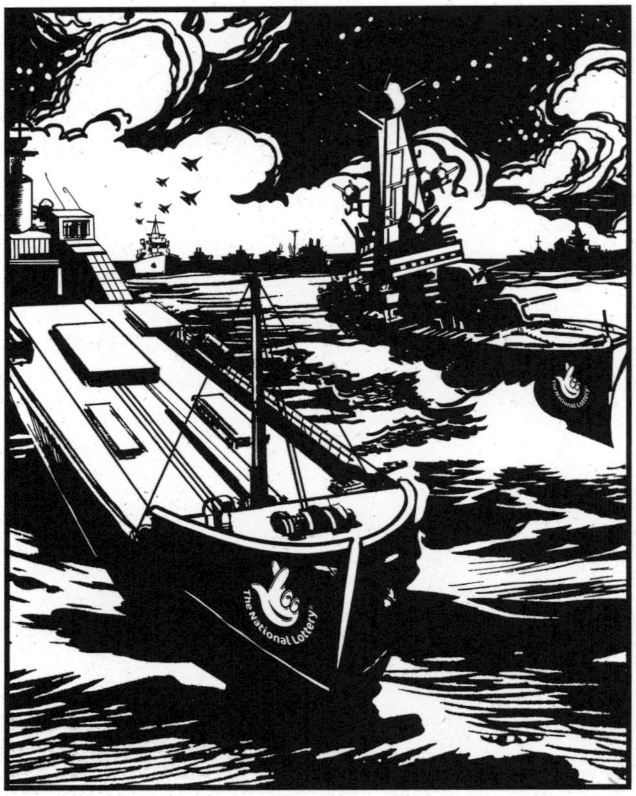

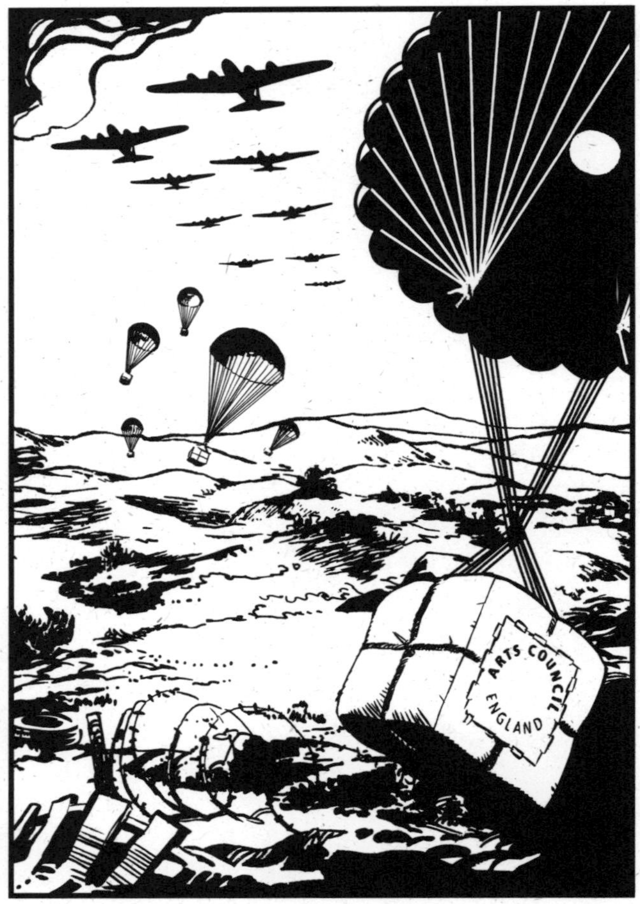

24 hours later...

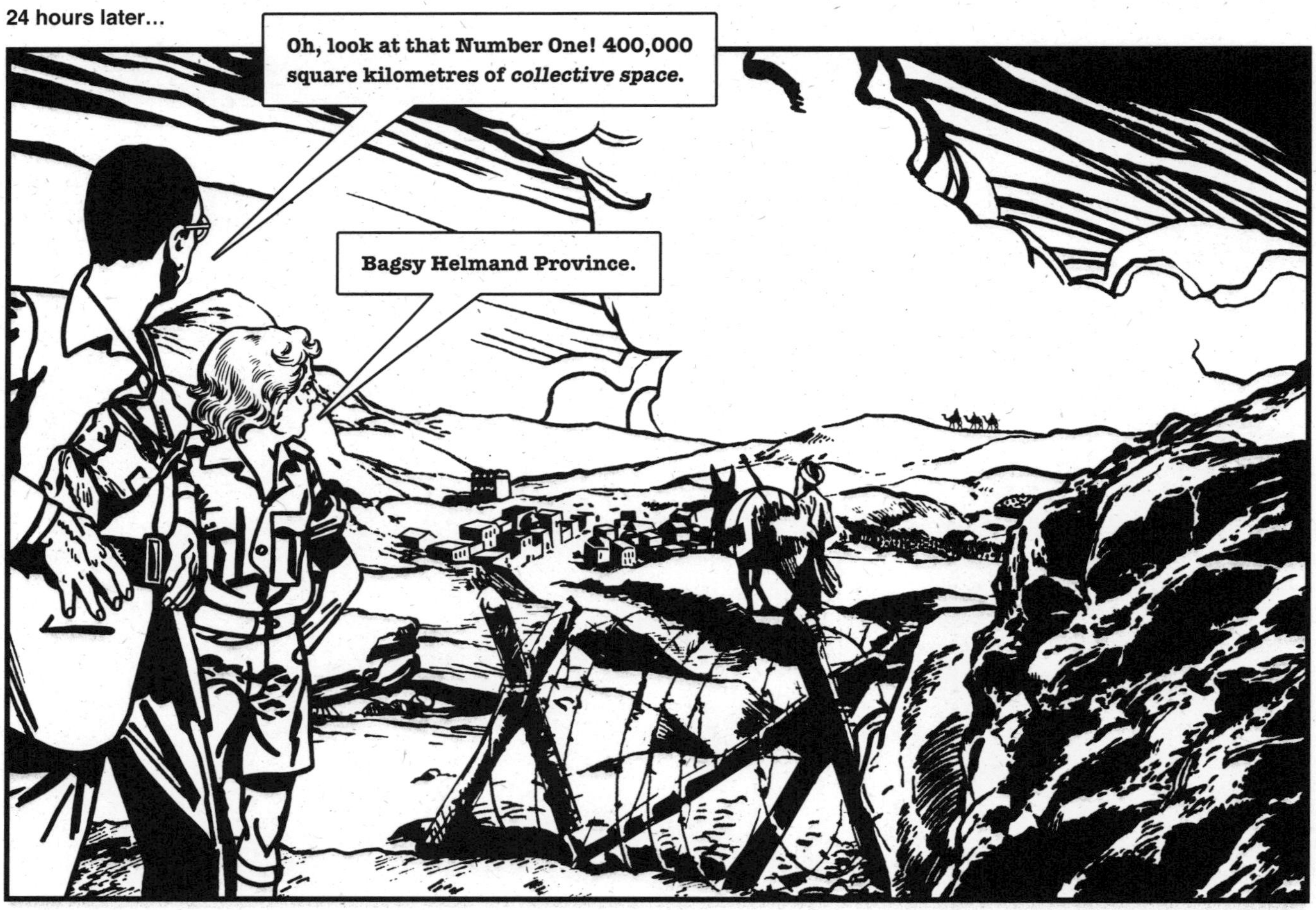

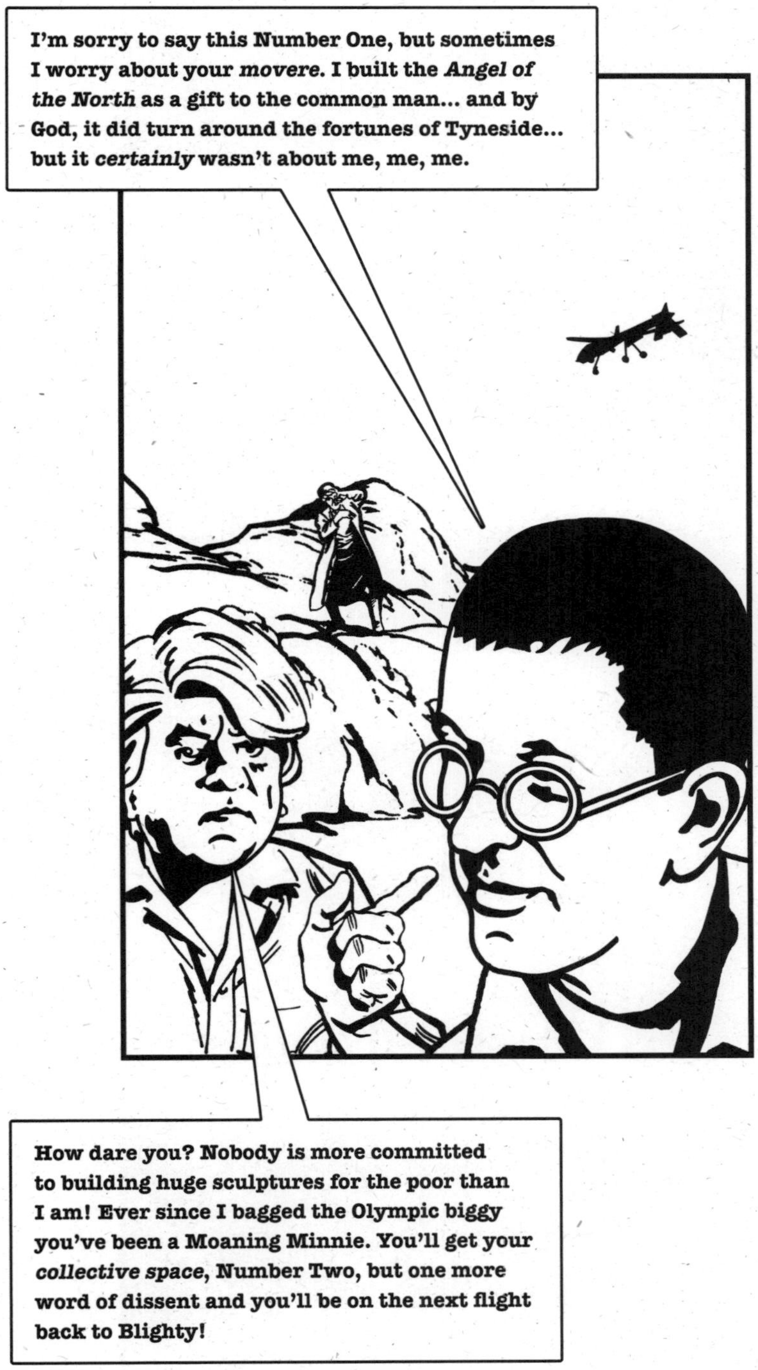
I'm sorry to say this Number One, but sometimes I worry about your *movere*. I built the *Angel of the North* as a gift to the common man... and by God, it did turn around the fortunes of Tyneside... but it *certainly* wasn't about me, me, me.
How dare you? Nobody is more committed to building huge sculptures for the poor than I am! Ever since I bagged the Olympic biggy you've been a Moaning Minnie. You'll get your *collective space*, Number Two, but one more word of dissent and you'll be on the next flight back to Blighty!

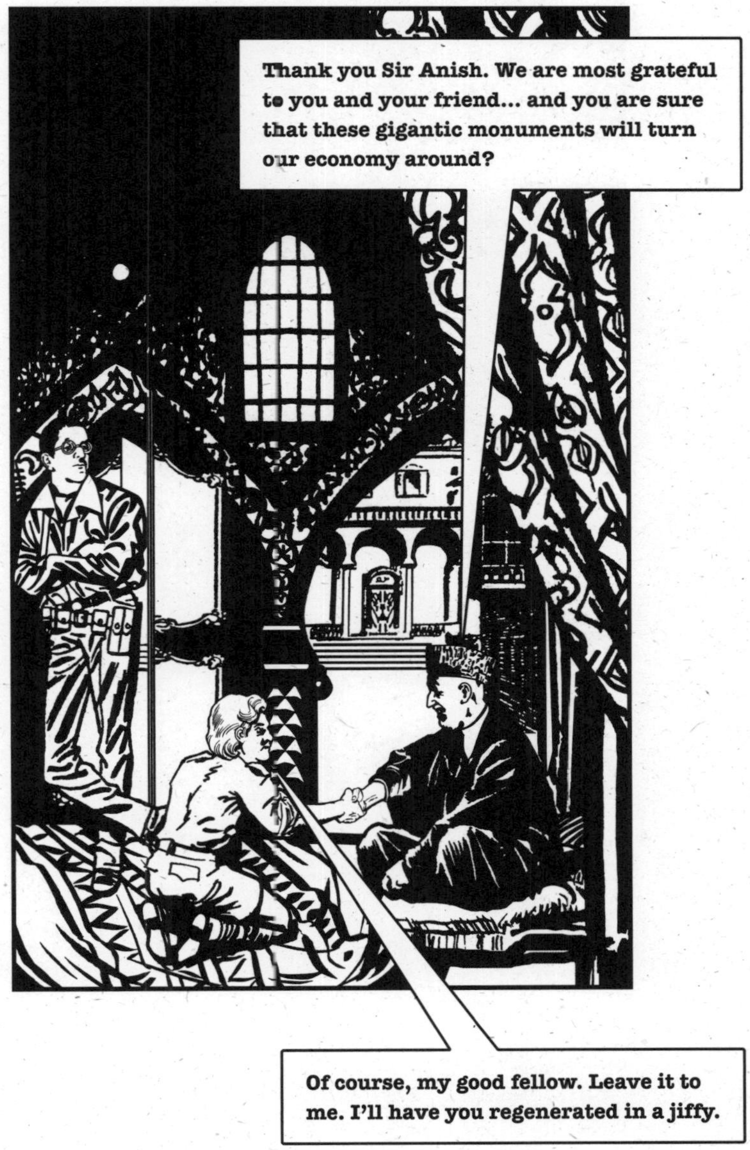
Thank you Sir Anish. We are most grateful to you and your friend... and you are sure that these gigantic monuments will turn our economy around?
Of course, my good fellow. Leave it to me. I'll have you regenerated in a jiffy.

The programme to build a New Afghanistan began with immediate effect…

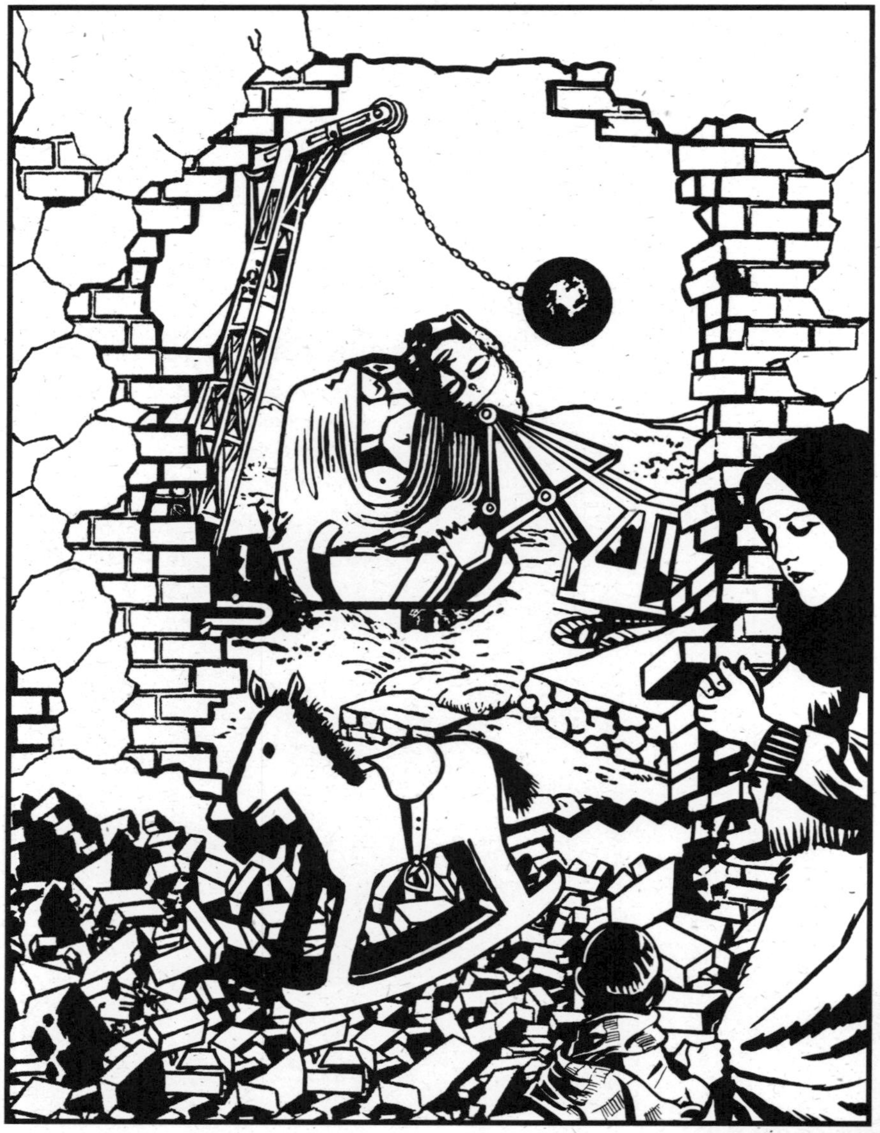

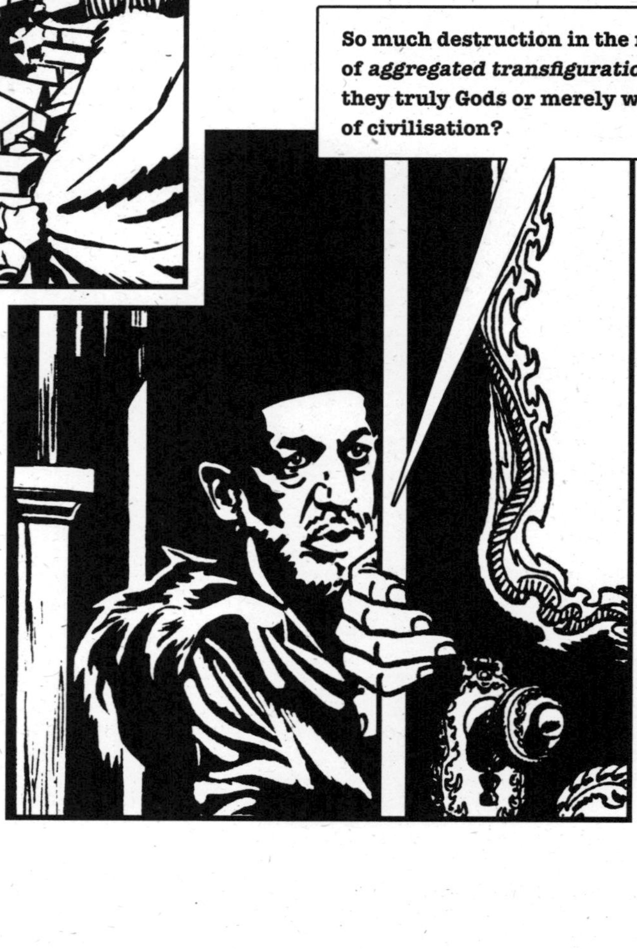

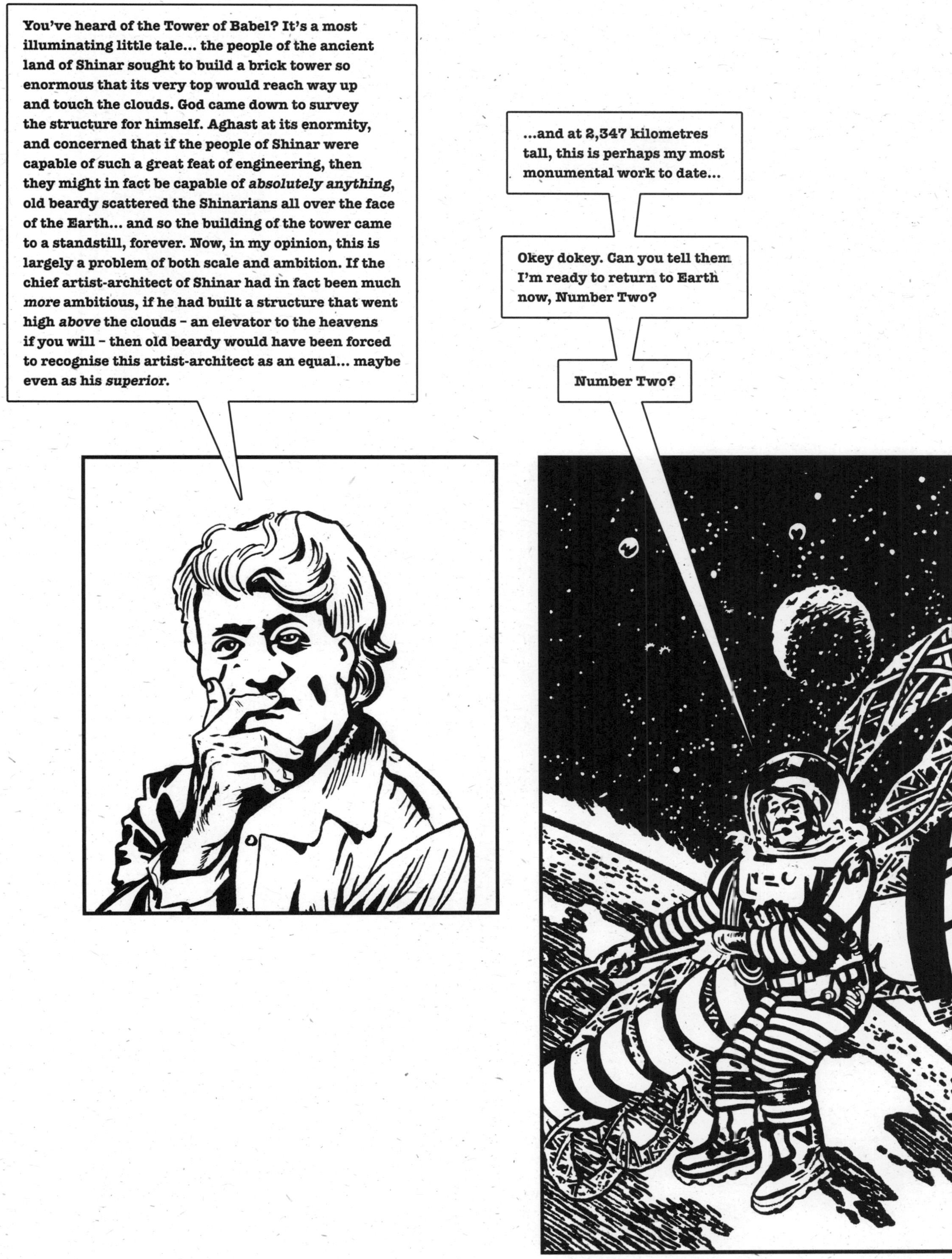
You've heard of the Tower of Babel? It's a most illuminating little tale... the people of the ancient land of Shinar sought to build a brick tower so enormous that its very top would reach way up and touch the clouds. God came down to survey the structure for himself. Aghast at its enormity, and concerned that if the people of Shinar were capable of such a great feat of engineering, then they might in fact be capable of *absolutely anything*, old beardy scattered the Shinarians all over the face of the Earth... and so the building of the tower came to a standstill, forever. Now, in my opinion, this is largely a problem of both scale and ambition. If the chief artist-architect of Shinar had in fact been much *more* ambitious, if he had built a structure that went high *above* the clouds – an elevator to the heavens if you will – then old beardy would have been forced to recognise this artist-architect as an equal... maybe even as his *superior*.
...and at 2,347 kilometres tall, this is perhaps my most monumental work to date...
Okey dokey. Can you tell them I'm ready to return to Earth now, Number Two?
Number Two?

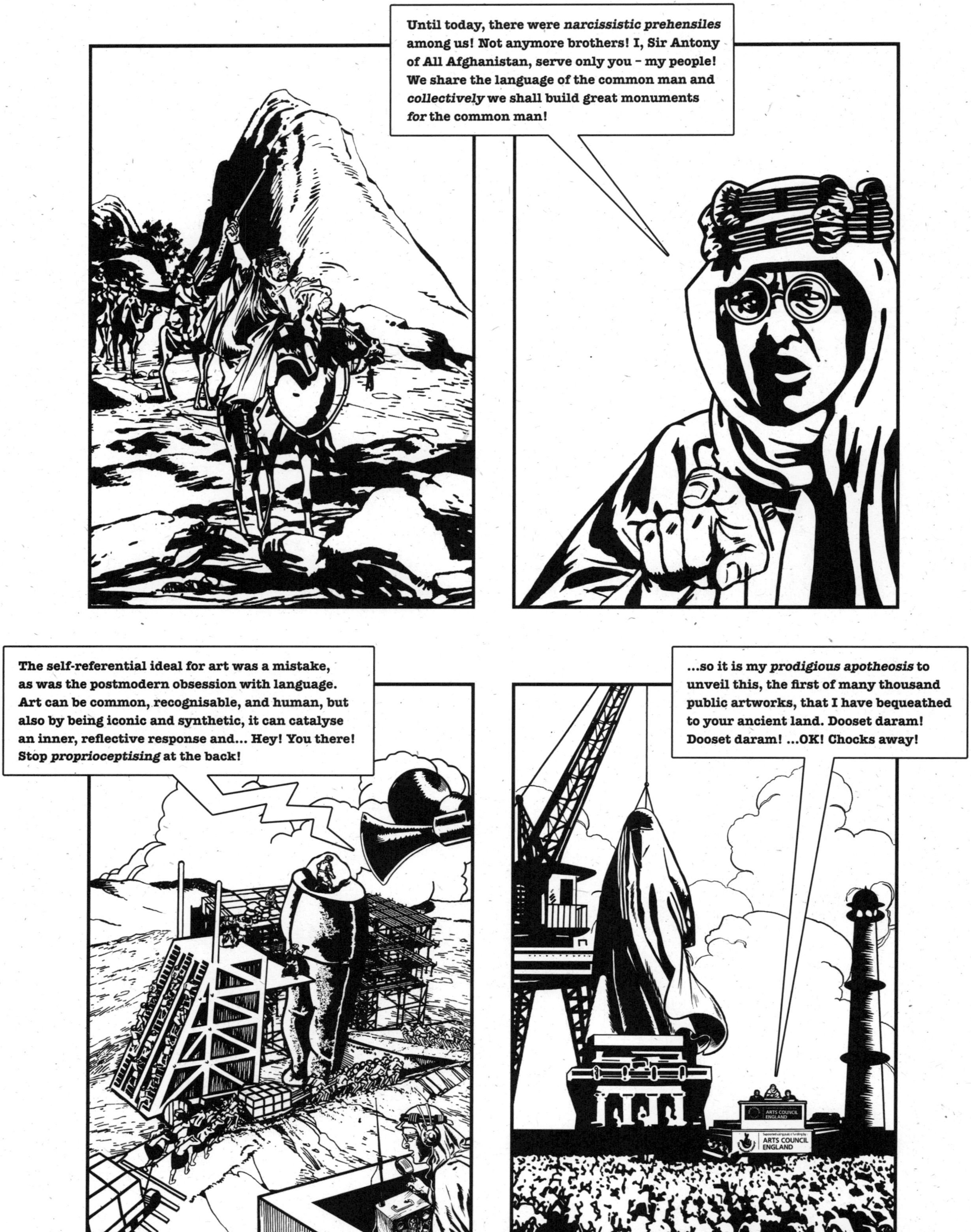
Until today, there were narcissistic prehensiles among us! Not anymore brothers! I, Sir Antony of All Afghanistan, serve only you – my people! We share the language of the common man and collectively we shall build great monuments for the common man!
The self-referential ideal for art was a mistake, as was the postmodern obsession with language. Art can be common, recognisable, and human, but also by being iconic and synthetic, it can catalyse an inner, reflective response and... Hey! You there! Stop proprioceptising at the back!
...so it is my prodigious apotheosis to unveil this, the first of many thousand public artworks, that I have bequeathed to your ancient land. Dooset daram! Dooset daram! ...OK! Chocks away!
ARTS COUNCIL ENGLAND
ARTS COUNCIL ENGLAND

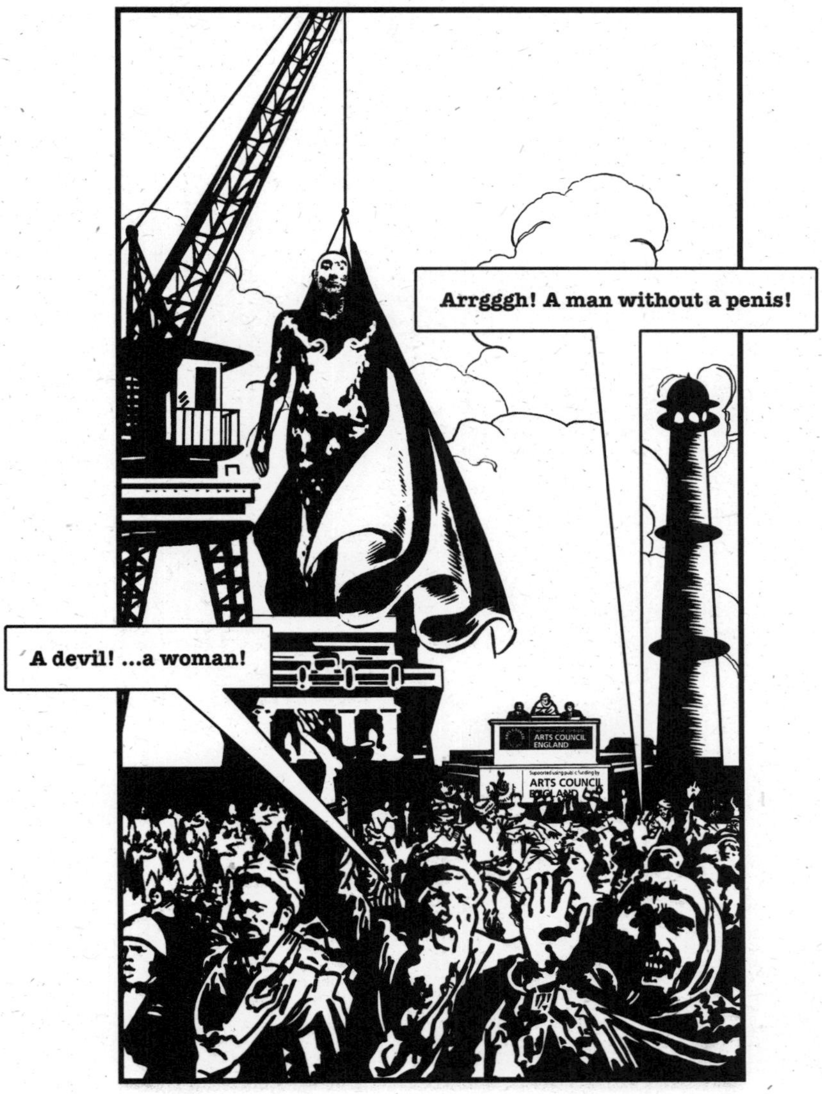
Arrgggh! A man without a penis!
A devil! ...a woman!

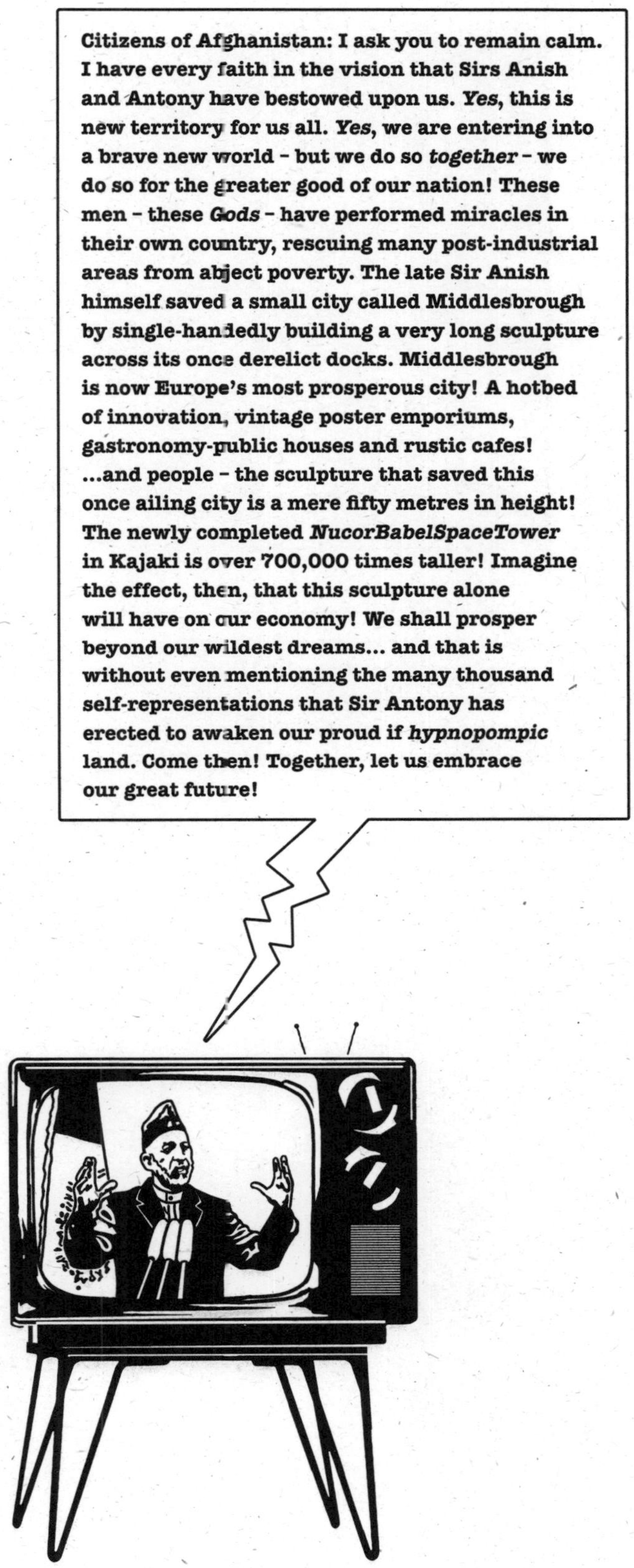
Citizens of Afghanistan: I ask you to remain calm. I have every faith in the vision that Sirs Anish and Antony have bestowed upon us. *Yes*, this is new territory for us all. *Yes*, we are entering into a brave new world – but we do so *together* – we do so for the greater good of our nation! These men – these *Gods* – have performed miracles in their own country, rescuing many post-industrial areas from abject poverty. The late Sir Anish himself saved a small city called Middlesbrough by single-handedly building a very long sculpture across its once derelict docks. Middlesbrough is now Europe's most prosperous city! A hotbed of innovation, vintage poster emporiums, gastronomy-public houses and rustic cafes! ...and people – the sculpture that saved this once ailing city is a mere fifty metres in height! The newly completed *NucorBabelSpaceTower* in Kajaki is over 700,000 times taller! Imagine the effect, then, that this sculpture alone will have on our economy! We shall prosper beyond our wildest dreams... and that is without even mentioning the many thousand self-representations that Sir Antony has erected to awaken our proud if *hypnopompic* land. Come then! Together, let us embrace our great future!

Following President Karzai's televised speech, calm was restored to the New Afghanistan. Very quickly the country began to prosper as its people embraced manufacturing, consumerism and the concept of credit card debt.

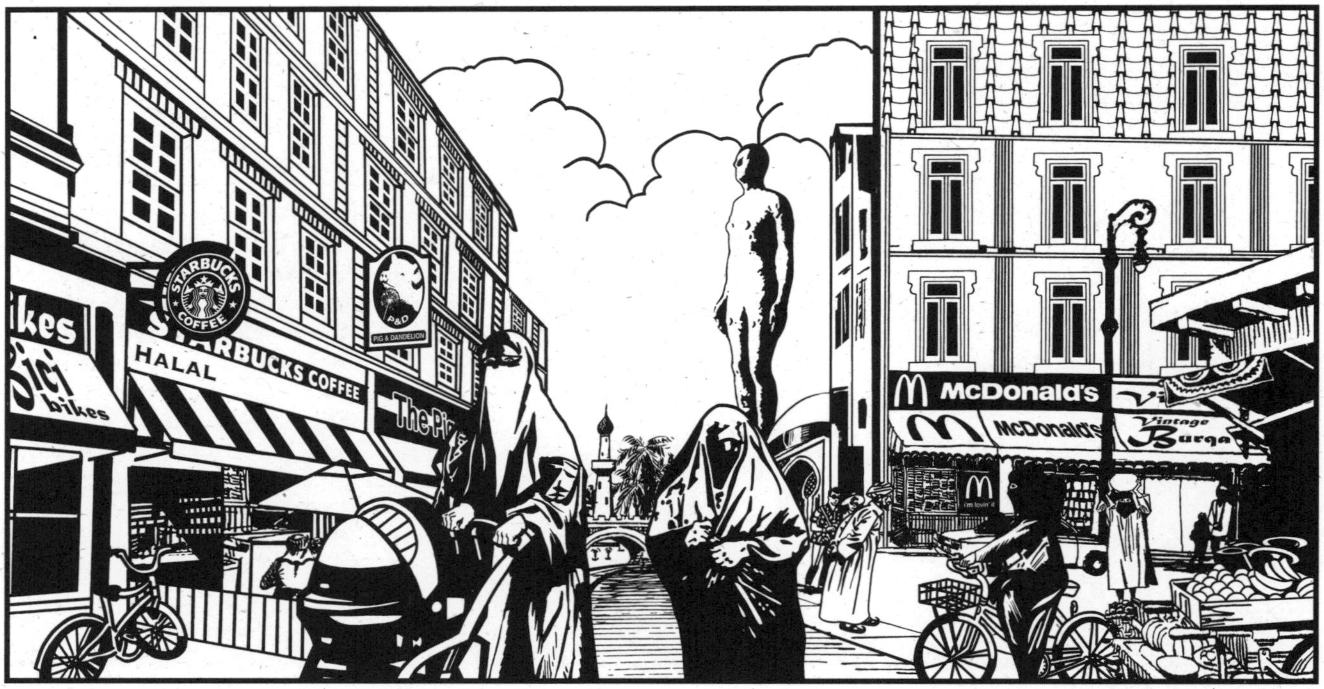

The sudden and unexpected worldwide popularity of Tarana Folk Rock meant that the New Afghanistan quickly became a festival hot-spot. Millions of tourists flooded the country, spending freely as they went…

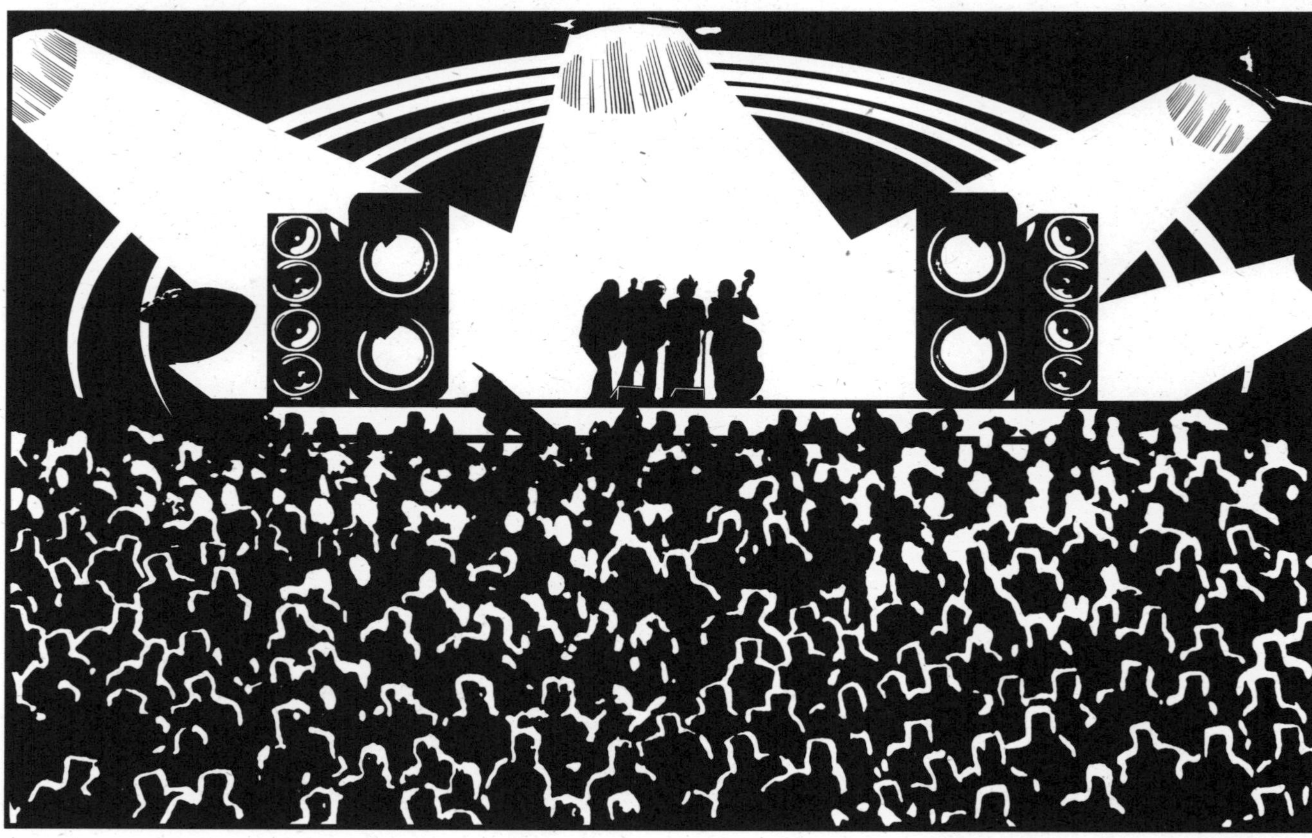

Back at the United Nations Headquarters...

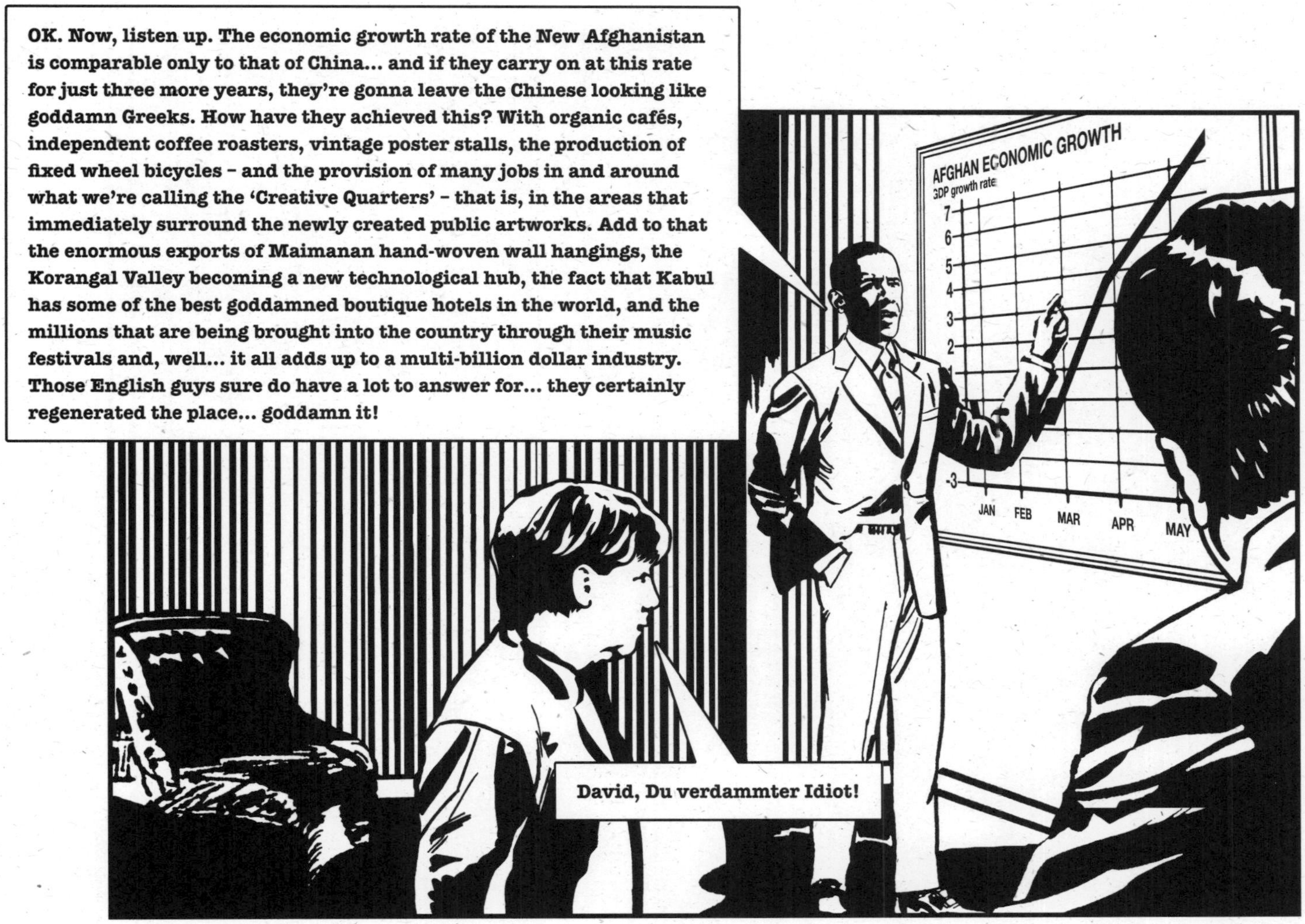

The rapid economic growth of the New Afghanistan sent shock waves through the West. Crisis meetings at the United Nations Headquarters quickly broke down into backbiting, obsequiousness and despair.

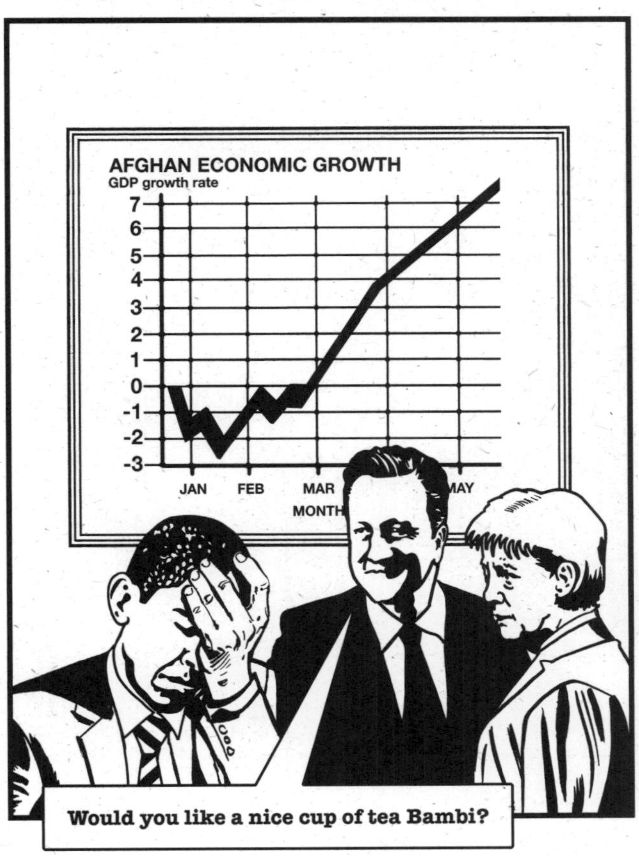

Once again, it fell upon the United States of America to rescue the Western world...

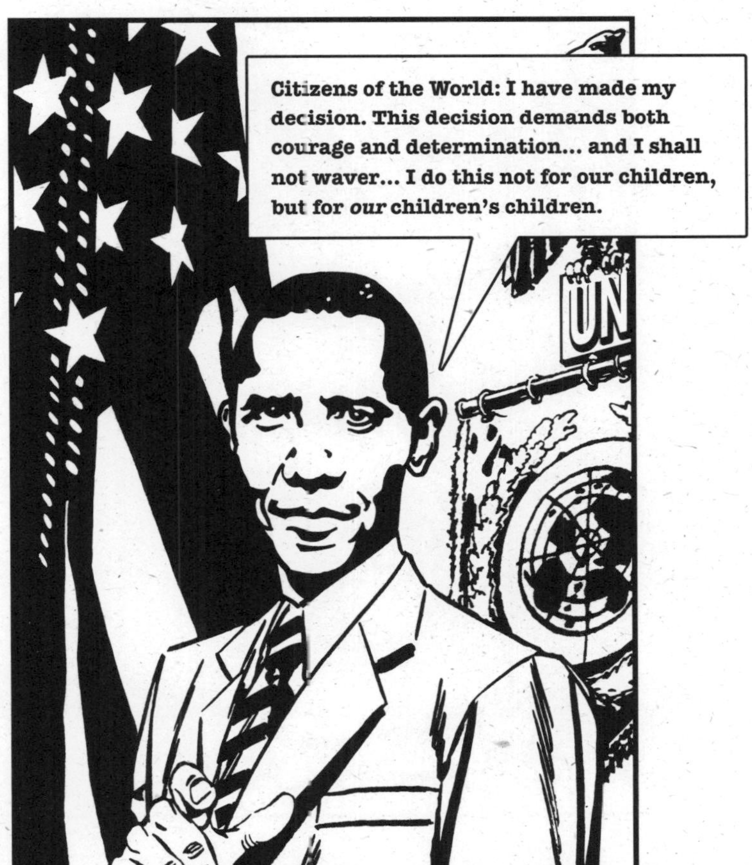

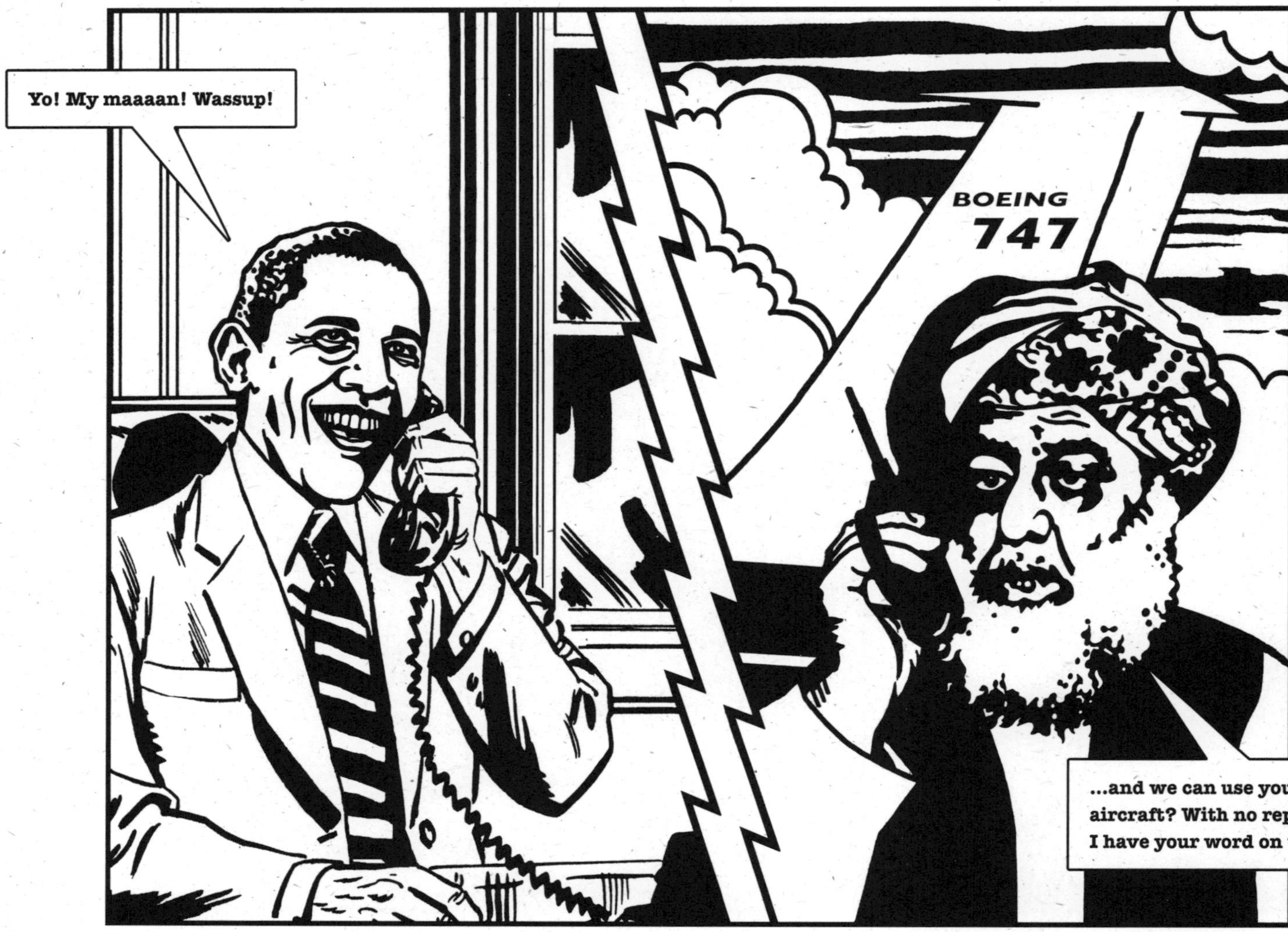
Yo! My maaaan! Wassup!
BOEING
747
...and we can use your aircraft? With no reprisals... I have your word on this?

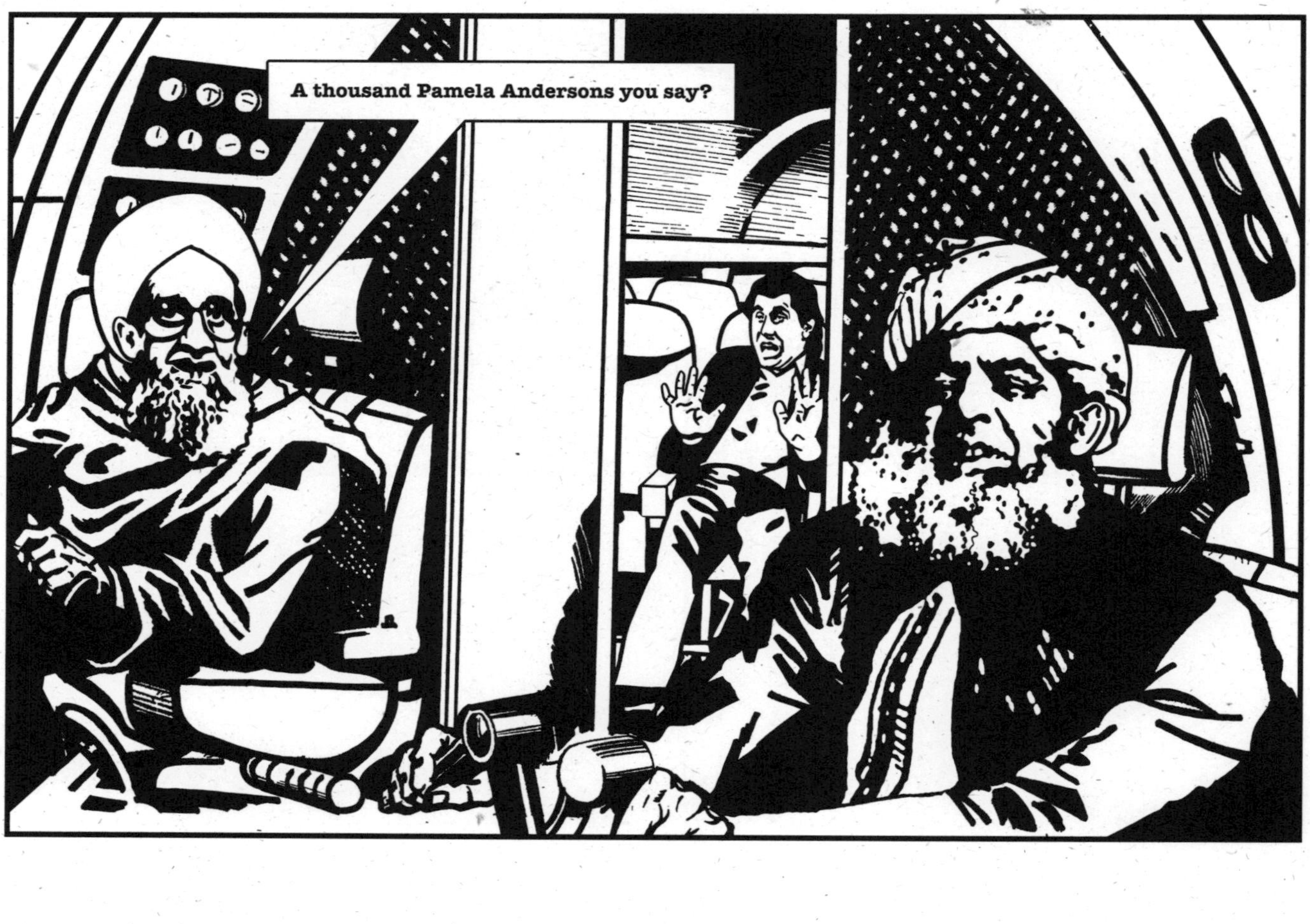
A thousand Pamela Andersons you say?

Hundreds of hijacked commercial airliners were used as missiles against the New Afghanistan, their combined destructive power the equivalent to three million tonnes of high explosives. Aviation fuel flooded the streets – the whole country became a blazing inferno.

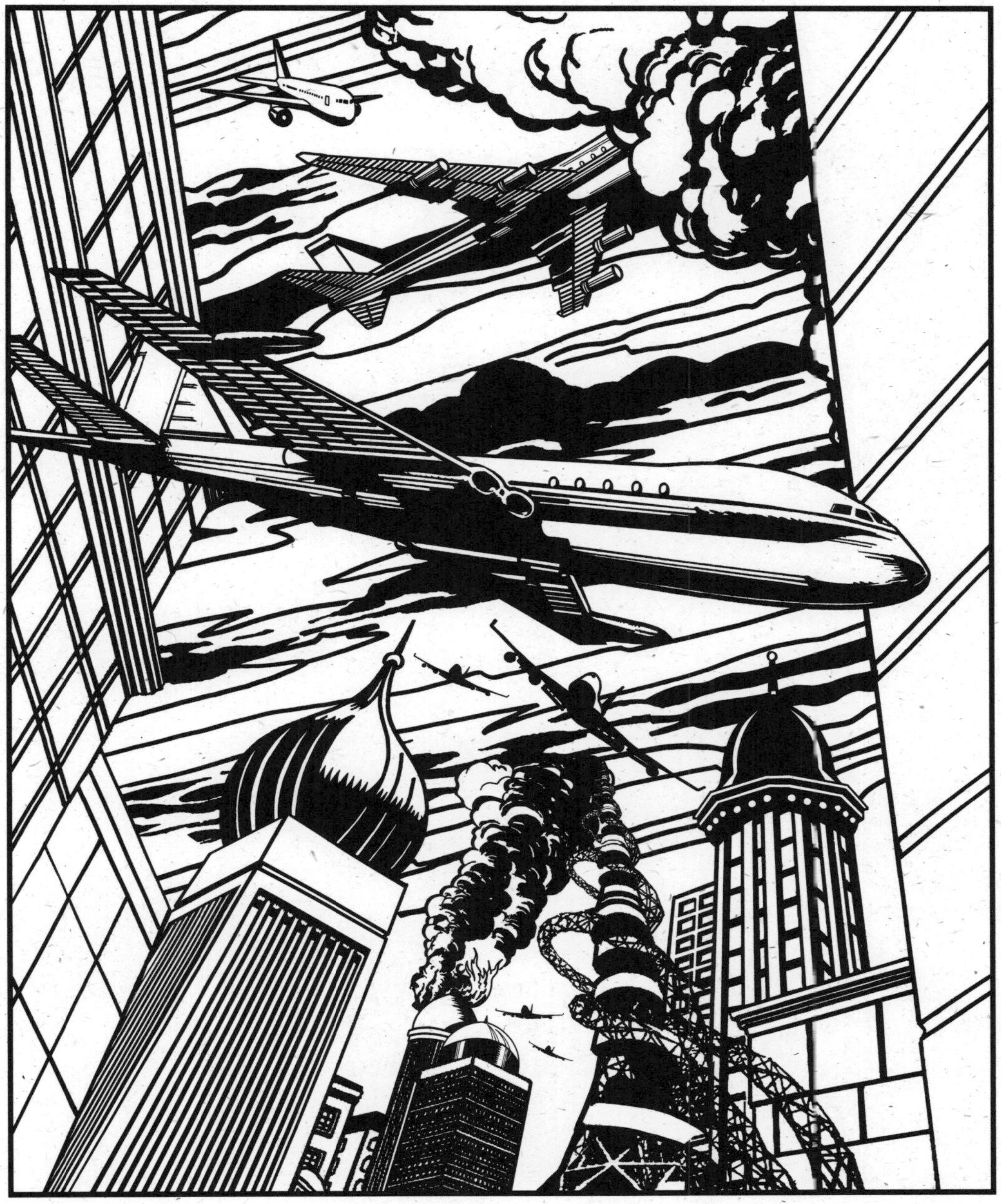

Afghanistan today…

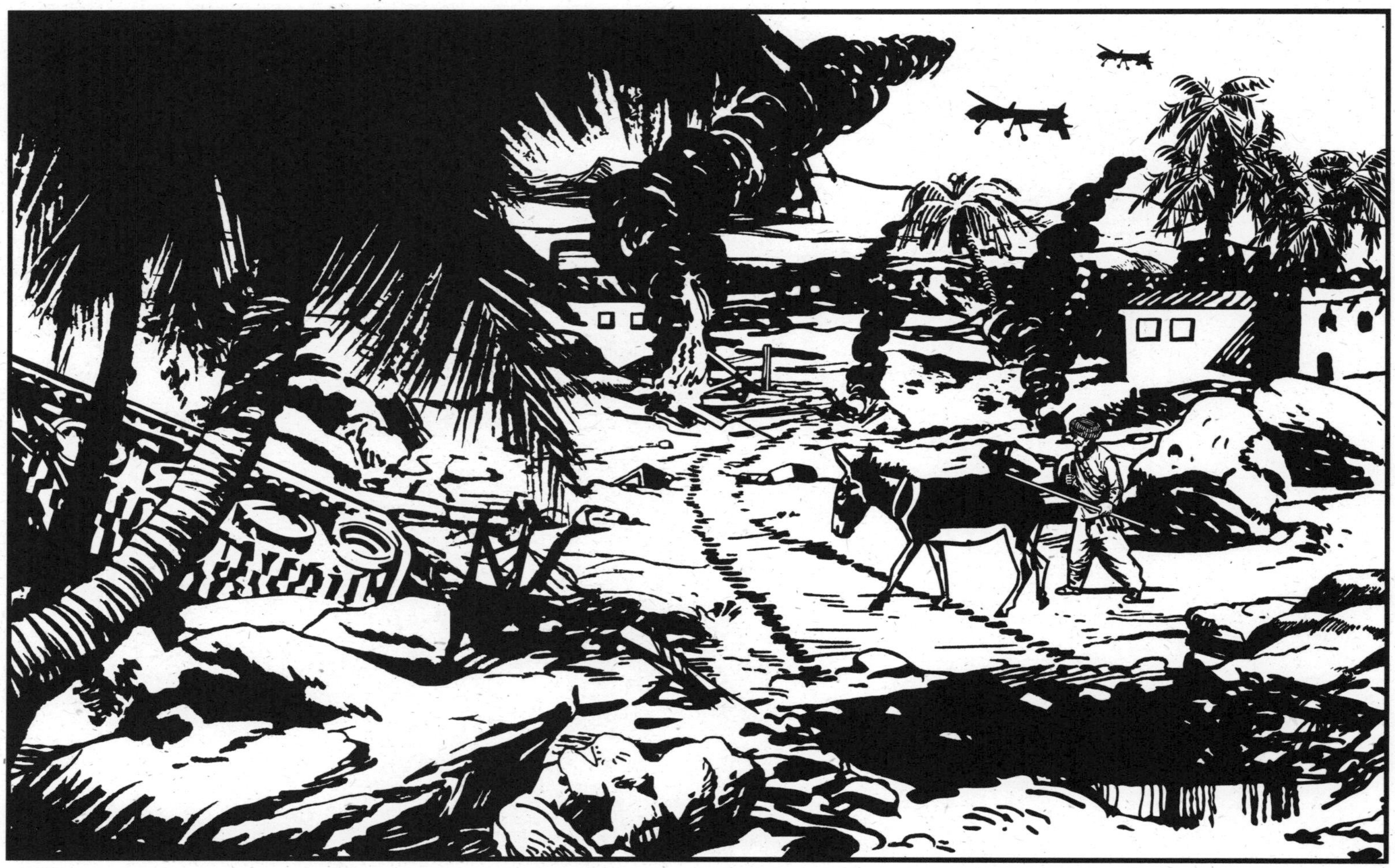

One only has to look at the impact that *Angel of the North* has had on the people of Newcastle. Antony is far too modest to repeat this, but the Chief Constable of Northumbria Police assured him that alcohol related crime on Tyneside has gone down by 14% since *Angel* was erected. Not only that, domestic abuse has decreased by 17% and car theft by 21%; most remarkably of all, employment has risen by an incredible 26% as a direct result of Antony's sculpture. *Temenos* will be twenty-eight metres taller than *Angel;* so one can only begin to imagine the effect that it's going to have on the people of Middlesbrough.

Anish Kapoor, *The Northern Echo*, 12 April 2010

THE EUROPEAN MONUMENT OF UNITY

'Europe is a small part of the world. If we have something to offer, it is our knowledge and leadership.

Around a century ago, one in five of the world's population were in Europe; today that figure is one in nine; in another century it will be one in twenty-five.

I believe we can, and should, play our part on the world stage; not for our own vanity, but because we have something to offer. We can show the world the strength that comes from uniting and the strategic interest in acting together. There has never been a more urgent and compelling time to do so.

We have more than forty active conflicts in the world at the moment. While these conflicts rage, whilst families are broken and homes reduced to rubble, I cannot come to you, almost sixty years after the birth of the European Union and pitch you peace. For the world is not at peace.

If we want to promote a more peaceful world, we will need more Europe and more Union… I do not want a Europe that stands on the sidelines of history. I want a Europe that leads. When the European Union stands united, we can change the world.'

Jean-Claude Juncker
President of the European Commission
Strasbourg, 9 September 2015

SECTION 3.1

Please provide a detailed Proposal (no more than 500 words) for the activity you want us to support. This is a very important part of your application. We will use your Proposal, along with your Projected Budget (Section 4), Public Benefit Analysis (Sections 5.1A to 5.9E), and Global Media Strategy (Section 6) to assess your activity's suitability for funding.

The European Monument of Unity (EMU) is a collaborative public sculpture, conceived on an immense scale, which seeks to explore, affirm and fortify the bonds between the diverse nations and people that comprise contemporary Europe, at a time when those bonds are under increasing internal and external pressure. Marked by humanity's highest achievements, and its lowest horrors, the history of our Continent is a history of shifts: between ignorance and enlightenment, poverty and plenty, tyranny and freedom, and conflict and peace. EMU looks to the future, a vision of European fraternity in an age of unprecedented change.

Rising vertically, EMU will be divided into a number of 'units' of equal size and dimensions*, each of them designed by an artist from one of Europe's constituent nations, who has been briefed to represent her homeland in the manner and material(s) of her choosing. Produced independently, with no conferring over content between artists, the resulting 'units' will be stacked one on top of the other to form a single, unified artwork, as in the Surrealist parlour game 'Exquisite Corpse'. The illustration that accompanies this proposal – in which a number of pre-existing contemporary public sculptures from across Europe have been fused into a compound vertical monument – gives an indication of the extraordinary, pan-Continental texture of the proposed project, and of the vitality of current European art practice.

While EMU's 'units' are likely, in the interests of diplomacy, to be arranged alphabetically by nation, this simple organizational logic will inevitably prompt thoughts of other, more complex logics. Arranged by the represented nations' GDP, or Net Migration Rate, or number of UNESCO World Heritage Sites, or carbon footprint, or military capacity, or Olympic gold medals, or by any one of hundreds of other possible metrics, the sequence of artworks would be different. Notably, even a random arrangement of the 'units' would be likely to give rise to narrative interest: historical rivals sharing an open border, say, or debtor nations morphing into their creditors.

In the spirit of the values that EMU promotes, we propose that the definition of 'European Nation' is understood in the broadest possible sense, encompassing not only EU member states, and EFTA and Schengen Agreement signatories, but also micro-states, states with limited diplomatic recognition, dependencies, special areas of internal sovereignty, non-state sovereign entities, and states identified as 'European' by academics and NGOs. Please see Appendix I for a list of nations invited to participate in EMU. By this tally, the monument will be comprised of the work of some 72 artists, although we are aware that this figure is open to change, and have made contingency for this in our Projected Budget (Section 4).

Participating artists for EMU will be selected in partnership with leading museums and cultural institutions across Europe, leveraging curatorial expertise on a Continental scale. The proposed site for EMU is the geographical centre of Europe, a designation currently claimed by Polotsk, Belarus; Saaremaa, Estonia; Tállya, Hungary; Bernotai, Lithuania; Suchowola, Poland; Krahule, Slovakia; and Rakhiv, Ukraine.

APPENDIX 1. PARTICIPATING NATIONS.

EU MEMBER STATES: Austria, Belgium, Bulgaria, Croatia, Republic of Cyprus, Czech Republic, Denmark, Estonia, Finland, France, Germany, Greece, Hungary, Ireland, Italy, Latvia, Lithuania, Luxembourg, Malta, The Netherlands, Poland, Portugal, Romania, Slovakia, Slovenia, Spain, Sweden, United Kingdom (comprising England, Scotland, Wales and Northern Ireland)

EUROPEAN STATES SIGNED TO THE EUROPEAN FREE TRADE AGREEMENT TREATY (NON-EU): Iceland, Liechtenstein, Norway, Switzerland

EUROPEAN MICRO-STATES: Andorra, Monaco, San Marino, Vatican City

OTHER EUROPEAN STATES, AS DEFINED BY WIKIPEDIA (ACCESSED SUMMER 2015): Albania, Armenia, Azerbaijan, Belarus, Bosnia and Herzegovina, Georgia, Kazakhstan, Macedonia, Moldova, Montenegro, Romania, Russia, Serbia, Turkey, Ukraine

STATES WITH LIMITED DIPLOMATIC RECOGNITION: Abkhazia, Kosovo, Nagorno-Karabakh, Northern Cyprus, Transnistria, South Ossetia

EUROPEAN DEPENDENCIES LOCATED IN THE CONTINENTAL GEOGRAPHIC ORBIT, EXCLUDING NON-CONTINENTAL ENTITIES SUCH AS GREENLAND, THE FALKLANDS ISLANDS, THE NETHERLANDS ANTILLES ETC.: Akrotiri and Dhekelia (British Overseas Territory), Faroe Islands (External Territory, Denmark), Gibraltar (British Overseas Territory), Guernsey (British Crown Dependency, including the islands of Alderney, Herm and Sark), Isle of Man (British Crown Dependency), Jersey (British Crown Dependency), Mount Athos (autonomous monastic state, Greece)

SPECIAL AREAS OF INTERNAL SOVEREIGNTY: Aland Islands (Self-governing area of Finland), Svalbard (Special Territory of Norway)

SOVEREIGN ENTITIES (NON-STATE): Sovereign Military Order of Malta

NON-EUROPEAN COUNTRIES THAT PARTICIPATE IN THE EUROVISION SONG CONTEST: Israel (comprising Israel and Palestine)

Tom Morton, *EMU Funding Application,* Laser print on paper, Two parts, Each 29.7 × 21 cm, 2016

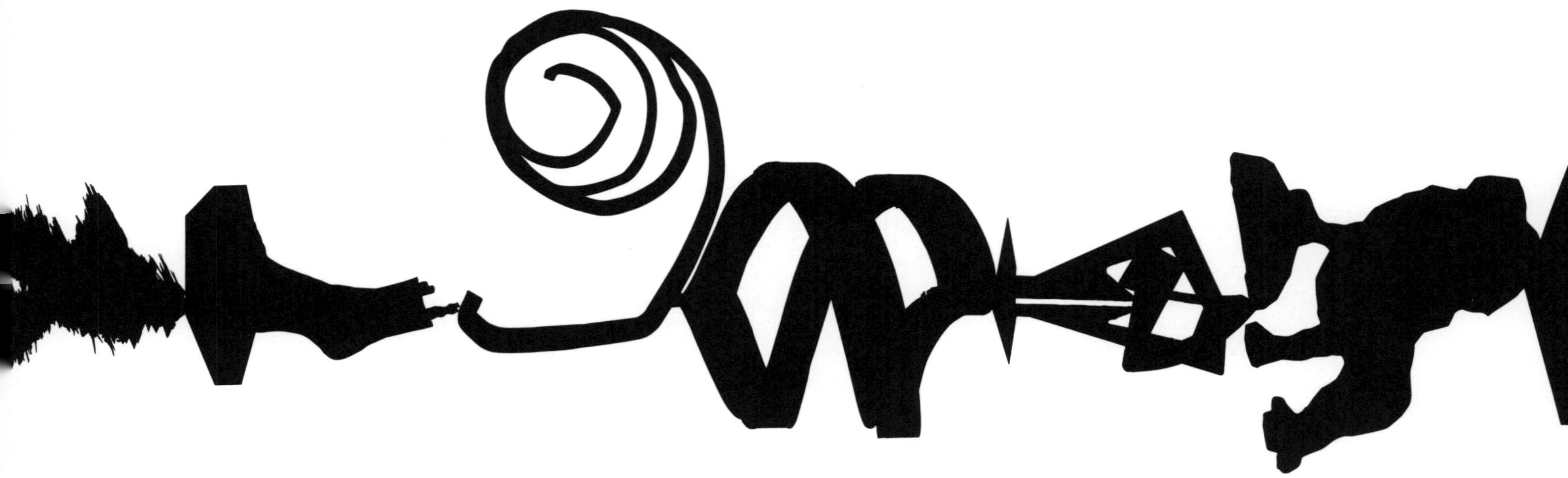

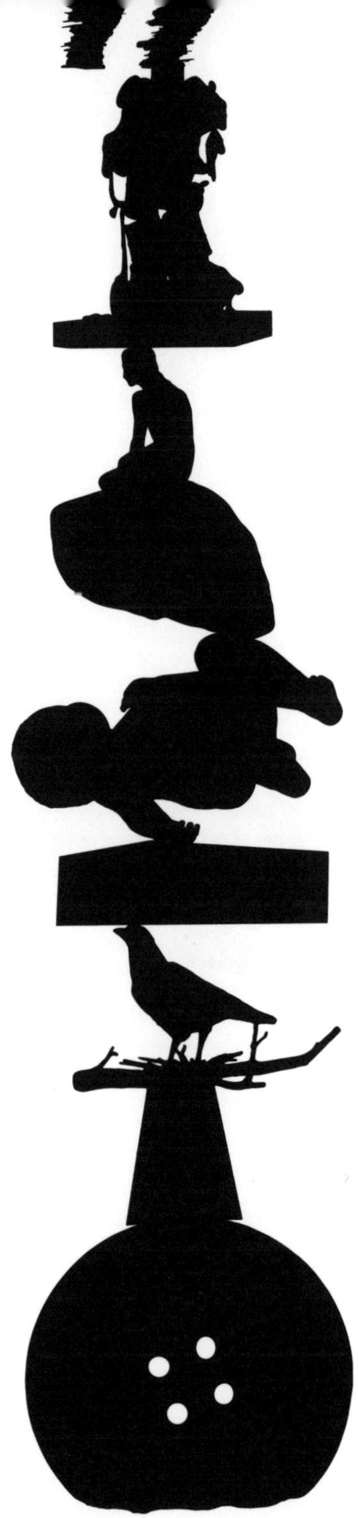

Figure 4: Final design proposal
Artist's impression of the *European Monument of Unity* scaled and ordered on a democratic basis to equally represent each nation in the European Union

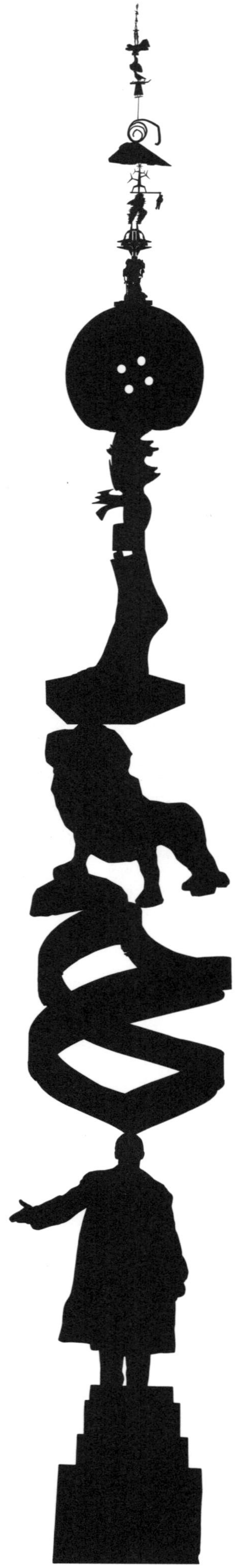

Figure 1: Early Design Proposal
Artist's impression of the *European Monument of Unity* scaled and ordered on the basis of population size for each nation represented in the European Union

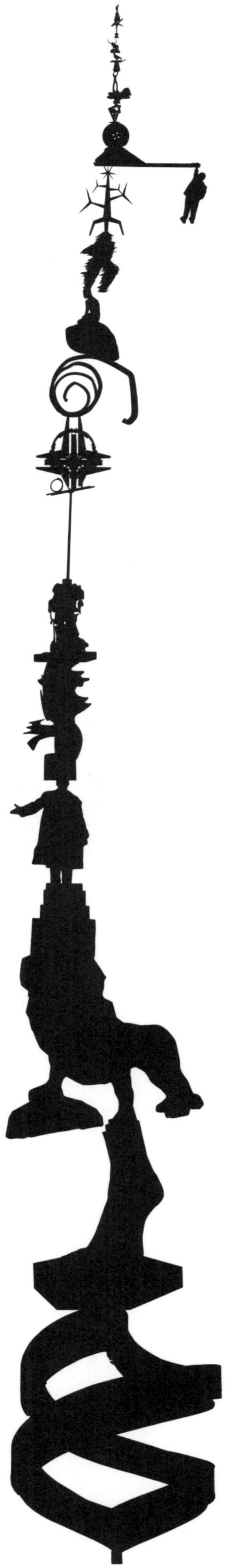

Figure 2: Early Design Proposal
Artist's impression of the *European Monument of Unity* scaled and ordered on the basis of Gross Domestic Product (GDP) for each nation represented in the European Union

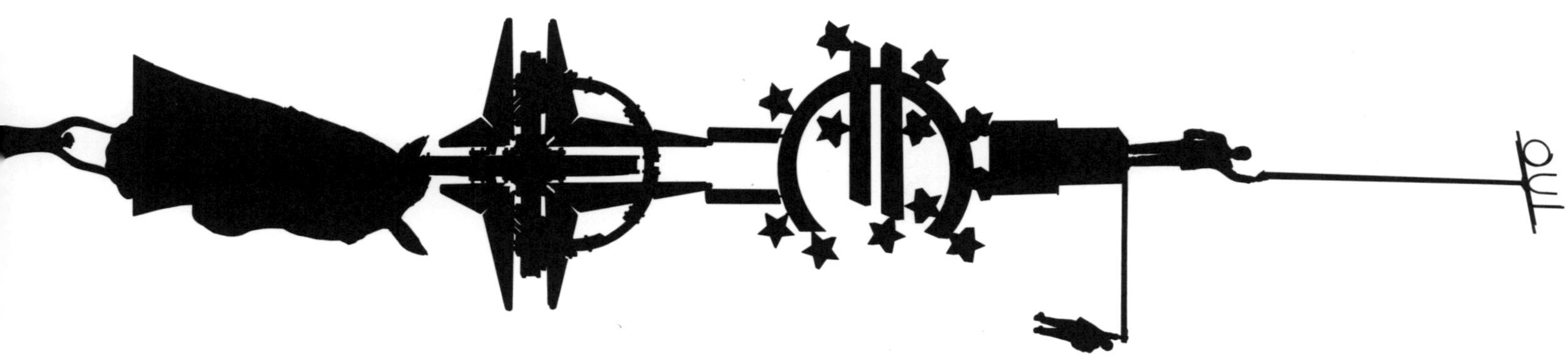

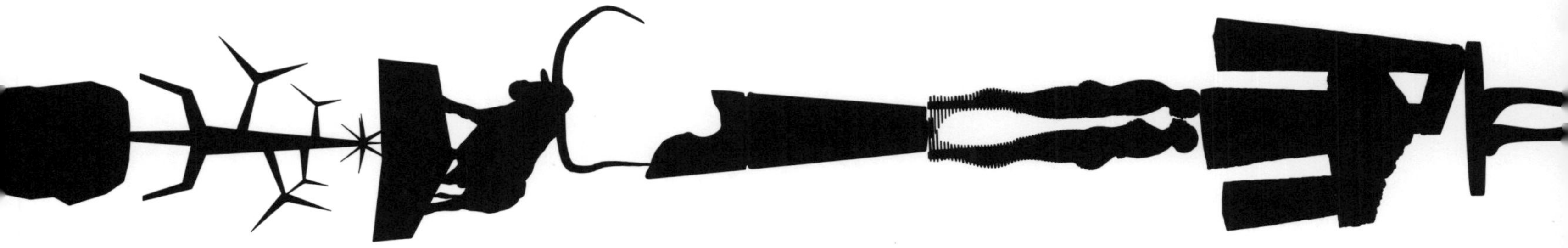

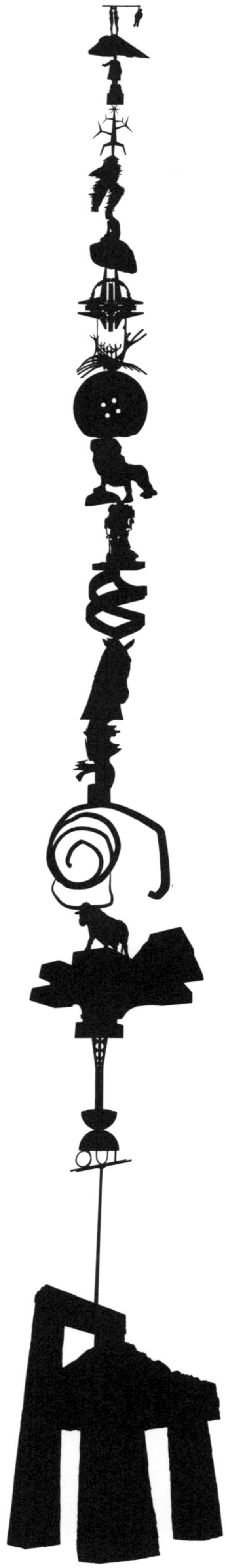

Figure 3: Early Design Proposal
Artist's impression of the *European Monument of Unity* scaled and ordered on the basis of immigrant population size for each nation represented in the European Union

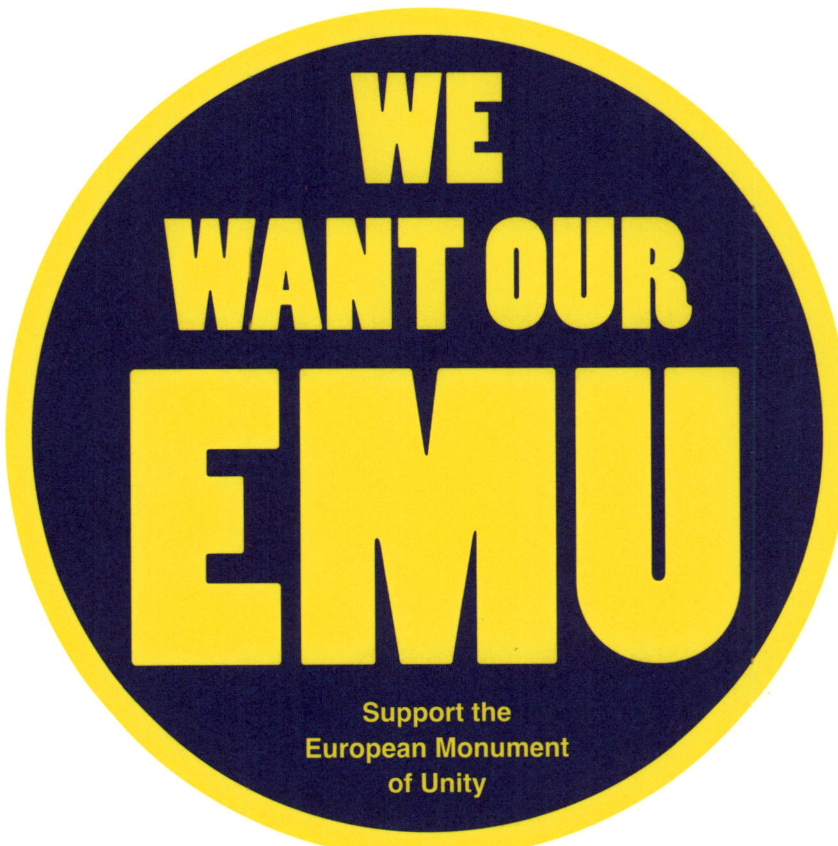
WE
WANT OUR
EMU
Support the
European Monument
of Unity

A ground effect vehicle (GEV) is one that attains level flight near the surface of the Earth, making use of the aerodynamic interaction between the wings and the surface known as ground effect. Best known are the Soviet ekranoplans, but names like wing-in-ground-effect (WIG), flarecraft, sea-skimmer, or wing-in-surface-effect ship (WISE) are also used. In recent years a large number of different GEV types have been developed for both civilian and military service. However, these craft have yet to enter widespread use.

Although they might look similar and have related technical characteristics, ground effect vehicles are not aircraft, seaplanes, hovercraft or hydrofoils, ground effect is a separate technology altogether.

The GEV is sometimes characterized as a transition between a hovercraft and an aircraft, although this is not correct as a hovercraft is statically supported upon a cushion of pressurised air from an onboard downward-directed fan. Some GEV designs, such as the Russian Lun and Dingo, have used forced blowing under the wing by auxiliary engines to increase the high pressure area under the wing to assist takeoff, however they differ from hovercrafts in that they still require forward motion to generate sufficient lift to fly.

• The health benefits of green space include: improved mental health and wellbeing for children, young people and adults; increased likelihood of physical activity across all age groups; reduced violence and aggression: a reduction in anti-social behaviour and incidence of crime in urban areas with green spaces; reduced health inequalities; improvement in air and noise quality.

• A study of 345,143 GP records in the Netherlands indicated that the annual prevalence rates for fifteen of twenty-four chosen disease clusters was lower where there was more green space within one kilometer. This correlation was strongest for anxiety and depression, and among children.

• The more time people spend outdoors the less stressed they feel – an important consideration given the cost to the UK economy of depression and mental illness, which has been calculated at 26.1 billion pounds.

• Survey results from 2009 showed that 87% of people had used green space in the previous year, and 79% in the previous six months, compared with 36% who visit concert halls and 27% who visit galleries.

• Houses close to parks are on average 8% more expensive than similar properties further away. Greener cities attract more visitors, whose spending on shopping and leisure generates job opportunities.

Visitor spending in Bilbao in the first three years after the museum opened raised over 100 million Euros (110 million dollars) in taxes for the regional government, more than enough to recoup construction costs. Last year more than one million people visited the museum, at least half of them from abroad. This was the third-highest number ever, so the building continues to attract visitors even though the collection on display is modest. Other cities without historic cultural centres now look to Bilbao as a model for what vision and imagination can achieve.

'The statue is beautiful. Mandela is a living symbol of the struggle for freedom. I think this monument will become an enduring emblem of the universal values he fought for.' – Cheryl Burke, 34, teacher, 29 August 2007.

THE EKRANOPLANTER

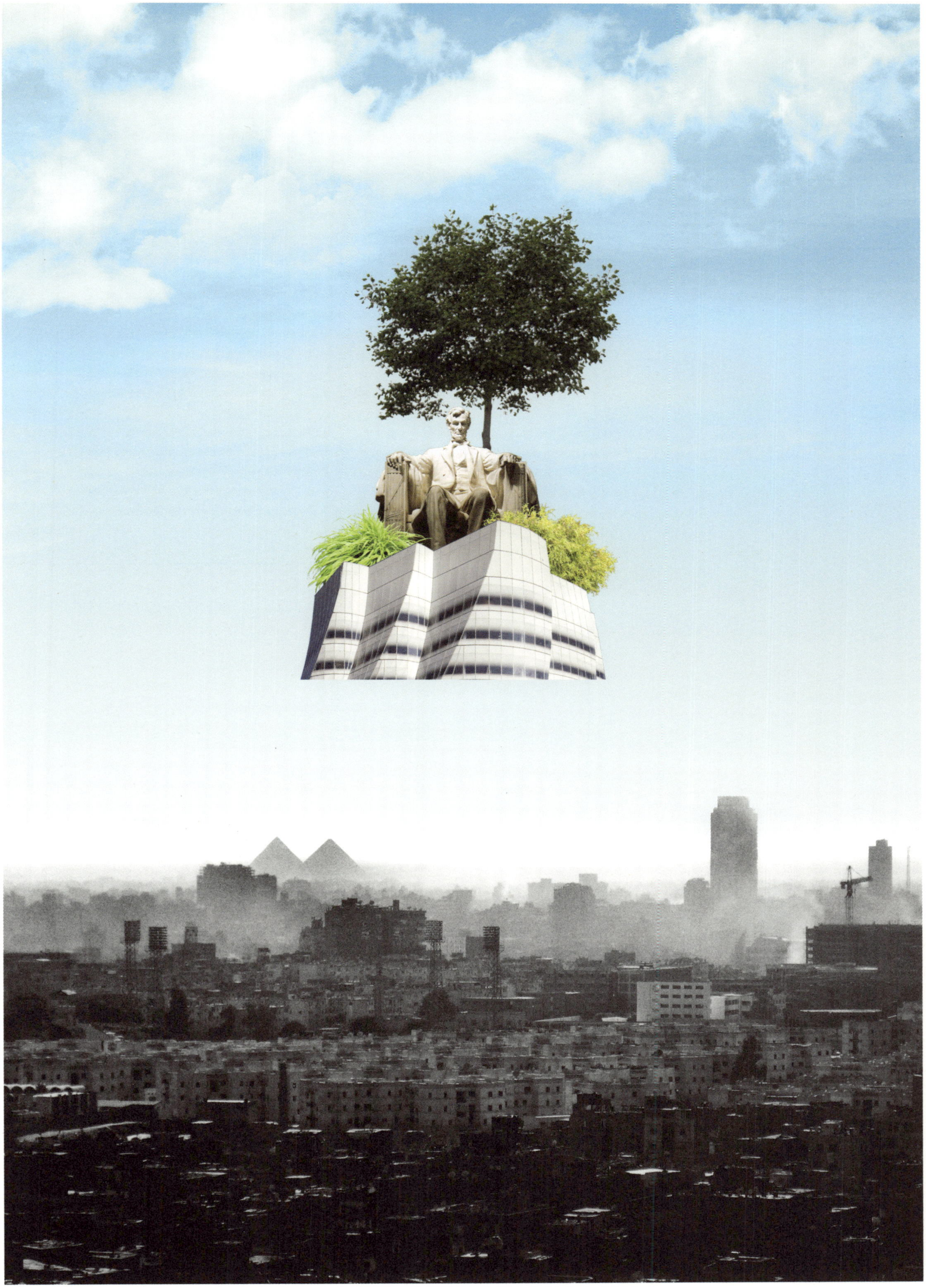

Ekranoplanter #1 (Cairo, Egypt), Photographic print on paper, 46 × 38 cm, 2016

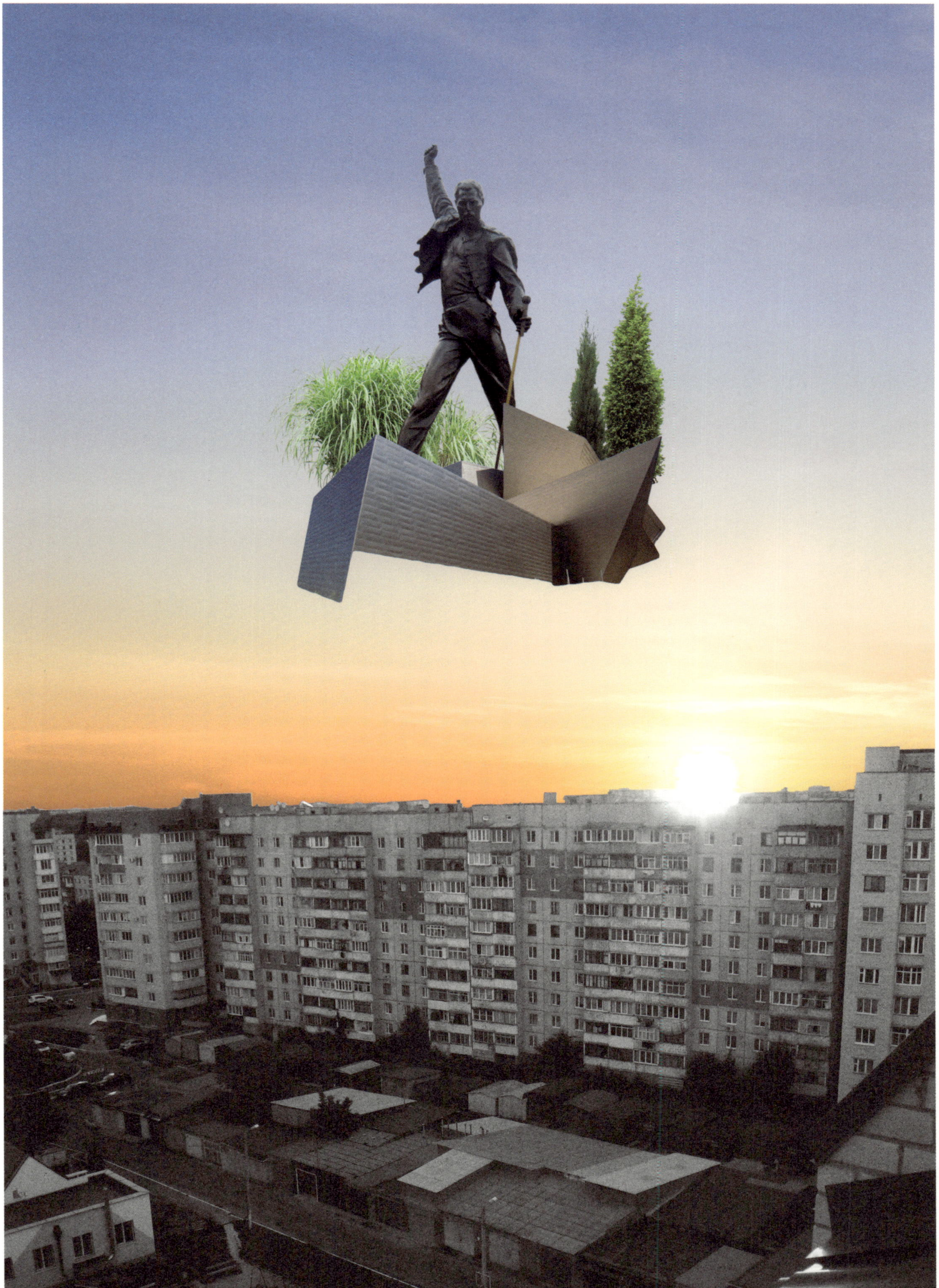

Ekranoplanter #2 (Caracas, Venezuela), Photographic print on paper, 46 × 38 cm, 2016

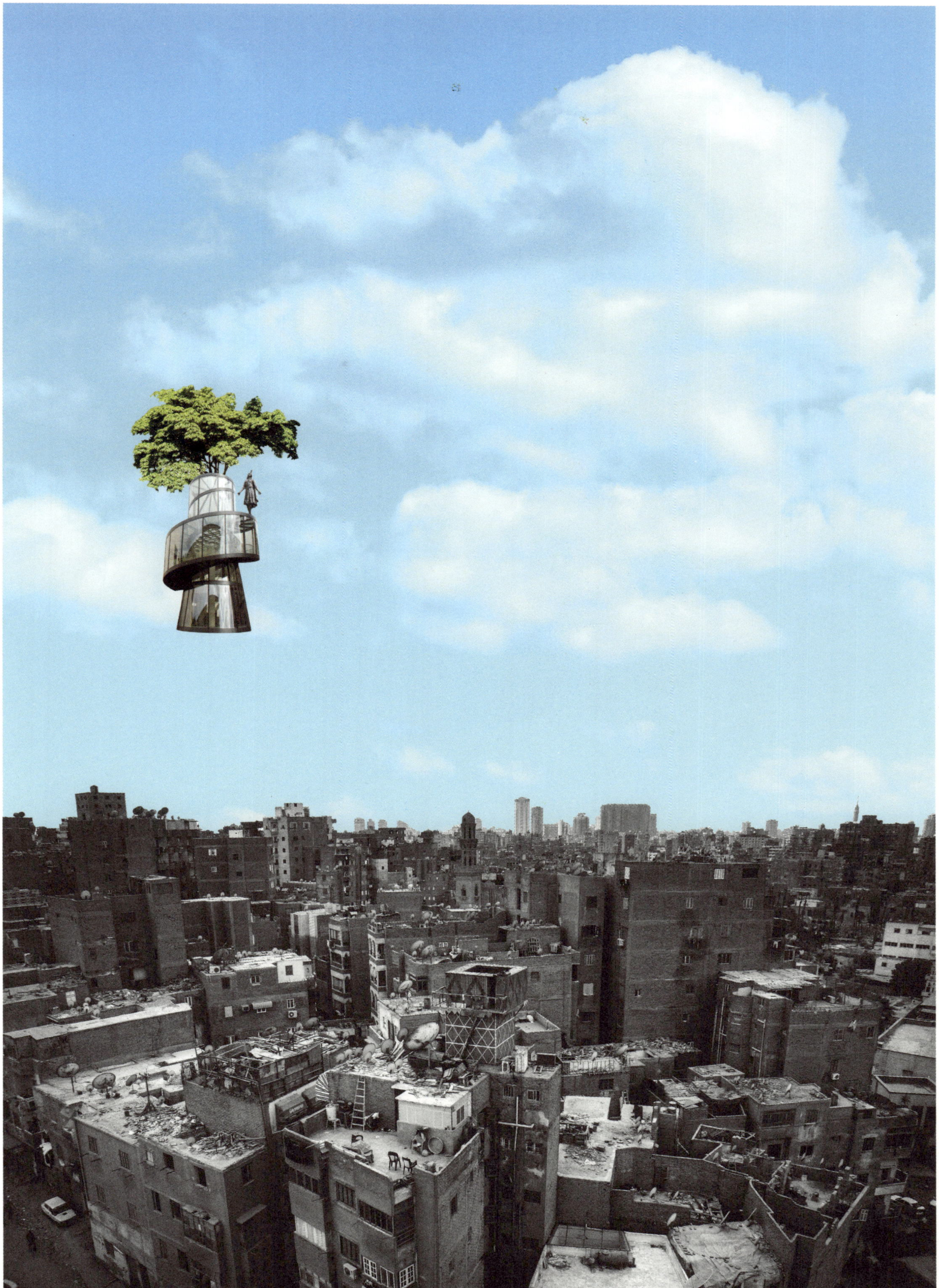

Ekranoplanter #3 (Dakar, Senegal), Photographic print on paper, 46 × 38 cm, 2016

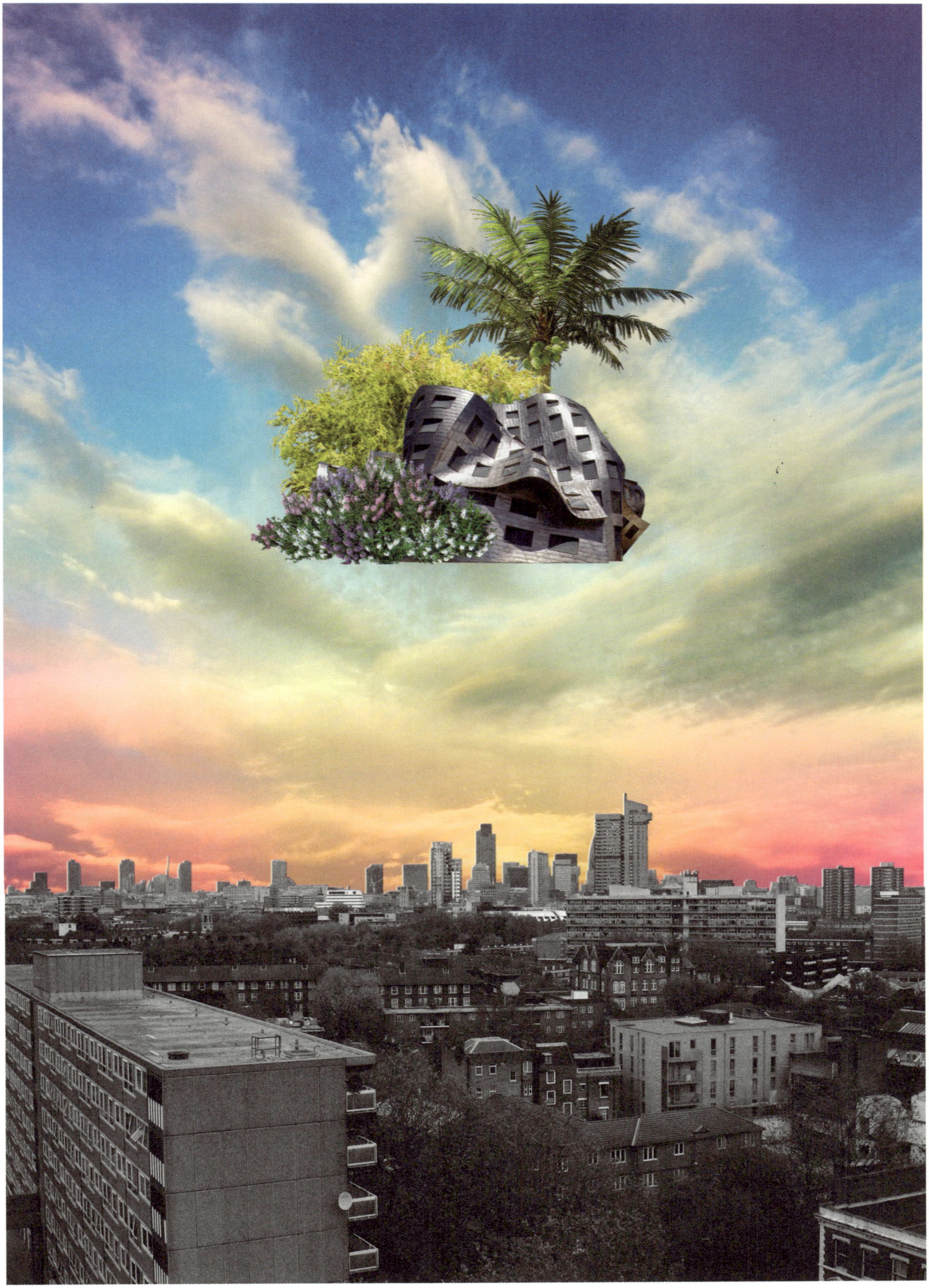

Ekranoplanter #4 (London, England), Photographic print on paper, 46 × 38 cm, 2016

INFINITE MONUMENT

'Can we all agree that the pair of shiny white shafts blazing heavenward adjacent to the ground zero site – calling it *Tribute in Light* somehow undermines its ghostly majesty – is the best public monument since Maya Lin wedged a black granite boomerang into the National Mall in 1982? Like minimalist set pieces, both invite expressions of personal grief without demanding the shedding of tears.

But carry such monumental simplicity to extremes, as Scott King does in the centerpiece sculpture of his wry solo exhibition 'Totem Motif' at Bortolami, and it becomes clear how easily such gestures can go awry. In a show preoccupied with man's outsized attraction to building outsized monuments, King offers a DIY memorial that reveals underlying tendencies toward public displays of affectation.

King's *Infinite Monument* is a modular tower of mirror-covered boxes, each slightly smaller than the one beneath, that can be stacked (using more or fewer boxes) to fit any space, theoretically reaching to the moon. Installed here, the piece nearly touches an HVAC duct. This one-work-fits-all ethos broaches a theme King explores in the photos and illustrations also on view at Bortolami: the naive wish that civic statuary might cure social ills through edification and contemplation, when most people just need clean water and a roof.'

'Scott King Takes Our Obsession With Monuments Down A Peg or Two', Jessica Dawson, *The Village Voice*, September 2014.

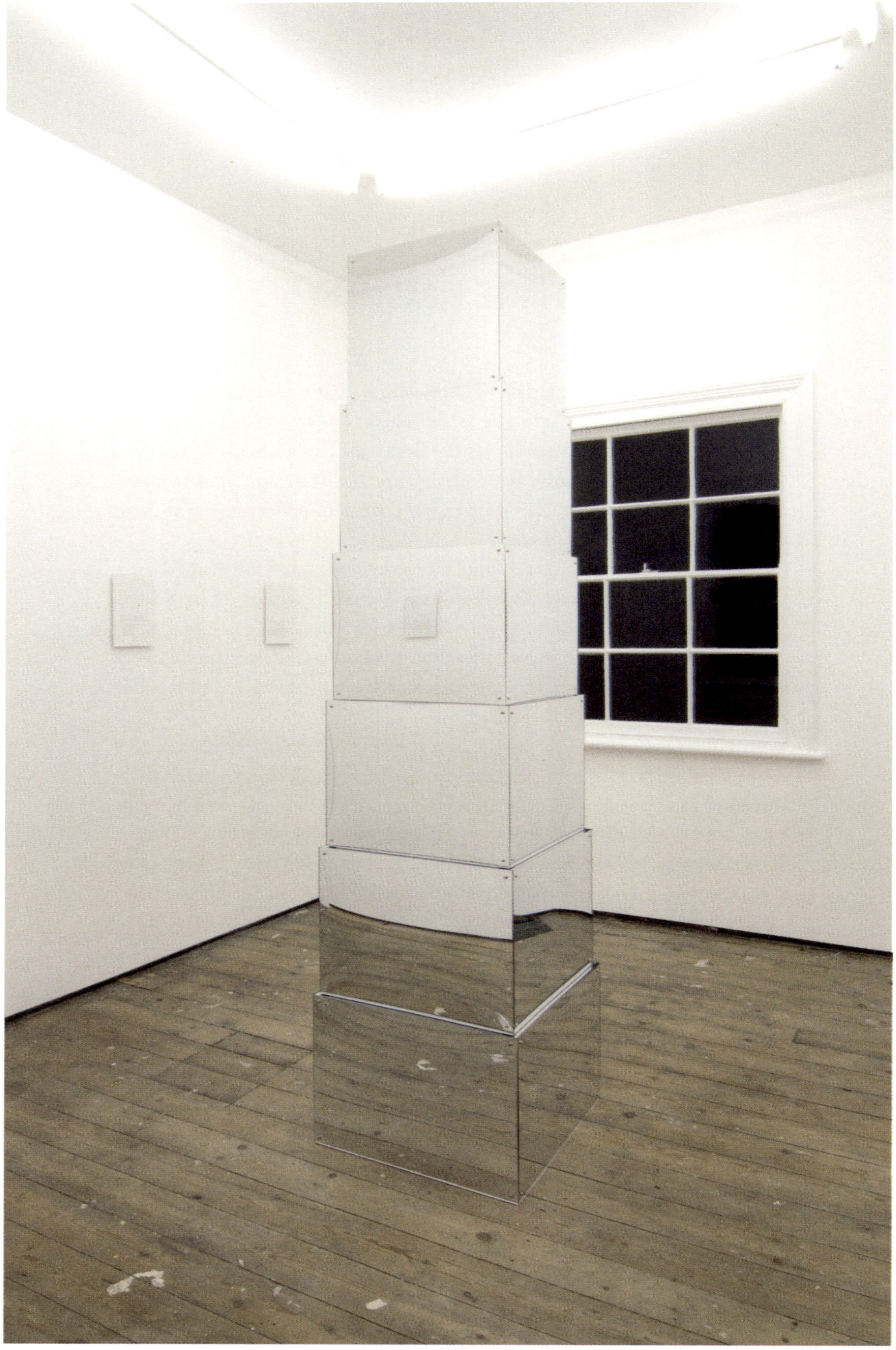

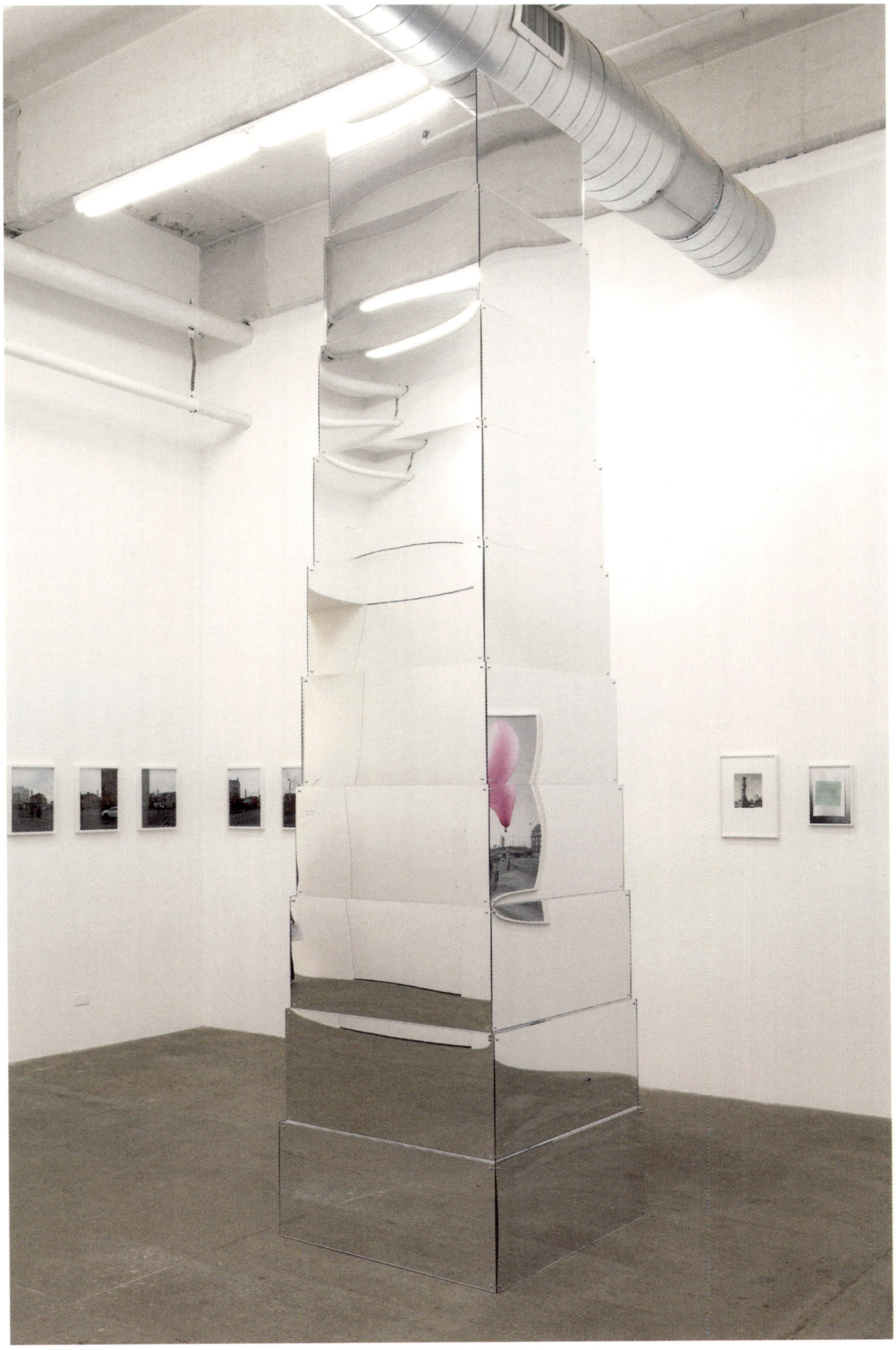

Infinite Monument – Parts 1 to 6 and Parts 7 to 16 (A 320 million dollar hotel on Broadway about halfway between Times Square and Central Park has eclipsed

a Marriott

at the Renaissance Center in Detroit to become the tallest single-use hotel in North America. Built and owned by G Holdings and managed by Interstate Hotels & Resorts, the towering property will house two brands across its sixty-eight floors: a 378-room Courtyard by Marriott and a 261-suite Residence Inn. 'This opening is a prime example of an ideal dual-branded hotel,' Janis Milham, senior vice-president of modern essentials and extended stay for Marriott International Inc (NASDAQ:MAR), said in a statement. She added that the building would be both brands' 'crown jewel' and an iconic addition to the New York City skyline. 'The new hotels' contemporary designs and stunning views coupled with our friendly associates will surely make the property a great ambassador for the bustling city.' The combined hotel at 1717 Broadway officially opened to the public on Dec. 29 with rates hovering around $300 per night. It boasts 6,000 square feet of meeting space, full-wall murals by abstract expressionist William DeBilzan and a fitness center on the 35th floor with floor-to-ceiling windows and an outdoor sundeck. The location in the heart of Midtown Manhattan offers guests convenient access to Carnegie Hall, the Broadway Theater District, Fifth Avenue, Rockefeller Center and Radio City Music Hall. Harry Gross, president and CEO of G Holdings, noted that the new Residence Inn Central Park and Courtyard by Marriott Central Park were the 'most innovative hotels' the company had built. 'In addition to fabulous views, a stellar New York City location and amenities galore, our 21st century telecommunications, with free international phone calls, digital systems and hi-tech wiring, set these hotels far above the standard that business travelers and tourists expect,' he said in a statement. At 750 feet (228.6 meters) high, the Courtyard-Residence Inn Central Park is twenty-three feet taller than the 727-foot (221-meter) Detroit Marriott at the Renaissance Center, according to the Chicago-based Council on Tall Buildings and Urban Habitat, or CTBUH. Neither building cracks the top ten in 'tallest hotels on the planet' list, which is dominated by skyscrapers in Dubai. A towering Four Seasons rising above Lower Manhattan will actually be taller than the new hotel in Midtown, but will include condos and therefore be ineligible for the title of tallest hotel in North America. Both properties reflect a surging demand for hotel space in the Big Apple. New York City welcomed a record 54.3 million visitors in 2013, and the hotel industry is racing to keep up with demand. According to analysts Smith Travel Research, occupancy rates were among the highest in the country last year at eighty-five percent / Ignoring an international outcry, Afghanistan's puritanical Taliban Islamic militia began demolishing statues across the country on Thursday, including two towering ancient stone Buddhas. Taliban Minister of Information and Culture Qudratullah Jamal told AFP the destruction of scores of pre-Islamic figures, designed to stop the worshipping of 'false idols,' had begun throughout the country. He said militiamen started wrecking the almost 2,000-year-old Buddhist masterpieces in the central province of Bamiyan, including the world's tallest standing Buddha measuring fifty meters (165 feet), after sunrise. 'The work started about five hours ago but I do not know how much of it (the two Bamiyan Buddhas) has been destroyed,' Jamal said. 'It will be destroyed by every means. All the statues are being destroyed.' He said Taliban soldiers were at 'work' in the Kabul museum and elsewhere in the provinces of Ghazni, Herat, Jalalabad and Kandahar. An edict announced Monday by the militia's supreme leader, Mulla Mohammad Omar, calling for the destruction of all statues in line with 'Islamic' laws, has caused shock around the world. Afghanistan is home to an array of pre-Islamic historic treasures from its days as a key stop on the ancient Silk Road and a strategic battleground for conquerers dating back to Alexander the Great and the Aryans before him. The two massive Bamiyan Buddhas, carved into a sandstone cliff near the provincial capital in central Afghanistan, stand fifty meters (165 feet) and 34.5 meters (114 feet) tall and were built around the second century. Appeals for their preservation have come from the United States, France, Germany, Thailand, Japan, Sri Lanka, Iran, Pakistan, Germany, Russia, India and UN Secretary General Kofi Annan. Koichiro Matsuura, chief of the UN Educational, Scientific and Cultural Organization (UNESCO), said he had convened an emergency meeting of members of the Organization of the Islamic Conference to try to stop the destruction. 'They are destroying statues that the entire world considers to be masterpieces,' Matsuura said. 'And this is being done in the name of an interpretation of the Muslim faith that is not recognized anywhere else in the world.' But Afghan Foreign Minister Wakil Ahmad Mutawakel said the edict was irreversible. 'Have you ever seen any decision of the Islamic Emirate (Taliban) reversed?' Mutawakel asked. The Taliban, or movement of religious students, seized Kabul in 1996 and have imposed a puritanical mix of Pashtun tribal and Sharia law in a bid to create their idea of a true Muslim state. Their regime is recognised only by Pakistan, Saudi Arabia and the United Arab Emirates, and is not represented at the United Nations nor the Organisation of the Islamic Conference. UN special envoy to Afghanistan Francesc Vendrell told AFP he discussed the edict with Mutawakel in Kabul on Thursday but was told 'the Islamic Emirate (Taliban) is not in the habit of rescinding their edicts.' 'I told him that the international community is baffled at the moment and it would create international outrage if the edict is carried out,' Vendrell said. Afghans, baffled at first by the decree and now its implementation, quietly and sadly condemned the destruction. 'Destroyed cities can be rehabilitated. But once the statues are gone, they can never be replaced,' said a resident of Kabul. 'It is not helping the war-wounded country.' Taliban officials also privately said they were not happy with Omar's decree, which is seen as absolute law in more than ninety percent of the country under the militia's rule. 'It is causing big damage to our history,' said a senior official, refusing to be named for fear of retribution from the hardline militia. 'The war had taken everything else. We had only these (monuments) which are now fading.' Another Taliban official added: 'Personally I am against a brick of Afghanistan being destroyed. It is very sad.'/ On the morning of Aug. 7, 1974, after months of preparation and years of dreaming, a French daredevil named Philippe Petit stepped into the sky above Lower Manhattan. For almost 45 minutes he ambled back and forth on a metal cable strung between the towers of the World Trade Center, a feat of illegal tightrope walking that, according to a New York Police Department sergeant who recounted Mr. Petit's act of physical poetry in dry press-conference prose, would more aptly be described as dancing. High-Wire Act for a Film Festival (April 18, 2008). For many years after, Mr. Petit's stunt was a cherished footnote in the annals of New York history, one of the touchstones of a crazy, awful, glittering era in the life of the city. The destruction of the twin towers in the terrorist attacks of Sept. 11, 2001, revived the memory of that earlier aesthetic assault on the buildings, which is now the subject of 'Man on A Wire', James Marsh's thorough, understated and altogether enthralling documentary. Wisely, Mr. Marsh, who based his film on a book Mr. Petit published in 2002, never alludes to Sept. 11. That would have been both distracting and redundant, since it's impossible, while watching a movie so intimate in its attention to the towers, not to be haunted by thoughts of their fate. But it is also worth recalling that the trade center inspired more love posthumously than while it stood. Mr. Petit was an exception. A zealous, daring wire walker – the French word funambule is a more lyrical, as well as a somewhat more ridiculous-sounding term – he conceived a passion for the structures even before they were built. As he recalls it (and as Mr. Marsh imagines the scene in one of many witty, unobtrusive re-enactments), the young Mr. Petit was flipping through a magazine at a doctor's office when he saw an article about plans to construct the two tallest skyscrapers in the world side by side at the bottom of Manhattan. In his mind, and then in a series of sketches and diagrams, he drew a simple line connecting the buildings and imagined himself perched atop it. / The Cristal Grand Ishtar Hotel is a hotel in Baghdad, Iraq located on Firdos Square. It is the tallest building in Baghdad, and the tallest structure in Iraq after the Baghdad Tower. Opened in 1982 as the Ishtar Sheraton Hotel & Casino, it was one of the most popular Western-run hotels in Baghdad until the Gulf War began in 1991, when Sheraton Hotels severed their management contract with the Iraqi Government, which built the property. The hotel continued to use the Sheraton name without permission for the following twenty-two years. While the hotel was briefly popular with foreign journalists and contractors after the 2003 invasion of Iraq, its occupancy level soon dropped sharply. The hotel, an obvious and imposing target, was periodically hit with mortar or rocket fire during the early years of the post-Saddam era. The structure was seriously damaged during a bomb attack in October 2005 and was closed for more than a year afterward. Thirty-seven were killed in a car bomb attack outside of the hotel on January 25, 2010 / The pyramid seems to have evolved out of the mastaba. During the first dynasties graves were marked by a man-high flat rectangular superstructure with sloping sides. Rather like the part of a sedan car that got the windows in it. King Djoser, first pharaoh of the third dynasty, got the idea of putting four of those on top of each other at Sakkara, to make a stairway to heaven. He later made the whole thing even bigger so he could manage six layers. It's called the 'stepped pyramid' and is believed to have sparked the idea of making a true pyramid. Djoser's pyramid still stands, but the structure has failed in places. Obviously mere piling-up of mastabas did not make for a solid enough building. Later kings tried to do better, but it took quite some experimenting before they got it right. Two obvious misses are the 'collapsed pyramid' at Meidum and the 'bent pyramid' at Dashur. The first was started as stepped and then the steps were smoothened. It's outer shell fell apart. The one at Dashur was constructed as smooth from the start, but the angle of the sloping sides had to be decreased drastically half-way, because the base could not carry the weight of the top. Why go smooth? The triangular shape mimics the Benben, a symbol of the universe, being both the primeval hill that rose above the waters at the moment of the Creation, and an image of the sun's rays shining down to create life. It was a gold-covered stone in the shape of a pyramid that was kept at Heliopolis in the temple of the sun. You also see it on top of obelisks. A pyramid made the ideal shape for resurrection of the dead king. It replayed the creation of the universe for his soul. The top would have been clad in bright metal (gold for Cheops, we know) and the sides were polished to a shine. A pyramid must indeed have looked like a divine shower of sunshine. In the dark, it still was the stairway to heaven too, of course. One way of becoming immortal was to go and live among the northern, undying stars. (The northern stars never set.) Also, it is the most stable shape if you want to go big. The sloping sides pressing inward balance the top pressing down and out, the down-pressure is divided over the broader base so that the weight-strength-ratio does not limit the size. From the Meidum pyramid we can see how the structure was conceived: blocks are piled up at an angle that is about half the slope of the sides, like columns leaning against each other being pushed inward at the bottom by the lower columns of the mantle. Think of the capital A. If a weight is put on top, the sides will bend. The mass in the centre stops the sides from bending inward, so they get pushed out. To stop that, you add weight to the sides to press back inward, the lower you get, the greater the pressure from what is above, so the more weight is needed. Why not build straight up or along the sides of the slope? Pressure straight down cannot be divided over *a broader base and will crush the lower stones in the center (the highest pile). Piling at the slope-angle will leave the sides unsupported at the base and the outer layers will slide off like unfastened shingles off a roof. The 'base-fattened-A' construction gets you the perfect balance between all those forces. / 'Nel progetto il Monumento Continuo, Superstudio si interroga con una immagine su quale mai differenza ci sia tra l'utopia quantitativa della griglia razionale di Coketown e l'utopia 'negativa' del Monumento continuo che si staglia sullo sfondo delle casette, sovrastandole come un infinito grattacielo disteso. Così l'immagine finale della sequenza riproduce una vista aerea del M.C. che attraversa la penisola di Manhattan, lasciando un vuoto 'archeologico' dal quale spuntano come rovine un fascio di grattacieli attorno al mitico Empire State, a testimonianza di come la città del moderno fosse ancora luogo di contraddizioni non composte dalla forza omologante della tecnica e della scienza'. Cristiano Toraldo di Francia Superstudio Firenze 1966 Adolfo Natalini Cristiano Toraldo di Francia Roberto Magris Piero Frassinelli Alessandro Poli Alessandro Magri / When LK Advani announced in all seriousness that the proposed Sardar Patel statue in Gujarat will be the tallest in the world, he sounded like a Dubai sheikh taking credit for the highest building, the biggest island, the largest aquarium. Something not for public good but for* The Guinness Book of Records. *Once complete, this 600-foot statue, Narendra Modi's brainchild, made of iron and concrete with a bronze outer layer, will shine in the afternoon light as it faces the Narmada Dam. But while a public commemoration of Patel as the architect of the Indian republic could hardly be underplayed, a display of such heedless gigantism does little to convey the man's stature. Since its estimated cost is a gigantic Rs 2,500 crore, many people argue that such money should instead go to public health, education and a tireless battle against poverty. Unfortunately, against the onslaught of wily political craft and expediency, they are fated to cry till hoarse. To assuage its own feelings of guilt, Gujarat government wants to assemble the statue from iron scrap contributed by the poor. This is an old devious strategy to strike at the moral Hindu heart. Like the Ram inscriptions on bricks planned for an Ayodhya temple, it seeks to present Patel's statue as a people's demand. A door-to-door campaign to canvass for necessary metal is being waged by an NGO called Citizens for Accountable Government. Almost two lakh collection boxes have been set up throughout India, and marathons called Run for Unity are being organised. Awarding the construction work to a company that engineered the world's highest tower in Dubai – the Burj Khalifa – signals seriousness of the intention. To give additional weight to Gujarat's biggest venture in public art, the statue will house a memorial, visitors' centre, hotel, convention facilities, amusement park and research institute – all the usual paraphernalia inserted when no serious usage is available. An open lift alongside the Sardar will carry tourists up to his head for a panoramic view. Despite its monumental size, this is timid art. A failure of the imagination, it dwarfs and cheapens the surrounding landscape and is a poor replacement for the real Sardar. For a man so decisive, his pose conveys both discomfort and tentativeness. Then there is the expressionless, mildly embarrassed face, as if caught at a road junction waiting for the traffic light to change. The utter silliness of this artistic approach is compounded by the misuse of materials, human skills and engineering to petty purpose. Its gullible acceptance is merely the result of political imposition, a tacit agreement between political zeal and trumped-up public expectation. Of course the idea of public deification is a familiar one and colossal statuary is nothing new to India. But in recent years, religious trusts emboldened by new technology and excess funds have gone on an especially conspicuous building spree. The fifty-eight foot Buddha in Hyderabad is dwarfed by the proposed Maitreya Buddha in Bodh Gaya at 150 feet, equivalent in height to the concrete Hanuman also coming up near Hyderabada. Such figurative statuary oscillates between the sublime to the ridiculous. Besides Lucknow's numerous Mayawatis and Ambedkars, some years back the Maharashtra government came up with a giant commemoration of Shivaji, a 310-foot-high statue set a mile into the Arabian Sea, a project now given an environmental nod. Is Kolkata then likely to ask for a 700-foot-high Mother Teresa in the Bay of Bengal? Will Tamil Nadu propose a 900-foot-high MGR along the coastline? Or Kerala a 1,000-foot Vasco da Gama? It is just a matter of time. Unfortunately, the equivalent of a sixty storey building rising out of the Narmada and towering over the countryside casts a long shadow on politicians' claim to art. Government coercion to make the public believe in the symbolic benefits of a 600-foot Sardar Patel, and in its own good intentions, should not worry exchequers as much as artists and environmentalists. Leaving aside the sheer audacity of public expenditure and the grotesque misuse of political power to electoral ends, the statue's conception raises questions of ecological malpractice and the visual destruction of landscape, not to mention those concerning the public's view of politics as art. The place of public sculpture will always be controversial in a country that still regards statues of political figures, living and dead, as the only form of public art. Without an informed choice in which the public selects its own art, how is the Patel statue any different from those of Lenin in Soviet Russia? If, however, even a small fraction of the budget for stone-faced political heroes were to be diverted into a more liberal – and liberating – form of public art, Indian cities and landscapes may become more engaging places. So as the sun goes down on the low hills around the Narmada dam, and as tour buses head home, Sardar Patel, bronzed and glinting in the evening light, will one day soon gaze desolately into the night, a great man reduced by human folly to an inert piece of stone, stranded forever on a small island in eastern Gujarat. / This is certainly one purchase where the buyer should beware. A couple of flatmates are hoping there will be a few brave souls left at the end as they auction a 'haunted' mirror which they claim has brought them nothing but misery. Student Joseph Birch, twenty, and painter Sotiris Charalambous, thirty-four, acquired the antique mirror when their landlord put it in a skip outside their in Muswell Hill, London five months ago. But ever since then, the pair claim they have been brought nothing but bad luck, misery, financial problems and illness. Mr Charalambous says it has caused him to wake up screaming with 'stabbing pains' in the night. He said: 'The landlord said keep it, I don't want it.' Joseph, an art and design student, and his flatmate began seeing 'flickering shadows' and 'glimpses of black darkness' in the mirror and orbs of light in the room. Since the walnut mirror was painted metallic silver by Sotiris two months ago, the flatmates began to suffer intense nightmares and their problems escalated. Joseph woke up covered in red scratchmarks in the middle of the night last week and both have had sleepless nights which they blame on the antique. But if that's the bad news, the good news is the mirror only has a few scratches and is not broken. They have placed the mirror on internet auction site eBay with a price of £100 but say it is 'only right' that a potential buyer knows about the problems it may bring. The flatmates have had a number of bids slightly below the reserve price so far. And one prospective buyer is even eyeing up the mirror as a gift for an ex. Sotiris said: 'I think someone could have been murdered in front of the mirror and that's why it has been haunting our house. 'I don't think the mirror likes it since I painted it silver. I took it to an antique dealer who said it was worth £100 once and that's why we're asking for the price, but we would ideally like it to go to someone who has experience of the paranormal.' The item has attracted interest from all over the country. People want to be scared. / The architect who won the competition to rebuild on New York's Ground Zero has revealed how the process degenerated into bitter feuds and childish squabbles among rival designers – though he rejects the notion that the new plan for the site is an uninspiring compromise. In a candid new book,* Breaking Ground, *Daniel Libeskind recounts what he calls his 'forced marriage' to David Childs, the favoured architect of the World Trade Centre site's developer, Larry Silverstein. He portrays Mr Childs as patronising and overbearing, and intent on eliminating as much of Mr Libeskind's vision as possible from the eventual design. Relations between the two architectural practices were so fraught that they 'recalled the orchestrated arrangements between North and South Korea at the very tense border at Panmunjom'. Since winning the competition last year, Mr Libeskind, designer of the Jewish Museum in Berlin, has been fighting to preserve what he can of his original concept, which had as its centrepiece a Freedom Tower, 1,776 feet high, to represent the date of the American declaration of independence. That symbolic height has been maintained, and the tower's cornerstone was laid in July. But much of the rest of the design has been heavily modified to meet Mr Silverstein's 'uncompromising demands for yet more office space without regard for the public plazas, parks, memorials and streets of the master plan', as Mr Libeskind puts it. Mr Childs's company, Skidmore Owings and Merrill (SOM), was hired directly by the developer – who told reporters he had an 'absolute right to choose the architects' – while Mr Libeskind won the prize from the Lower Manhattan Development Corporation. The consequent working relationship, Mr Libeskind writes, was often 'downright nuts'. He claims that no representative from his company was allowed to enter SOM's offices unless someone of equivalent seniority was present, and that for the majority of the time during their weekly meetings, Mr Childs would 'chatter on about where he'd just been or would lecture me on architecture'. 'He gave me the patronising look reserved for the village idiot,' he notes on another occasion, describing it as 'weird to inhabit David Childs's universe, where everybody knew his or her prescribed place… Childs wasn't interested in what we were working on; he was proceeding with plans for the building he had proposed to Larry Silverstein many months before.' The process was only kept on track at all, he says, because of the forceful intervention of George Pataki, the governor of New York state. The collaboration was undoubtedly a clash of cultures between the black-suited European architect, poetic and sometimes baffling in his pronouncements about the site, and the no-nonsense American commercial designer. Elizabeth Kubany, from Mr Childs's company, said Mr Libeskind's account was highly partisan. 'We're not going to respond to it point by point,' she said. 'Certainly there are many things in it that are half true. We have a building that we're trying to build, so all of this time spent talking about the process seems counterproductive to us.' A spokesman for Mr Silverstein called the plans for the site 'spectacular', adding: 'We regret that Daniel Libeskind feels the need to attack so many of the participants in that effort.' Mr Libeskind seemed more conciliatory yesterday. 'I compromised here and I negotiated there… but I believe in [the project],' he told the Associated Press news agency. 'You have to be flexible. You have to be able to accommodate future needs. At the same time, you have to create a plan that has integrity and strength and that can withstand all these changes. I think when it's built, people will forget the squabbles.' That perspective is far from unanimously shared among design experts. 'It's like that old cliche about a camel being a horse designed by a committee,' said Paul Goldberger, the New Yorker magazine's architectural critic. 'We now have the camel of skyscrapers. Do you ask Matisse and Dalí to collaborate on painting a picture together? No.' / Vladimir Tatlin's tower in St Petersburg was never built – yet it has inspired generations of artists. Why does it still have such mystique, asks Brian Dillon),* Mirrored acrylic, aluminium and stainless steel, Sixteen of an infinite number of parts: 61 × 61 × 40 cm, Leading towards infinity, 2014

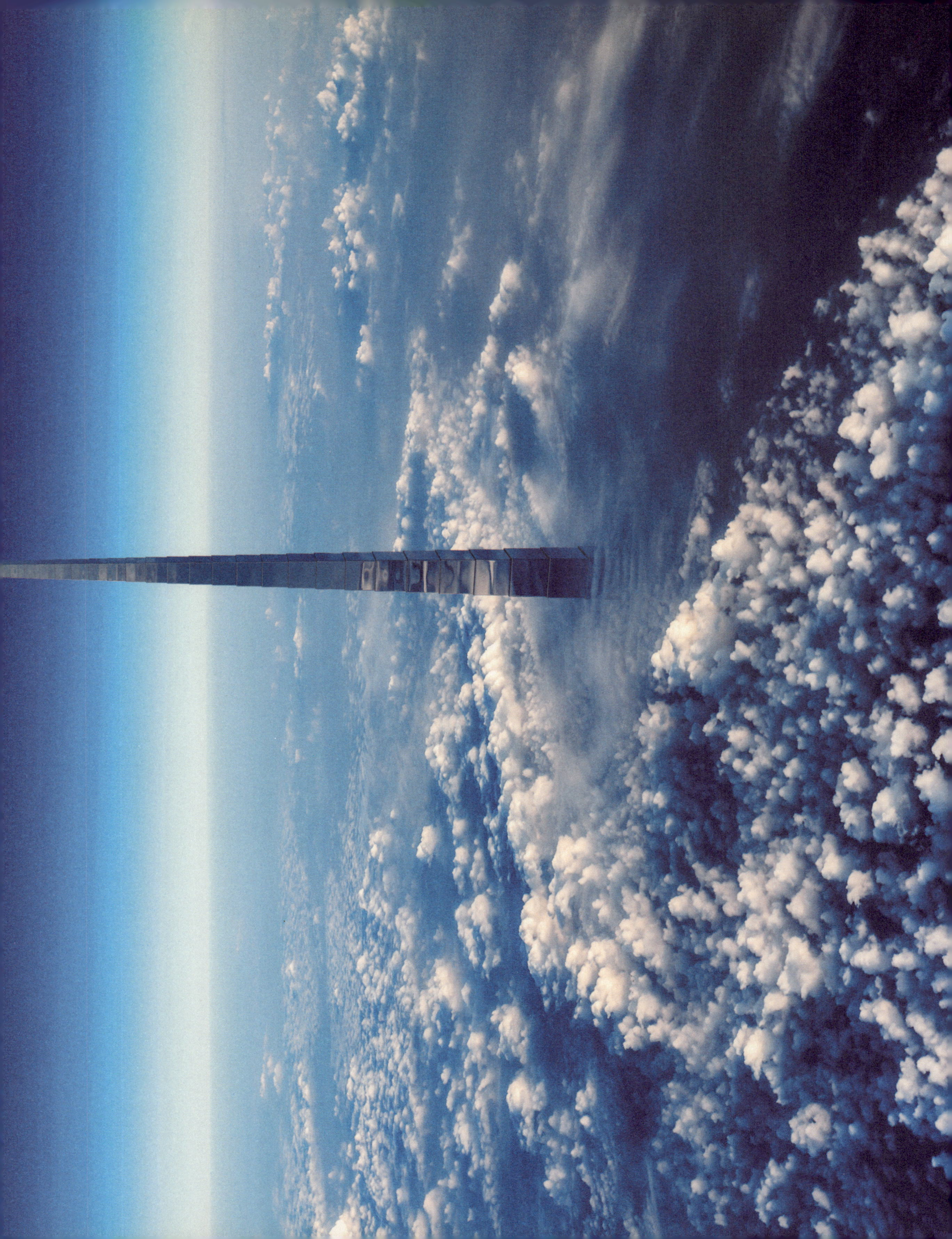

Artist's Impression of *Infinite Monument*, Photographic print on paper, 31.7 × 24.5cm, 2016. King intends to build this modular structure in Mesopotamia at the site of the fabled Tower of Babel. If the Tower of Babel has been associated with known structures according to some modern scholars, notably the Etemenanki, a ziggurat dedicated to the Mesopotamian god Marduk by Nabopolassar, king of Babylonia (c. 610 BC), then King's work will effectively collapse myth, reality and time by combining the language of pre-historical edifices, Minimalist sculpture and contemporary architecture in a single monolithic device.

NEW YORK RURAL

Illustrations by Will Henry

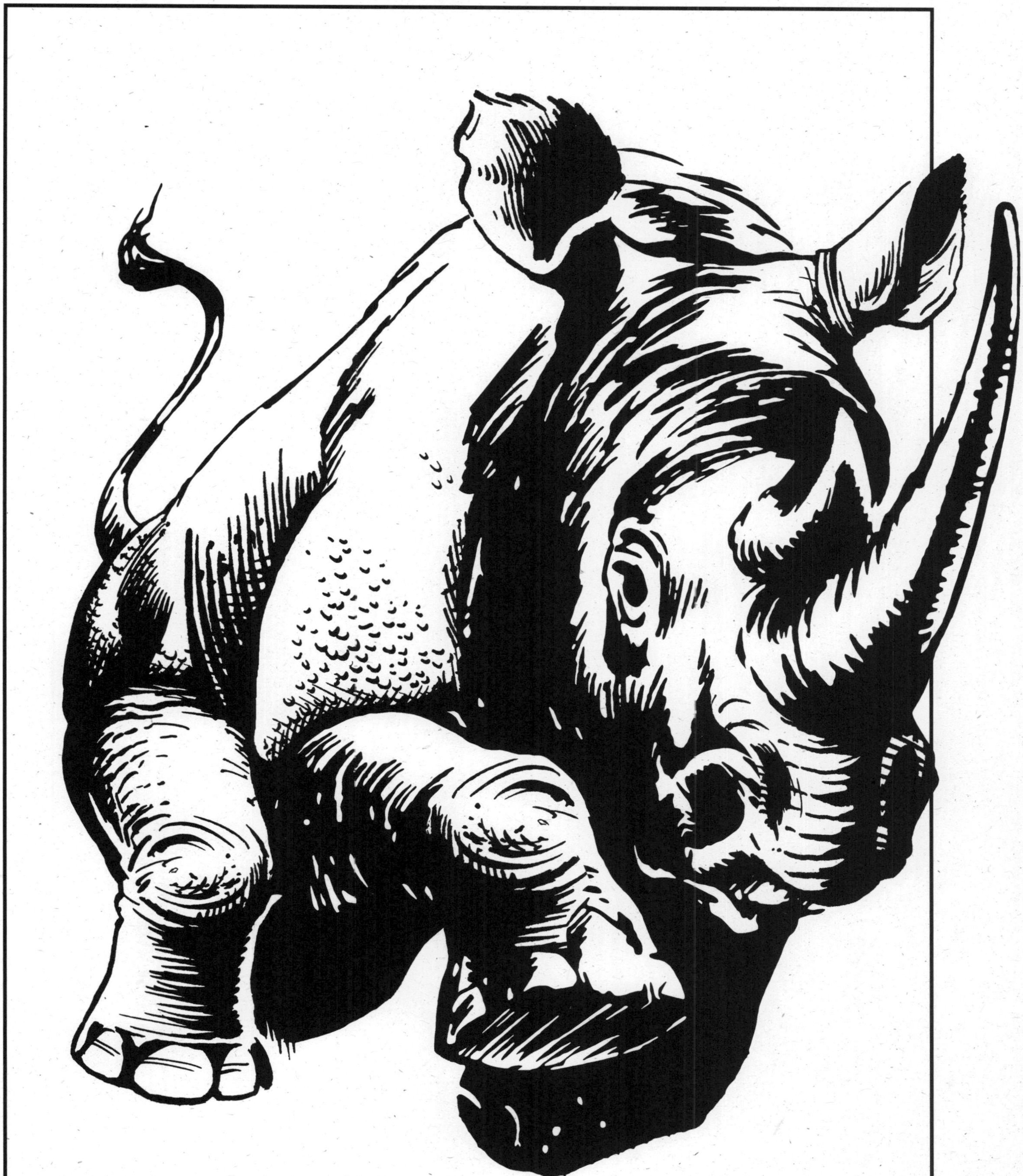

New York Rural, Digital prints, Forty-three parts, 2016

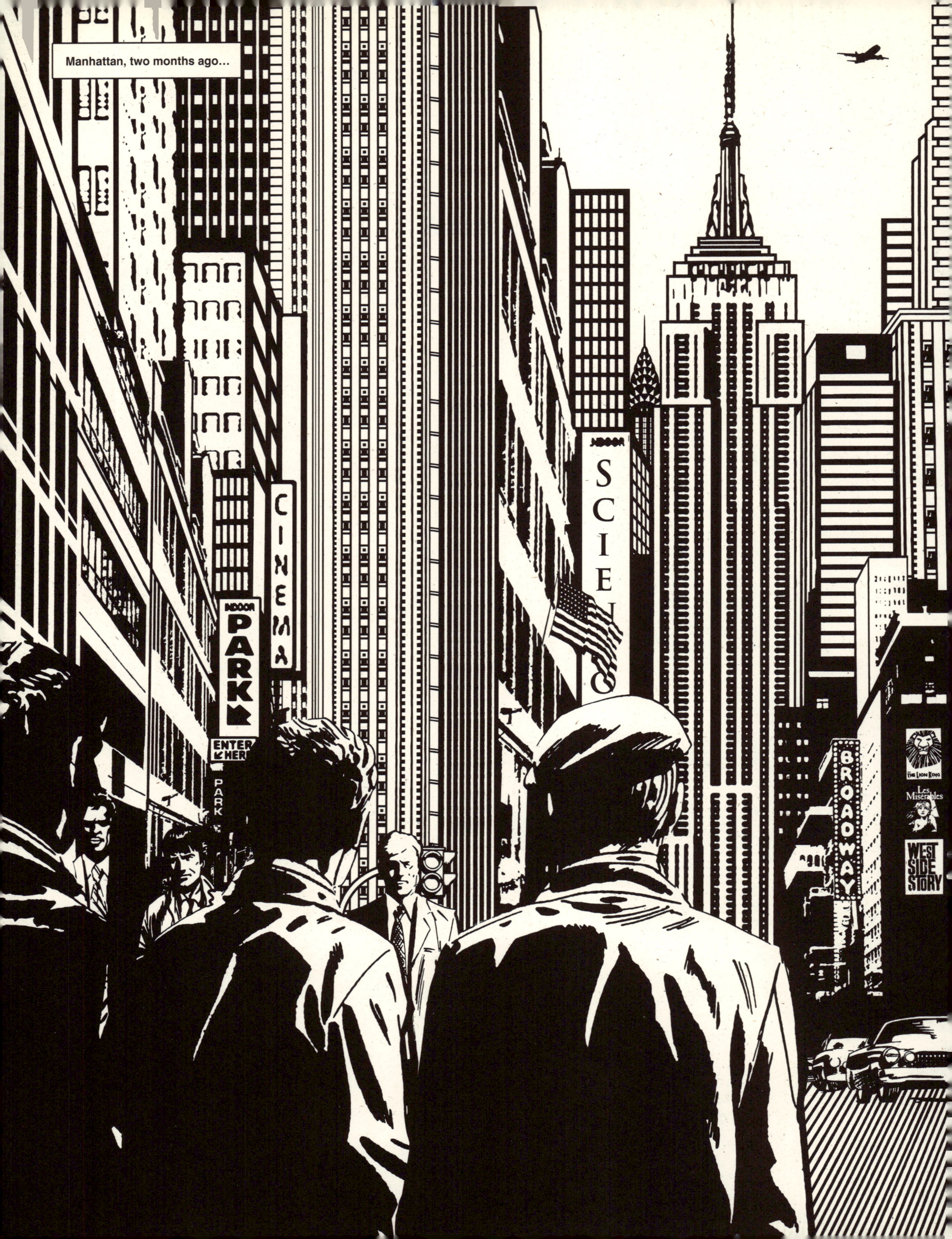
Manhattan, two months ago...
CINEMA
INDOOR
PARK
ENTER HERE
BROADWAY
THE LION KING
Les Misérables
WEST SIDE STORY

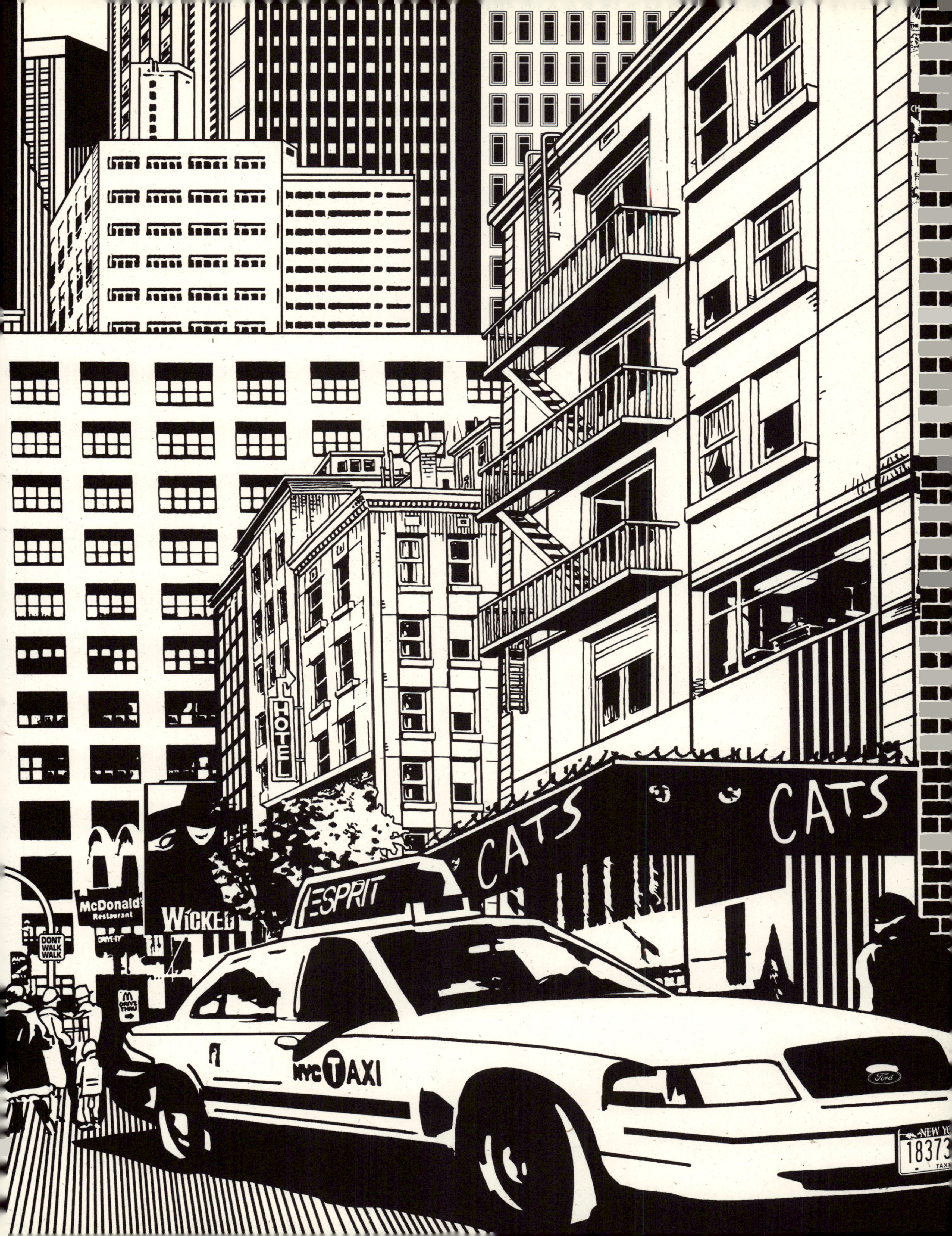
HOTEL
CATS
CATS
ESPRIT
McDonald's
Restaurant
WICKED
DONT WALK
NYC TAXI
NEW YO
18373

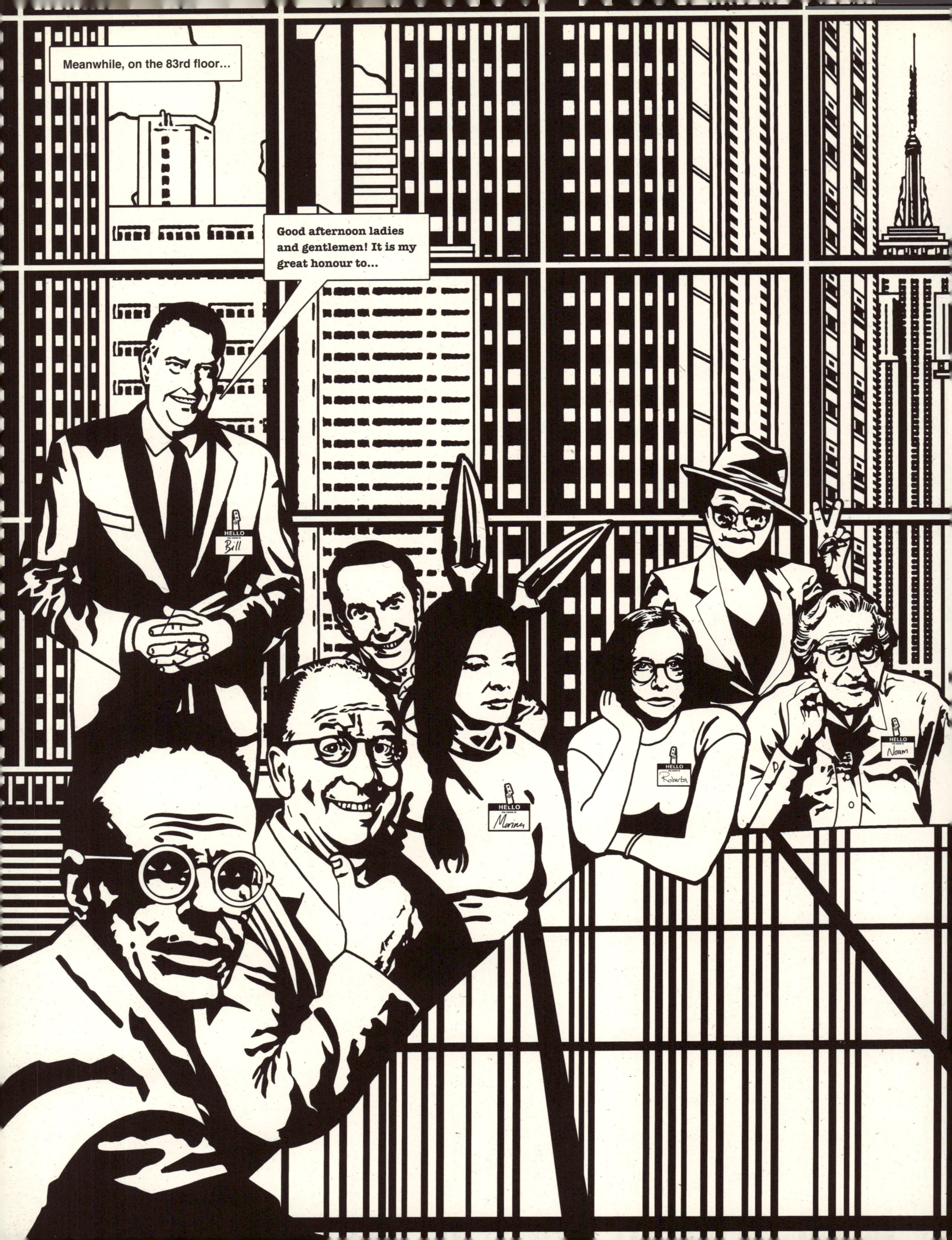
Meanwhile, on the 83rd floor...
Good afternoon ladies and gentlemen! It is my great honour to...
HELLO
Bill
HELLO
Marina
HELLO
Roberta
HELLO
Noam

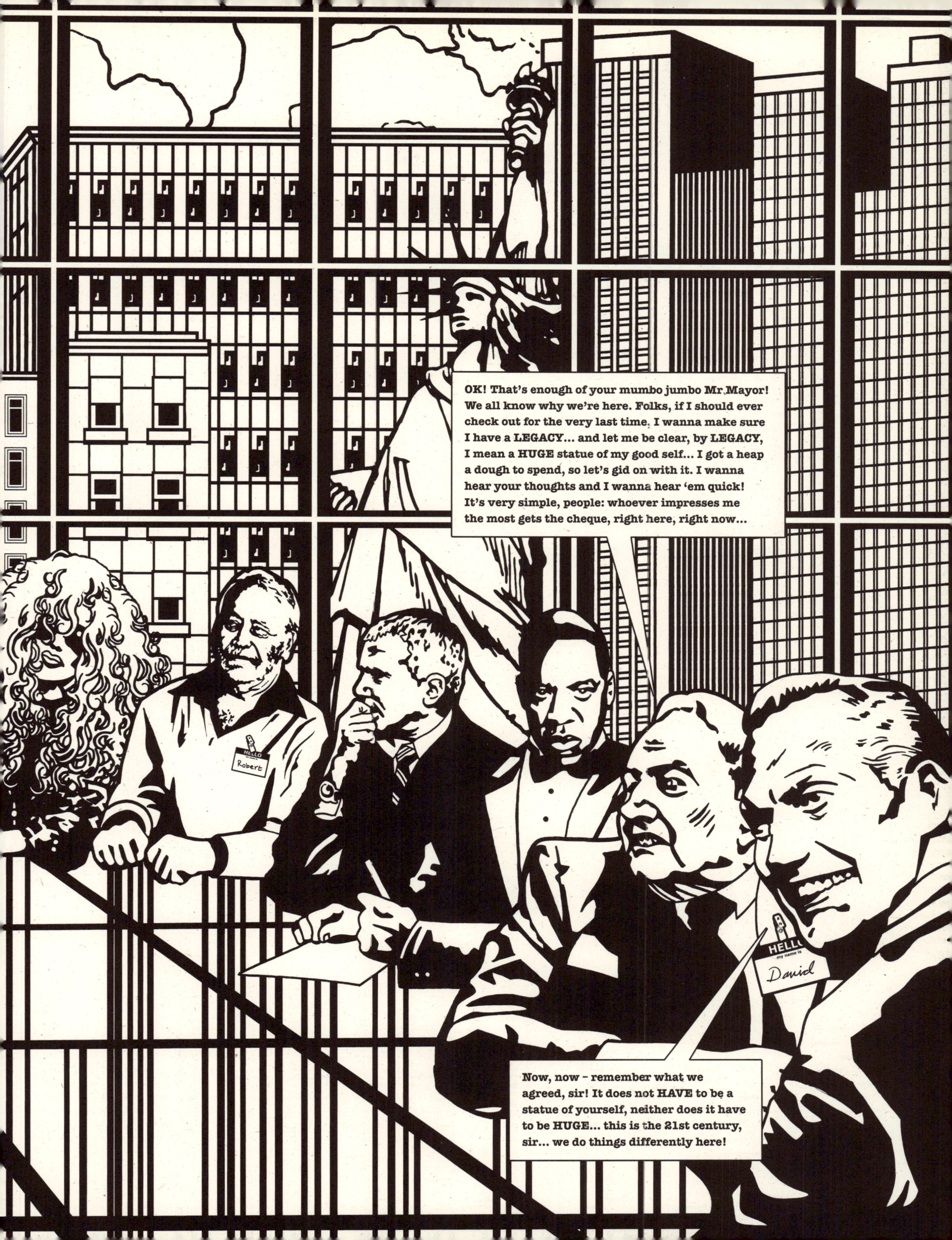
OK! That's enough of your mumbo jumbo Mr.Mayor! We all know why we're here. Folks, if I should ever check out for the very last time, I wanna make sure I have a LEGACY... and let me be clear, by LEGACY, I mean a HUGE statue of my good self... I got a heap a dough to spend, so let's gid on with it. I wanna hear your thoughts and I wanna hear 'em quick! It's very simple, people: whoever impresses me the most gets the cheque, right here, right now...
HELLO
Robert
HELLO
my name is
David
Now, now - remember what we agreed, sir! It does not HAVE to be a statue of yourself, neither does it have to be HUGE... this is the 21st century, sir... we do things differently here!

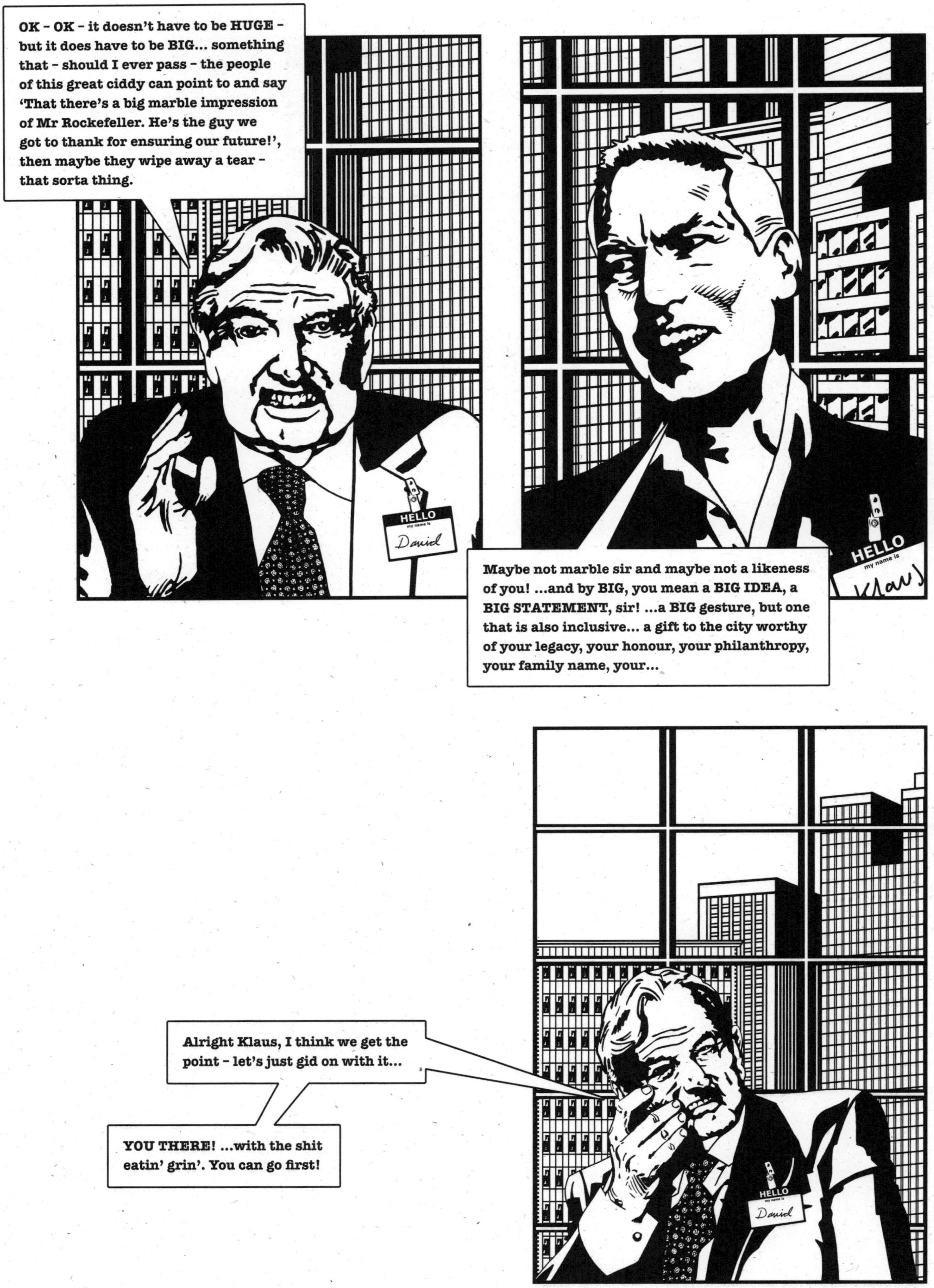
OK - OK - it doesn't have to be HUGE - but it does have to be BIG... something that - should I ever pass - the people of this great ciddy can point to and say 'That there's a big marble impression of Mr Rockefeller. He's the guy we got to thank for ensuring our future!', then maybe they wipe away a tear - that sorta thing.
HELLO
David
Maybe not marble sir and maybe not a likeness of you! ...and by BIG, you mean a BIG IDEA, a BIG STATEMENT, sir! ...a BIG gesture, but one that is also inclusive... a gift to the city worthy of your legacy, your honour, your philanthropy, your family name, your...
HELLO
Alright Klaus, I think we get the point - let's just gid on with it...
YOU THERE! ...with the shit eatin' grin'. You can go first!
HELLO
David

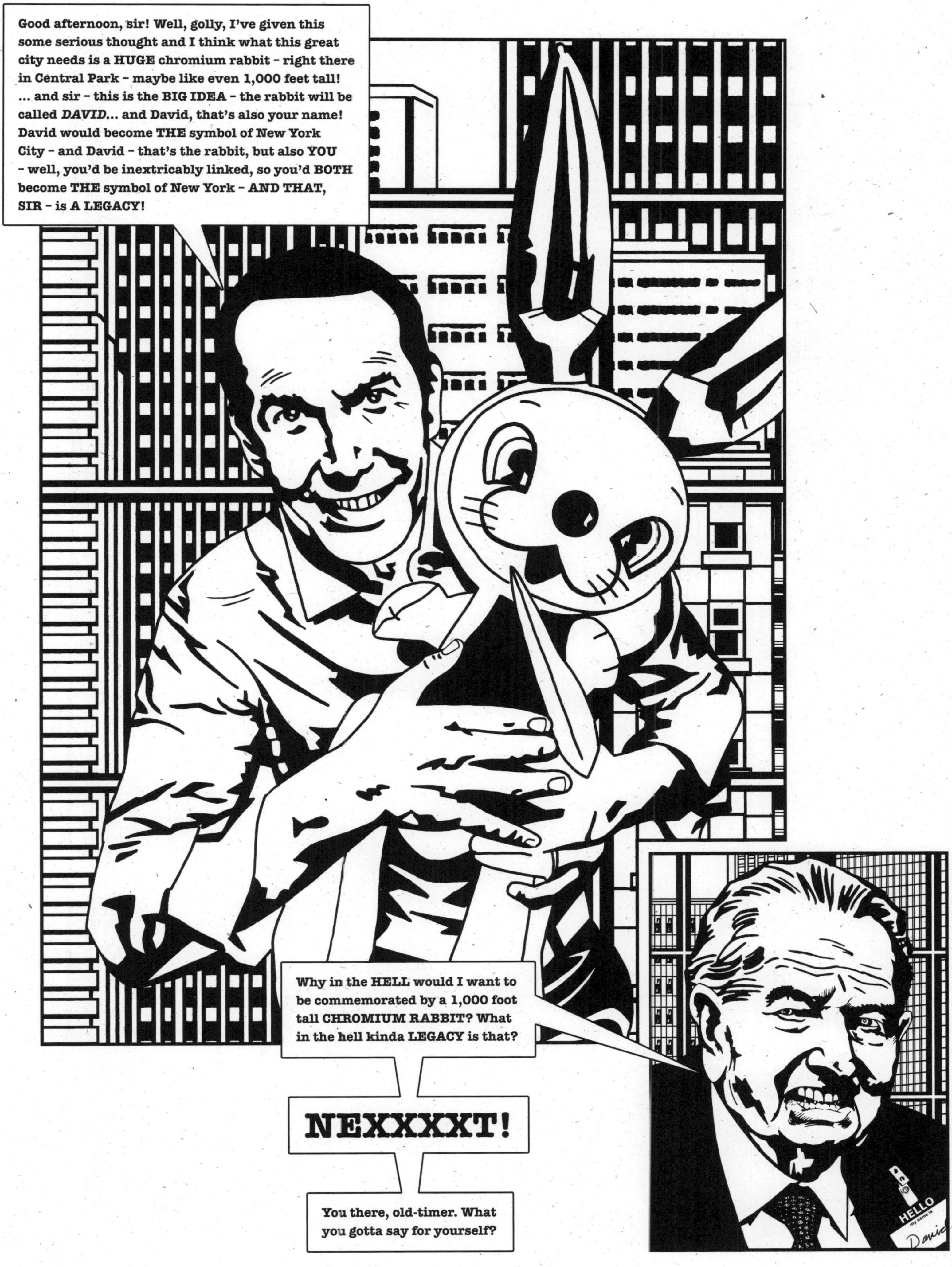
Good afternoon, sir! Well, golly, I've given this some serious thought and I think what this great city needs is a HUGE chromium rabbit - right there in Central Park - maybe like even 1,000 feet tall! ... and sir - this is the BIG IDEA - the rabbit will be called DAVID... and David, that's also your name! David would become THE symbol of New York City - and David - that's the rabbit, but also YOU - well, you'd be inextricably linked, so you'd BOTH become THE symbol of New York - AND THAT, SIR - is A LEGACY!
Why in the HELL would I want to be commemorated by a 1,000 foot tall CHROMIUM RABBIT? What in the hell kinda LEGACY is that?
NEXXXXT!
You there, old-timer. What you gotta say for yourself?
HELLO
my name is
David

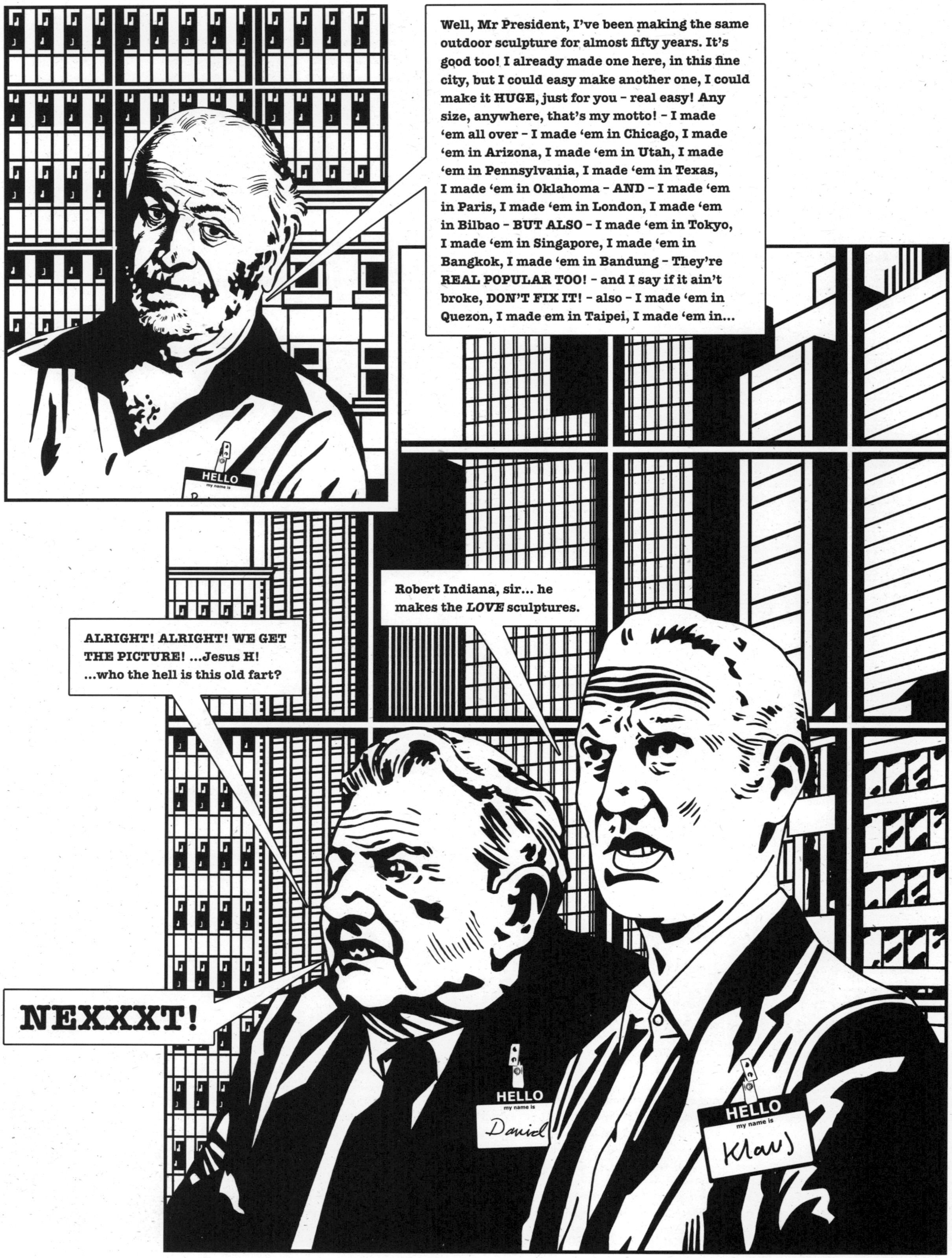
Well, Mr President, I've been making the same outdoor sculpture for almost fifty years. It's good too! I already made one here, in this fine city, but I could easy make another one, I could make it HUGE, just for you – real easy! Any size, anywhere, that's my motto! – I made 'em all over – I made 'em in Chicago, I made 'em in Arizona, I made 'em in Utah, I made 'em in Pennsylvania, I made 'em in Texas, I made 'em in Oklahoma – AND – I made 'em in Paris, I made 'em in London, I made 'em in Bilbao – BUT ALSO – I made 'em in Tokyo, I made 'em in Singapore, I made 'em in Bangkok, I made 'em in Bandung – They're REAL POPULAR TOO! – and I say if it ain't broke, DON'T FIX IT! – also – I made 'em in Quezon, I made em in Taipei, I made 'em in...
ALRIGHT! ALRIGHT! WE GET THE PICTURE! ...Jesus H! ...who the hell is this old fart?
Robert Indiana, sir... he makes the *LOVE* sculptures.
NEXXXT!

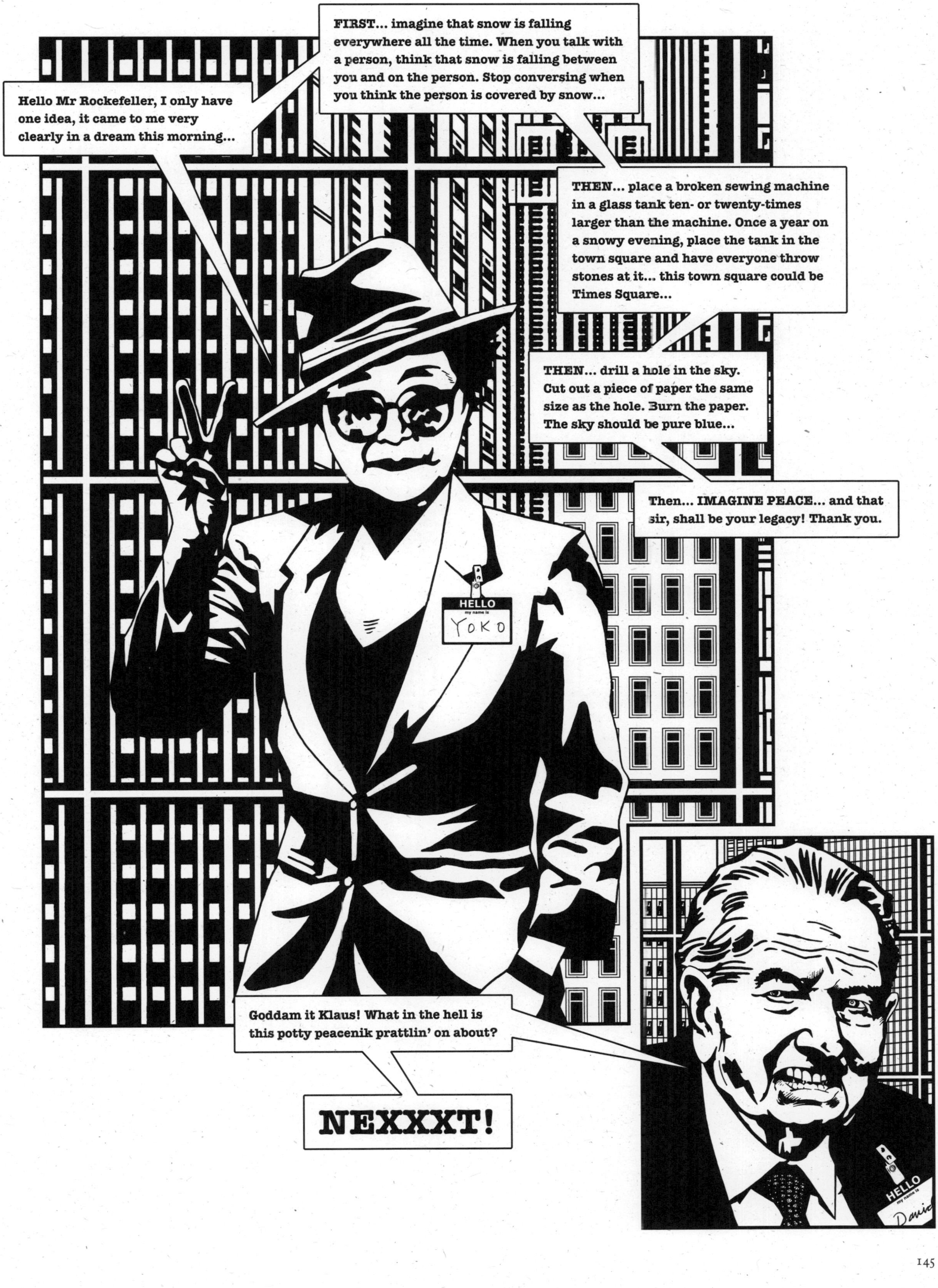
Hello Mr Rockefeller, I only have one idea, it came to me very clearly in a dream this morning...
FIRST... imagine that snow is falling everywhere all the time. When you talk with a person, think that snow is falling between you and on the person. Stop conversing when you think the person is covered by snow...
THEN... place a broken sewing machine in a glass tank ten- or twenty-times larger than the machine. Once a year on a snowy evening, place the tank in the town square and have everyone throw stones at it... this town square could be Times Square...
THEN... drill a hole in the sky. Cut out a piece of paper the same size as the hole. Burn the paper. The sky should be pure blue...
Then... IMAGINE PEACE... and that sir, shall be your legacy! Thank you.
HELLO my name is YOKO
Goddam it Klaus! What in the hell is this potty peacenik prattlin' on about?
NEXXXT!
HELLO my name is David

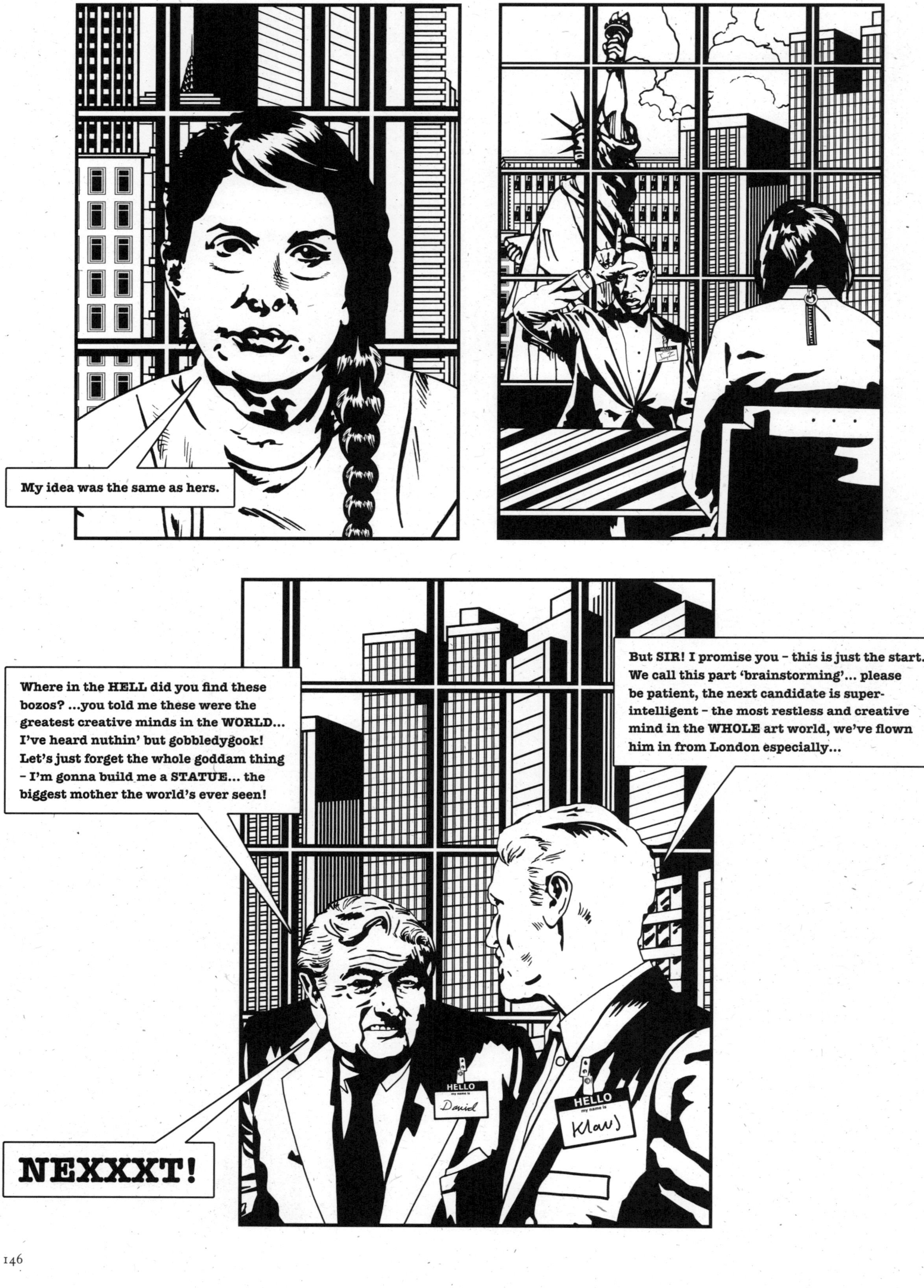
My idea was the same as hers.
Where in the HELL did you find these bozos? ...you told me these were the greatest creative minds in the WORLD... I've heard nuthin' but gobbledygook! Let's just forget the whole goddam thing – I'm gonna build me a STATUE... the biggest mother the world's ever seen!
But SIR! I promise you – this is just the start. We call this part 'brainstorming'... please be patient, the next candidate is super-intelligent – the most restless and creative mind in the WHOLE art world, we've flown him in from London especially...
HELLO
Daniel
HELLO
Klaus
NEXXXT!

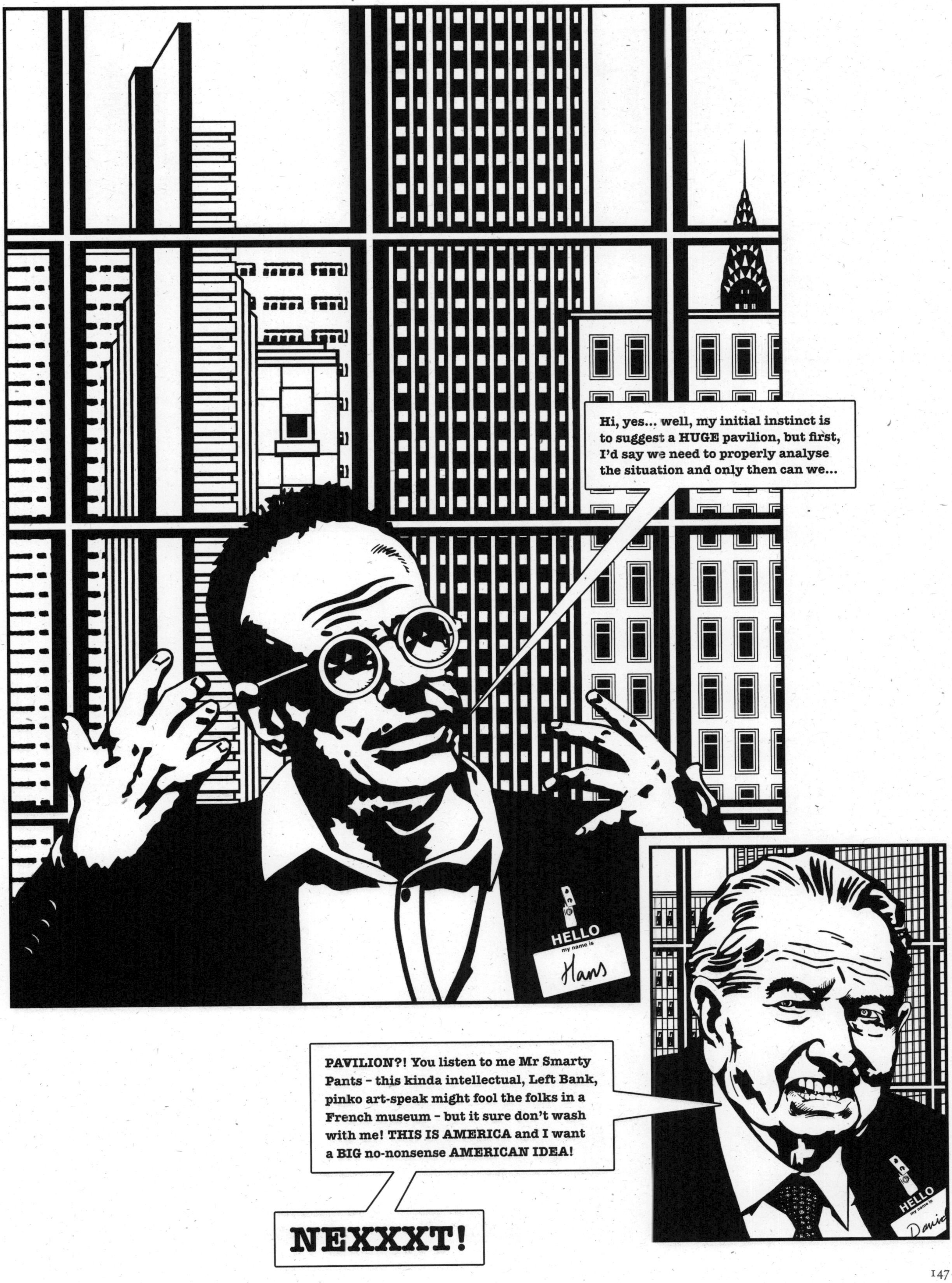
Hi, yes... well, my initial instinct is to suggest a HUGE pavilion, but first, I'd say we need to properly analyse the situation and only then can we...
HELLO my name is Hans
PAVILION?! You listen to me Mr Smarty Pants – this kinda intellectual, Left Bank, pinko art-speak might fool the folks in a French museum – but it sure don't wash with me! THIS IS AMERICA and I want a BIG no-nonsense AMERICAN IDEA!
NEXXXT!
HELLO my name is David

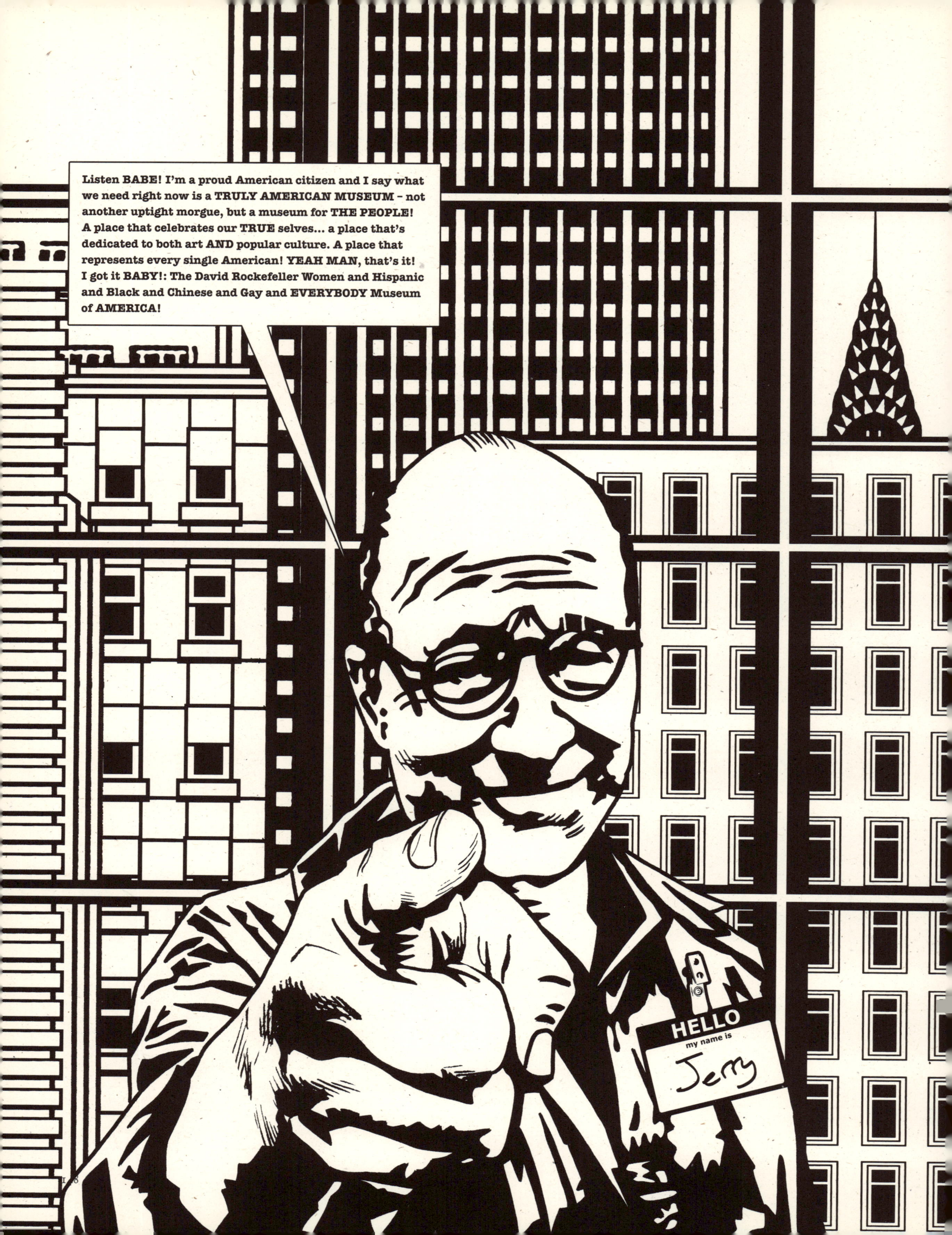
Listen BABE! I'm a proud American citizen and I say what we need right now is a TRULY AMERICAN MUSEUM – not another uptight morgue, but a museum for THE PEOPLE! A place that celebrates our TRUE selves… a place that's dedicated to both art AND popular culture. A place that represents every single American! YEAH MAN, that's it! I got it BABY!: The David Rockefeller Women and Hispanic and Black and Chinese and Gay and EVERYBODY Museum of AMERICA!
HELLO
my name is
Jerry

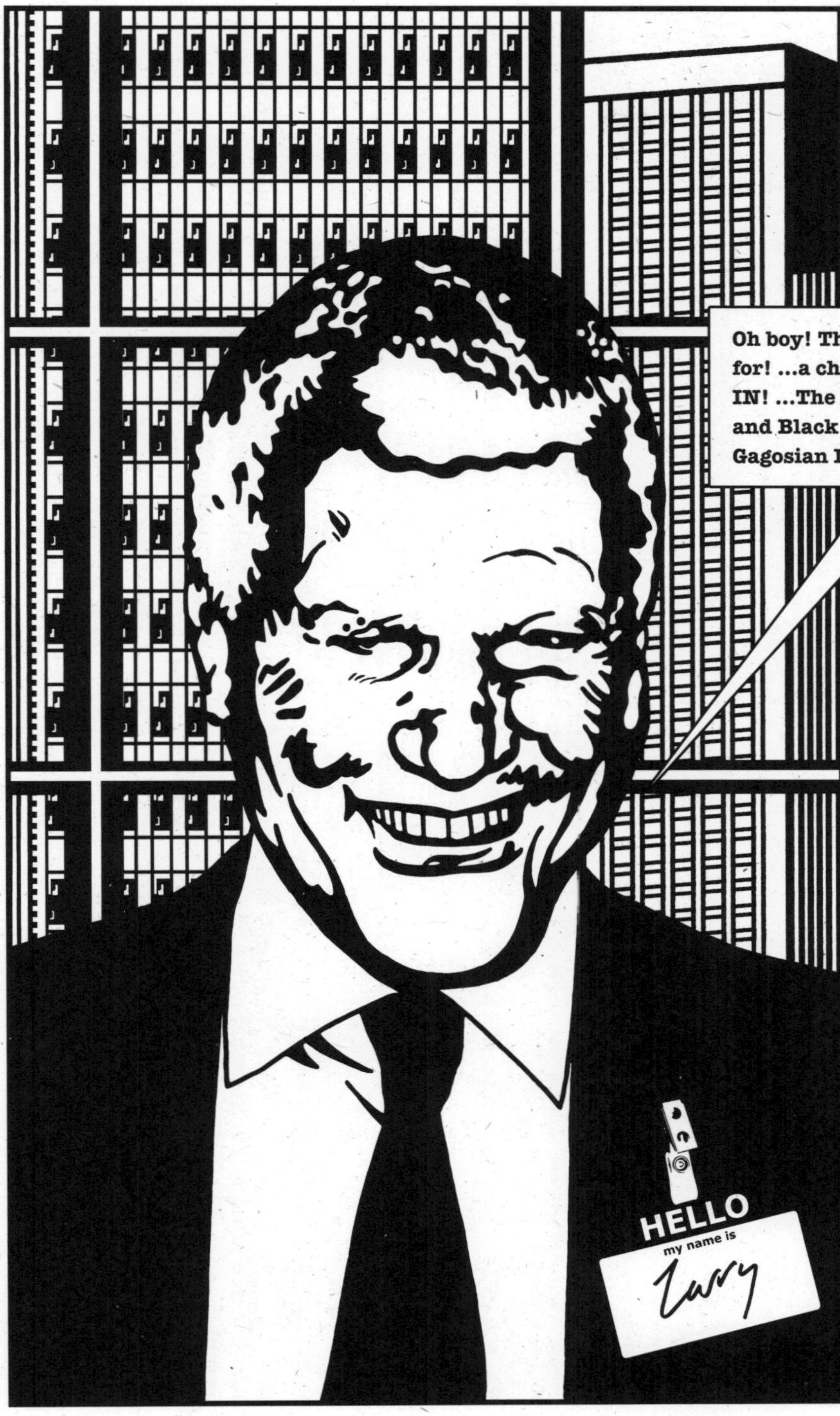
Oh boy! This is what I've been waiting all my life for! ...a chance to give something back! Count me IN! ...The David Rockefeller Women and Hispanic and Black and Chinese and Gay and EVERYBODY Gagosian Museum of AMERICA!
HELLO
my name is
Larry

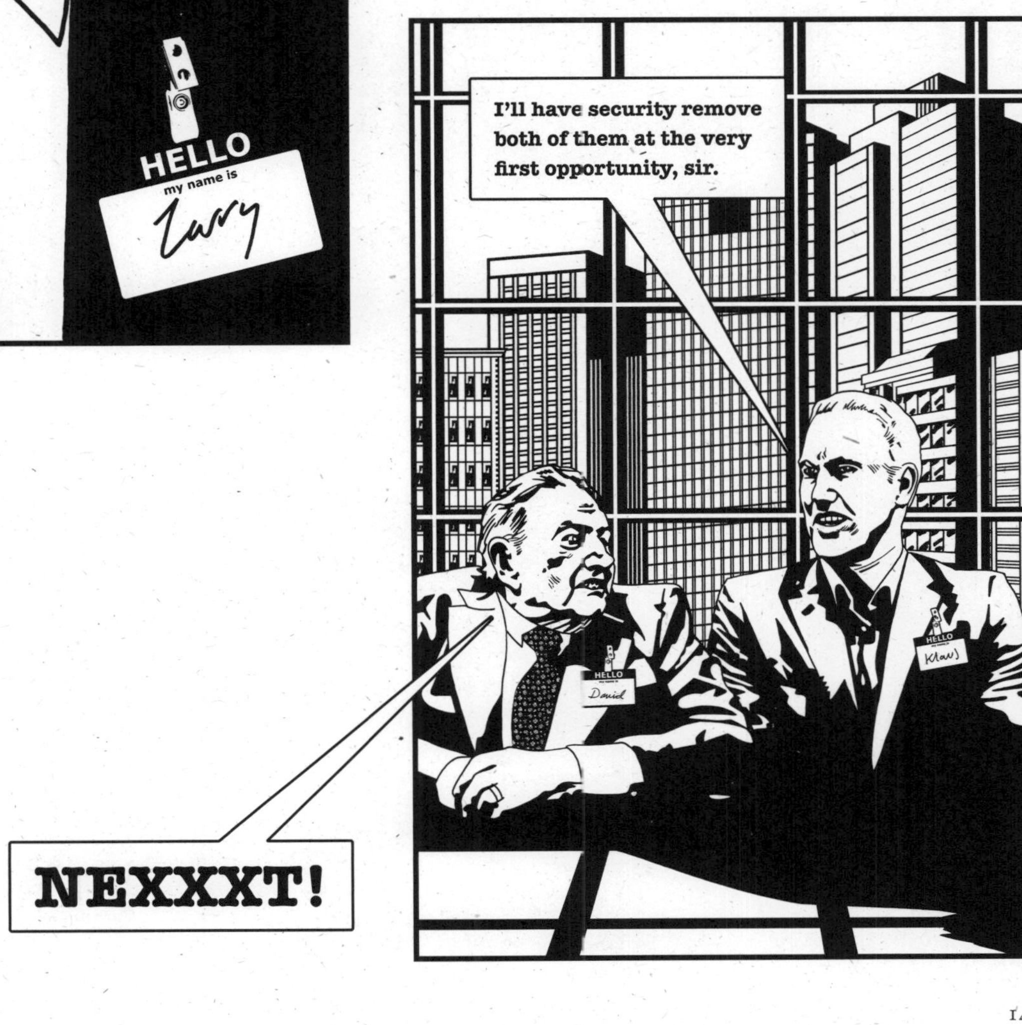
I'll have security remove both of them at the very first opportunity, sir.
NEXXXT!

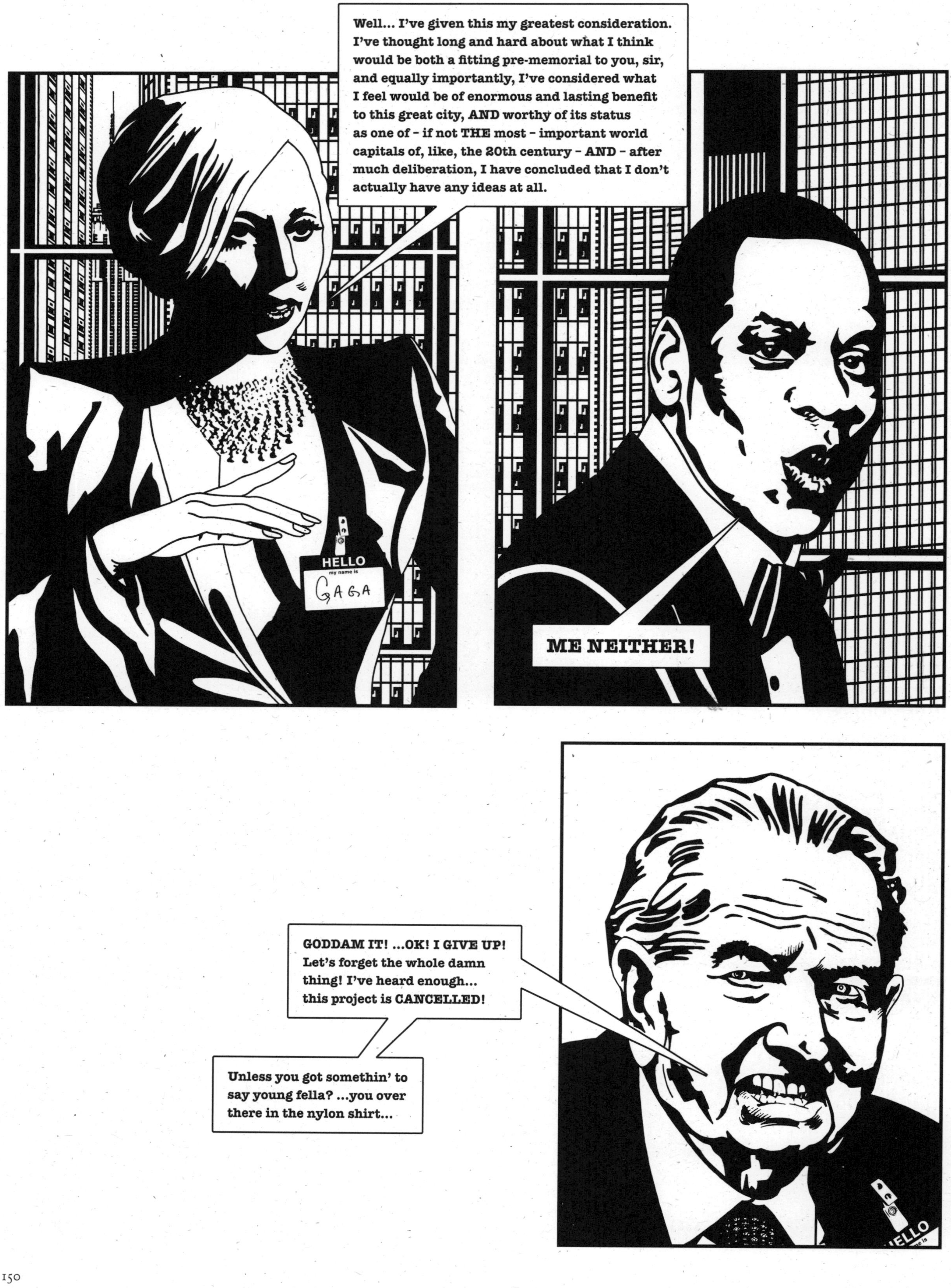
Well... I've given this my greatest consideration. I've thought long and hard about what I think would be both a fitting pre-memorial to you, sir, and equally importantly, I've considered what I feel would be of enormous and lasting benefit to this great city, AND worthy of its status as one of - if not THE most - important world capitals of, like, the 20th century - AND - after much deliberation, I have concluded that I don't actually have any ideas at all.
HELLO
my name is
GAGA
ME NEITHER!
GODDAM IT! ...OK! I GIVE UP! Let's forget the whole damn thing! I've heard enough... this project is CANCELLED!
Unless you got somethin' to say young fella? ...you over there in the nylon shirt...

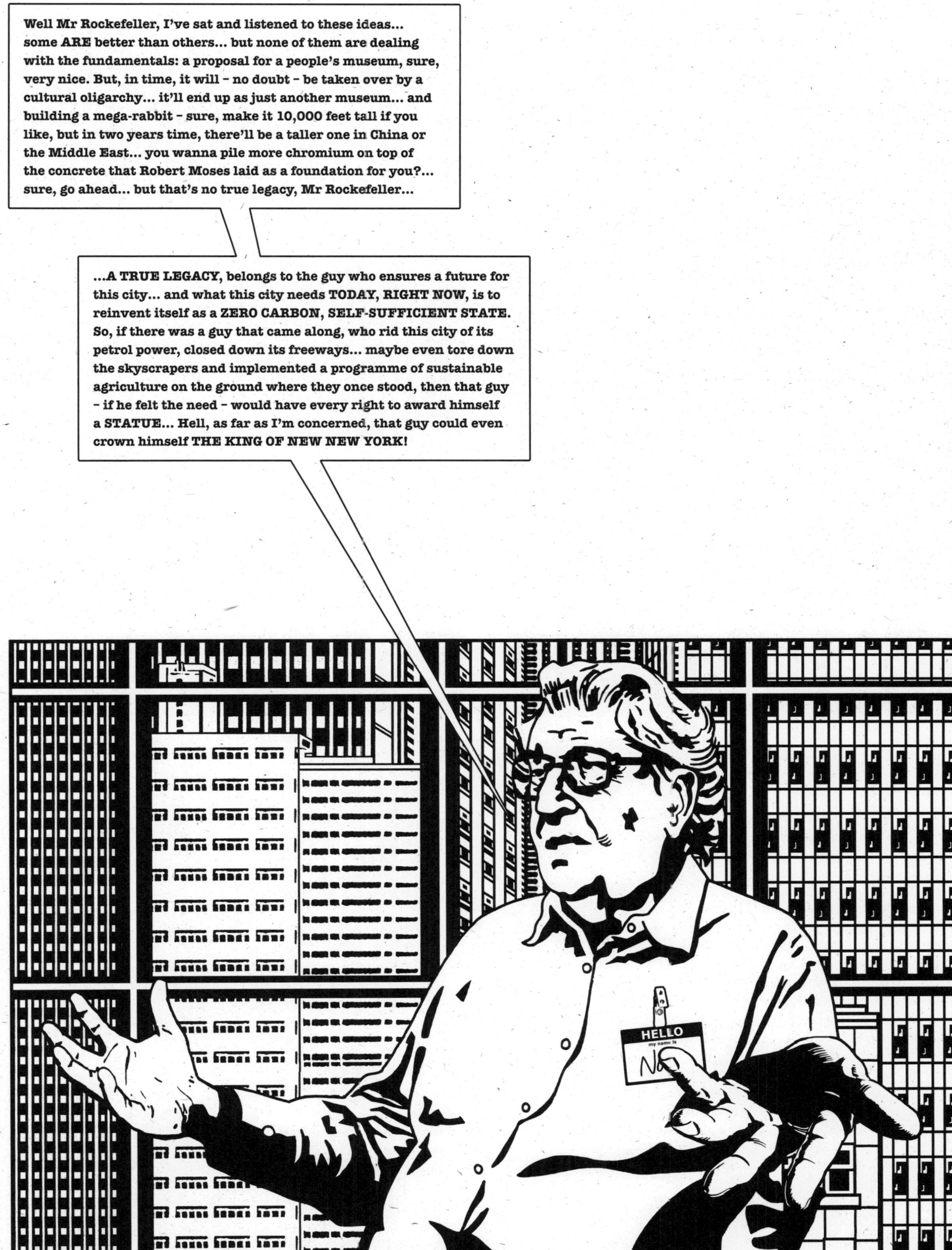
Well Mr Rockefeller, I've sat and listened to these ideas... some ARE better than others... but none of them are dealing with the fundamentals: a proposal for a people's museum, sure, very nice. But, in time, it will - no doubt - be taken over by a cultural oligarchy... it'll end up as just another museum... and building a mega-rabbit - sure, make it 10,000 feet tall if you like, but in two years time, there'll be a taller one in China or the Middle East... you wanna pile more chromium on top of the concrete that Robert Moses laid as a foundation for you?... sure, go ahead... but that's no true legacy, Mr Rockefeller...
...A TRUE LEGACY, belongs to the guy who ensures a future for this city... and what this city needs TODAY, RIGHT NOW, is to reinvent itself as a ZERO CARBON, SELF-SUFFICIENT STATE. So, if there was a guy that came along, who rid this city of its petrol power, closed down its freeways... maybe even tore down the skyscrapers and implemented a programme of sustainable agriculture on the ground where they once stood, then that guy - if he felt the need - would have every right to award himself a STATUE... Hell, as far as I'm concerned, that guy could even crown himself THE KING OF NEW NEW YORK!
HELLO
my name is

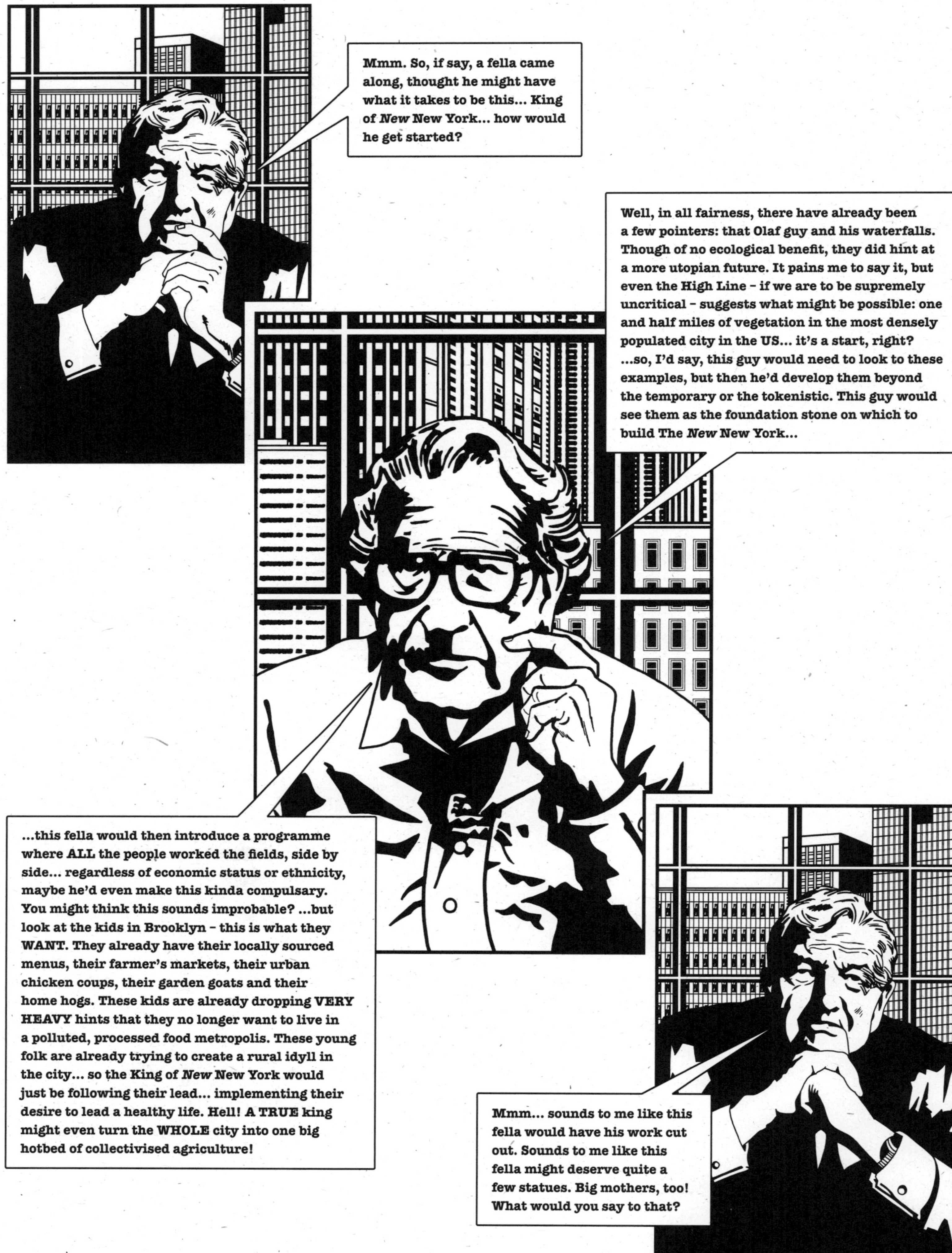
Mmm. So, if say, a fella came along, thought he might have what it takes to be this... King of *New* New York... how would he get started?
Well, in all fairness, there have already been a few pointers: that Olaf guy and his waterfalls. Though of no ecological benefit, they did hint at a more utopian future. It pains me to say it, but even the High Line – if we are to be supremely uncritical – suggests what might be possible: one and half miles of vegetation in the most densely populated city in the US... it's a start, right? ...so, I'd say, this guy would need to look to these examples, but then he'd develop them beyond the temporary or the tokenistic. This guy would see them as the foundation stone on which to build The *New* New York...
...this fella would then introduce a programme where ALL the people worked the fields, side by side... regardless of economic status or ethnicity, maybe he'd even make this kinda compulsary. You might think this sounds improbable? ...but look at the kids in Brooklyn – this is what they WANT. They already have their locally sourced menus, their farmer's markets, their urban chicken coups, their garden goats and their home hogs. These kids are already dropping VERY HEAVY hints that they no longer want to live in a polluted, processed food metropolis. These young folk are already trying to create a rural idyll in the city... so the King of *New* New York would just be following their lead... implementing their desire to lead a healthy life. Hell! A TRUE king might even turn the WHOLE city into one big hotbed of collectivised agriculture!
Mmm... sounds to me like this fella would have his work cut out. Sounds to me like this fella might deserve quite a few statues. Big mothers, too! What would you say to that?

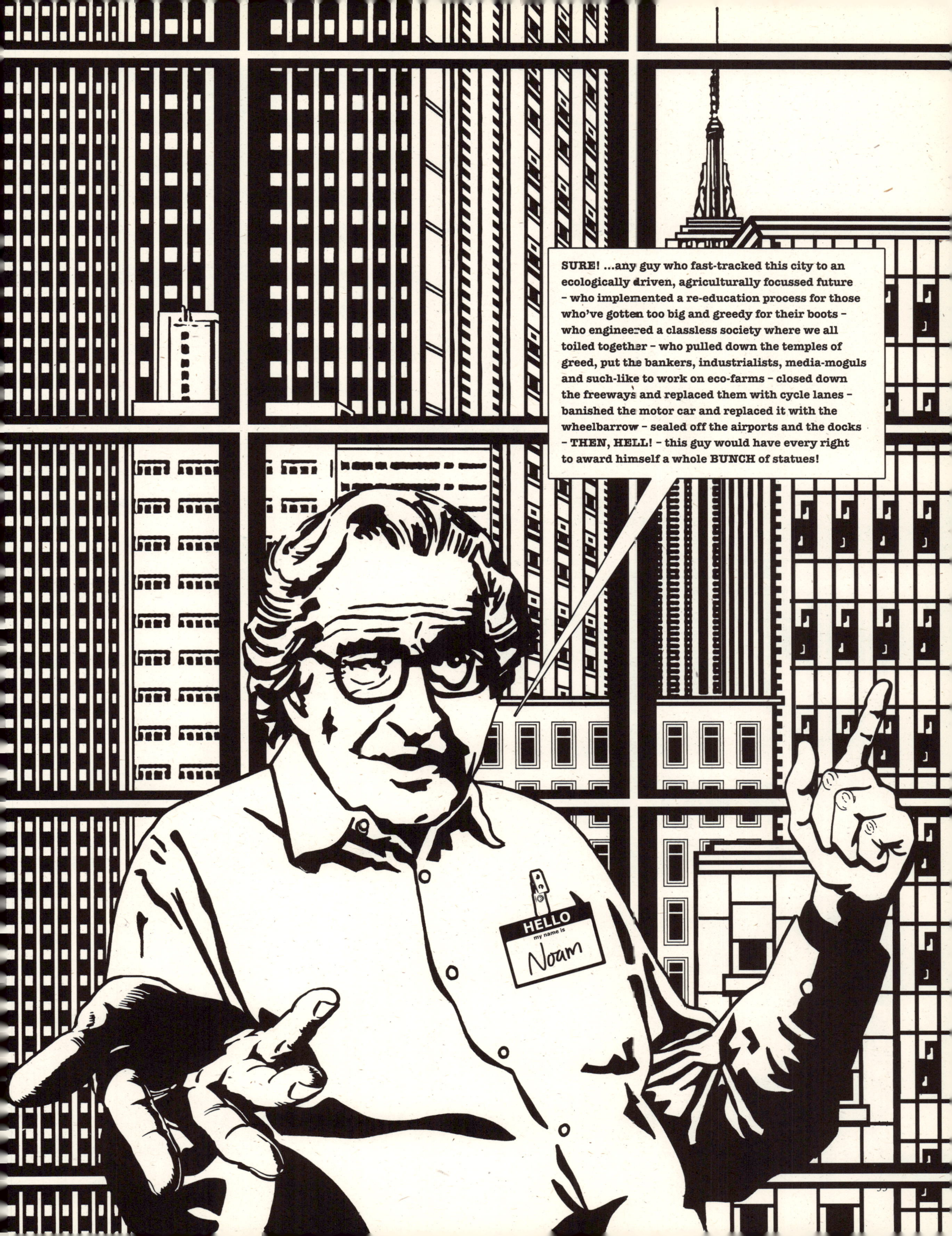
SURE! ...any guy who fast-tracked this city to an ecologically driven, agriculturally focussed future – who implemented a re-education process for those who've gotten too big and greedy for their boots – who engineered a classless society where we all toiled together – who pulled down the temples of greed, put the bankers, industrialists, media-moguls and such-like to work on eco-farms – closed down the freeways and replaced them with cycle lanes – banished the motor car and replaced it with the wheelbarrow – sealed off the airports and the docks – THEN, HELL! – this guy would have every right to award himself a whole BUNCH of statues!
HELLO
my name is
Noam

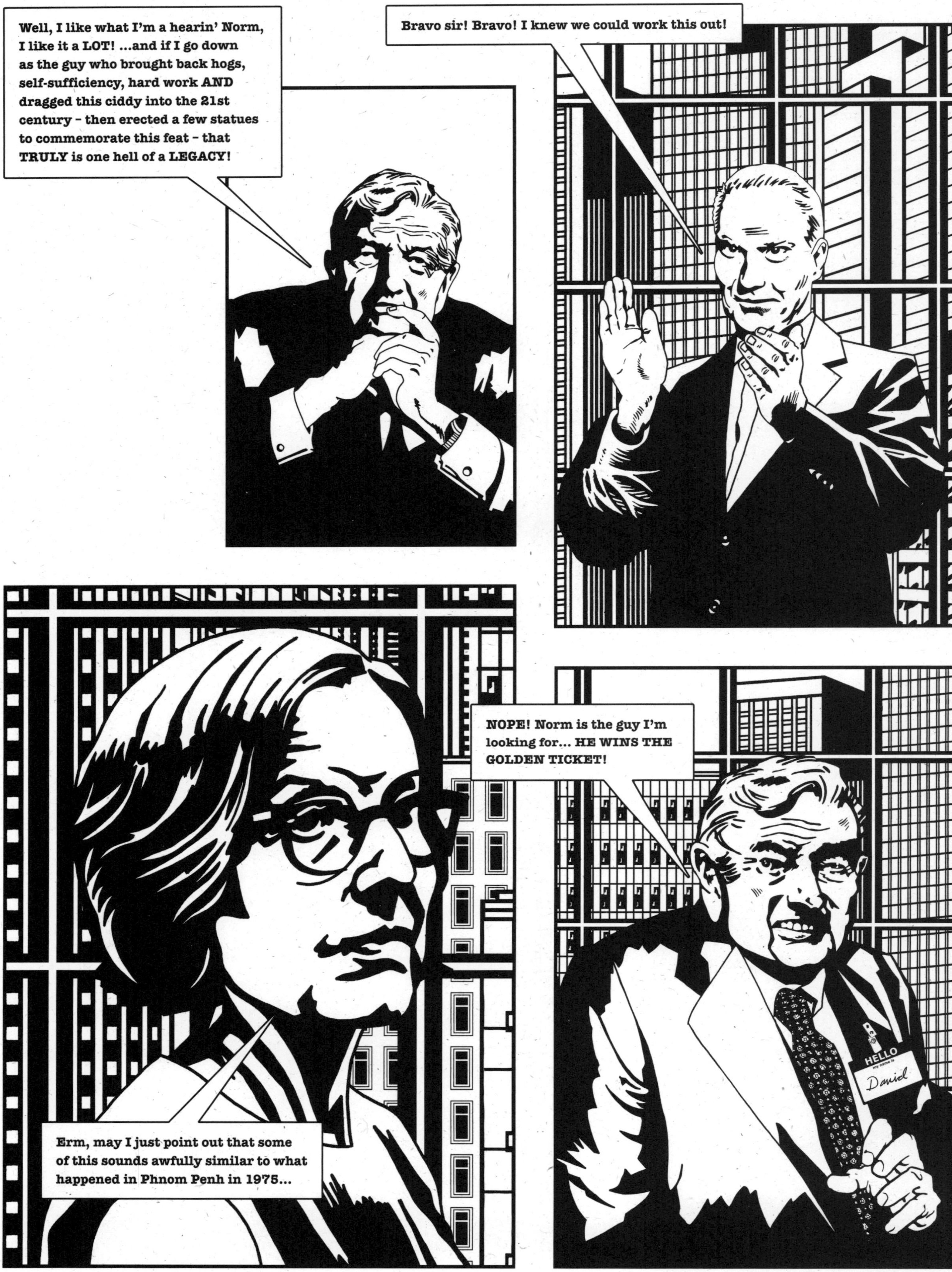
Well, I like what I'm a hearin' Norm, I like it a LOT! ...and if I go down as the guy who brought back hogs, self-sufficiency, hard work AND dragged this ciddy into the 21st century – then erected a few statues to commemorate this feat – that TRULY is one hell of a LEGACY!
Bravo sir! Bravo! I knew we could work this out!
Erm, may I just point out that some of this sounds awfully similar to what happened in Phnom Penh in 1975...
NOPE! Norm is the guy I'm looking for... HE WINS THE GOLDEN TICKET!
HELLO
David

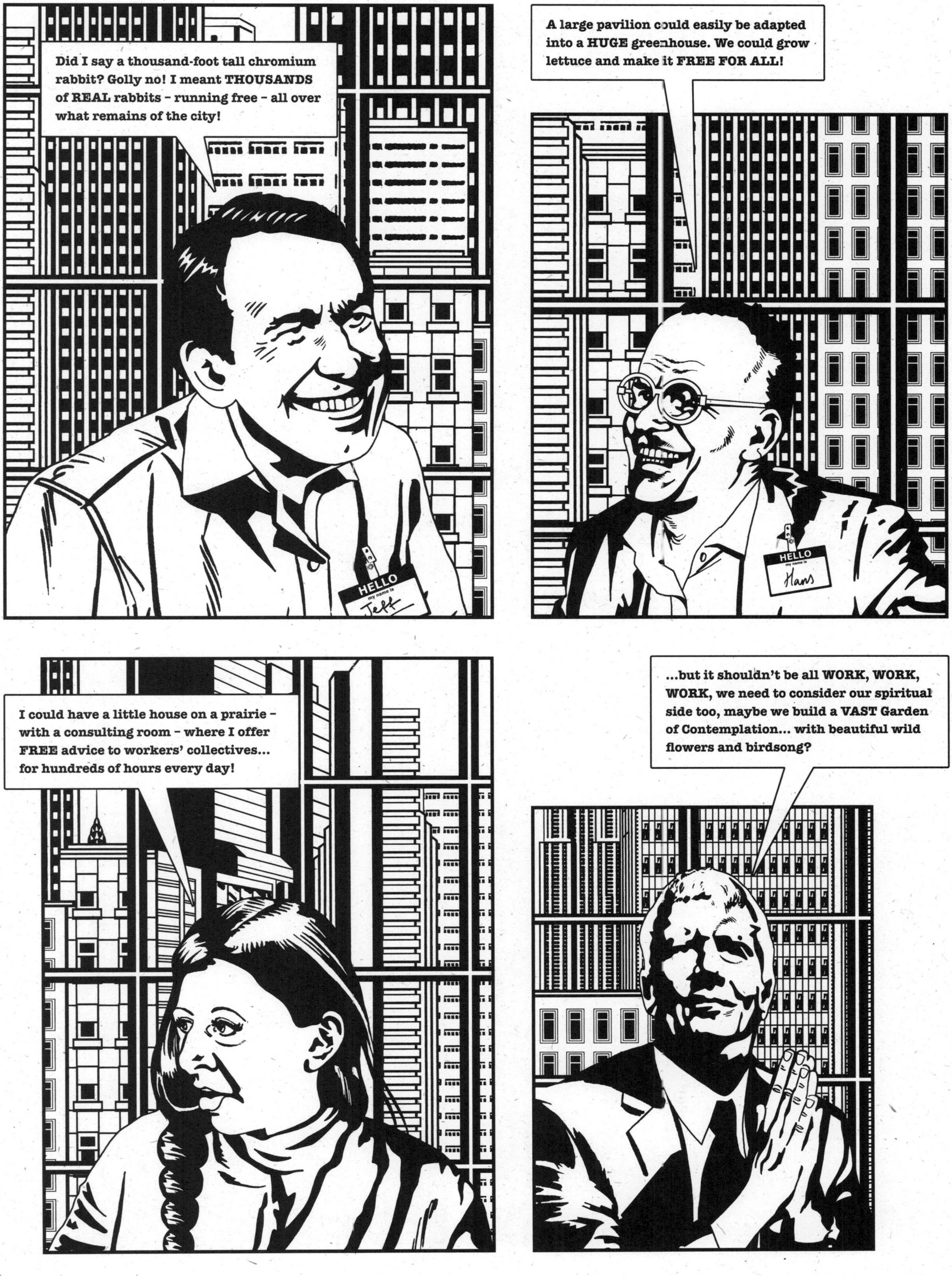
Did I say a thousand-foot tall chromium rabbit? Golly no! I meant THOUSANDS of REAL rabbits – running free – all over what remains of the city!
HELLO
Jeff
A large pavilion could easily be adapted into a HUGE greenhouse. We could grow lettuce and make it FREE FOR ALL!
HELLO
Hans
I could have a little house on a prairie – with a consulting room – where I offer FREE advice to workers' collectives... for hundreds of hours every day!
...but it shouldn't be all WORK, WORK, WORK, we need to consider our spiritual side too, maybe we build a VAST Garden of Contemplation... with beautiful wild flowers and birdsong?

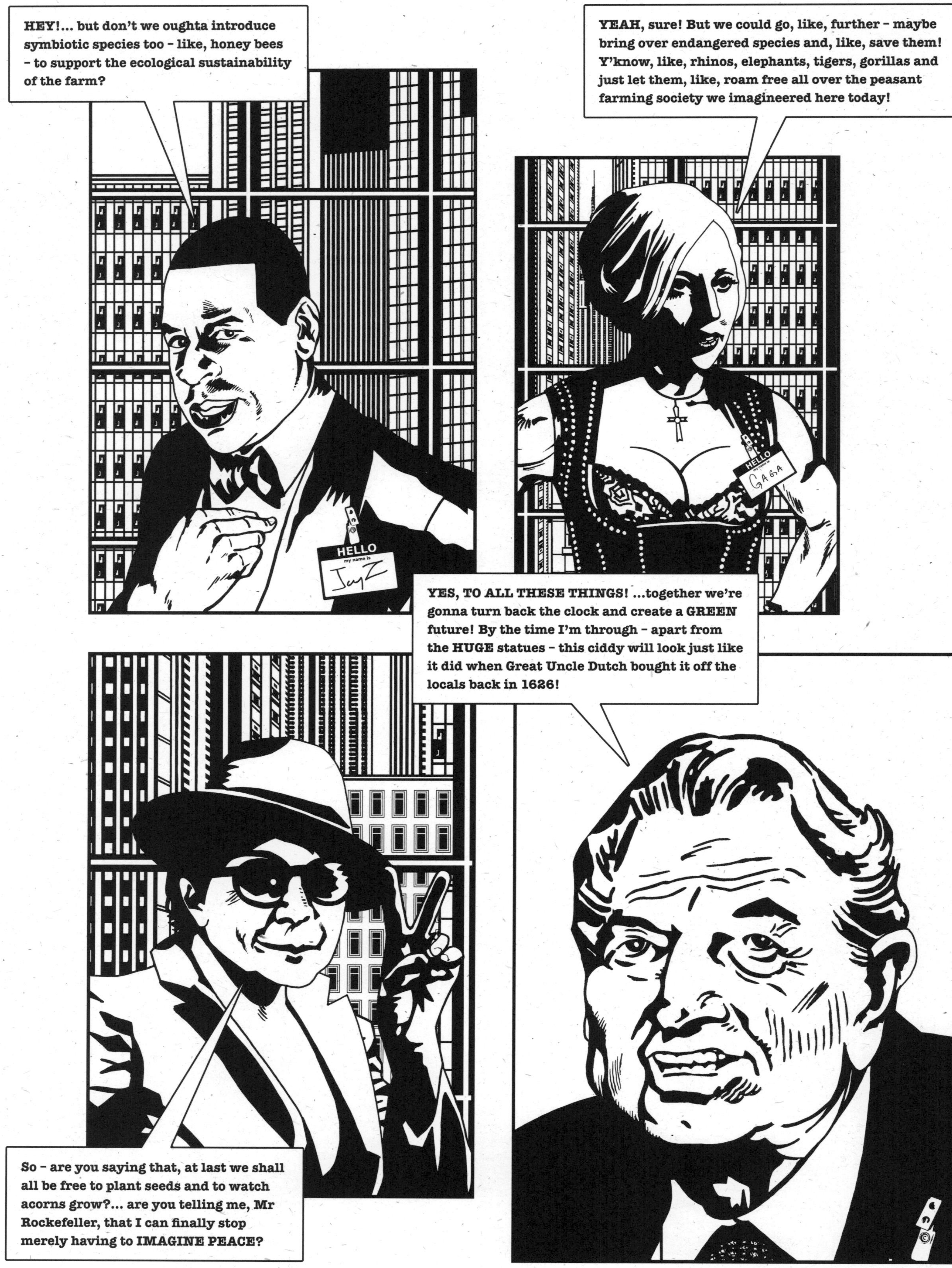
HEY!... but don't we oughta introduce symbiotic species too – like, honey bees – to support the ecological sustainability of the farm?
HELLO my name is JayZ
YEAH, sure! But we could go, like, further – maybe bring over endangered species and, like, save them! Y'know, like, rhinos, elephants, tigers, gorillas and just let them, like, roam free all over the peasant farming society we imagineered here today!
HELLO GAGA
YES, TO ALL THESE THINGS! ...together we're gonna turn back the clock and create a GREEN future! By the time I'm through – apart from the HUGE statues – this ciddy will look just like it did when Great Uncle Dutch bought it off the locals back in 1626!
So – are you saying that, at last we shall all be free to plant seeds and to watch acorns grow?... are you telling me, Mr Rockefeller, that I can finally stop merely having to IMAGINE PEACE?

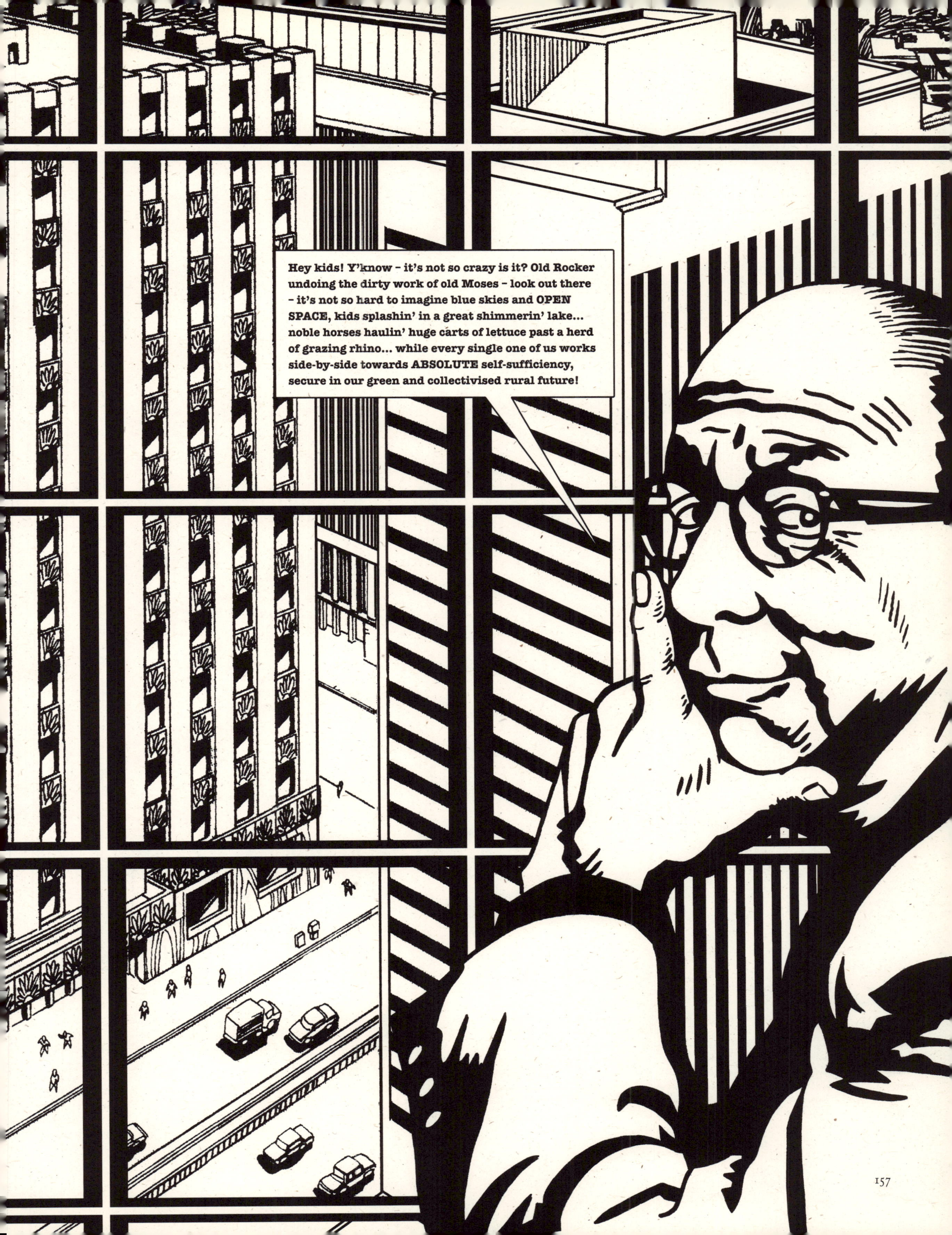
Hey kids! Y'know – it's not so crazy is it? Old Rocker undoing the dirty work of old Moses – look out there – it's not so hard to imagine blue skies and OPEN SPACE, kids splashin' in a great shimmerin' lake... noble horses haulin' huge carts of lettuce past a herd of grazing rhino... while every single one of us works side-by-side towards ABSOLUTE self-sufficiency, secure in our green and collectivised rural future!

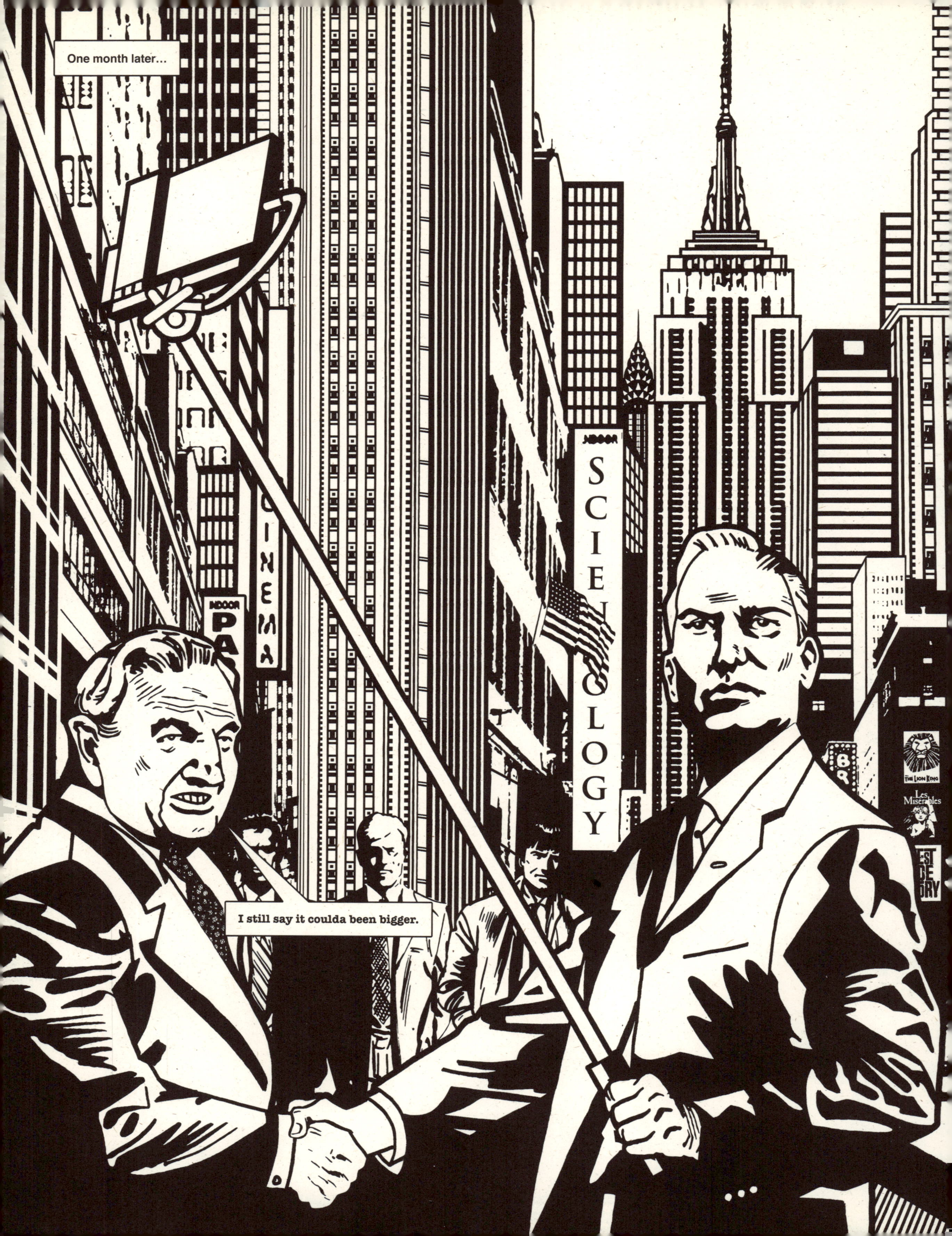
One month later...
INDOOR
CINEMA
SCIENTOLOGY
THE LION KING
Les Misérables
I still say it coulda been bigger.

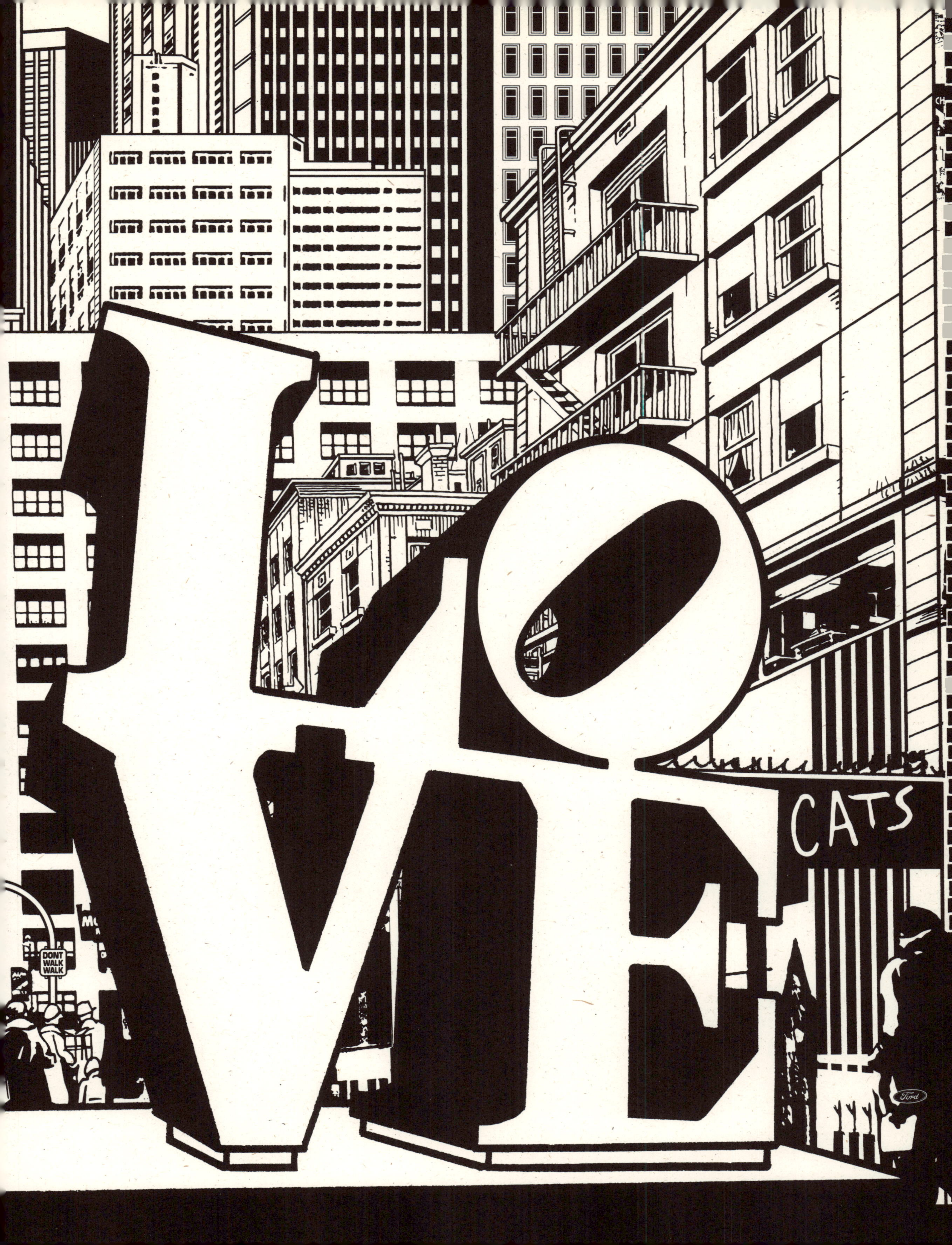
LOVE
CATS
DONT
WALK
WALK

THE END

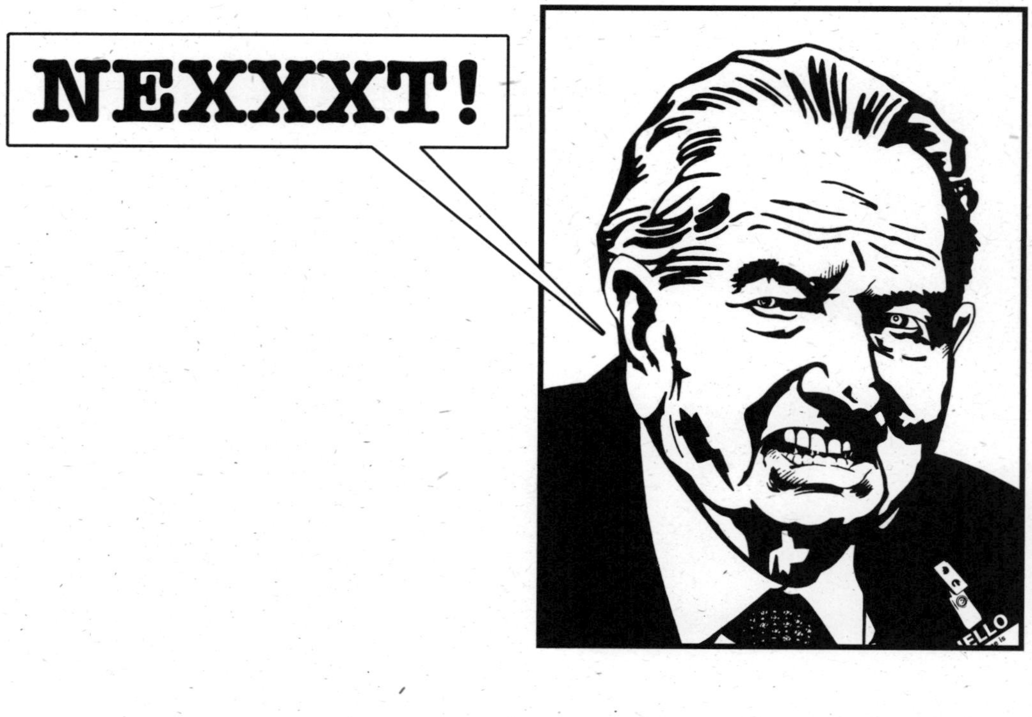

The Sculpture Park is dedicated to helping people improve their mental health and well-being; our purpose is to make a real and lasting difference to everyone we support.

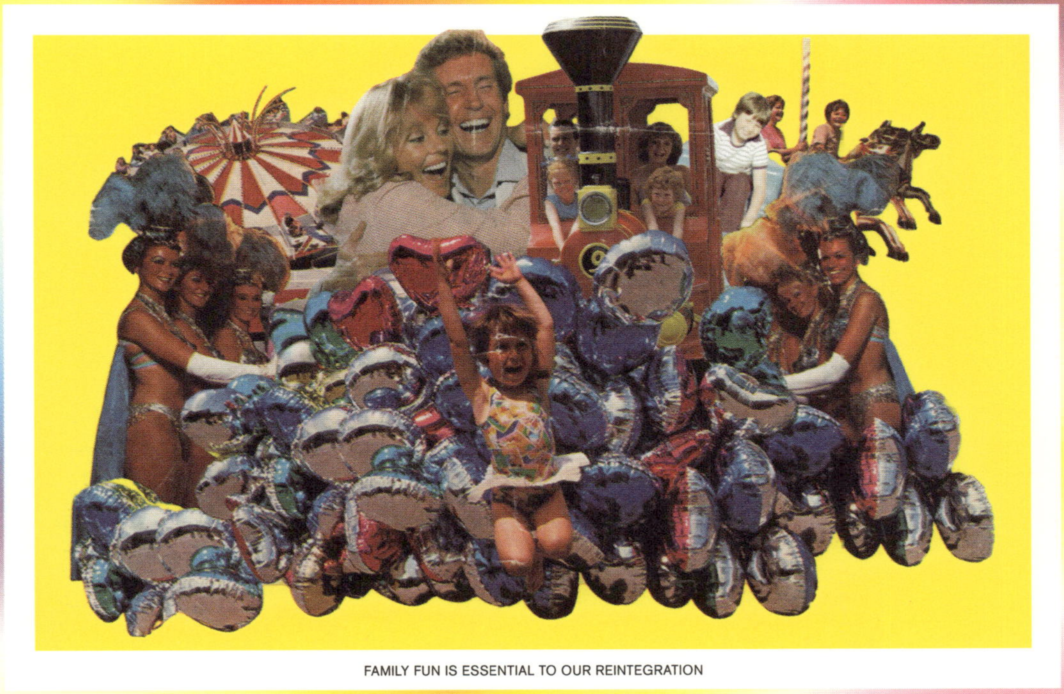

Postcards from The Sculpture Park, Offset litho prints, Each: 14 × 9 cm, 2016

Since our first site opened near Lucerne, Switzerland in 1952, The Sculpture Park has gone on to establish itself in twenty-three countries, across five continents, now treating over 100,000 people worldwide every year.

The Sculpture Park is a world leader in the provision of behavioural care.

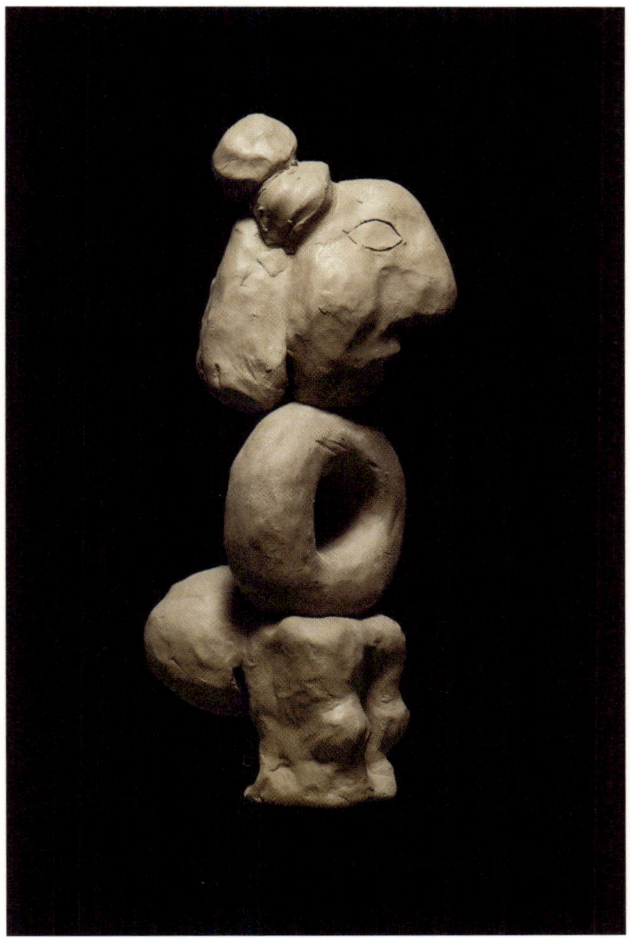

WORK IS CENTRAL TO OUR RECOVERY

We understand that in order for people to achieve high quality clinical and behavioural outcomes they need individually crafted programmes, suiting their specific needs.

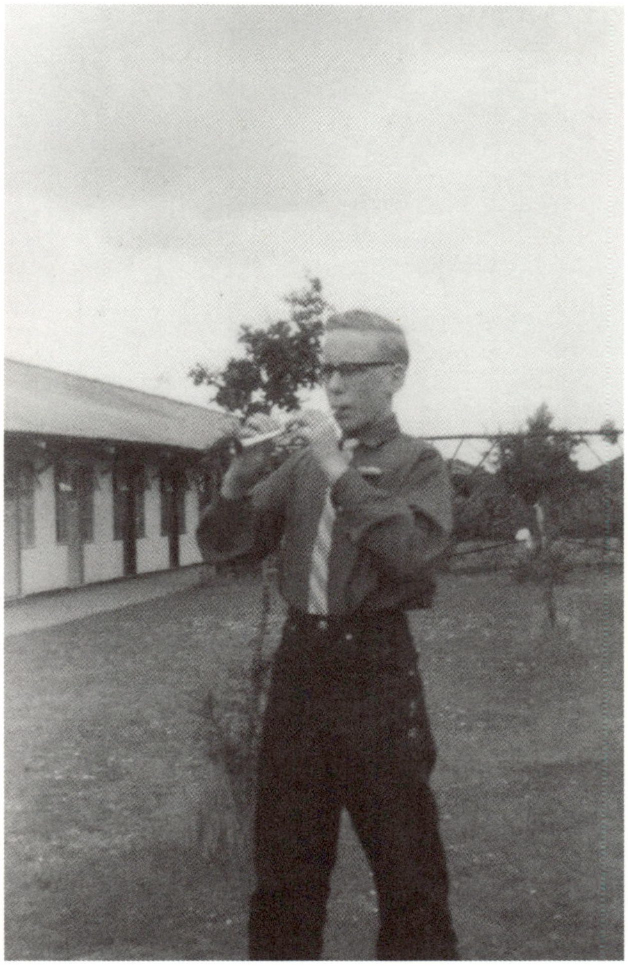

PARTICIPATION IN ALL FORMS OF SELF-EXPRESSION IS ENCOURAGED

The Sculpture Park has established an unrivalled reputation for delivering a real and lasting difference to its service users.

New Values: An International Public Art[1] for the Future

by Andrew Hunt

'Everything that has ever been called folk art has always reflected domination.'[2] – Theodor Adorno

Scott King *Public Art* was developed over a two-year period between early 2014 and 2016. Aside from compiling King's works on the subject of public sculpture and the connected themes of architecture and new galleries, this book was informed by two moments in local UK history, namely the shift between the New Labour and Conservative governments' effects on culture and the visual arts. King's work has been actively examining art in the public realm for some time, and by presenting his full spectrum of projects that analyse shifts in its purpose, we aim to broaden a discussion to an international level, so as to ask questions about what might inform the production of large-scale artworks and galleries in the future.

If it's true that we're at the end of 'public sculpture' in the UK as we've know it since the mid-1990s – i.e. the construction of large totemic artworks as a focus for the regeneration of post-industrial areas and a hub for community engagement, transformation and processes of social healing – then this book attempts to imagine a range of critical and satirical alternatives. King's proposals exist as direct graphic devises, and their aim isn't so much to be realised, but held as fanciful ideas. Like Claes Oldenburg's Pop drawings, or Conceptual Art's ability to propose impossible scenarios, King's exaggerated schemes present an unattainable yet imaginative transition towards a redeemed way of working under current ideological circumstances.

The current political position in the UK in the late 2010s reflects what might be called a 'purer form of neo-liberalism'. As is well known, after 2008, governments in the EU didn't act to rectify the failures of the financial sector, instead they enforced austerity measures on the public sector, and this has had huge consequences for the support of publicly funded arts organisations, which in turn has affected what constitutes public sculpture, especially in the UK. The large monuments constructed in the late 1990s and 2000s have disappeared leaving in their wake new forms of uncritical socially-engaged practices, low-level temporary developments and community engagement for straightened times.

In the book *Cultural Capital* (2014), the historian Robert Hewison describes the rise of funding for culture during the late 1990s and 2000s as part of New Labour's mission to transform economically decimated areas of the UK.[3] Claire Bishop's condemnation of capitalist forces in the commissioning of this public sculpture and buildings criticised the way in which Tony Blair's government saw culture, and increasingly contemporary visual art, as a cheap way of making visible a sense of 'care', a synthetic veneer of social engagement in 'hard-to-reach', disadvantaged locations. As Bishop made clear in her 2012 book *Artificial Hells: Participatory Art and the Politics of Spectatorship*, Blair viewed culture as a cost-effective way of creating the impression of social cohesion, while covering up policies that were actually undermining it. In Hewison's view, the subsequent coalition government's austerity measures between 2010 and 2015 represented a new 'age of lead', in which cuts to the public sector led to a spiralling destruction to forms of creativity.

This is a period that is familiar to me personally because I ran a small publicly funded regional gallery between 2008 and 2014 and was a close witness to the increasingly alarming changes in public subsidy, a situation that many arts professionals will be familiar with.[4] Reflecting on this period in the wake of the Conservative government's full-blown rise to power in the summer of 2015 has been fascinating, especially within the entwined, circular issues contained in King's work, which alongside public sculpture, contains an analysis of the nature of art made for 'the public' in all its forms.

Since 2010, alongside a reduction of permanent public sculpture, we have seen a dramatic shift away from large-scale capital projects, by which I mean buildings for new arts venues. The period between the 1990s and 2011 that saw Tate Modern, Baltic, Ikon, mima (Middlesbrough Institute of Modern Art), Nottingham Contemporary, the New Art Gallery Walsall, Firstsite and Turner Contemporary built, has been replaced by small grants by ACE to organisations to improve existing facilities. The focus away from new buildings isn't necessary a bad thing. New public art galleries and sculpture were effects not only of New Labour's policy towards regeneration and the 'creative industries', but also, if we take a long view, an overcompensation by the British art establishment for the perceived lack of opportunities for artists in the UK in the 1980s, when the heart of the commercial visual art industry was in New York and Cologne.

Of course, this was evident in the simultaneous rise of the yBa movement, where media-friendly late Conceptual Art became window dressing for property in the British capital. Historically, gambling through the National Lottery in the early 1990s help fund new buildings, and it's in this recent historical moment in which we can begin to see the problems that eventually led to the situation in which artists have been priced out of London. It's no coincidence that the property developer Baron Palumbo, for instance, who chaired the Arts Council of Great Britain during this time, was instrumental in making the decision that Lottery money should fund buildings rather than artists. Palumbo is an art collector, an architecture connoisseur, a property collector, and a life peer.

With this in mind, I'd like to discuss a line that runs through the interconnected political, cultural and historical tropes of King's proposals for public sculpture and buildings, which were generated during the period of this book's production. If King's examination of monuments previously dwelt on Antony Gormley's *Angel of the North* (1998) and Anish Kapoor's *ArcelorMittal Orbit* (2012),[5] as well as historical structures such as Blackpool Tower and Watkin's Folly in Wembley (which aimed to become London's answer to the Eiffel Tower), then what is remarkable is his examination of recent low-level town planning. This shift in urban regeneration has a preoccupation with green cities and new parks, exemplified in the High Line in New York and the proposed Garden Bridge for the Thames in London, due for completion in 2017.

In his unrealised artwork *Nice Cities (Flower Solutions to World Problems)* and *Infinite Monument* (2014), for example, King envisages parks and monuments taken to their logical extreme, in the same manner as the radical architectural firm Superstudio, whose research around the 'architecture of the monument' and 'technomorphic architecture' led to their *Continuous Monument* (1969), a work that proposed the entire planet be covered in a single endless black and white gridded monument. If Superstudio's penchant for envisioning immense, aspirational mega-structures is a trait visible in the early work of architects such as Zaha Hadid, Rem Koolhaas and Rafael Viñoly (Viñoly designed the ill-conceived building for Colchester's Firstsite) – who took the style of Superstudio to create exactly what Superstudio stood against: monumental architecture designed to glorify its owners – then King translates this into an ever-expanding arrangement of 'natural' low-level foliage in *Nice Cities*. This is a design that's as much a futuristic corporate vision of the English Garden City movement, as it is a reference to crummy B-Movies, via its arbitrary evocation of the uncontrollable, ever-expanding amorphous substance in *The Blob*, the 1958 horror/science-fiction flick directed by Irvin Yeaworth. King's idea places alien shrubs at the locations of high-profile world disasters, which succeed in encroaching on the planet to such a degree that they eventually cover its entire surface. Superstudio's projects contain a disregarded critical aspect in the way they staged their projects in public spaces, such as the radio broadcast for *12 Ideal Cities*, which was transmitted to fixed radio receivers during their Mana Art Gallery exhibition in Rome in 1971. Similarly, King's ever-expanding mirrored *Infinite Monument*, which is situated at an imagined site of the Tower of Babel in Mesopotamia – a region currently controlled by ISIS – is so large it reaches outside the earth's atmosphere, and presents a 'worst-case scenario' that comments on incongruous architecture and public art's false role as social healer.

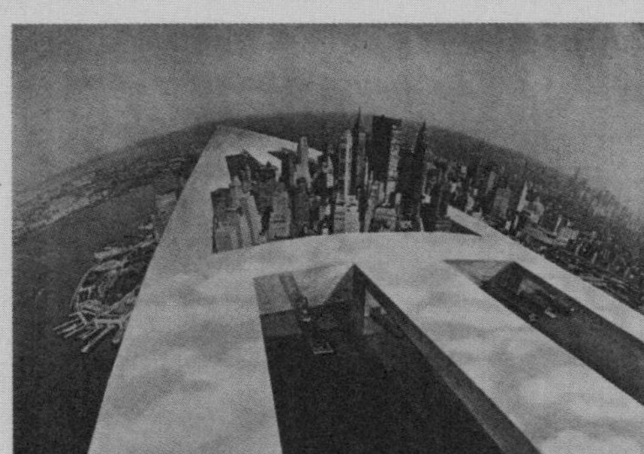

Superstudio, *Continuous Monument: An Architectural Model for Total Urbanization*, 1969

In a more literal manner, King's *A Balloon for Britain* (2012) describes an attempt to 'make pretty' desolate post-industrial areas in the UK by floating large party balloons over each site. These works sit in the Pop tradition of the fantastic, affirmative and excessively glossy within a divisive politics of regeneration by illustrating an idea to improve each of Britain's ten poorest towns, including Caerphilly, Dundee, Hull, Knowsley, Middlesbrough, Nottingham and Sunderland. Each coloured balloon hangs over a rough, pixelated Xerox-style landscape reduced to a trace of its already deprived self – Hull becomes banal satellite nothingness, Sunderland a 'nowhere' destination – that's brightened by the stark treatment of corporate advertising. Public art becomes a hollow, plastic recovery reflecting pop environment gentrification. Drawings and sketches for monuments that refer to the innocuous attempts of the British Government to resolve socio-economic problems though art, simultaneously hold a down-at-heel British Pop realism, more indicative of an overcast Yorkshire sky rather than Californian sunshine.

***

If the split-narrative of Owen Hatherley's introduction to this book examines the history of public art in the UK and its current ideological predicament, then I'd like to suggest King provides a similar series of semi-fantastic alternatives to the dominant focus on a new conservative accent on the utility of art. Again, this is a utility that began with the concept of public art as an economic driver in poor locations (represented in works by Gormley and Kapoor) and has morphed into an art whose pure use comes in an uncritical form of socially engaged architecture. In the US, curators such as Nato Thompson have addressed a prevailing artistic dilemma in which the language of folk protest, activism, subcultures, and society have mingled with the creative industries, to produce a situation in which traditional alternatives have been recuperated. In Thompson's view, this isn't a moment of defeat. Instead it's a 'fairly dismal moment' of 'total and utter co-optation'[6] that ultimately produces an optimistic situation in which we can begin to identify destructive power relationships, so as to open gaps that might forge real change. For me, a similar new approach within the institutions of public art (in all of its guises from public sculpture, socially-engaged practice and public galleries) is needed, in which critically independent activities acknowledge the pressures currently placed on artists and curators.

In a previous essay titled 'Public Art Attack' in the British magazine *Art Monthly* (Issue 380, October 2014), I referred to the complex relationship between public art, property and social cleansing with reference to Mike Nelson's failed Heygate Estate project in London's Elephant and Castle, and a wider art-historical context connected to Gordon Matta-Clark's building cuts of the early 1970s and Mike Kelley's *Mobile Homestead* from 2013. It's worth repeating some of the mains points of this text. Matta-Clark's 'anarchitecture' called for a process of de-structuring by focusing on existing edifices in neglected areas, while Kelley's full-scale replica of the 1950s Westland suburban Detroit home he grew up in was produced and relocated to the city centre in a provocative reversal of the 'white flight' that followed the uprisings known as the 12th Street riot in 1967. Kelley's work was a challenge to a city decimated by economic change, and it was his view that 'one always has to hide one's true desires and beliefs behind a facade of socially acceptable lies' to produce a confrontational work. In my view, Nelson's troubled project, which aimed to construct a pyramid from the debris of a demolished housing estate so as to produce a temporary monument that would act as a centre for protest, echoed these historical examples within the frame of a contemporary British political context of gentrification and resettlement in London, and had much in common with King's book *Anish and Antony Take Afghanistan* (2014), which is reprinted in full in this publication.

The premise of King's satirical book is that Kapoor and Gormley ('two giants of British public art') might solve the financial and political problems of Afghanistan by invading the country and erecting massive new sculptures. Apart from ridiculing the UK sculptural elite's unquenchable hankering for ever-larger monuments under the guise of connecting with the communities of specific locales, such as Gormley's *Angel* and Kapoor's *Tees Valley Giants* (2008), King's imagined re-invasion of Afghanistan in 2014 to solve the damage done by NATO forces in the country since 2001, through 'art' rather than 'war', became a metaphor for the history of change in the North East of England from the early 1980s to the present day. UN think-tank language is deployed in this cartoon to construct a resolution for a decimated world region, and culture is shown as a parallel 'Band-Aid solution' to cover up the crimes of impoverishment enacted by Margaret Thatcher on the communities in the UK through the destruction of industry and the subsequent commissioning of spectacularly tall 'cod-avant-garde artworks'.

King's project, which runs with issues of power, taste and local pride connected to national ambition, war and cultural imperialism, initially took place as an exhibition called 'Totem Motif' at Wolfgang Tillmans' gallery Between Bridges in Berlin in May and June 2014 (the invitation card pictures two young women staring up in wonder at a tall modernist sculpture by Henry Moore, an image that is reproduced on page two of this publication) and was published as a small book by JRP-Ringier during the same year. It was subsequently shown in London during November and December 2015 at Herald Street, with its opening accidentally coinciding with the Paris attacks in November.

The style of this boys-own *Victor*-style 'comic' pervades subsequent works connected to urban renewal and power. *I Dream of Dalstonia* (2016), for example, presents ex-Tory minister William Hague's recruitment of an aggressive 'hipster militia', which invades Middlesbrough on Penny Farthings to force local communities to construct gourmet cafés, pop-up craft beer stalls, fixed-wheel bicycle emporiums, and impose mandatory activities such as tending vegetable gardens.

In this world, Greggs, Wetherspoons and JD Sports are demolished and banned for their unhealthy influence on local communities. This theatrical camping-up of public art, taste and issues of class in end-game capitalism via the self-conscious and highly debunked style of a Situationist cartoon is a device that admits its own unfeasibility by reference to the failure of the Situationist International in the early 1970s and the defeat of the British left in the mid-1980s. Yet King's energetic fabrication allows us to examine the lasting effects of public art during a period in which public money is disappearing to suggest a productive way forward, simply through his transparent concept of 'de-regeneration', which allows for an emotive deconstruction of regeneration and cultural duplicity.

GARDENS

'And then all wars ended / Arms of every kind were outlawed and the masses gladly contributed them to giant foundries in which they were melted down and the metal poured back into the earth / The Pentagon was turned on its side and painted purple, yellow & green / All boundaries were dissolved / The slaughter of animals was forbidden / The whole of lower Manhattan became a meadow in which unfortunates from the Bowery were allowed to live out their fantasies in the sunshine and were cured / People swam in the sparkling rivers under blue skies streaked only with incense pouring from the new factories / The energy from dismantled nuclear weapons provided free heat and light / World health was restored / An abundance of organic vegetables, fruits and grains was growing wild along the discarded highways / National flags were sewn together into brightly coloured circus tents under which politicians were allowed to perform harmless theatrical games / The concept of work was forgotten.'[7]

The transition from formal sculpture to collaborative architecture can be seen as a generational one that presents the language of mid-twentieth century folk protest robbed of its transformative potential. A counter-culture that initially provided a massive shift in society has been emptied of content and incorporated into privileged lifestyle choices to dovetail with austerity, nostalgia and aspiring small commerce in a synthesis of alternative styles and stoic pragmatism favoured by small-time entrepreneurs. This new transatlantic tendency around fantasy folk-pop appears minus Woody Guthrie's anti-fascism and Morrissey's vegetarianism or his refusal to participate. In the UK, David Cameron has previously spoken of his like for The Smiths, while George Osborne has praised NWA (the LA rap act that have transformed themselves into billionaire tech magnates and Coors Light spokespeople), which is referred to in the opening gambit to *I Dream of Dalstonia*, where the British Prime Minister is pictured DJ-ing in front of a portrait of Margaret Thatcher dressed in a shirt that reads 'Music is the Weapon'.[8]

This culture extends to the new picturesque. In the States, the romantic pastoral view of New York's High Line, the recent creative transformation of an elevated section of a disused New York Central Railroad spur called the West Side Line into an urban garden, is similar in nature to the view of the reinvention of post-industrial architecture in Tate Modern's two-stage development. Spreading out for 1.45 miles above the city, with five million visitors per year and rising, this metro-garden knits past, present and future histories of the city, in an attempt to form a new use for a defunct structure. Back in London, The Garden Bridge planned for the Thames, headed by the architect Thomas Heatherwick and the actress Joanna Lumley, sees an extension of this urban-rural phenomenon. Heatherwick and Lumley's pay-to-enter structure in central London points to the transformation of city gardens into new 'utopias' for profit, alongside the commercial makeover of the Southbank Centre nearby.

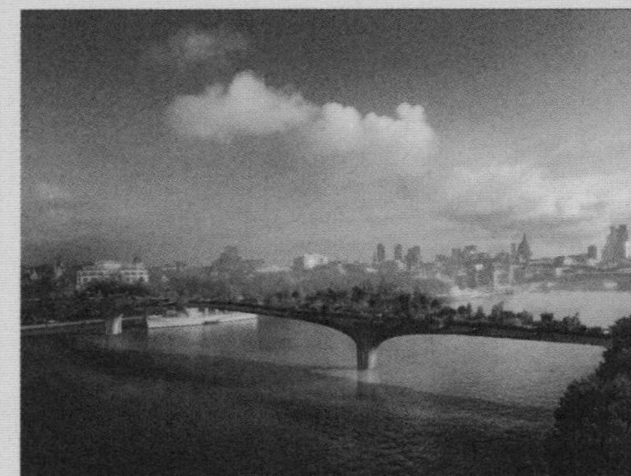

The Garden Bridge.
Courtesy The Garden Bridge Trust

In the US, where terms such as 'urban prairie' designate the desolation of cities such as Detroit, the phrase 'ruin-porn' has been invented to describe a fetish of untouched post-industrial desolation, and buildings such as Detroit's Michigan station are regularly photographed for their twentieth century architectural integrity. In this context, Matta-Clark's 'anarchitecture' and Robert Smithson's concept of entropy take on new meaning within the historical perspective of urban Land Art. Oddly, video games such as *Fallout 4* (2015) show a mid-twentieth century North American landscape populated by fin-tailed cars and a futuristic optimism held in stasis within the parallel reality of a Cold War nuclear attack that actually took place, a situation in which we're free to enjoy the experience of wandering in the devastation of a radioactive American Pop environment. The idea of the post-industrial landscape as urban prairie, and the simultaneous regeneration of cities with gardens, shows a conflation of ideas of freedom, tourism, nostalgia, dystopia and the ever-increasing presence of the market in the public sphere.

Prior to the rise of the urban garden, the British contemporary art group Freee produced a billboard project that was located at the corner of Corporation Street and Alma Street in Sheffield during April 2004. Originally commissioned by Ixia (formerly the Public Art Forum) the work read: 'The economic function of public art is to increase the value of private property'. The simple truth held in this statement is comparable with the subsequent relationship of public art with urban villages alongside civic activism's stylistic roots in 'localism', which claims that small businesses, ethical shopping and community initiatives can stop corporate globalisation. Despite making the lives of some people better, public sculpture and small businesses don't challenge the drive for profit that damages small communities. Instead, one can claim that localism is fixated on an outdated economic model where small firms must play by the same rules as large ones, cutting costs and exploiting workers: combined with public art, this system drives up the cost of property, and therefore becomes a strategy for neo-liberal economics, not an alternative to it.[9]

The related need to create a village in the face of the global, and the increased use of gardens in public art commissions, if taken to the logical extreme of Superstudio's *Continuous Monument* and Marshall McLuhan's 'global village' – an oxymoronic theory in which communication systems develop to such a degree that the world's population becomes closer and physical distance is erased – in King's view, would eventually translate as a monoculture of unified bourgeois-folk colonies across western civilisation.

King's term for this coalescing of gardens, art, museum commissioning – such as Adam Cruzvillegas' 2015 Tate Modern Turbine Hall project *Empty Lot*, which presented a floating floor comprising 240 raised, triangular empty planters intended for seed-bombing by visitors[10] – and regeneration, is 'Mumfordisation'. Based on the pop band Mumford and Sons' fascination with the language of folk-protest, this term, rendered as a dictionary definition, was produced as a warning for the town of Southend-on-Sea during the opening of Focal Point Gallery's new premises in late 2013. The artwork, *Excerpts from A Better Britain, Southend*, which was positioned on a banner that hung from the town's high street railway bridge, read:

'Mumfordised / (see also Mumfordisation): Describing the successful transformation of a once rundown urban area into an inner-city rural idyll. Mumfordisation most commonly begins with a single (non-chain) coffee shop acting as a nucleus, around which other businesses spring up – vintage and cycling shops, real ale pubs, rustic cafes – until the whole area is transformed. A fully successful transformation then becomes known as a Mumford Quarter. The ultimate goal of Mumfordisation is to reconstruct whole cites as a series of interlocking hamlets; and though there are not yet any completely Mumfordised cities as such, there are adjoining areas of London that, as acknowledgement of their commitment to Mumfordisation, are now demanding to be officially rebranded as Stoke Mumford Newington and Hackney Mumford Village.'[11]

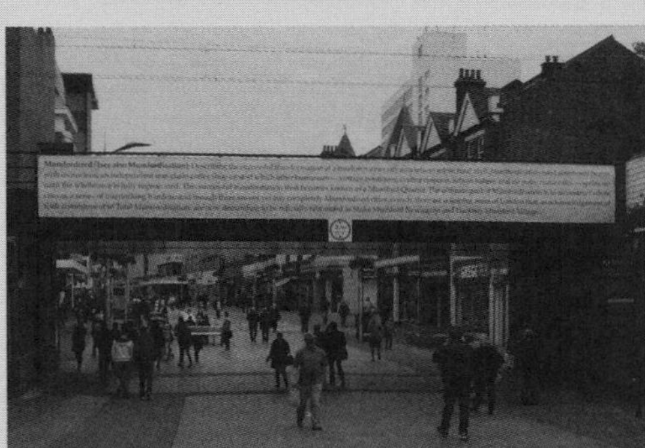

Scott King, *Excerpts from A Better Britain, Southend*, 2013

King's viewpoint on the group was furthered in an unlimited letterpress print that bore the slogan 'Stop! Mumford And Sons'. In response to the question 'what is your opinion of the band?' during a 2013 interview, King answered in a typically candid manner:

'They are shit. They represent everything that is wrong with this country today. They are a bunch of public schoolboys pretending to be hillbillies aren't they? I think that's quite funny, Etonians taking on bluegrass or Woody Guthrie or whatever they imagine they are doing – the sons of investment bankers taking a genre that was explicitly about poverty and making it into a multi-million pound phenomena. This whole country is slowly being Mumfordised. Even places like Margate now have a Mumford Quarter that sells lattes, vintage posters and rustic lunches. Everything presented as "real" and "authentic" – real ale, hand cut chips – gastro pubs stuffed with broken furniture on stripped wooden floors – everything "hand reared" and localised – you can no longer buy mussels, cod, pork or crab in these pubs – only Shetland Isle Mussels, Peterhead Cod, Suffolk Pork and Dorset Crab. There is an overwhelming folksy, middle class, twee faux-local attitude that means many urban areas are rebranding themselves as "villages": people in cities lusting after allotments, going to farmer's markets in their wellies – the Mumfords are the house band for this desire to create the rural idyll in cities. Bring back The Wurzels, I say. The Wurzels were much better than Mumford & Sons.'[12]

Leaving 'Mumfordisation' aside for a moment, it's interesting that the US counter-culture of the 1950s, 1960s and 1970s holds many fantastic references to cities becoming gardens, from the album cover notes of Terry Riley's *A Rainbow in Curved Air* (1969) to the recently-deceased jazz musician Ornette Coleman's album *Science Fiction*, which contains a stunning blast of energy in a track called *The Jungle is a Skyscraper* (1972). If New York's vitality, as King has previously suggested, is held in its ability to act as a 'twentieth century museum',[13] then Charles Baudelaire and Walter Benjamin's idea that the modern city appears as a series of unified 'Wunderhammers' – shop-fronts and advertising in the constantly ever-evolving spectacle – now, somewhat unexpectedly incorporates public art and gardens as other elements of the urban-modern project.

New publications such as *Hippie Modernism: The Struggle for Utopia* (2016) point to an increased analysis of the ideal metropolis, while, in turn, Kim Gordon's 2015 exhibition 'The City is a Garden' at 303 Gallery in New York, commented on the contemporary predilection for new urban 'parks'. Elucidating on the artist's assessment of New York as a gentrification mecca, this latter project showcased Gordon's signature text-focused painting style, which had developed into crumpled sculptural objects placed on the gallery floor. Named after 'condo developments' and the slogans that they use – Gordon's 'hedge sculptures' included titles such as *Bauhaus Inspired Living*, *The Highline*, *Fortress of Glassitude* and *Chelsea Enclave* – they comment on how the city has reached a point of commercial climax. Gordon has said of this recent transformation of the city:

'If you walk through the Lower East Side, you keep bumping into parks and suddenly there are four planters in the middle of the street that weren't there. Mayor Bloomberg brought in the whole beautification of the city and has made it about upping the ante for consumerism, and there are all of these condos. I've never seen so much building going on. The people buying the condos aren't necessarily going to live there – they're out of country-ers. So the hedges are representative of that. Second, they also bring in how art is part of that whole consumerism. At art events, they often use these hedges, and they're instant walls. It almost represents some kind of class. I feel like they could be at MoMA, but I also like that they look like furniture, so it's almost like an indoor sculpture garden.'[14]

Gordon's ideas are taken further in an interview with Lynda Morris's in this book. Using Hannah Arendt's *The Origins of Totalitarianism* – which examines colonialism, the historical search for gold and the use of enforced famine on populations – alongside Mike Davis' research into how museum buildings in LA have displaced Latin American communities and purged them from city centre areas, she points to the duplicitous nature of contemporary culture, grand architecture and public art, which has had an adverse effect on communities both in the UK and the US, while simultaneously using the moral rhetoric of education and opportunities for all. If European countries previously controlled the populations of their colonies through starvation (such as in the Congo[15] and Ireland in the nineteenth century), then public art, the building of new galleries and the regeneration in the city through gardens, paradoxically contributes to the removal of local or 'indigenous' poor communities.

King's cartoon *New York Rural* (2016) takes this narrative as its starting point. As the third work produced with illustrator Will Henry, an imaginary committee is formed consisting of curators (Klaus Biesenbach and Hans Ulrich-Obrist), celebrity artists (Yoko Ono, Marina Abramović and Jeff Koons), musicians (Lady Gaga and Jay-Z), a Marxist theorist (Noam Chomsky), and two critics (Roberta Smith and Jerry Saltz) who sit alongside New York's Mayor Bill de Blasio and the project's chief donor, the centenarian David Rockefeller, in an attempt to facilitate a new public artwork for New York City. Despite his advanced age, Rockefeller aggressively chairs the meeting (at one point he shouts at Koons: 'You there with the shit eatin' grin, you can go first') until a breakthrough comes when Chomsky suggests the construction of a series of farms run by workers' collectives in an environment inspired by Olafur Eliasson's' waterfalls, a setting that reminds the celebrated academic of America before it was colonised. This satire enters dark territory, however, when the idea of going 'back to the land' starts to reveal itself as none other than Pol Pot's ill-fated project to relocate the urban population of Democratic Kampuchea to the countryside.

***

Going back to London's planned Garden Bridge, one can see a knitting of Land Art, architecture, urban planning and spectacular park design. New bridges for the Thames were mooted as far back as 1986 in Richard Rogers' Royal Academy exhibition 'London as it Could Be', plans that subsequently appeared in Rogers' book *A New London* (1992).

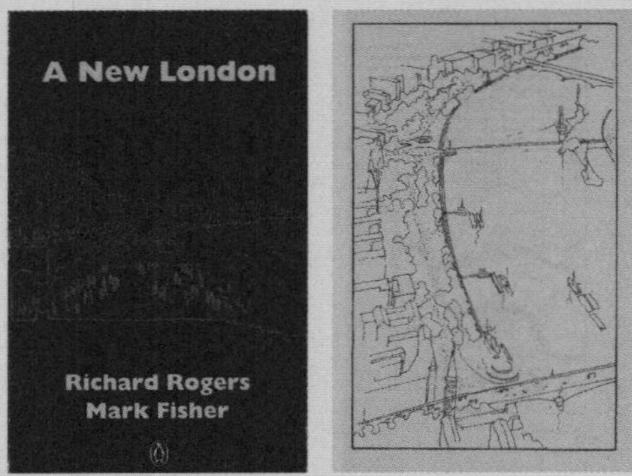

Mark Fisher and Richard Rogers, *A New London*, Penguin, 1992. Courtesy Penguin Books

In *A New London*, Rogers (who initially came from a utopian tradition of thinking in architecture) describes the dream behind his informal illustrations and initial vision for various structures. The London Olympics is discussed, while a forerunner to the Millennium Bridge can be clearly seen in one of the drawings, which in 1990 retained some of its optimistic flavour. In 2016 however, its real purpose can only be described as a commercial enterprise that disregards the interests of local communities in Lambeth. It's hard to see it as anything other than a private park for tourists and central London's wealthy inhabitants.

If the domestic nature of The Garden Bridge links to desires held in British television shows such as *The Great British Bake Off* (baking), *The Great Pottery Throw Down* (ceramics) and *Grand Designs* (rural property developing) then BBC Two's *The Secret History of the English Garden* represents a new shift in 'aspiration', that great Blairite buzzword. On Sunday 2 November 2015, *Gardeners' World* presenter Monty Don interviewed Peregrine Cavendish, the current Duke of Devonshire at Chatsworth House. Both men stood behind one of Cavendish's employees, who dutifully removed a tree in the distance that blocked a sweeping view of the grounds. Cavendish proudly commented on this fine-tuning of his estate: 'it's Land Art really isn't it?'

This self-conscious remark reveals a shift in utopian artistic models of the 1960s towards a narrowing relationship with traditional landscape painting. If, for example, as Morris states in her interview, the beautiful simplicity of the small drawings by Richard Long in the late 1960s (diagrams on school notepaper that contain holes from a compass alongside collaged maps, for example) were transformed after 1979 into large professional photographs behind glass (after the artist had started to work with the dealer Anthony D'Offay), then Cavendish's comment dovetails with a specific type of expansion of historical Conceptualism.

In the past, as a cultural philanthropist, Cavendish's son William has commissioned artists to work with Lismore Castle in Ireland, which sits in Jacobean gardens in the Blackwater Valley. The castle contains its own contemporary gallery, Lismore Castle Arts and so the family's equation of Land Art with the ambitious landscape created by Capability Brown for Chatsworth is perhaps no surprise. In fact Long was invited to produce an exhibition at Lismore in 2006, in which he used mud from the River Blackwater nearby. He also reinstalled his artwork *Cornwall Slate Line* (1990) within the castle's gardens.

It's clear that the artist has worked intimately with this region of Ireland, having walked extensively in the area, and that the Devonshire family are deeply engaged with contemporary art. However, one might also see Land Art in stately homes as a tasteful way to introduce artists as the new Capability Browns of the early twenty-first century. With Lawrence Weiner's work being commissioned to fill Blenheim Palace, the stately home in Oxfordshire, in late 2015, with the project 'Within a realm of distance: Lawrence Weiner at Blenheim Palace',[16] we can again see that architecture, grand houses and interior décor go hand-in-hand in a further shift away from the modest pieces of paper and proposals that Morris speaks of in her interview.

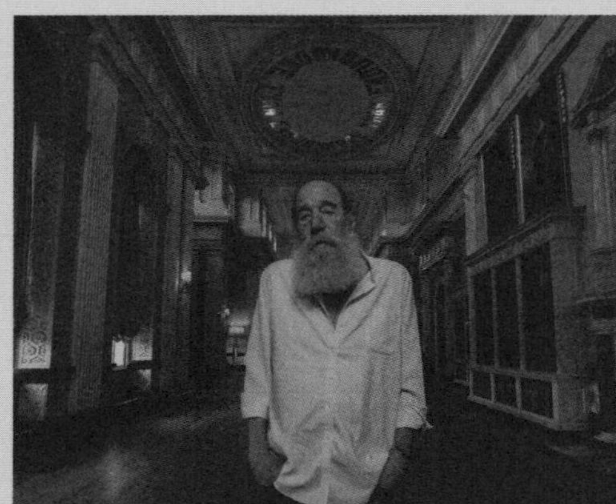

'Within a realm of distance: Lawrence Weiner at Blenheim Palace'. Photography: Hugo Glendinning. Courtesy Blenheim Art Foundation

It's important to mention that these points connect with the narrative of British artist Tris Vonna-Michell's book *Capitol Complex / Ulterior Vistas* (2014).[17] Vonna-Michell's publication provides two stories via a spoken word soundtrack and a separate script. One describes the poverty that currently surrounds Le Corbusier's famous architectural master plan for the city of Chandigarh in Punjab (Vonna-Michell's work intends to form a critique of the parallel ideologies of contemporary architecture and cultural regeneration), and another that ruminates on historical landscape gardens and contemporary property developers in Essex (the artist has family ties in both Punjab and Essex).

Capitol Complex is much like King's cartoons, in that it reflects on connected local moments across international borders in modern and rural contexts through a semi-fictional narrative.[18] The difference with Vonna-Michell's work is that a more reflective register of meaning replaces satire. *Capitol Complex*, for example, exposes the alienating effects of large architectural plans on the communities they serve in Chandigarh, while *Ulterior Vistas* follows the journey of a driven estate agent who orates a prospectus based on a grand eighteenth century English Landscape Garden. The conceptual framework for this sound work, as well as the book's photographic montages, derives from the work of English landscape architect, and fellow Essex resident Humphry Repton (Repton lived in Gidea Park), whose famous Red Books (produced between 1795 and 1816) contain bespoke architectural propositions and landscapes that improved the estates and pleasure grounds of his potential clients. Repton's before-and-after illustrations were a key feature of his work, as were his verbal presentations, and Vonna-Michell's tribute connects to contemporary questions around property, architecture, city planning and redevelopment.

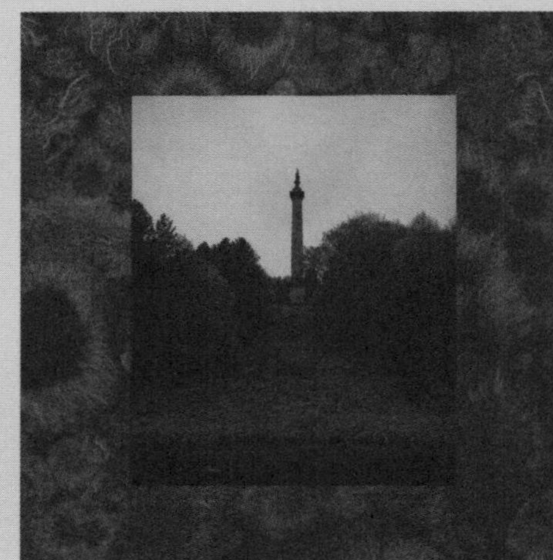

Tris Vonna-Michell, *Capitol Complex / Ulterior Vistas* (detail), Book containing two inserts and a ten-inch vinyl record, 2014

Through its mechanical score and the movement of the ten-inch record that contains its soundtrack, Vonna-Michell's narrative literally 'revolves' around the main government buildings in Chandigarh. After concentrated listening, it becomes clear that the work addresses ideas of Western colonial control that surround Le Corbusier's iconic urban modernist masterpiece. The urgency of the artist's voice also equates the wily estate agent or the Essex market trader with the earnest delivery of the frantic rapper and the concrete poet in a fictive system that analyses how cultural regeneration enhances desire and helps to condition any perception of place. The artist's pitch literally promises 'the earth' (to property investors and Essex's incoming residents, the latter, paradoxically, the newly displaced, socially-cleansed populace of London), as it covers absurd features such as iguanas, hills, swans, castles, casinos, as well as unethical advantages such as how to exploit local farmers.

Perhaps if Art & Language recognised Land Art as a continuation of the tradition of landscape art in the late 1960s, and foresaw its future transformation of scale forty-years later, then Long's work may have already been connected to problematic issues of class at its inception. Read in this way, Long's diagrammatical sketches perpetuate the legitimacy of the 'natural' landscape in a rural conservatism disguised as radical Conceptualism. However unlikely in may seem, apart from acting as a landscape gardener for the aristocrasy, Long's role becomes analogous to that of a tenant farmer. Due to global markets, many farmers in the UK receive European subsidies to bolster their unsustainable businesses: if they went bust, they'd leave the landscape bare of animals and crops. Therefore aid creates the illusion of economic stability and perpetuates the traditional appearance of the English countryside. If tenant farmers' now play the role of glorified gamekeepers, then it's fair to say that Long performs a similar part in an artificial landscape that sustains the fantasy of rural England savoured by our art establishment.

THE WATKINS FOLLY

As I mentioned earlier in this essay, King's favourite equivalent to the legacy of New Labour is Watkin's Folly. In 1890, a monument called 'The Great Tower of London' was planned as the British capital's answer to the Eiffel Tower. As the centrepiece to a huge funfair in Wembley Park, it was commissioned by the railway entrepreneur Edward Watkin, who was also responsible for an expansion of the Metropolitan Railway and a failed attempt to dig the first channel tunnel.

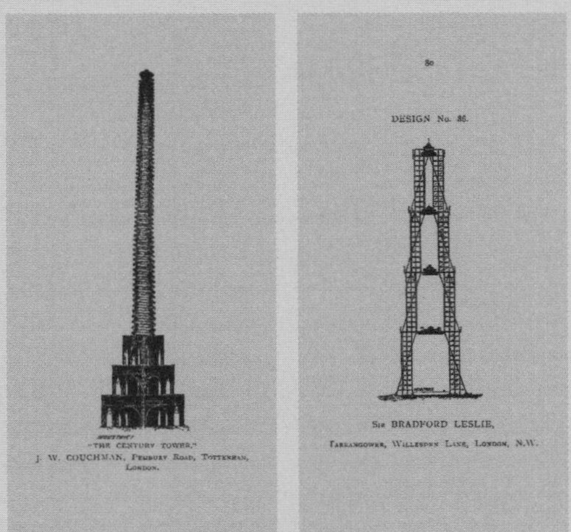

Two entries to a competition to design a new tower in London. Design No. 64, 1890

A catalogue of entries for the competition to design this tower shows a wonderful array of drawings, such as the 'Century Tower', which is reminiscent of a huge metal screw. The London Vegetarian Society's outline for an aerial colony contains hanging vegetable gardens with a one-twelfth-scale replica of the Great Pyramid on its summit. Despite these imaginative ideas, a more traditional plan, 'Design No. 37' by Stewart, McLaren and Dunn, was awarded the 500 guinea prize-money. Construction began in 1892, however the development soon ran into problems. After reaching forty-seven metres in height, not only did the project run out of money, The Metropolitan Tower Company in charge of the construction realised that the site was built on marshland. The tower subsequently subsided and had to be abandoned. It remained a spectacle in the park for a number of years before being deemed unsafe and dismantled in 1904.[19] Wembley Stadium was built over the site for the 1923 British Empire Exhibition and the Folly's original foundations were discovered when the football ground was re-built in 2000.

Watkin's Folly, or the 'London Stump' as it became known, contains all of the elements of New Labour's approach to statement public art projects. Cultural competition, monumental gigantism, and the attempt to create tourist destinations as hubs for economic change in previously isolated locations are key to projects from both eras. Watkin's monument was going to be the centre of a huge theme park, as were the Millennium Dome and the Olympic Park one hundred years later. This parallel extends to Blackpool Tower, which was successfully built in the same era as Watkin's failed enterprise and which proved to be an extremely effective attraction for British holidaymakers at the turn of the nineteenth century. Kapoor's *ArcelorMittal Orbit* in Stratford and *Temenos* in Middlesbrough, and Gormley's *Angel* in Gateshead echo the same historical trajectory. Blackpool however is currently the second poorest town in the UK. We can now see the Tower as a totem of social inequality, economic injustice and failed regeneration. The wealth that was once brought to the area slowly left, and a long process of erosion took place.

King's photographic *Study of Blackpool Tower* (2014) is a stark reminder of the dilapidation that now exists in the town. Visiting to interview the band Sleaford Mods, King circumnavigated the iron monument, as he puts it, as 'an objective way to document the surrounding misery'.

An article by the English journalist and broadcaster Paul Mason's in *The Guardian* on 1 December 2015[20] revealed the fact that there's a gap of sixteen years in the lifespan between the population of Blackpool and Wokingham in Berkshire, and King's creation of his own fantasy public art 'think tank', *A Balloon for Britain*, appears to address this issue of inequality. The sardonic joy of King's petrified balloon sculptures also connects and jars inadvertently with the impermanence of Swedish curator Maria Lind's 'Made to Fit, or The Gathering of the Balloons' written for *e-flux*'s *Supercommunity* series of online essays in mid-2015. Lind speaks of the difference between 'size' and 'scale' and the free distribution of information in art. By prioritising the dispersal of ideas in education and participation over the physical domination of large artworks, through the example of a small boy chasing a balloon in the streets of Paris, her model of idea-seeds being blown far and wide hints at alternative modes of production that undermine the pomposity of fixed art and architecture:

'While maintaining its nuances and contradictions, the art of the dandelion needs amplification. It doesn't need a bigger size or massive scale, but an accumulation of discrete entities passing the ball between each other. It requires distributed sensibilities that erupt and consolidate at certain moments in particular places. It needs active circulation, not unlike in the 1956 children's film *The Red Balloon*.'[21]

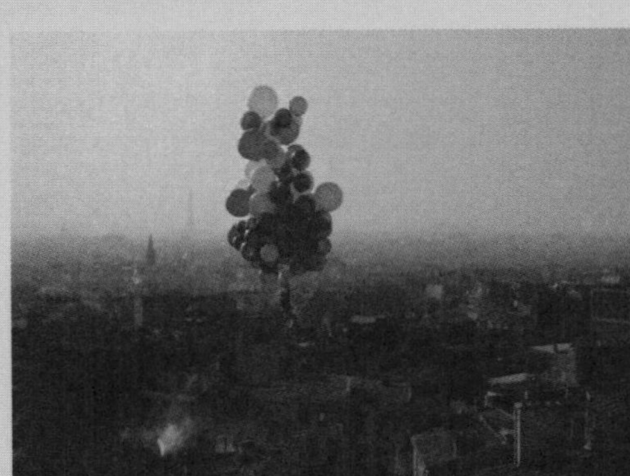

Film still from *The Red Balloon*, 1956

I DREAM OF DALSTONIA

Moving on, I would like to discuss King's aforementioned *I Dream of Dalstonia*,[22] which presents a 'what if' scenario that charts the progress of a 'hipster militia's' invasion of Middlesbrough to revitalise it after Kapoor's *Temenos* failed to work.

Among other things, this cartoon is a thinly veiled attack on a new preference for a 'radically useful art' within public art institutions. The idea of use in art has always been problematic because it is seen to oppose disinterested forms of thought represented by the Kantian tradition of purposeful-purposelessness. Much like the recent commodification of thought represented by British university education's co-option by the market, the belief in free philosophical propositions inherent to artworks appears to be eroded within this context.[23] In the press text to one of mima's projects called 'Localism', for example, a description of 'use' is given:

'True to its new vision as the useful museum, mima is taking a radical approach to curating with Localism. This is an exhibition for and about Middlesbrough and Teesside, an industrial area in the northeast of England that is increasingly vulnerable to the uncertainties of a globalized world. In the mid-19th century, the region exploded into a world centre of steel production; today, it faces a challenging economic situation.'[24]

This development shows a distinct shift away from the large static works by Gormley in Gateshead and Kapoor in Middlesbrough as a way of connecting with the history of mining and the steel industry, as well as the difficult economic situation in the North East of England. Its rhetoric is 'correct', yet the work's reliance on art's 'use' is a worrying element, which becomes more disturbing through what appears to be its attempted fusion with the 'radical museology' recently espoused by Claire Bishop and the curator Charles Esche, which aims to address the real potential of animating local political histories with museum collections against neo-liberal forces.[25] Essentially, mima's conflation of 'use' value with Bishop and Esche's formula for locally relevant museums could serve to diminish engagement with aesthetic autonomy, disinterested thought and therefore the possibility of real change.

King's impossible semi-abstract floating public buildings in *The Ekranoplanter* (2016) function within this absurd language of power, in which an organisation such as mima champions the 'small' and the 'local' yet simultaneously operates from a gigantic palace of culture built in a previous economic era. King transforms his new spectacular Bilbao-like monuments that contain a variety of fashionable foliage into mundane social essentials such as libraries, hospitals and fire stations that fit with the rhetoric of useful culture. As designs, however, they are entirely non-functional and completely useless. These are warped edifices that point to the rise of architecture and the systematic decimation of the public sector, the welfare state and enlightenment forms of thinking.

Similarly, *I Dream of Dalstonia* plays with London-based Assemble's version of Victorian philanthropy in the regions, as a do-it-yourself, self-organised, pre-welfare state model that plugs the gaps left by a lack of government care. From this perspective, Assemble's real use is similar to the large monuments of the 1990s and 2000s, in that their highly symbolic work serves as marketing to cover up new policies imposed by government to destroy social housing. Their work is actually 'useful' as a veneer behind which the conservative government can operate with less fear of criticism.

Assemble's *Granby Four Streets* project, which centred around regenerating a cluster of terraced houses in Toxteth is described on the company's website:

'Over the past 10 years they [the residents] have cleaned and planted their streets, painted the empty houses, organized a thriving monthly market, founded a Community Land Trust and shown their area in a different light. Assemble worked with the Granby Four Streets CLT and Steinbeck Studios to present a sustainable and incremental vision for the area that builds on the hard work already done by local residents and translates it to the refurbishment of housing, public space and the provision of new work and enterprise opportunities.'[26]

Phrases such as 'architectural and cultural heritage', 'resourcefulness' and 'DIY spirit' feature heavily, while markets and indoor botanical gardens are included in Assemble's photographic documentation.

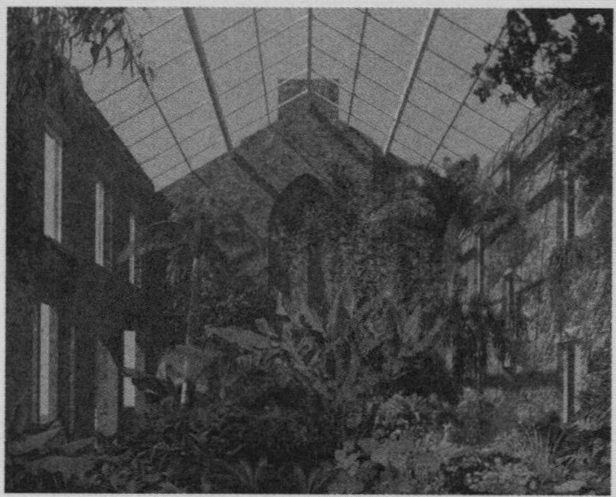

Assemble, *Granby Four Streets* (detail), 2015

After being awarded the Turner Prize in December 2015, various journalists claimed that the yearly event had started to represent a move against the art market because Assemble work as architects, are 'community-oriented', and had sold inexpensive objects directly from the Turner Prize exhibition. In four positive articles on this subject alone in *The Guardian* the following day, the accent was placed fully on Assemble's generosity. One piece, however, asked a question about Assemble's commissioning process:

'I ask, for example, what if a hypothetical super-rich client asked for a luxury house with all the trimmings and an underground swimming pool? Would they take on such a project? Schulz [one of Assemble's members] explains that when work comes in, an email goes round, and everyone has the chance to express interest. "We can't say whether we'd do it or not. It doesn't sound like our kind of thing – but we wouldn't rule it out."'[27]

Although their work may be read as a rejection of the art market and the practice still lacks ARB (Architects Registration Board) registration, the 'alternative' they present is profitable, sustainable and less precarious than choosing a career as a visual artist. With the Tate's historical embrace of architects as trustees, this new winning 'art form' of the Turner Prize might be more traditional than the mainstream media might think.

It might also be interesting to ask if Assemble's Turner Prize exhibition at Tramway in Glasgow was really for 'the people' after all. In a review of the activist and curator Nato Thompson's book *Seeing Power* in the curatorial journal *The Exhibitionist*, Zachary Cahill raised an important point in relation to the elitism of socially engaged artworks:

'While he [Thompson] was staging his political art exhibition The Interventionists, the museum also had a German painting show on view. He was surprised to learn that audiences felt, perhaps counter-intuitively, that the socially-engaged art was elitist, while the expensive German paintings from the Rubell Family Collection were something they could connect with.'[28]

This is a situation in which argument and counter-argument prevail. Tate's viewpoint would be that Assemble educate the general public about what might constitute art, and create awareness around contemporary social issues. Yet this debate between the boundaries of art and architecture conveniently avoids addressing stark issues of class in Assemble's work, and it's easy to see the group as the direct descendants or progeny of Gormley and Kapoor.[29] In this respect one might claim that Assemble are nothing other than the fag end of the New Labour era in an impending 'Mumfordised world'.

THE FUTURE

Similar to Assemble, Scott King synthesises two disciplines. Instead of creating modest and sensible rudimentary structures in the real world as art, he uses his dual roles as graphic designer and contemporary artist to construct glossy illogical scenarios that reveal the ways in which public art is employed in contemporary society. Of course, both Assemble and King are moralists and follow an ethical approach to life, yet the difference with King is that his work advocates that artists, curators and public commissioners break with their instrumental role in line with corporate interests, to create a situation in which art in the public realm holds valuable new forms of critical independence.

A more shadowy alternative is provided by King's *Long Live Death* (2012), in which Nelson's Column is combined with Gormley's *Angel* in a Wagnerian view of a future. In this scenario, the government have decided that the north of England no longer deserves large monuments, and in one fell swoop they've all been moved south where they're more valuable for votes and the tourist economy.[30]

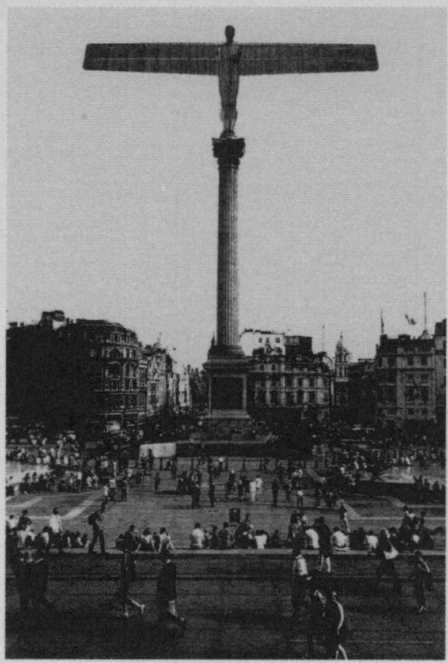

Scott King, *Long Live Death*,
Inkjet print, 219 × 150 cm, 2012

In all seriousness, King's work shows that we're living in a period of extreme politics and extreme fashion, where each side eliminates the other to provide an infinitely recuperated politics. In much the same way as the utopian glimpse that theorist Theodor Adorno spoke of, which suggests that successful artworks offer a window onto a transformed social and political reality, one that's inconceivable in the irredeemable present, King's graphic works 'advertise' fantastic events that are either impossible or endlessly deferred.

By colliding public art, fashion, and the politics of regeneration to encapsulate a self-defeating series of projects, *Public Art* emits a melancholy so profound that we're left with a strange sense of optimism, one that comes from the realisation we're being told the truth about our world. Whatever happens, we live in hope of a better future, and in essence, King's work is a phenomenology of advanced reification that yields a popular utopian possibility, however damaged this desire might be.

1. My use of the term 'Public Art' within this essay intends to describe public sculpture in all of its forms, alongside contemporary art that is available to view in the public realm, including within galleries and museums.

2. Theodor Adorno, *Minima Moralia: Reflections on a Damaged Life*, 1951. I'd like to outline my reasons for using this popular quote by Adorno at the start of this essay. Firstly, Adorno's text aimed to state that folk art's opposition was always shaped by the ruling culture it resisted. Read in 2016, Adorno's statement reflects a governing culture's subsequent appropriation of folk art as part of its complex ruling ideology. Thirdly the inclusion of this quote aims to echo King's concern that prevailing philosophers and theorists are used by academics to validate their sometimes-spurious ideas. By way of example, a text-work in King's book of fabricated citations *Quotations* (2011) reads: 'The very idea of using another's words in order to authenticate one's own thoughts or position seems really quite repulsive to me. Recently, I scarcely seem to be able to open a novel or browse a museum catalogue without seeing my own words reprinted there: servile, meaningless and stripped of context. I appear to have become the principle propagandist for every imbecile that ever picked up a pen or a paintbrush. Walter Benjamin, Portbou, 24 September 1940.'

3. Robert Hewison's book starts from New Labour's ceaseless promotion of the visual and performing arts, museums and galleries, 'as a stimulus to national economic revival, a post-industrial revolution where spending on culture would solve everything, from national decline to crime'. Hewison, Robert. *Cultural Capital: The Rise and Fall of Creative Britain*, Verso, 2014. Back cover.

4. Focal Point Gallery in Southend-on-Sea, which is co-funded by Arts Council England (as a National Portfolio Organisation) and Southend-on-Sea Borough Council.

5. On 20 October 2015, BBC London News revealed that Kapoor's *ArcelorMittal Orbit* at the Olympic Park was losing £10,000 per week, and had lost £520,000 since it had opened in 2014, and called it 'a pointless monument at vast taxpayers' expense'. Similarly on 21 October 2015, *The Independent* led with 'Mayor's "vanity project" loses £10,000 a week', and continued: 'Orbit, the UK's tallest sculpture at 1,145 m, was expected to generate a profit of almost £1.2 m in its first year. But the attraction, which reopened at the start of April 2014, lost £520,000 as only 124,000 people visited between then and March 2015.'

6. Nato Thompson, *Seeing Power*, Melville House Publishing, 2015. Page 12.

7. Terry Riley, album cover notes from *A Rainbow in Curved Air*, 1971.

8. See Stuart Heritage's 'NWA, Breaking Bad and Bake Off: was there any pop culture the Tories didn't ruin in 2015?' in *The Guardian*, 29 December 2015: www.theguardian.com/culture/2015/dec/28/tory-party-patronage-ruins-popular-culture

9. Greg Sharzer, *No Local*, Zero Books, 2012.

10. In his blog 'Unleash the badness! Why the art world needs more sleaze and less morality' on 29 December 2015, *The Guardian* journalist Jonathan Jones claimed that 2015 was marked by politics and ideology that was smothering the art world in good intentions. 'The Venice Biennale was oh so serious. The Tate Modern Turbine Hall's latest project was unveiled and turned out to be a garden deck with weeds growing in pots – a work whose ecological message is banal and visually null' [...] 'Now we're back in smallville, in that eternal province where culture is rational, sombre, serious and ethical. A teacher's dream, a true artist's nightmare.' See: www.theguardian.com/artanddesign/jonathanjonesblog/2015/dec/29/unleash-the-badness-why-the-art-world-needs-more-sleaze?CMP=twt_a-artanddesign_b-gdnartanddesign/artanddesign/2015/oct/12/abraham-cruzvillegas-tubine-hall-tate-modern-hyundai-commission-review

11. Scott King, *Excerpts from A Better Britain, Southend*, 2013.

12. '"THIS WHOLE COUNTRY IS SLOWLY BEING MUMFORDISED": Q&A WITH ARTIST SCOTT KING ON THE STATE OF POPULAR CULTURE', The Vinyl Factory, 2013. See: www.thevinylfactory.com/vinyl-factory-releases/this-whole-country-is-slowly-being-mumfordised-qa-with-artist-scott-king-on-the-state-of-popular-culture/

13. From a conversation with the writer, June 2015.

14. Humberto Leon, 'Kim Gordon and Humberto Leon Talk Art in NYC, Pop-Culture Feminism, and Hillary for President', Opening Ceremony: Culture, June 4, 2015. See: www.openingceremony.us/entry.asp?pid=11252

15. Within the context of gallery sponsorship and human rights issues, a 2012 series of exhibitions by the Institute for Human Activity (IHA), which artist Renzo Martens directs, attempted to reverse global inequalities by proposing a gentrification program on a former Unilever plantation in Congo, 800 kilometres from Kinshasa, on a tributary of the Congo River. This project links the brutality of historical colonialism and contemporary museums. IHA's press material consisted of the following passage: 'Unilever, well known for sponsoring Tate Modern's Unilever Series, founded its first palm oil plantation in 1911, after which Congolese inhabitants were coerced into forced labour. Today, few of the workers have access to clean water, electricity, or sanitation, and still produce the ingredients for Unilever's Blue Band. In the summer of 2013, Canadian palm oil operator Feronia forced the IHA to leave its settlement and the communities with whom it had been working. From its New Settlement in exile, plantation workers continue the Critical Curriculum and are developing a critical apparatus to think through their fears, dreams, complicity and resistance, and the role of art. A new series of sculptures, made out of river clay, reflect upon the mystery of money – some people appear to create money seemingly out of thin air, even as the workers themselves do not have enough to feed their children. The Institute for Human Activities asserts that even when art critically engages with global inequalities, it ultimately brings beauty, jobs, and opportunity to places like the Lower East Side in New York and Berlin-Mitte. To counteract this situation, the IHA has built a settlement in the Congolese rainforest where art can fully deal with its dependencies on these very inequalities, turn gentrification into a tool for economic justice, and recalibrate art's critical mandate.'

16. Mark Hudson, 'Lawrence Weiner, Blenheim Palace, review: "off the wall"', *The Telegraph*, 2 November 2015. Hudson suggests that Weiner may have produced a work that was critical of the Blenheim Palace site: 'The suspicion that Weiner may be providing a subversive counter-commentary to this grandiose dynastic message builds as you look up at the library cupola where the words "More Than Enough" feel like a comment on the surrounding magnificence.'

17. This work was developed as a wider response to the construction of Focal Point Gallery in Southend-on-Sea. See my Focal Point Gallery: A New Institution?' in *Architecture and Culture*, Vol.4, Issue 1, 'Architecture and the Spaces of Information', (Dr. Ruth Blacksell and Dr. Stephen Walker, Eds), Routledge, 2016.

18. King's work is similar in nature to Jonathan Swift's book *A Modest Proposal for Preventing the Children of Poor People From Being a Burthen to Their Parents or Country, and for Making Them Beneficial to the Publick*, which is commonly referred to as *A Modest Proposal*, published anonymously in 1729. Swift suggests that the impoverished Irish might ease their economic troubles by selling their children as food for rich ladies and gentlemen. This satirical hyperbole mocks heartless attitudes towards the poor, as well as Irish policy in general. In English writing, the phrase 'a modest proposal' is now a conventional allusion to this style of straight-faced satire.

19. For more information see Fred. C. Lynde's *Descriptive Illustrated Catalogue of the Sixty-Eight Competitive Designs for the Great Tower for London*, Isha Books, 2013.

20. Paul Mason, 'We need to be shocked into action about why wealth still dictates life expectancy', *The Guardian*, 1 December 2015.

21. Maria Lind, 'Made to Fit, or the Gathering of the Balloons', Supercommunity, *e-flux journal 56th Venice Biennale*. August 25, 2015 – Day 80.

22. *I Dream of Dalstonia* was initially titled *Welthauptstadt Dalstonia*. Dalston, the area in east London, which has been increasingly transformed into a prime location for London's young white bourgeois community is combined with *Welthauptstadt*, part of the name 'Welthauptstadt Germania', which refers to the projected renewal of Berlin during the Nazi period, part of Adolf Hitler's vision for the future of Germany after the planned victory in World War II. As is well known, Albert Speer, the 'first architect of the Third Reich', produced many of the plans for the rebuilt city in his capacity as overseer of the project, only a small portion of which was realised between the years 1937 and 1943 when construction took place.

23. Scott King's work addresses the double bind of a public art that is intrinsically entwined with state marketing and advertising. His proposals appear as graphic design solutions for poor areas, and represent the fantasy of healing through culture rather than large-scale social investment. The government's gradual release of its social responsibility is realised in its full fantastic horror in King's work. However cynical this may appear, his work holds a yearning for a truly effective socially engaged art, one that's situated in a philosophically disinterested argument.

24. From the press text of mima's project 'Localism', 10 October 2015 to 7 February 2016. See www.visitmima.com/whats-on/single/localism/

25. See Claire Bishop, *Radical Museology*, Koenig Books, 2013, Ekaterina and David Riff's interview with Charles Esche 'What More Do You Want Than Freedom?' in *Self-Organised*, edited by Stine Hebert and Anne Szefer Karlsen, Occasional Table, 2013, and Esche's text 'Coda: The Curatorial' in *The Curatorial*, edited by Jean-Paul Martinon, Bloomsbury, 2013.

26. From the press text of Assemble's project *Granby Four Streets*. See www.assemblestudio.co.uk/?page_id=862

27. Charlotte Higgins 'Turner prize winners Assemble: "Art? We're more interested in plumbing"', *The Guardian*, 8 December 2015. See www.theguardian.com/artanddesign/2015/dec/08/assemble-turner-prize-architects-are-we-artists

28. Zachary Cahill, 'Save the Republic! Art and Politics with Hal Foster and Nato Thompson'. See www.the-exhibitionist.com/save-the-republic-art-and-politics-with-hal-foster-and-nato-thompson/

29. In Kriston Capps' interview with Anish Kapoor 'Sculptor Anish Kapoor on Public Art, Copycats, and His Beef With Chicago Mayor Rahm Emanuel' on citylab.com on 4 December 2015, one of the artist's arguments for the value of his public sculpture *Cloud Gate* (2006) in Chicago appeared to be it's impact on property prices in the city: 'By the way, it brings a great deal to Chicago. Property values in that area have gone up, I don't dare to guess how many fold, but many fold.' See www.citylab.com/design/2015/12/sculptor-anish-kapoor-on-public-art-copycats-and-his-beef-with-chicago-mayor-rahm-emanuel/418746/

30. Perhaps in line with the vision of *Long Live Death*, the late Brian Sewell once provocatively commented on *Angel of the North* and Gateshead in the *London Evening Standard*: 'I think it is probably the emptiest, most inflated, most vulgar of his [Antony Gormley's] works… Gateshead is a self-inflicted wound. Bomb it, then you will change it. It is an awful place… most of the North is awful.'

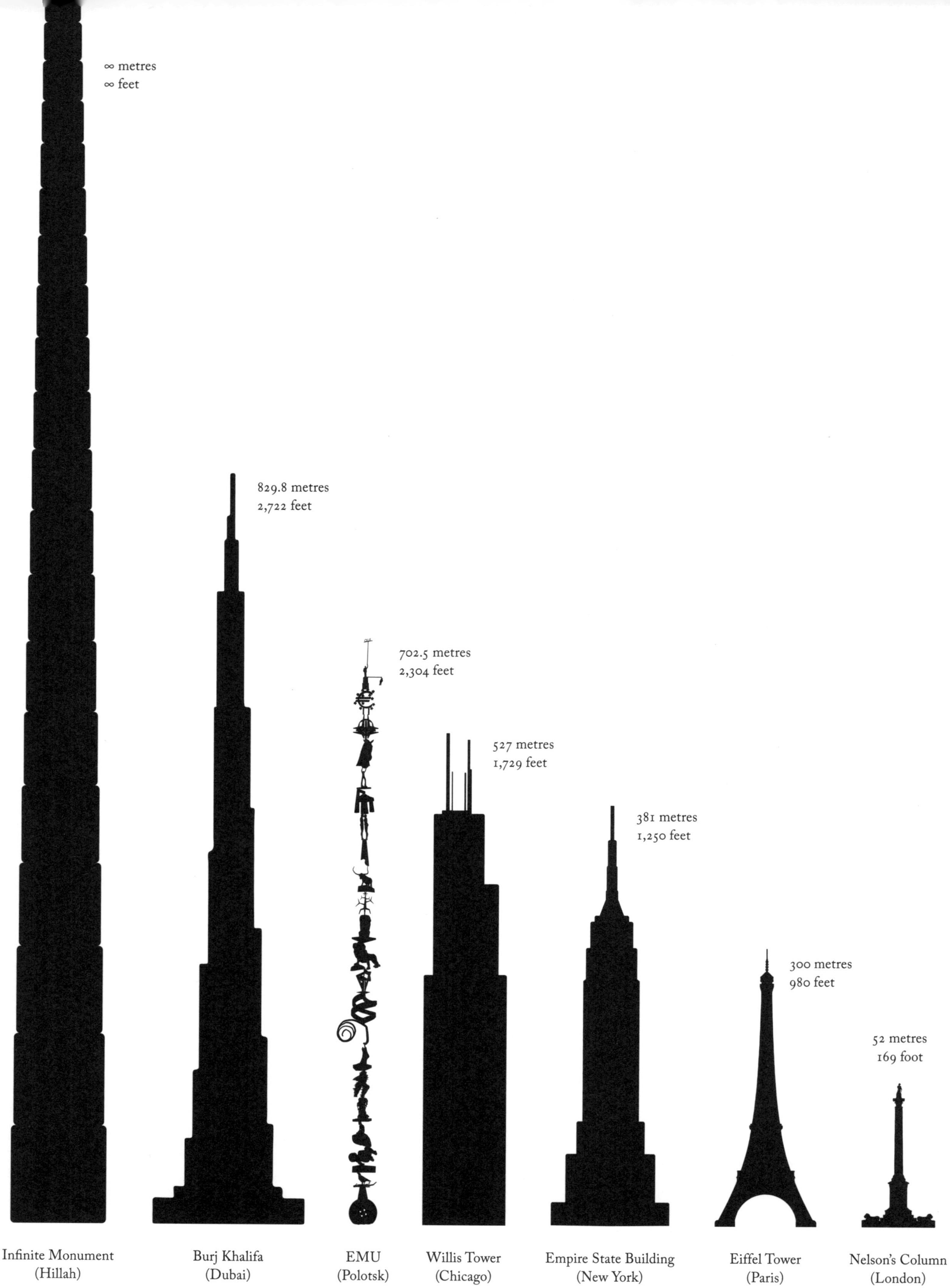
∞ metres
∞ feet
829.8 metres
2,722 feet
702.5 metres
2,304 feet
527 metres
1,729 feet
381 metres
1,250 feet
300 metres
980 feet
52 metres
169 foot
Infinite Monument
(Hillah)
Burj Khalifa
(Dubai)
EMU
(Polotsk)
Willis Tower
(Chicago)
Empire State Building
(New York)
Eiffel Tower
(Paris)
Nelson's Column
(London)

BIOGRAPHIES

Owen Hatherley was born in Southampton, England in 1981. He received a PhD in 2011 from Birkbeck College, London, for a thesis on Constructivism and Americanism. He writes regularly on architecture and cultural politics for *Architects Journal, Architectural Review*, *Icon*, *The Guardian*, the *London Review of Books* and *New Humanist*, and is the author of several books: *Militant Modernism* (Zero, 2009), *A Guide to the New Ruins of Great Britain* (Verso, 2010), *Uncommon – An Essay on Pulp* (Zero, 2011), *A New Kind of Bleak – Journeys through Urban Britain* (Verso, 2012), *Across the Plaza* (Strelka, 2012), *Landscapes of Communism* (Penguin, 2015) and *The Ministry of Nostalgia* (Verso, 2016). He also edited and introduced an updated edition of Ian Nairn's *Nairn's Towns* (Notting Hill Editions, 2013). He lives in Woolwich and Warsaw.

Will Henry is an illustrator who lives and works in London. He previously worked with King on *Anish and Antony Take Afghanistan*, JRP|Ringier, 2014.

Robert Hewison is an independent writer, curator, journalist and consultant, who specialises in the field of cultural policy. He studied at Oxford University, where he gained his doctorate, and Ravensbourne College of Art & Design. He has published more than twenty books on aspects of nineteenth and twentieth century British cultural history, among them *The Heritage Industry* (1987), *Future Tense: A New Art for Nineties* (1990), *Culture and Consensus: England, Art and Politics since 1940* (1997) and *Ruskin on Venice: 'The Paradise of Cities'* (2010). An authority on John Ruskin, he has held chairs at Oxford, Lancaster and City Universities. He has written on the arts for *The Sunday Times* since 1981. He is an Associate of the think tank Demos, and has been a consultant to the Heritage Lottery Fund, the Royal Shakespeare Company and the Clore Leadership Programme. His most recent work, *Cultural Capital: The Rise and Fall of Creative Britain* was published by Verso in November 2014.

Andrew Hunt is a curator and writer based in London. He completed his PhD at the University of Reading in 2015 and is currently a Research Fellow in the Faculty of Art, Design & Architecture at Kingston University. Between 2008 and 2014 he was Director of Focal Point Gallery (FPG) in Southend-on-Sea, Essex. Between 2005 and 2008 he was Director/Curator of the International Project Space, Birmingham, and in 2012 a member of the Turner Prize jury. He is founder of the Slimvolume imprint, which to date has published editions and books by over 250 artists. He is author of numerous catalogue essays, and contributes to journals such as *Art Monthly*, *Domus*, *Frieze*, *Mousse Magazine* and *TATE ETC.*

Scott King was born in 1969 in Goole, East Yorkshire, England. He previously worked as Art Director of *i-D* and Creative Director of *Sleazenation* magazines. King has also designed record sleeves for the Pet Shop Boys, Suicide, Earl Brutus and Morrissey amongst many others, and in 2013 he finally made a record of his own entitled *You're My Favorite Artist* (Vinyl Factory). For almost twenty years, King has created work under the banner *CRASH!* with historian Matthew Worley. King's work has been exhibited internationally in both commercial galleries and institutions and he has produced several books, including *Anxiety & Depression* (2009), *Art Works* (2010) and *Anish & Antony Take Afghanistan* (2014), all with JRP|Ringier. Scott King is currently Professor of Visual Communication at University of the Arts London.

Tom Morton is a writer, curator and Contributing Editor of *frieze*, based in Rochester, UK.

Lynda Morris was born in Scotland in 1947 and has two children. She studied art in Canterbury and worked at the ICA, London, from 1969 to 1971. Her 1973 RCA thesis researched Art & Language, Joseph Beuys and The Projects Class. From 1971 to 1974 she worked for Nigel Greenwood and organised the 'Book as Artwork 1960–72' exhibition with Germano Celant. She wrote for *Studio International*, *The Listener* and *Art Press*. She was Richard Hamilton's assistant for his 1973 Guggenheim exhibition. As Exhibition Organiser at the Midland Group, Nottingham, between 1976 and 1979, she worked on 'Towards Another Picture' with Andrew Brighton. For nineteen years she organised 'EAST*international*' in Norwich, with assistants including Tim Wilcox, Josephine Lanyon, Kirsty Ogg, Andrew Hunt, Michelle Cotton and Kaavous Clayton. She organised 'Picasso: Peace and Freedom' (Tate Liverpool, 2010), and is now working on Picasso and Africa after 1945. She curated 'Vanley Burke: By the Rivers of Birminam' (mac Birmingham, 2012), which travelled to Johannesburg in 2014. She developed 'Conception, the Conceptual Documents 1968–72' with Catherine Moseley (2000) and *Unconcealed: The International Network of Conceptual Artists 1967–1977* (Ridinghouse, 2009) from Sophie Richard's PhD 'Dear Lynda…' commissioned by Matthew Higgs for White Columns, New York in 2012, travelled to Chelsea, Dundee, Norwich, Berlin and Birmingham. She has lectured at the Getty Museum (2009), LACMA (2012) and DIA Beacon (2014). She curated 'Documenting Cadere 1972–78' (MoMA Oxford, 2012) and 'Genuine Conceptualism' (Herbert Foundation, Ghent, 2014).

Matthew Worley has worked with King as *CRASH!* from 1997. He currently works as a historian at the University of Reading and has published several books and articles on British politics and culture in the twentieth century. His most recent project is focused on the relationship between punk, politics and youth culture in the late 1970s and early 1980s. Articles relating to this can be found in *History Workshop Journal*, *Twentieth Century British History* and *Contemporary British History*. A book will be published in 2017.

Public Art
Scott King

The artist would like to dedicate
this publication to Tess and Iris

Edited by Andrew Hunt and Scott King
Designed by Scott King
and Fraser Muggeridge studio
Design assistance by Rhys Atkinson
and Callum Griffiths
Cover photography by David Gill
Transcription of interviews with Robert Hewison
and Lynda Morris by Sophie Sleigh-Johnson
Copy editing by Andrew Hunt
and David L Hayles
Printed by SIZ Industria Grafica
in an edition of 1,000

Published by Slimvolume, 2016

Scott King and Slimvolume would like to thank:
Rhys Atkinson, Between Bridges, Bortolami Gallery, Jessica Dawson, David Gasi, David Gill, Tom Godfrey and Joshua Lockwood, Callum Griffiths, Luke Hall, Owen Hatherley, David L Hayles, Will Henry, Herald St, Robert Hewison, JRP|Ringier, Simon Martin, Lynda Morris, Tom Morton and his students at Christie's Education, Fraser Muggeridge, Djordje Ozbolt, Serpentine Gallery, Sophie Sleigh-Johnson, Luke Stephenson, Brian Sweeney, Nick Wesley and Matthew Worley.

ISBN: 978-1-910516-01-0

Distributed by:
Cornerhouse Publications Ltd
HOME
2 Tony Wilson Place
Manchester M15 4FN
United Kingdom
www.cornerhousepublications.org

Published by:
Slimvolume
57c Davisville Road
London W12 9SH
United Kingdom
www.slimvolume.org

Slimvolume #3

slimvolume

The Elephant Trust

The Henry Moore
Foundation

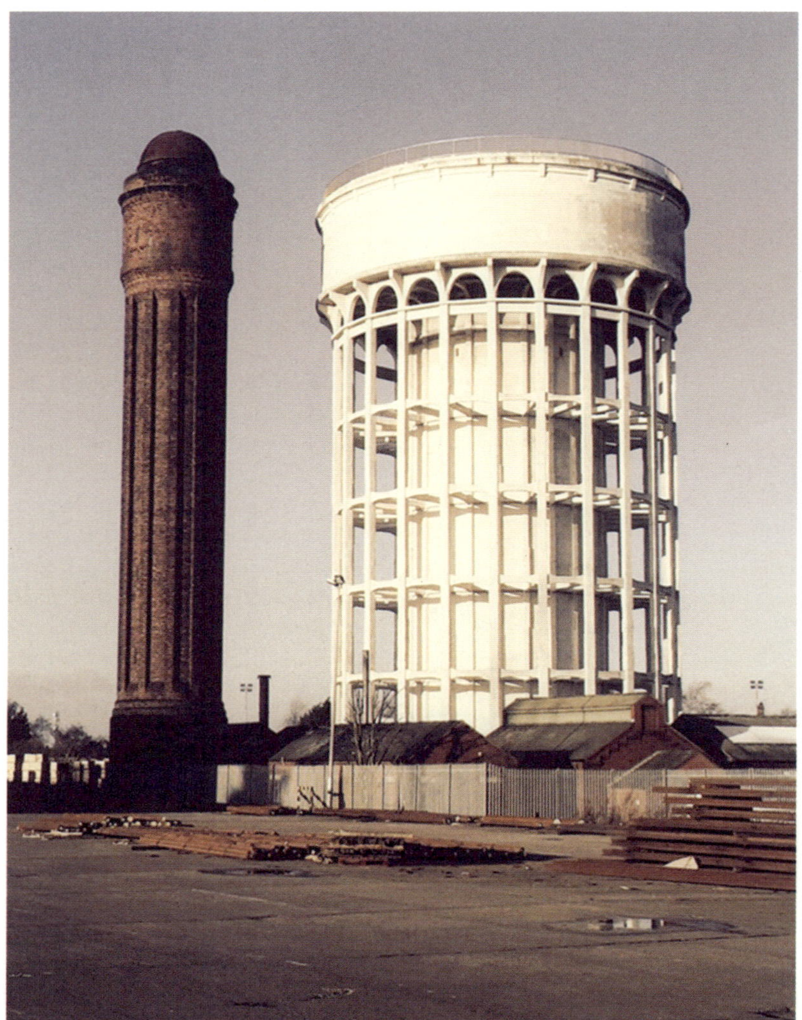